Developments in American Poli

Developments titles available from Palgrave Macmillan

Maria Green Cowles and Desmond Dinan (eds)
DEVELOPMENTS IN THE EUROPEAN UNION 2

Patrick Dunleavy, Richard Heffernan, Philip Cowley and
Colin Hay (eds)
DEVELOPMENTS IN BRITISH POLITICS 8

Alistair Cole, Patrick Le Galès and Jonah D. Levy (eds)
DEVELOPMENTS IN FRENCH POLITICS 4

Paul M. Heywood, Erik Jones, Martin Rhodes
and Ulrich Sedelmeier (eds)
DEVELOPMENTS IN EUROPEAN POLITICS

Stephen Padgett, William E. Paterson and Gordon Smith (eds)
DEVELOPMENTS IN GERMAN POLITICS 3*

Gillian Peele, Christopher J. Bailey, Bruce Cain and B. Guy Peters (eds)
DEVELOPMENTS IN AMERICAN POLITICS 5

Stephen White, Judy Batt and Paul Lewis (eds)
DEVELOPMENTS IN CENTRAL AND EAST
EUROPEAN POLITICS 4*

Stephen White, Zvi Gitelman and Richard Sakwa (eds)
DEVELOPMENTS IN RUSSIAN POLITICS 6*

If you have any comments or suggestions regarding the
above or other possible *Developments* titles, please write to
Steven Kennedy, Palgrave Macmillan, Houndmills,
Basingstoke RG21 6XS, UK or e-mail s.kennedy@palgrave.com

---

* Rights World excluding North America

Developments in American Politics 6

edited by
Gillian Peele
Christopher J. Bailey
Bruce Cain
and
B. Guy Peters

palgrave
macmillan

First published 2010 by
PALGRAVE MACMILLAN

Palgrave Macmillan in the UK is an imprint of Macmillan Publishers Limited, registered in England, company number 785998, of Houndmills, Basingstoke, Hampshire RG21 6XS.

Palgrave Macmillan in the US is a division of St Martin's Press LLC, 175 Fifth Avenue, New York, NY 10010.

Palgrave Macmillan is the global academic imprint of the above companies and has companies and representatives throughout the world.

Palgrave® and Macmillan® are registered trademarks in the United States, the United Kingdom, Europe and other countries.

ISBN 978–0–230–57682–7   hardback
ISBN 978–0–230–57683–4   paperback

This book is printed on paper suitable for recycling and made from fully managed and sustained forest sources. Logging, pulping and manufacturing processes are expected to conform to the environmental regulations of the country of origin.

A catalogue record for this book is available from the British Library.

A catalog record for this book is available from the Library of Congress.

10 9 8 7 6 5 4 3 2 1
19 18 17 16 15 14 13 12 11 10

Printed in China.

Contents

List of Tables, Figures, and Maps

Tables

Figures

Map

The United States: states, state capitals, and main cities

Key:
- Major cities/conurbations
- State capitals

Preface

This is the sixth volume of *Developments in American Politics*. It addresses a variety of issues in American politics at a time of potentially great change. The election in 2008 of Barack Obama as president was obviously historically significant in terms of both racial and broader politics. Individual chapters in the book explore the political landscape that Obama inherited, the policy dilemmas he confronts, and the way he has set about addressing them. As with previous volumes our aim has been to provide students with a stimulating and accessible account of key aspects of contemporary American politics that does not assume prior knowledge but does complement introductory material available elsewhere. Although our primary focus is on recent developments in the United States, we have taken care not to neglect the historical context of current issues and debates and the institutional continuities and constraints that mark the American governmental system.

We have again been fortunate in attracting an outstanding team of contributors from both sides of the Atlantic. In order to make the book user friendly and to convey the color and idioms of American politics, we have used American spelling throughout. The major references to works cited in the chapters are collected together at the end of the book where there is also a short guide to further reading for each of the chapters.

The editors would like to thank our publisher Steven Kennedy for his continuing help and encouragement. We also thank our anonymous reviewer for the constructive comments which have helped us in the process of refining this book. Thanks are due also to our colleagues at the University of Oxford, at Keele University, at the University of California at Berkeley, and at the University of Pittsburgh. Many thanks also to Sheryn Peters who assisted Guy with the index. We are especially grateful also to the research and organizational assistance provided by David Greenberg during the early stages of the book and to Mrs Glynis Beckett of Lady Margaret Hall for her crucial secretarial expertise and support.

GILLIAN PEELE
CHRISTOPHER J. BAILEY
BRUCE CAIN AND
B. GUY PETERS

Notes on the Contributors

Dorie E. Apollonio is Adjunct Professor, University of California, San Francisco.

Christopher J. Bailey is Professor of American Politics, University of Keele.

Bruce E. Cain is Robson Professor of Government, University of California at Berkeley.

Tim Conlan is Professor of Government and Politics at George Mason University.

Louis Fisher is a specialist on the separation of power with the Congressional Research Service.

James F. Hollifield is Professor of Political Science and Director of the Tower Center Southern Methodist University.

Timothy Lynch is Senior Lecturer in US Foreign Policy, University of London.

George Mackenzie is an Analyst with AARP and a Visiting Professor at the University of California in Washington DC.

Thomas Mann is a Senior Fellow in Governance Studies at the Brookings Institution, Washington DC.

Paul Martin is Fellow and Tutor in Politics, Wadham College, Oxford.

Jonathan Parker is Senior Lecturer in American Politics at the University of Keele.

Gillian Peele is Fellow and Tutor in Politics, Lady Margaret Hall, Oxford.

B. Guy Peters is Maurice Falk Professor of American Government, University of Pittsburgh.

Jon Roper is Professor of Politics, University of Swansea.

Alan Ware is Professor of Politics, Worcester College, Oxford.

Abbreviations and Acronyms

AAA	American Automobile Association
AARP	American Association of Retired Persons
ABA	American Bar Association
ABC	American Broadcasting Corporation
ACES	American Clean Energy and Security [Act] 2009
ACLU	American Civil Liberties Union
AEI	American Enterprise Institute
AFDC	Aid to Families with Dependent Children
AIG	American International Group
AILA	American Immigration Lawyers Association
AIPAC	American Israel Public Affairs Committee
ARRA	American Recovery and Reinvestment Act
AUMF	Authorization for the Use of Military Force
BCRA	Bipartisan Campaign Reform Act
BRIC	Brazil Russia India China
CBO	Congressional Budget Office
CBP	Convention Against Torture
CBS	Columbia Broadcasting System
CDS	Credit Default Swaps
CEO	Chief Executive Officer
CEQ	Council on Environmental Quality
CIA	Central Intelligence Agency
CNN	Cable News Network
CSRT	Combatant Status Review Tribunals
CWA	Concerned Women of America
DC	District of Columbia
DHS	Department of Homeland Security
DNC	Democratic National Committee
DREAM	Development Relief and Education for Minors Act 2009
DTA	Detainee Treatment Act 2005
EPA	Environmental Protection Agency
EU	European Union
FAIR	Federation for American Immigration Reform
FBI	Federal Bureau of Investigation
FCC	Federal Communications Commission
FDIC	Federal Deposit Insurance Corporation
FEC	Federal Election Commission
FECA	Federal Election Campaign Act 1974
FISA	Foreign Intelligence Surveillance Act 1978

FY	Fiscal Year
GDP	Gross Domestic Product
GGOOB	Get Government Off Our Back
GOP	Grand Old Party (Republican Party)
HAVA	Help America Vote Act 2002
ID	Identity (as in Real ID ACT)
IIRIRA	Illegal Immigration Reform and Immigrant Responsibility Act 1996
IOU	I owe you
INA	Immigration and Nationality Act 1965
INS	Immigration and Naturalization Service
IRCA	Immigration Reform and Control Act 1986
IRS	Internal Revenue Service
LCV	League of Conservation Voters
LPR	Legal Permanent Resident
LULAC	League of United Latin American Citizens
MALDEF	Mexican American Legal Defense Fund
MBS	Mortgage Backed Securities
MCA	Military Commissions Act 2006
NAACP	National Association for the Advancement of Colored People
NAFTA	North American Free Trade Agreement
NASA	National Aeronautics and Space Administration
NATO	North Atlantic Treaty Organization
NMD	National Missile Defense
NPT	Nuclear Non-Proliferation Treaty
NRA	National Rifle Association
NSA	National Security Agency
NBC	National Broadcasting Corporation
NCLB	No Child Left Behind
NRDC	Natural Resources Defense Council
OASDI	Old Age Survivors and Disability Insurance
OLC	Office of Legal Counsel
OMB	Office of Management and Budget
PAC	Political Action Committee
POW	Prisoner of War
PPIP	Public Private Investment Program
PRC	People's Republic of China
RNC	Republican National Committee
RGGI	Regional Greenhouse Gas Initiative
RPS	Renewable Portfolio Standards
SAW	Special Agricultural Worker
SCHIP	State Children's Health Insurance Program
SCIRP	Select Committee on Immigration and Refugee Policy
SOS	Save Our State

SSI	Supplemental Security Income
TANF	Temporary Assistance to Needy Families
TARP	Troubled Assets Relief Program
UCA	Unanimous Consent Agreement
UCMJ	Uniform Code of Military Justice
UCS	Union of Concerned Scientists
UFW	United Farm Workers of America
UN	United Nations
US	United States
USSR	Union of Soviet Socialist Republics
VA	Veterans Affairs
WASP	White Anglo Saxon Protestant
WCI	Western Climate Initiative
WMD	Weapons of Mass Destruction

Chapter 1

Introduction: The Legacy of the Bush Years

Gillian Peele, Christopher J. Bailey, Bruce E. Cain, and B. Guy Peters

When Barack Obama's administration took office in January 2009 it was for many Americans a decisive and much welcomed break with the past. George W. Bush, who had entered the White House amid intense controversy about the validity of his 2000 electoral victory, left it with approval ratings of 22 percent, the lowest of any president according to a CBS poll taken on January 16, 2009. The eight-year Bush presidency was widely condemned as a failure not merely by political opponents but by many on the right who blamed Bush personally for the collapse of the Republican vote (Edwards, 2008; Tanner, 2007).

Yet the newly elected president was not able to begin writing on a clean slate. The country Obama now has to lead, its institutions and its politics as well as its public policies have all been by shaped by the events that occurred and the decisions taken over George Bush's two terms in the White House from 2001–09. In this Introduction we examine the legacy of the Bush years in order to set the scene for the chapters that follow.

The manner of Bush's achievement of the presidency in 2000 itself left important legacies for American democracy. The long and tortuous saga of determining who had in fact "won" the 2000 election cast doubts on the legitimacy of the Bush presidency and had two further consequences. First, the arguments about the counting of the vote, the adequacy of election machines, exclusion from the polls, and standards for determining vote validity drew attention to the complex and diverse character of an American electoral system which draws on a range of sources and varies markedly from state to state. Despite efforts to improve aspects of the electoral machinery over the immediate post-2000 period, especially through the 2002 Help America Vote Act (HAVA), faith in the American electoral system was dented by the experience of the 2000 election. Although fears that the system would again be deficient in 2008 proved largely unfounded, the saga of Bush's first election placed a large question mark over the adequacy of the US electoral system.

Second, the resolution of the 2000 presidential election in the Supreme Court also had wider implications for the legitimacy of the political system. *Bush* v *Gore* displayed to the public a Supreme Court apparently divided on party political lines, and one where a Republican-appointed majority seemed determined to hand the presidency to George W. Bush, adopting whatever arguments were convenient for the purpose. Whether fairly or not, it was inevitable that the Court's standing would be damaged as a result.

Once in the White House as a result of the Supreme Court's decision, Bush's presidency initially appeared dedicated to an ambitious conservative domestic agenda, until it was overtaken by the terrorist attacks on the New York twin towers in September 2001. That attack turned his administration into a wartime presidency, and set the stage for a foreign policy which would become deeply unpopular at home, involving as it did the commitment of American troops to Afghanistan and Iraq, and separate him from allies abroad. And, although there was early sympathy with the United States across the world after 9/11, Bush's subsequent approach to international affairs, with its emphasis on the United States' right to engage in unilateral preventive military action, generated increasing anti-Americanism. The Bush doctrine, as it came to be known, while not a completely new departure, seemed to represent a step change in America's handling of foreign policy and military strategy.

The 9/11 attacks also opened a period in which national security concerns would loom large in the domestic arena. The passage by wide margins and without much debate of legislation to "provide tools required to intercept and obstruct terrorism" in the so-called Patriot Act of 2001 strengthened the powers available to law enforcement agencies in a number of respects, including the powers to conduct wiretaps and other surveillance operations on citizens, and to detain and deport immigrants suspected of being involved with terrorism. At the same time the various national security agencies were restructured and a new Department of Homeland Security set up. The Patriot Act was seen by many critics, such as the American Civil Liberties Union (ACLU), as deeply flawed not least because of its overly broad and loose drafting, the threat to privacy, and the absence of judicial checks and safeguards on the use of the powers. The new emphasis on executive power, taken together with the Bush administration's own preference for secrecy, prompted extensive concern about the protection of individual liberties and constitutional propriety.

9/11 was not however the only crisis to beset the Bush presidency. Indeed the Bush presidency was in many ways one that was defined by external events not of his choosing. Less than a year after a successful re-election bid in November 2004 in which Bush claimed he had earned some political capital, Hurricane Katrina struck the Gulf Coast, devastating much of the area including the city of New Orleans. The incompetence with which the disaster was handled and Bush's own apparent detachment from the crisis were seen by many observers, including some Bush advisers such as Don Bartlett and Matthew Dowd, as the final nail in the coffin for the reputation of the Bush presidency. Apart from the administrative chaos that marked the handling of Katrina, many critics also noted that the disaster had racial, class, and political overtones. New Orleans, the city hardest hit by the disaster, epitomized a culture which was far removed from that of the Grand Old Party's (GOP's) natural constituency, and most of the city's inhabitants were black.

The final crisis to hit the Bush administration was one that forms a dark backdrop to the Obama administration. The implosion of the country's financial institutions in 2008 as a result of complex lending and investment decisions, especially on the mortgage market, presented Bush with a massive crisis. Although the crisis was global in spread, it rocked the United States, which witnessed the collapse of a number of familiar firms including Bear Stearns, the country's fifth largest investment bank, Lehman Brothers, and the mortgage companies Fannie Mae and Freddie Mac. Bush's intervention took the form of a massive $700 billion bailout for the financial industry (the Emergency Economic Stabilization Act 2008) which only got through Congress on the second attempt. On taking office Obama was faced with the need to frame a massive stimulus package, and inevitably encountered continuing problems such as the need to rescue the automobile giant General Motors.

Bush's own ambition for his presidency was deeply partisan, although like many presidents he came to the Oval Office promising to be a unifier. Together with Karl Rove, his key electoral strategist, Bush wanted to engineer a long period of Republican hegemony and to restructure the state, cutting back on social expenditure and reducing taxation in a bid to encourage entrepreneurial activity and free up the market. His detached style of governance was very different from his predecessor Bill Clinton and from his successor Obama. Critics noted that he displayed little intellectual curiosity or interest in the details of policy-making, and had a liking for orderly, short meetings where the points to be decided could be reduced to a few key items. Initially he countered the charge of inexperience by relying on seasoned administrators – many from his father's administration. However personal loyalty also figured highly in his calculations, and over time – and especially between the first and second administrations – there was a growing dependence on an inner circle of loyalists. The powerful role that Dick Cheney built up as vice president was central to the style of the administration, and left a new model for the handling of that office (Gellman, 2008).

Bush's conception of the constitutional role of the presidency clearly departed markedly from the shared powers model of checks and balances that the majority of scholars have seen as essential to the workings of the American system. Bush embraced a strong vision of presidential power and a unitary theory of the executive, which built on approaches to the office seen under Richard Nixon and later Ronald Reagan (Aberbach and Peterson, 2005; Nathan, 1975; Nathan, 1983). It was a plebiscitary theory of government that endowed the executive branch with the obligation to protect the nation, and derived from that obligation the right to resist control by other branches. There is now a mass of evidence of how scornful the Bush administration and its legal advisers were of the legitimacy of congressional restrictions on executive power. (See Louis Fisher's discussion in Chapter 15.) Bush himself expressed his view that he was the ultimate arbiter of the constitution and its meaning in a number of ways, but especially through the sweeping use of signing statements and the explicit distinction between those laws or parts of laws that needed to be implemented and those that did not. Not surprisingly, many critics were quick to point to the emergence of a "new imperial presidency," echoing the critique that had been leveled against the presidential styles of Lyndon Johnson and Richard Nixon (Rudalevige, 2005). Yet it should be noted that the precedents set by George W. Bush are available for use by his successor, and that Obama, while he may avoid some of the more flagrant abuses of executive power, has not rejected all of the arguments deployed by Bush, and indeed has already incurred criticism for his (or his Department of Justice's) deployment of arguments which suggest reliance on a strong view of executive authority to justify secrecy. Obama has also issued signing statements in relation to the legislative spending authority.

Despite the circumstances of the 2000 election (and the narrowness of the country's electoral divisions), Bush's ideological ambition and style of government meant that there was no real attempt to build cross-party consensus, and the administration's approach was intensely partisan. That partisanship inevitably affected the operation of Congress, and the inter-branch relationship between executive and legislature. In the House, the Republicans who had taken control in 1994 retained their majority when Bush won the presidency in 2000, and indeed kept it for six of the eight years of his presidency. Under Newt Gingrich's leadership after 1994, House Republicans had been aggressively ideological, giving priority to party goals rather than institutional ones. That remained a feature of the post-2000 period, leading many critics to note a decline of comity and reduced attention to such constitutional responsibilities as effective oversight of the administration as the Republican majority mobilized behind Bush's program. In the Senate, where the Republicans also had a majority from 2001 until 2007, there was also a lack of attention to the scrutiny function in such matters as appointments and science and medical policy.

With the 2006 election there was a shift to Democratic Party control of Congress, and consequential reassertion of some elements of the legislature's constitutional role as a check on the executive. The way the Republicans had used power when they were in the majority nevertheless left a bitter legacy of distrust between the parties. But the intense partisanship also damaged the reputation of Congress with the general public. Indeed by quite startling margins polls underlined the public distrust of Congress as an institution. Thus a May 13, 2009 poll for Rasmussen, quoted in *The Bulletin,* revealed that only 13 percent of Americans rated Congress as the institution of federal government they would trust most, while by two to one Americans thought that no matter how bad things were, Congress could make them worse. Half the respondents thought elections were rigged in favor of incumbents, while more than half thought most members of Congress cheated on their taxes, and two-thirds of respondents thought their own economic judgment better than that of Congress (see Tremoglie, 2009).

The Bush years thus saw a dangerously weakened role for Congress, as the president asserted executive powers and the Republicans in the legislature acquiesced in much of the president's policy. The Bush years also saw intensely partisan controversy surrounding nominations to the federal bench, as Democrats, although a minority in the Senate for much of his presidency, used the procedural device of the filibuster to delay or block Bush's judicial nominations. Indeed the determination of Democrats in the Senate to block Bush's judicial nominees by using the filibuster threatened to provoke major retaliation, as Senate leader Bill Frist threatened what came to be known as the "nuclear option," the reform of the Senate's filibuster power. In the end the threat was deflected by the ad hoc coalition of Democrats and Republicans, known as the "Gang of 14," who broke party lines to moderate Democratic obstruction of judicial nominees and to oppose any move to weaken the filibuster weapon.

The controversy over the filibuster not merely underlined how stark the partisan divisions had become in Congress; it also signaled how politicized the process of appointing to lower federal positions had become. Bush, like his father and Ronald Reagan, saw the federal bench as an important element in the strategy for institutionalizing conservative values, and he relied for advice on nominees not on the American Bar Association (ABA), but on the Federalist Society and other conservative judicial groupings.

At the level of the Supreme Court, Bush got his choice of chief justice, the relatively young John Roberts, and associate justice, Samuel

Alito – though not until after he was forced to withdraw the nomination of Harriet Myers.

One of the issues that has confronted the courts in recent years has been that issue of federalism – the respective powers of state and federal government. Although he was a former governor of Texas and a self-proclaimed "faithful friend of federalism," Bush espoused "big government" policies which expanded federal grants in aid, increased new mandates and federal pre-emption of state authority, and expanded the federal government's role in relation to the states. This transformation of conservatism produced an approach to federalism which, as Timothy Conlan notes in Chapter 10, was in marked contrast to the emphasis on the devolution of power and federal restructuring of the Nixon and Reagan years.

More ominously perhaps for the health of federalism in the longer run was the financial situation of the states by the end of the Bush presidency. The level of federal aid to state and local governments grew rapidly under George W. Bush, with increased regulation and federally driven initiatives especially in the policy areas of education, health care, homeland security, and electoral reform. The recession and credit crisis has seriously weakened the states' ability to raise revenue, as income and sales taxes have declined and the costs of many state-provided services have spiraled. Only those states that have revenues derived from natural resources have been to some extent sheltered from the financial storm.

President Bush has also of course left a significant policy legacy on both the domestic front and internationally. On the domestic front there was his determination to push through tax cuts in the early period of his presidency. These tax cuts in the years 2001–03, when taken together with expanded defense spending, have created yawning budget deficits which will likely run far into the future.

It was however in the field of foreign policy that the most controversial legacies were constructed. Mention has already been made of the Bush doctrine, and the tilt towards a strong emphasis on the United States' right to use preemptive force to defend itself from attack. In the immediate aftermath of the 9/11 attacks the United States launched a war in Afghanistan, known as Operation Enduring Freedom. By 2002, however, the President was also making a strong argument in favor of war in Iraq on the grounds that the Iraq dictatorship had weapons of mass destruction. This invasion was undertaken without extensive international support, and although the United States succeeded in toppling the regime, the military conduct of the campaign and the strategy for establishing a viable government in place of Saddam Hussein became hopelessly bogged down. The cost in money, lives, and American reputation was devastating, detracting from the anti-terrorism struggle elsewhere and incurring deep public hostility. In the election campaign of 2008 Obama promised a timetable for the withdrawal of American troops, but it remains to be seen how easily he can deliver on this, as well as on his other promises.

The chapters in this new volume of developments all address the institutional and political problems that Obama has inherited from his predecessor, and explore their implications for the governance of the United States. As before, each chapter has been written specifically for this volume, and apart from the editors, the team of authors is wholly new.

In Chapter 2 Gillian Peele examines the extent to which there is a new political agenda in the United States as a result of the Obama election victory. She examines the opportunities for Obama to change the direction of American public policy, especially in such controversial areas as health care. She sets the discussion against the background of shifts in the ideological balance of the United States, and the changing role played by race and religion in shaping American values. She argues that for Obama, despite the new opportunities, the constraints on freedom of action are very evident. Those constraints spring from the disaggregated policy process and the range of veto players in the American system, as well as from the diverse character of American society and the sheer difficulty of the problems that were in store for Obama on taking office.

The making of Obama's electoral victory and the mandate that provided are analyzed in Chapter 3 by Bruce Cain. Cain notes the way in which some specific features of the 2008 elections – especially the collapse of public funding and the way the Democratic primaries evolved – will have to be addressed in the coming years. 2008 was an election that raised as many questions as it answered, and leaves important unfinished business for the parties.

In Chapter 4, Alan Ware looks more broadly at the character of the contemporary party system. He finds that the team-like character of parties has increased in recent years, partly because of the changed behavior and appeal of party leaders, and partly because of the long-term working through the political system of southern realignment, which sorted out previous anomalies inside Democratic and Republican ranks. Party conflict is a much more important feature of the system today than for many years. But Ware is not entirely sure that it will endure. As he notes, there is a possibility that the clarity of party today could be replaced, especially given the complexity of the different arenas created by the constitution. For the moment, however, party and partisanship are central features of the polity.

Parties are not the only players in the political system of the United States. Interest groups, as Dorie Apollonio notes in Chapter 5, play a large role in American politics, and one, she suggests, that is often more significant than that of political parties. Not only have such groups increased in number and influence over the twentieth century, new tactics (such as the use of front groups to hide funding from unpopular sources such as tobacco firms) now allow lobbies to circumvent a good deal of restrictive legislation. While there are occasions on which public concern results in efforts to limit the influence of these groups, American political culture is often more suspicious of big government than of private business. Apollonio asks, however, whether the financial crisis that engulfed the United States from the end of the Bush presidency may have made certain business activities unpopular and cast suspicion on the private sector's ethics more generally. If so, this cultural shift may have created a new opportunity for interest group reform, although, as her chapter hints, that moment might not merely be short-lived, but the mechanisms of regulation will have to be chosen with care.

The mass media are also key players in their own right in the political system, and in the United States, as in most democracies, technology is transforming their role. Obama's victory was in many ways the product of new media developments, and the 2008 elections stand out as the point at which the Internet came into its own. Yet, as Jonathan Parker makes clear in Chapter 6, Obama's victory was the result of a hybrid strategy, mixing old tactics and new technology in a powerful campaigning and fund-raising drive. Beyond the Obama campaign, the election also witnessed the ability of new media to affect the reputation of candidates, as clips of Sarah Palin interviews – real and spoof – were viewed repeatedly on YouTube. The primary focus of Parker's chapter is however the continuing transformation of the structure of the American media, involving the decline of traditional media (especially newspapers and magazines, but also network news) and the rise of new media in the form of cable and Internet. As Parker notes, the current economic downturn has reinforced the decline, and has had a devastating effect on newspapers, reducing their advertising and forcing them to lay off staff. (Such a familiar title as the *Christian Science Monitor* has become an Internet-only paper, and other newspapers and magazines have closed altogether.) The majority of today's citizens are getting their information about politics from the Internet, and the candidates and parties as well as other political players will have to adjust.

Obama's approach to the presidency is discussed by Jon Roper in Chapter 7. He makes it clear, as does Bruce Cain, that Obama's campaigning style was different from anything that had gone before. In power, Roper suggests, Obama has already displayed many of the qualities that analysts such as Fred Greenstein have used to judge what makes for presidential success (Greenstein, 2004). Among the criteria that Greenstein sees as crucial to a president's ability to achieve his goals are the power to communicate, and the key attributes of cognitive skill and emotional intelligence. Roper underlines also Obama's ability to prioritize by putting the $787 billion stimulus package of domestic spending, benefit expansion, and tax cuts at the top of his agenda, and applauds his willingness to compromise to secure the passage of key elements of that package into law as the American Recovery and Reinvestment Act (ARRA) in February 2009. It is of course entirely possible that much of the admiration for Obama's self-presentation will wear off with time and as his administration encounters political roadblocks. Initially, however, his handling of the presidential campaign and the presidency has proved intriguing.

The realities of American politics were to the fore in the debate about the economic recovery legislation. One of the features of congressional response to the Obama stimulus package was the extent to which the vote on it was almost entirely partisan, despite Obama's initial hope that national rather than party goals would prevail in its consideration. Thomas Mann takes up this theme in his assessment of the current congressional mood in Chapter 8. His earlier analysis of Congress as a "broken branch" underlined the constitutional and political dangers associated with the last decade's changes in congressional behavior (Mann and Ornstein, 2008). Here he traces the evolution of some of those changes through the 110th Congress to opening of the 111th Congress, focusing on such issues as leadership and mobilization in the legislature as well as wider issues of legislative capacity.

In Chapter 9, Paul Martin takes up the debate about the role of the Supreme Court in American politics. He argued that under Bush the Supreme Court did indeed finally achieve a conservative ideological majority with the appointments of John Roberts and Samuel Alito, although he acknowledges that the tangible results of this shift have thus far been disappointing for conservatives. Martin stresses the extent to which the Court (and indeed the legal system generally) should not be seen as an isolated institution, but as one where there is interplay between the branches. He examines in this respect the Court's somewhat weak response to Bush's aggressive constitutional agenda on war powers, but also looks in detail at the congressional reaction to a conservative decision by the Court on equal pay. Here Congress was able swiftly to overturn a restrictive Supreme Court in legislation (the Lily Ledbetter Fair Pay Act 2009) in a manner comparable to Congress's overturning of conservative interpretations of civil rights legislation in the 1990s. As Martin also shows, Supreme Court litigation can be encouraged by judicial signals – as occurred in *D.C. v Heller* – and we now see the elaboration of conservative rights claims (such as the right to bear arms) receiving support from the bench. This adds a new dimension to the tussle between liberals and conservatives over such issues as abortion rights, the death penalty, and affirmative action. More generally Martin thinks the current Court, at least before any reshaping achieved by Obama, to be more friendly to business interests than it once was, and more skeptical of claims to executive power.

Economic crises traditionally produce a shake-up of governmental organization. In Chapter 10, Tim Conlan's discussion of federalism explores the implications of Obama's initiatives and priorities on inter-governmental relations. He argues that Obama's commitment to health care (where he signed in his second week of office a massive expansion of the State Children's Health Insurance Progam (SCHIP) that Bush had twice vetoed), combined with new spending of the economic stim-ulus package and the other financial requests in the regular budget, will push the curve of federal spending sharply upwards again. This additional money, while important for states, is also likely to further tilt the balance of the federal system in a centralizing direction, and taken together with the political constraints on state autonomy, limit the states' room for maneuver. Moreover, the way in which money has been given under the American Recovery and Reinvestment Act (ARRA) has introduced new administrative requirements of accountability and transparency on the state recipients.

The economy was clearly the most urgent problem facing Obama when he took office. In Chapter 12, George McKenzie analyzes the causes of the 2008 financial crisis and explores the economic tools available to Obama as he tries to ameliorate America's economic woes. McKenzie explains the difficulty of turning an economy like that of America around quickly, noting the intricate nature of the budgetary process and the impact on the economy of longer-term structural prob-lems such as the funding of Social Security. McKenzie's conclusions are largely pessimistic as he notes the rising level of public debt. But he also notes that lessons had been learned from the Great Depression (when credit was tightened rather than relaxed), and he observes that some of the structural problems – notably Social Security – could be eased if there was the political will to do so. Equally McKenzie sug-gests that the kind of "loose rein" free market capitalism associated with the 1980s is unlikely to operate in the same way in future, as the public demands closer and tighter regulation of financial institutions. The fact that the era of light-touch regulation is over can indeed already be seen in the United States by the proposal to tighten the way credit cards work and the report that senior administration officials were considering a major financial regulatory reform package with a single agency to regulate the banks (Appelbaum and Goldfarb, 2009). The package was also thought to include new regulation to cover derivatives and hedge funds, and a new agency to protect the consumers of financial products.

The gloomy economic situation that Obama encountered in January 2009 clearly limited the scope that he had to tackle other domestic policies. Yet, as Guy Peters shows in Chapter 13, there are vitally important issues in relation to social policy that demand attention. The reform of health care is clearly an issue that Obama was especially committed to pursuing. Peters argues that, contrary to received wisdom, America has a sizeable welfare sector, although it is distinguished from its European counterparts by variation because of the states' participation, by means testing and by the reliance on social insurance. There are clearly structural problems with many of the American programs – especially Social Security, where the demographic trends suggest that the system is facing bankruptcy – and there are also problems of perception and public opinion. The social security system could be repaired by the injections of new tax revenues; the health system could be reformed if the shibboleths of socialized medicine and freedom of choice were resisted. But the challenge of reform is severe also because of the diversity of the system, especially the number of both public and private interests involved, and the fact that whatever solutions are found are likely to involve cost.

Few policy areas have showed as much of a break with the past as that of environmental policy under Obama. Chris Bailey shows in Chapter 11 how Bush conducted an "unprecedented assault" on the environment, weakening key legislation and failing to address central environmental problems. Much of this was done "under the radar" by low profile rule-making changes which were protected from the gaze of public opinion. Obama by contrast has made the environment a key theme, appointing a team with outstanding expertise, reversing Bush's rule changes and promoting a major comprehensive energy plan. Yet, as Bailey hints, the prospects for promoting more effective environmental policy making should not be overestimated. The policy area is a complex one with multiple actors; and, although public opinion is supportive of environmental initiatives, that support might not be very deep – especially in a recession. Equally the recent congressional partisanship has made the achievement of legislative consensus difficult, so that recourse has often to be had to executive rules rather the more stable legislative enactment. Finally, framing policy is itself complex: there is a new generation of tools different from the command and control approach of earlier decades, but it is not clear how well they work. Nevertheless for the Obama team the environment has taken on a new urgency, and the administration's collaborative international style should revive American participation in the attempt to find global solutions to problems of climate change and conservation.

In Chapter 14, Timothy Lynch looks at the prospects for the future of American foreign policy after Bush. As he argues, the expectations riding on Obama's shoulders were very high. Obama was looked to as a savior to wipe out the sins of his predecessor and push the "reset" button on American foreign policy. However, as Lynch argues, the same defining features mark the world Obama has to inhabit as marked the world under Bush. It remains characterized by American primacy, by unipolarity, by global terrorism and nuclear proliferation, and by only a limited capacity for international organizations to achieve effective solutions to problems. Lynch expects continuity in Obama's handling of such problem areas as Iran, Russia, and China, although he notes that there will be differences of emphasis, tone, and style. Although Obama has not adopted the grand strategy of a war on terrorism, he subscribes to its component parts. And although a liberal in the Senate, Obama is now navigating between a liberal and a realist perspective, which leaves him very close in practical terms to the policy agenda of his predecessor. Of course there may be some major changes (such as Cuban policy), but for the most part the emphasis is on continuity, not change.

In the last two chapters the authors address two issues of major and wide-ranging significance for the future of American policy. In Chapter 15, Louis Fisher examines the extent to which Bush's highly questionable interpretation of his executive powers has threatened civil liberties. Fisher examines the handling of such issues as extraordinary rendition and eavesdropping by the Bush administration, to show how Bush based these highly suspect policies on a claim to constitutional authority which Fisher strongly believes is unwarranted. Yet what is interesting in the survey of this material is the extent to which Obama, though he has taken some bold steps such as announcing the close of Guantánamo, has not entirely stepped back from the strong doctrines espoused by Bush. Indeed the intriguing question that emerges from Fisher's chapter is not so much whether Bush's alternative to the Madisonian system of checks and balances was flawed, but whether, if it had not been promoted so crudely, it would have gained more consent. Put rather differently, to what extent is the Madisonian system compatible with the modern requirements of a war on terror?

Finally, in Chapter 16, James Hollifield addresses a topic that has not been directly covered in previous editions of *Developments in American Politics* – immigration. Hollifield shows how different models of immigration have dominated American thinking at different times, and he explains carefully the reasons that it is such an intractable issue in domestic politics. Yet, as Hollifield underlines, and the point is echoed in Gillian Peele's chapter, immigration is in the process of transforming the United States – culturally, politically and socially – and posing huge questions about American identity.

These issues will doubtless continue to be debated throughout the Obama administration and beyond. We hope that the treatment given them here will be helpful not just to those formally studying American politics, but also to anyone with an interest in the future of a world shaped by its most powerful country.

Chapter 2

A New Political Agenda?

Gillian Peele

Introduction

Political scientists have frequently emphasized the extent to which the American system combines periods of stability with periods of significant change (Baumgartner and Jones, 1993). The 2008 elections in the United States clearly signaled a dramatic change in the nation's political balance, and held out the promise of a new political agenda, which would differ radically in many ways from that of President George W. Bush's administration. By electing the Democrat Barack Obama, American voters transferred power to a president whose youth and ethnicity made him a distinctive occupant of the Oval Office, and whose message to the electorate invoked the rhetoric of change and hope. Once into the Obama presidency, however, the policy consequences of the 2008 elections became somewhat blurred. Critics had pointed to the way Obama's campaign emphasized his personal charisma at the expense of the issues, and some had underlined the point that, far from being a dangerous radical, Obama was a highly pragmatic centrist in the tradition of John Kennedy and Bill Clinton (Street, 2009). Although there were some early symbolic policy reversals of Bush's executive orders, and notable differences of style and tone, commentators, whether sympathetic or not, began to point up the continuities in some substantive policy areas as much as the disjuncture between Obama and Bush. (See for example Chapter 14 by Lynch on foreign policy in this book.) In this chapter I examine the contemporary American policy agenda and the opportunities for policy change that Obama enjoyed on taking office, as well as the constraints on his administration's ability to shift direction. I do this by examining first the new actors in control of the policy process. Then I examine the shifts in ideological mood and political climate that seemed to mark the election, focusing especially on the cleavages of race, ethnicity, and religion in American culture. Finally I examine the constraints on Obama's freedom of maneuver, and the institutional and cultural factors that present barriers to change in the American political system.

It is of course sometimes argued, especially by writers on the left of the political spectrum, that the American political system is calculated to exclude from high office those who are committed to genuine and radical reform of the country. This is an important argument, and one to which I return briefly at the end of the chapter. However, my primary focus here is on the middle-level questions relating to the extent to which the Obama presidency entails a new political agenda for the United States.

Any incoming administration has to recognize that there are powerful factors limiting the likelihood of radical reform in the policy process, even if it is clear that sweeping change is what a new president really wants. Incremental decision-making and inertia are more normal hall-marks of the routine operation of large organizations, public or private. Powerful existing interests impose constraints on the government's freedom of action. Public opinion may be volatile or incoherent. In addi-tion the policy problems themselves may prove intractable, especially if the resources of the government are limited. In the United States, as I argue in the second part of the chapter, the highly disaggregated system of government can make it vulnerable to gridlock even when there is ini-tially an apparently strong political mandate for change. In addition the diversity of the country's social composition makes forging and maintaining a consensus a challenge for any president.

Obama's new team

How a president thinks about the governing process, and the team he selects to help navigate the shark-filled waters of the political system, are important elements in his ability to be a successful leader and to shape the policy agenda (Kingdon, 1984). The Obama transition was generally agreed to be an unusually well-organized and effective opera-tion under John Podesta, a former Clinton chief of staff and the presi-dent and CEO of the Center for American Progress. Among the early appointments announced was that of Rahm Emanuel as Chief of Staff; Emanuel's hardball reputation suggested the newly elected president placed a premium on expertise and pragmatism. Although the Obama administration was given a degree of cooperation from the outgoing administration, there was a keen awareness of Bush's determination to use his remaining time to promulgate executive orders and shift policy in directions that reflected his agenda. By the same token the incoming President was keen to use his executive powers to implement a changed agenda on such issues as abortion, stem cell research, and environmental issues as quickly as possible.

Initially Obama made rapid progress with cabinet appointments, although the pace slowed as he experienced a series of difficulties with nominees felled by integrity issues. The failed nomination of Thomas Daschle as Health and Human Services Secretary because of tax issues was especially embarrassing, as health care was high on Obama's agenda; but embarrassing too was the loss of New Mexico Governor Bill Richardson as Commerce Secretary as the result of a corruption probe. Daschle and Richardson's nominations were both withdrawn, causing some disruption to the cabinet selection process. Other controversial nominations – such as that of Timothy Geithner, who admitted a series of errors on his tax returns – got through.

Part of the problem for Obama as he formed his administration was that he had promised a new, cleaner approach to government. One aspect of this embrace of transparency was a more stringent vetting of nominees. Not merely was this a time-consuming process, it was one that publicly tripped up some nominees. The time factor became a major problem once Obama took office and found that many of his chosen sub-cabinet appointees could not be put in place quickly. Indeed by August 2009 there were reports that a substantial number of appointments had not been filled, leaving key posts to remain empty, be filled by non-political civil service appointees, or remain staffed by appointees from the Bush administration.

Obama's cabinet and other executive appointments brought to the policy process a new team of players, although many of the individuals had clocked up a good deal of experience in earlier administrations. Although Obama had exploited the novelty of his candidacy in the campaign, he had no wish to bring an "outsider" team to his administration. Much was made of Obama's admiration for Lincoln's inclusion of competitors in his cabinet, and *Team of Rivals,* a best-selling book by Doris Kearns (2005), was scoured for hints about Obama's approach to government. There were early suggestions that some key posts might go to Republicans. In fact only Ray Lahood, as Secretary of Transportation, and John McHugh as Army Secretary, were Republicans – both had been Grand Old Party (GOP) legislators. However, there were some key figures from the Bush administration who were asked to stay on – Robert Gates (a registered independent) stayed at Defense; Sheila Bair stayed at the Federal Deposit Insurance Corporation (FDIC), and in the summer of 2009 Ben Bernanke was given another term as chairman of the Federal Reserve Bank. The "team of rivals" did however incorporate his close competitor for the Democratic nomination – Hillary Clinton – at State.

Modern presidents always feel the need to make their appointees reflect the diversity of American society. Obama was no exception to this rule. Women were well represented in the top positions, with four women given full cabinet posts and two others posts of cabinet rank. (By comparison Clinton had five female cabinet secretaries, of whom four served simultaneously, while Bush had six, of whom five served simultaneously in the second term.) Apart from Hillary Clinton at State, Janet Napolitano took over Homeland Security, Kathleen Sibelius took over Health and Human Services, Hilda Solis took on Labor, and Lisa Jackson became head of the Environmental Protection Agency. Other key female appointments included Susan Rice, who became Ambassador to the United Nations, and Valerie Jarrett who helped organize the transition and became a senior policy advisor. Hispanics were represented by Ken Salazar at Interior and Asian Americans by Eric Shinseki at Veterans Affairs and Steven Chu at Energy. African American appointees included Lisa Jackson and Eric Holder, who became the first black Attorney General.

In some areas the expertise and commitment of the Obama appointees represented a very marked change from the Bush team. At the Department of Energy, for example, the appointment of physics Nobel laureate Steven Chu was a clear signal that, as Obama put it, "my Administration will value science" (Kintisch, 2008). Obama promised that "we will make decisions based on the facts, and we understand that the facts demand clear action" (quoted in Kintisch, 2008). His valuing of science was emphasized by the publication in March 2009 of his memorandum to the heads of departments and agencies to protect scientific integrity. Obama's emphasis on science was calculated to reverse what had been dubbed a "war on science" in the Bush White House, which had put politicized appointees into a number of scientific and medical posts, had restricted stem cell research on ethical grounds, and had endorsed theories such as intelligent design, which went against the views of the mainstream scientific community (Mooney, 2005). During the transition, it became clear that Obama would act quickly to reverse a host of executive orders and administrative regulations that had been used by Bush to limit stem cell research and to restrict abortion access (Connelly and Smith, 2008). And indeed Obama did take action very soon after his inauguration to change policy on abortion and stem cell research, following those executive orders with his memorandum on the role of science in government.

The economic team appointed by Obama was noteworthy for the extent of the professional economic expertise it deployed, and for the extent to which it drew on people who had worked in the Clinton administration, especially with Robert Rubin. It was also a team that was pro-market, and perhaps insufficiently distanced from policies that had contributed to America's financial meltdown. As the *Economist* pointed out in November 2008 when the team was announced, Lawrence Summers, who became Obama's Director of the National Economic Council, had as Clinton's Treasury Secretary backed the 1999 repeal of the Glass–Steagall legislation, which since the New Deal had kept commercial and investment banks separate. Christina Romer, who became Obama's chair of the Council of Economic Advisers, had in her academic writings argued that raising taxes retarded growth.

If the economic team seemed oriented to the center, so too did the foreign policy appointees. Although Obama had promised to reshape the American foreign policy process, and had undertaken to disentangle the United States from military involvement in Iraq, he put in key foreign policy positions three people who seemed to be to his right: Hillary Clinton as Secretary of State, a former Marine general, Jim Jones, as National Security Adviser, and Bush appointee Robert Gates as Secretary of Defense. Continuity and expertise, not new departures, seemed to be the dominant motif.

The election also reinforced Democratic control of Congress. In both the House and the Senate, Democratic leaders and committee chairs acquired enhanced capacity to shape the legislative outcomes, and the Democratic position in the Senate was further strengthened when Arlen Specter (R-Pennsylvania) switched parties in April 2009, pushing the Democrats close to a filibuster-proof majority in the Senate, although the loss of Massachusetts in 2010 threatened that aspiration. Nevertheless, the Obama administration was aware that even in such favorable political circumstances there was need for good legislative liaison, and the choice of Phil Schiliro was widely seen as a shrewd one. It should also be noted that, while Obama himself has relatively little Congressional experience, the new vice president, Joe Biden, has long experience as a senator, having served since 1973.

The mandate

The assumption of any new administration is that it should move fast to take advantage of the electoral victory and a "honeymoon" period, which may be brief. It was clear that Obama had won decisively in 2008, but how to interpret the spectacular nature of the Democratic victory in winning the presidency and Congress gave many commentators pause for thought. While some saw in the new coalition put together in 2008 the elements of a long-term realignment, other critics urged caution. While it is true that Obama's 2008 victory was built on improved performance among many – indeed almost all – sections of the electorate by comparison with Kerry's 2004 vote, the economic circumstances of the 2008 election were extremely propitious for the Democrats. The spectacular financial meltdown of 2008, which had destroyed institutions such as Bear Stearns, Lehman Brothers, and Fannie Mae and Freddie Mac, threatened economic collapse on a scale not seen since the interwar period. At the time of the 2008 elections unemployment stood well over 6 percent, though in some states it was considerably higher. By August 2009 it was 9.7 percent.

The Democrats were also blessed by a poor Republican campaign performance especially at the presidential level, the product of McCain's financial weakness, poor GOP organization and a failure to match Obama's skilful exploitation of new technology, especially the Internet, to boost support. While there are factors, such as the growing Hispanic population and support among younger voters, that point to a strengthening of the Democratic Party's long-term electoral position, it is far too early to predict that such factors will reliably work to their advantage in successive elections (Judis and Tuxeira, 2002).

A changing political climate

The 2008 elections also saw a tangible shift of mood in the United States. The Democratic Party, which had been out of power at the executive level since 2000, was resurgent, and its recapture of the White House changed the hopes and expectations not merely of its voters, but also of the host of liberal advocacy groups, organized interests, and think tanks which looked to Democrats rather than Republicans to advance their causes. Unions, a part of the traditional Democratic coalition, expected more access and pro-union policies. Although his economic team was not obviously "labor-friendly," Obama took swift action by executive order to reverse Bush policies on federal contracting which were seen as unfair to unions. Corporate business anticipated a chillier climate. (Interestingly, although the Obama cabinet hardly seemed hostile to business, it contained few if any corporate CEOs.) The conservative-leaning think tanks such as the AEI, Cato, and Heritage, which had all been crucial to Republican policy development over the period since 1980, similarly expected to be marginalized and to redirect their energies to developing alternative policies.

These right-leaning think tanks are part of an extensive and well-funded network of conservative groups and institutions that had been built up using money from such backers as Richard Mellon Scaife and John Olin. There was little comparable counter-mobilization by liberals until the early years of the twenty-first century. Indeed much of the debate inside the Democratic Party over the 1990s had been about how to repackage and reposition the Democrats at the center of American politics to maximize electoral appeal (Baer, 2000). However, after the Kerry defeat in 2004 Democrats and liberals became more serious about putting together a counter-organization. Rob Stein, a Democrat strategist, and Simon Rosenberg of the New Democratic Network began to mobilize to bring liberal-leaning groups together in a new coalition, which could counter the juggernaut of the right. It has been estimated that the new organization – the Democracy Alliance – since its foundation has given over $100 million to sympathetic liberal nonprofit organizations, including Emily's List, People for the American Way, and the New Democratic Network itself. With a Democratic administration in Washington such "not for profit" groups are likely to have much greater access and political success, and a different range of think tanks and policy institutes will be favored from those that enjoyed access under Bush. Thus such policy institutes as the Brookings Institution, the Center on Budget and Policy Priorities, the Century Foundation, the Urban Institute, and the Center for American Progress will have greater opportunities to shape the policy agenda, and may be tapped for personnel by the Obama administration.

Ideology – the death of conservatism?

The 2008 elections seemed to confirm an ideological shift away from the conservatism that had dominated the public philosophy of the United States since the late 1970s to a rekindled progressivism. On such issues as the proper role of government, on the economy, on health care reform, and on foreign policy, the public seemed to be rejecting the values that had dominated political discourse since the 1980s. Obama's stands on a number of specific policy issues did not merely seem radically different from those of Republicans, he seemed to project a new set of political ideals, a progressivism which emphasized equality and rights, concern about poverty, and recognition of the role that the public sector had to play in promoting those values.

While the precise shape of this new progressivism was not immediately obvious, the bitter recriminations and squabbling inside the conservative movement and the Republican Party highlighted the extent to which conservatism was a diminished force. For both the GOP and the wider conservative movement the 2008 elections underlined a loss of unity and direction which had been increasingly apparent throughout the Bush presidency.

American conservatism, which had become increasingly self-confident since the Reagan presidency, found itself divided between its several strands. The big government conservatism espoused by George W. Bush, and manifested especially in his controversial education policy – the No Child Left Behind legislation – and the introduction of a new medical prescription subsidy for seniors, antagonized those who believed in small government, deregulation, and balanced budgets. The emphasis on faith and morality, and the family values agenda of the social conservatives, antagonized libertarians. And a deep chasm opened up between neoconservatives who approved of Bush's expansive foreign policy and the more cautious traditional conservatives who wanted to see American foreign policy kept free of costly entanglements. These divisions not only led to a good deal of polemical agonizing as conservatives rushed to distance themselves from the Bush administration; the end of the Bush presidency also saw much speculation about whether the conservative movement had died or been killed.

For the Republican Party itself, charting a course forward from 2008 was painful. The party organization needed rebuilding in the aftermath of 2008, but the most important issue was the future direction of the GOP, and whether it was to reach out beyond its narrowing base of supporters even if that meant compromising its conservative principles. This issue saw public bickering after the election, as moderates such as former Secretary of State Colin Powell and Utah Governor Jon Huntsman urged a broadening of Republican appeal, while figures such as Dick Cheney and the flamboyant talk radio host Rush Limbaugh urged cleaving to the right. (Huntsman's selection by Obama as US Ambassador to China was interpreted by many not just as a clever display of bipartisanship, but also as a shrewd move to stymie a potential Republican presidential challenger.)

The Republican Party recognized the need for an image makeover, and in January 2009 elected its first African American chairman, Michael Steele. However barely a few weeks into his tenure Steele found maintaining unity in the Party problematic, and after a brush with Rush Limbaugh about who spoke for the Republicans, embarrassing controversy over the issues of abortion and same-sex marriage, and restrictions on his financial power within the GOP organization, it looked as though his period in the post would certainly be fraught and might be short-lived.

The question of whether or not to move the Republican Party to a more centrist position was thus one that generated intense disagreement on the right. Nor was this surprising. Republicans who looked at what their party supporters wanted were likely to be convinced that adhering to principled conservatism was necessary. Thus a Rasmussen Report in January 2009 found that 43 percent of Republicans thought their party had been too moderate in the previous eight years, and 55 percent thought it should become more like Sarah Palin. Only 17 percent thought it had become too conservative (Rasmussen Reports, January 2009).

Those who looked beyond that narrow base to the wider public were more likely to find a much more complex picture. First, as a Pew poll in May 2009 showed, although Republicans were at a low ebb on nearly every dimension – image, morale, and demography – their decline did not translate into automatic Democrat gains. In fact the largest section of the American electorate by May 2009 appeared to be those who labeled themselves independent (Pew Center, 2009). Thus while it appears true that Democrats and Republicans are more deeply divided than in the past, the largest section of the public appears to identify itself as independent (36 percent), in comparison with 35 percent who are Democrats and 23 percent Republican. Even if this group is best seen as partisan-leaners rather than truly independent, it points up the fact that partisan Democrats are in a minority in the electorate. What is even more problematic is that this body of independent opinion is internally divided about the role of government, about the handling of poverty, and about a host of other issues.

A new America?

Behind the Democratic triumph of 2008 there thus lies a much more confusing spectrum of attitudes amongst the general public, a complexity which Obama's policies will have to navigate. For example, while 86 percent agree that government ought to do more to make health care accessible and affordable, nearly half (46 percent), according to a 2009 Pew report (Pew Center, 2009), are concerned about the government becoming too involved in health care. And on some issues opinion is very fluid. Public attitudes towards protecting the environment at the expense of growth and jobs have proved vulnerable to the economic downturn. In 2007 66 percent said that the environment should be protected even at the expense of jobs and growth; in May 2009 that figure was down to 51 percent.

The health care debate itself is an interesting example of how even presidents near the beginning of their term of office can lose the ability to frame the debate. During the summer of 2009, as Obama tried to advance the proposals for health care reform through such devices as town hall meetings, the critics of reform often hijacked these grassroots discussions. It was not merely that Obama had difficulty getting his message across; it was also that some ideas, especially the notion that greater government involvement would lead to "death panels," became lodged in the public consciousness. After a speech to Congress on the issue and an appearance on television, Obama seemed to recapture the initiative, but by mid-September public opinion seemed evenly divided about both the plan itself and Obama's handling of the issue (Cohen and Balz, 2009).

Obama's ability to set the agenda also encountered obstacles in relation to financial reform, where the momentum for greater regulation of financial services began to meet resistance as the consciousness of the 2008 meltdown dimmed. The context of America's financial crisis also changed voters' priorities in other ways. Whereas in 2004 a plurality of voters named moral values as the most important issue facing the electorate, by May 2009 only 10 percent did so, and 50 percent put economic issues as their key concern. The so-called "hot-button issues" which have been such a central part of the Republican appeal in recent years appear to have lost some of their force, so that Republicans may have to devise another line of attack.

A divided America?

Behind these shifts in immediate public priorities, there are two longer and broader changes which seem to be reshaping Obama's America – changes in the role played by race and ethnicity, and changes in the role played by religion.

Race and ethnicity

Race is not the only major social cleavage in the United States, but it is the most tragic and the most deeply ingrained. The symbolism of America's election of its first black president was and is profound. It occurred less than 50 years after the Voting Rights Act of 1965 finally signaled federal determination to enforce the right to vote for African Americans, and while segregation and the civil rights movement were both within living memory. On one level America has obviously become a more tolerant and equal society than ever before, and has transcended its most shameful historical legacy. On another level, however, there are still important questions to be asked about ethnic cleavages in American politics.

How far race had an impact in the campaign itself is debatable. In the early stages of the primary there was doubt about how genuinely Obama appealed to African Americans. Was Obama not "black enough," or was his color a handicap? Obama projected himself as a "post-racial candidate," avoiding the issue and distancing himself from the appeal of black activists such as Al Sharpton and Jesse Jackson. At the same time Hillary Clinton at points in the primaries seemed to suggest that race could be a handicap for Obama. Obama's campaign thus seemed to many to be caught between de-emphasizing his identity and mobilizing a powerful constituency on his behalf.

Obama was forced to address the race issue when the press began to analyze the sermons of the black pastor of his Chicago mega church, Jeremiah Wright. Wright had been highly critical of the United States' international and domestic policy record, especially its treatment of its black citizens, and had even suggested that the country had partly brought the 9/11 attacks on itself. In one sermon Wright suggested that the words "God damn America" should replace "God Bless America" because of the country's record of killing the innocent. Obama was forced to address the race issue and dissociate himself from Wright's comments, which he did in a careful speech –"A More Perfect Union"– in Philadelphia in March 2008. Obama also discontinued his membership of the Chicago church.

Unraveling the overall impact of race in the election itself is problematic, not least last because it is difficult to get an accurate figure of those whose vote against Obama was motivated by race. However estimates put this at about 7–8 percent of the vote, which was more than counterbalanced by the increase in black turnout, and the shift of certain groups of white voters to Obama.

Although the circumstances of the 2008 election and Obama's candidacy obviously highlighted the position of African Americans in the wider society, there was a range of other ethnic tensions that surfaced from time to time. Latinos and African Americans have frequently clashed over public policy as well as in everyday social settings. Other ethnic groups in tense urban situations have targeted Asian minorities; and anti-Semitism has surfaced among ethnic minority leaders. More generally it was evident that although the constitution's promise of equality looked closer than ever to being met as far as legal and politics rights were concerned, the reality of social and economic inequality remained. Ambiguity about the significance of the Obama victory can be gleaned from a May 2009 Pew Center for the People and the Press survey. It found that after a few months of the Obama presidency, blacks had acquired a more positive view of American society and a more positive view of voting. Yet only a third (31 percent) of Americans believed that discrimination against blacks was rare; and far more African Americans than whites still believed that the status of blacks had not improved much. Black and white Americans differed sharply over the degree of effort they needed to put into the fight against discrimination and in the choice of tools to be used in that battle.

Clearly the Obama candidacy generated intense opposition in some quarters. There were many reports of race crimes during the election. And the outburst of Senator Joe Wilson during Obama's address to Congress in September 2009 prompted extensive reflection on the continuing impact of racism in American society.

Religion

In the immediate aftermath of the elections there was also speculation about the role of religion in American society. Religion has always played a major role in American society, and denominational affiliation was frequently a marker of political allegiance. Three features of religious observance in the United States today are especially noteworthy. First there is the sheer diversity of religious belief and practice across the United States. In addition to the divisions between religious traditions there is enormous diversity within those traditions, as a Pew report written for the State Department noted in 2008 (Pew Foundation, 2008). Thus within the Protestant community there are sharp divisions between the mainline churches, the evangelicals (who now constitute about half of all protestants), and the black churches, which claim about 13 percent of protestants. The Roman Catholic Church is now the biggest single denomination, but without the new members brought by post-1965 immigration it too would have been in decline.

The post-1965 immigration also brought to the United States a significant number of adherents of religions outside the Judaeo-Christian tradition, and as Diana Eck and others have observed, their presence is now obvious from the proliferation of temples and mosques in the United States (Eck, 1997). But there are divisions within non-Christian communities – Jewish, Muslim, and Buddhist groups – which further complicate America's religious landscape Importantly it also appears that the percentage of Americans who consider themselves unaffiliated to any religion has been rising, along with a propensity for Americans to shift religious affiliation over their lifetime (Pew Foundation, 2008a).

A second important aspect of religion in the United States in the last 30 years or so has been its visible politicization. Although there have always been links between religious adherences and voting behavior, the most marked impact of religion in the late twentieth century was the rise of the so-called new Christian right. This mobilization went through several stages.

At the time of the Reagan election of 1980 a good deal of attention was paid to newly formed groups such as the Moral Majority and Christian Voice, which under the leadership of entrepreneurial pastors such as Jerry Falwell sought to reshape the political agenda to take account of traditional moral values, including opposition to abortion and homosexuality. A decade later much of the original new right religious organization had been replaced by politically more sophisticated leaders (such as Ralph Reed of the Christian Coalition), better organization, and a strategy that integrated it more effectively with the interests and organization of the Republican Party. Although the factionalism which religious right mobilization brought to the Republican ranks both nationally and at the grassroots was sometimes disruptive, it also provided a reliable core of activists. With the election of George W. Bush to the White House in November 2000, the country acquired a president whose Bible-based style of Christianity had significant consequences, both on issues such as abortion and scientific research, and on appointments, where a number of fundamentalists and evangelicals were given key positions. Bush also wanted to involve the churches and other faith-based communities more effectively in the provision of social and welfare services. In part this played into his interest in developing an ideology of compassionate conservatism that could reach out to minority groups in society. Although Bush's establishment of an office of faith-based initiatives in the White House incurred skepticism, it is significant that Obama, whose electoral campaign emphasized religious values, has retained it (Kuo, 2006; Steinfels, 2009).

The third consequence of America's religious make-up is the presence of moral and lifestyle issues at the center of its political agenda in recent years. Such issues have always of course had a place in American politics: the anti-slavery movement in the nineteenth century and the prohibition movement in the first part of the twentieth century drew heavily on religious sentiment. But the late twentieth century saw renewed concern with such divisive themes as abortion, feminism, family values, homosexuality, gay marriage, pornography, and censorship, as well as euthanasia and the morality of stem cell research.

The question of polarization is one on which much ink has been spilt in recent years. For some, the United States had over the early years of the twenty-first century become a starkly and narrowly divided country, polarized around cultural, religious, and moral issues such as abortion and gay marriage as opposed to economic cleavages (Nivola and Brady, 2006, 2008). For others the division of the United States into two nations, red and blue, is exaggerated, at least among the mass of voters if not the political elites. Thus for Morris Fiorina, for example, much of the discussion of polarized politics is the product of a series of errors including distortion by the media (Fiorina, 2005). Fiorina's thesis is that America is a country where there may be polarization among partisans and activists, but where there is also a vast amount of consensus at the level of the ordinary citizen, with a tendency for religious observance to be correlated with political preference and voting behavior.

The situation with regard to religious and moral values is not however static. As noted earlier, Obama early in his presidency took decisive steps on morally sensitive issues, legalizing funding for stem-cell research and liberalizing abortion rules. On other moral issues, however, Obama's positions are not entirely predictable and are certainly not consistently liberal. For example, although he is opposed to discrimination against gays, his religious views make him opposed to same-sex marriage. He is not opposed to the death penalty.

As far as the general public is concerned there is evidence that opinion on some of the most flammable moral issues in recent American politics such as gay marriage has moved in recent years. A July 2009 Pew study of gay marriage reported earlier findings that, although opponents of gay marriage still outnumbered supporters by 54 percent to 35 percent, the figures had shifted since 2004, when the opponents outnumbered supporters by 60 percent to 29 percent (Pew Forum on Religion and Public Life, 2009). To some extent the impact of such issues may have been blunted by economic issues; generational change has also made opinion more liberal.

Certainly there is evidence of change within America's religious communities, although the issue remains highly divisive. Evangelicals for example have become notably more diverse in their views in recent years, with younger evangelicals exhibiting greater tolerance on issues such as gay marriage, and placing new emphasis on themes such as environmental protection, global warming, and poverty. The simple portrayal of evangelical Christians as a solid block of conservative activists is increasingly unconvincing. Commentators are thus divided on the future impact of the Christian right. For some, such as E. J. Dionne, the new right's position in recent years was anomalous; the movement will inevitably become less powerful, as a broader range of religious sentiment engages in public life (Dionne, 2008). For others the obituaries of the movement have been premature in the past and may be again.

All of these factors pointed to a complex context for context for policymaking and political competition. It appears to be one in which, while partisan attitudes may still be sharply divided, there is also a good deal of movement and fluidity, although not necessarily coherence among the electorate because a sizeable bloc of independent-minded voters makes opinion difficult to mobilize behind partisan leadership.

Continuing constraints

Obama's change agenda faces other constraints. These constraints are present on a number of levels. There is the constraint imposed by the sheer diversity of American society, which makes forging a consensus at the national level challenging. There is the constraint of the American political institutions, where the checks and balances of separated institutions may produce gridlock. The federal system itself produces many "veto players" who can block change, and different arenas make the integration of policy initiatives less than straightforward. And there is the constraint imposed by the peculiar slate of policy problems that America faces as it enters the second decade of the twenty-first century. I discuss each of these constraints briefly below.

American society

If American political institutions and an ingrained suspicion of government place constraints on the political agenda, so too does the complexity of American society. Twenty-first century America is a society of kaleidoscopic diversity. That diversity of interest and its mobilization have inevitably made the creation of consensus at the federal level a challenge.

Any assessment of American social complexity needs to start with its demographics. Although population growth rate is slowing, the United States remains a society that is growing rapidly in absolute terms, fueled by immigration, legal and illegal, as well as by natural increase. Two authors writing for the Pew Hispanic Center in 2008 estimated the American population would rise to 438 million in 2050 from 296 million in 2005 (Passel and Cohn, 2008). As the Census Bureau noted in 2008, by mid-century the American population would have changed in several other respects too. By 2050 the population would have become markedly older: one in five Americans would be over 65 by 2050. The ethnic composition of the United States would also be very different by 2050. On Census Bureau estimates the non-Hispanic white population is projected to decline to 46 percent of the population by 2050 – down from 66 percent in 2008. Hispanics are projected to double as a proportion of the whole from 15 percent in 2008 to 30 percent in 2050, so that by the middle of the twenty-first century one in three Americans will be Hispanic. Black Americans will rise from 14 percent of the population in 2008 to 15 percent in mid-century, and American Asians will climb from 5.1 percent to 9.2 percent. American Indians and Eskimos will rise slightly as proportion of population to constitute 2 percent of the whole by mid-century (Census Bureau, 2008).

Immigration in large part accounts for the country's population growth, and indeed it is significant that the remaking of America through immigration in the late twentieth century may be compared to the waves of immigration to the United States at the very beginning of the twentieth century (Gerstle, 2001; King, 2000, 2005). In 1900 some 10 percent of the population was foreign born, a figure which rose to 14.7 percent by 1910. After periods of immigration restriction during the inter-war and immediate postwar period, the figure soared again, stimulated especially by the liberal immigration legislation of 1965 which abandoned national origin quotas. Passel and Cohn in 2008 reckoned that by 2050 one in five Americans would be an immigrant, compared with one in eight (12 percent) in 2005 (Passel and Cohn, 2008). The debate about immigration is properly the subject of another chapter (see Hollifield, Chapter 16), but here it is important to underline the extent to which America's demographic mix has provoked controversy about the United States' identity, as well as about measures for dealing with illegal immigration.

The concern with American identity is fueled by the fact that ethnic minorities are destined to become the majority by 2042, and that of the different groups, the Hispanic community is expected to become the dominant ethnicity by 2050. This huge growth – involving a tripling of the Hispanic community between 2009 and 2050, when one in three Americans will be Hispanic – has profound implications for the character of the United States. The possible consequences of this ethnic shift include a threat to the use of English as the primary language of the United States, as well as the possibility that this large section of the population may be imperfectly integrated into the political system, with relatively low levels of participation. For some commentators, such as the late Samuel Huntington, the shift also threatens to undermine the values of the United States (Huntington, 2004).

In terms of the voting preferences of ethnic minorities in the United States, Obama clearly was their preferred candidate by a huge margin, taking some 96 percent of African American votes and 67 percent of Latino votes, as well as the overwhelming majority of the smaller Asian and Native American communities.

The other side of this rise of the ethnic minority population is of course the decline of the dominance of the white population. There has been something of a backlash in recent years, as some states have tried to pass legislation to make English the official language, and groups have mobilized against immigration and against the provision of social services and education facilities to the children of illegal immigrants (Lichtman, 2009). Indeed the applicability of health care provision to illegal immigrants became a factor in the debate about extending coverage in 2009.

Ethnicity, although a powerful cleavage, is not of course the only one. Religion has already been mentioned, but in addition we see throughout American society politically significant identities built on gender, age, geography, and sexual preference.

Women have become a major political force in recent years, and gender remains an important cleavage in American society. Although they were granted the vote in 1920, there was until quite recently only limited representation of women in major political office. Even in the early twenty-first century women struggled to achieve equality in the social and economic sphere. Women's organizations have long been active in politics but they are politically very diverse. Women's groups such as the National Organization of Women (NOW) and the National Women's Political Caucus (NWPC) are firmly in the Democratic and liberal camp. In 2008 Hillary Clinton's campaign for the presidency was symbolically important, although some doubted the extent to which Clinton herself seriously championed women's issues. Women's groups are now looking to Obama to make judicial appointments sympathetic to liberal women's concerns, and to promote social and economic equity for women. His first pick of a liberal Hispanic woman, Sonia Sotomayor, to fill the vacancy left by Justice Souter's retirement, is unlikely to disappoint them, although it has predictably generated intense rumblings from groups opposed to her jurisprudence.

Liberal women's groups have come through a difficult period. Although they made much headway in the 1970s on political claims and substantive issues such as the right to an abortion, the conservative swing after the 1980 election of Reagan put them on the defensive. The loss of the Equal Rights Amendment under Carter was emblematic of a shifting political climate. Liberal women's legitimacy was challenged from the 1970s by right-of-center organizations and leaders, who claimed to represent the female mainstream more accurately than the liberal groups did. Such groups have included Concerned Women for America (CWA) and the Independent Women's Forum (IWF), and a myriad of groups with a strong traditionalist family agenda (Schreiber, 2008). McCain's selection of Sarah Palin was a carefully calculated effort to enthuse the core Republican base and shape an appeal to conservative women. That said, there have also been substantial gains for women in recent years. At the level of political representation there are now many more female congressmen and senators, including the Speaker, Nancy Pelosi. (In the 110th Congress elected in 2006 there were 16 women in the Senate and 75 in the House; these figures rose to 17 and 75 in the 111th Congress elected in 2008, the highest number ever.) Hillary Clinton as Secretary of State joins a succession of powerful women in that post, and Obama has, as noted earlier, appointed other women to key roles in his administration.

With Obama's election, NOW identified a women's agenda consisting of several different kinds of initiative that it wanted to see pursued. The agenda covered economic justice, reproductive rights and sexual health, equality rights and an end to sex discrimination, health care for all, and measures to stop violence against women. In addition NOW wanted more protections for the lesbian gay and transsexual communities, educational equity, the promotion of diversity, an end to racism, and greater media fairness and accessibility.

While age may seem too general a category to form the basis of mobilization in the United States, as in other western societies, there has been increasing mobilization of senior citizens. In the United States the American Association of Retired Persons (AARP), which was formed in 1958, has become a very powerful pressure group on issues such as pensions and social security, health care, and medical provision. This development in turn reflects the changing demography of the United States and other western countries where there is an aging population. It has been estimated that there are some 37 million people aged 65 or over in the United States, but that by 2030 one in five of the population will be 65 or over.

From the beginning of the Republic regional divisions within the United States have been highly salient, and the north/south divisions were both the cause of a civil war and the source of enduring differences. Other regional divisions retain significance – especially when economic and political divisions appear to overlay cultural ones. For many observers there is in the United States a division between America's cultural elite, located on the eastern seaboard and in the larger cities, and small-town America. During the primaries Obama was criticized for saying that residents of small-town America tended to cling to guns, or religion, or antipathy to people not like them, out of bitterness about lost jobs. This remark brought much criticism, but it highlighted a perception of a cultural chasm in the United States. Today the South still stands out politically as the shrinking base of Republican electoral support and the source of many of the GOP's standard bearers in Congress.

Sexual preference has also become an important source of identity within the United States, especially in the cities. The gay movement has a wide agenda, which has moved from a call for legal equality in such fields as property rights and employment, through concern with health care, and on to gay marriage.

The shift from a liberal and permissive environment to one of conservatism in the 1980s put the gay movement on the defensive, and the Bush administration was seen increasingly hostile to gay rights. In 2004 the Republican Party included opposition to gay marriage in its electoral platform, echoing President Bush's endorsement of a constitutional ban forbidding gay marriage. As a result, the Log Cabin group (the gay Republican faction) refused to endorse President Bush for re-election. The emphasis on traditional morality formed part of an electoral strategy designed to solidify key Republican supporters.

Willingness to recognize same-sex marriage and same-sex civil partnerships is increasing, albeit slowly. Traditionally liberal areas such as New England have made the running, and six states allow gay marriage. In California the situation has been complicated by the passing by referendum of Proposition 8, which in 2008 overturned the California Supreme Court's recognition of same-sex marriages. The California Supreme Court then in turn upheld that proposition. Many other states have passed constitutional amendments confining marriage to unions between a man and a woman.

Obama's victory was relished by the gay movement, which is overwhelmingly liberal and Democrat in orientation. In the transition Obama promised to promote a number of measures which would secure gay support, including an expansion of the scope of anti-hate crime legislation, renewed opposition to workplace discrimination, support for civil unions and equal access to the privileges of marriage, a ban on any constitutional amendment against same-sex marriages, and an expansion of adoption rights for gay couples. Soon after the election Hillary Clinton announced a change of policy to allow same-sex partners of State Department employees equal treatment with married partners.

The policy process

The American system is one of checks and balances, with multiple veto players and multiple access points for interest groups. Although the importance attributed by political scientists to organized interests in the political process has waxed and waned, it is difficult to deny the prominence of pressure groups and lobbies at all levels of the American system. One reading of the role of pressure groups sees in their diversity in the United States a recipe for a healthy pluralistic politics. Other readings attribute to them many more toxic consequences, from gridlock to corruption. Regardless of the perspective taken, it must be admitted that getting momentum in the American system is not easy.

The institutional structure of American government does not aid informed decision-making, control, or leadership. The executive branch is itself a labyrinthine structure, which needs careful organizational management to ensure that it works efficiently. Indeed, the first problem that confronts an incoming president is how to organize his advisory coordinating units to reflect his personal style, and strike the right balance between informational overload and exclusion from key stages of the policy process. He also needs, as Andrew Rudalevige has emphasized, to strike a balance between expertise and responsiveness – between advisors who have appropriate knowledge, and those who are loyal to him personally (Rudalevige, 2009).

Congress is a powerful veto player in the system, and individual congressmen and senators are highly responsive to shifts in public opinion. Whatever its nominal party composition, pressure groups are able to mobilize in campaigns around issues that might have the effect of driving elective politicians away from a controversial stand. The existence of the filibuster in the Senate gives substantial power to determined minorities to frustrate the majority.

The policy process is not only about policy-*making*, of course. It is also about implementation. Here too the American system presents its own difficulties, with federal bureaucracy having to coordinate policy with state and local actors, and the courts may overturn or constrain policy. It is important also to remember that the courts, state, and local authorities will not necessarily march to the same tune as a president. Indeed these competing authorities will often be the product of quite different political impulses. In the United States legitimacy is frequently contested.

Federalism can encourage experiment and creativity, but it can also present obstacles to reform. The political dynamics of state and local government is often counter-cyclical in relation to federal government, thereby establishing tensions in the governing process. Governance at the state level is itself proving problematic for a number of states. In California the difficulty in setting a budget has been compounded by the state's constitutional and budgetary provisions and its commitment to direct democracy, which allows many policy issues to go to referendum. As a result government requests for additional funding failed, prompting the need for draconian cuts that will not merely affect substantive programs and employment, but seem set to trigger asset sales and drastic reductions in prison populations.

California's financial difficulties (which are to some extent replicated in many other states) point up another important feature of much of the American government: its vulnerability to surges of populism, which can cripple government and effective policy-making. The widespread use of referenda and initiatives, and the power of recall, are examples of this aspect of American government generating what some have called "hybrid democracy" (Bowler and Glazer, 2008). So too is the more recent vogue for term limits. Agenda-setting within the United States is thus not the prerogative of elected political elites. And although it could be argued that the opportunity for direct intervention by the people keeps America's political institutions responsive to the electorate, and may have other positive effects such as boosting political interest (Nicholson, 2008), it is also the case that the financial power of organized interests can use the device of direct democracy to mobilize on its own behalf. Regardless of the interests served by direct democracy, the way these instruments of popular democracy work can be extremely disruptive and an impediment to accountable government.

Running through much of recent American history has been a profound hostility to government itself, and especially to the federal government in Washington DC (Phillips, 1994). Indeed some observers saw in this sentiment in the 1990s (and encapsulated in Gingrich's Contract with America) a force sufficiently strong to unite the many disparate elements of the conservative coalition and give it a powerful popular appeal (Balz and Brownstein, 1996). Certainly waves of antigovernmental populism are a regular feature of American politics, and can produce institutional changes – such as the vogue for term limits at the state level – that have a profound effect on policy and government.

The problems

Alongside the constraints posed by America's institutions and the myriad claims of pressure groups, there are the constraints on a president's agenda imposed by the severity of the policy problems themselves. Few presidents have taken power with such an unremittingly bleak "in tray" of issues, most notably the war in Iraq and the consequences of the financial meltdown of 2008. So severe were the problems faced by Obama in 2009 that many commentators drew parallels with Franklin Roosevelt's advent to power in the aftermath of the Great Depression. Alongside the dominant issues of the economy and foreign policy, the Obama administration faced a host of enduring domestic problems, including the difficulty of managing health care and social security, educational under-achievement, crime, immigration, environmental issues, and the stubborn persistence of poverty.

The failure to make more progress in remedying social and economic inequality is in many ways the direct product of conservative capture of the political agenda in recent years. Some tools such as affirmative action, which might have been used to counter inequality, became suspect as a result of conservative arguments. American tax policies and the general free market orientation of the policy process took certain kinds of redistributive policies off the agenda and reinforced existing income inequalities. And the advent of poor economic conditions harmed those already at or near the poverty line, especially ethnic minority groups, as is always the case.

In the campaign, as Rudalevige noted, Obama tended to emphasize "inspirational competence" rather than a specific policy agenda (Rudalevige, 2009). During the health care debate some critics thought that Obama was being too aloof from the specifics of the debate – perhaps for fear that failure would damage his presidency, as the health care issue had dented Clinton's reputation.

Conclusion

Obama came to power with an agenda that is ambitious and promises substantive change. In many respects he had an unusual window of political opportunity to shape public policy. On many other levels, however, he is constrained by a number of daunting powerful factors, which reflect American political culture, the structure of American society, and the architecture of American constitutional design. As far as American culture is concerned, Obama's ideological path has been steered towards the center of the political spectrum, not just by the need to win a majority of the electorate and to raise the money needed to fight a presidential campaign, but also by the need to find consensus to enact legislation. The structure of American society creates a tension between an apparently vibrant pluralism, where conflicting interests are played out in the democratic process, and a powerful set of dominant elites whose interests prevail regardless of electoral change. The architecture of American constitutional design, with its Madisonian barriers against majoritarianism, has the effect of making the process of government one of slow negotiation rather than swift decision-making. Taken together these factors operate as a safety-lock on the exercise of power, limiting the ability for comprehensive reform but limiting also the potential threat to minority interests. It remains to be seen whether the style of government that results remains as able to satisfy the American public in the twenty-first century as it did in earlier periods.

Chapter 3

The Electoral System and the Lessons of 2008

Bruce E. Cain

Given the memorable 2008 presidential campaign and the significance of America electing its first black president, it would be easy to over-look the continuities between this election and the past. But in fact, the 2008 presidential contest illustrates several recurring themes about recent American elections.

To begin with, procedural issues continue to bedevil American national elections despite the multiple waves of reform in recent decades. Even the seemingly simple task of counting votes accurately, something that was not widely acknowledged in America as problem-atic until the 2000 Florida presidential election controversy, proved elusive once again. Months after the 2008 presidential election was resolved, Minnesota was still embroiled in litigation over counting ballots in a close senatorial race which left the prospect of a filibuster-proof US Senate hanging in the balance.

Second, for all the drama and media emphasis on the minutiae of campaign decisions and candidate performance, the state of the economy and larger partisan forces usually trump tactics in deter-mining the final outcome of national elections. This is less true of pri-maries, where candidates of the same party compete against each other and policy differences are often minimal, but it is very much the norm in general elections. While such factors as the tactic of choosing Sarah Palin as John McCain's running mate, the quality and number of tele-vision advertisements, the winners and losers of debate outcomes and the like, may have influenced the size of the final vote margin in 2008, the odds were strongly against the Republican nominee McCain from the start because of the bad economic conditions, disillusionment with a prolonged and costly war, and the incumbent president's deep unpopularity.

Last, as with President Obama's predecessor George W. Bush in 2004, the meaning of his electoral mandate was open to wide interpre-tation. The voting majority was clearer about what it rejected than what it embraced, leaving the Obama administration and Congress with the task of defining the election's meaning for themselves.

The unresolved issues of nomination

There is no process in American politics, including the Electoral College, more convoluted and obscure than the presidential primary system. Because so many critical details of the selection process are left to the individual states, presidential candidates must cope with a complex, confusing, and varying array of rules. Subject to only a few limitations from the national party organizations, states independently design such critical parameters of the nomination process as the schedule, whether to hold caucuses or run elections, the specific formulae for allocating delegates, and the administration of vote casting and counting (Smith and Springer, 2009).

Scheduling issues have become particularly problematic for the political parties, because there are clear "first-mover advantages" to those holding the earliest primaries (Busch, 2009). States that hold their contests at the beginning of the primary process receive more attention from the candidates and have a more decisive role in the winnowing process. As this influence advantage has become more evident to other states over the years, the primary schedule has shifted forward in two senses: the first contests (that is, Iowa and New Hampshire) are held earlier than before, and an increasing number of states have moved into the January–March window. Iowa and New Hampshire have declared their resolve to remain at the head of the line, rebuffing arguments that their populations are unrepresentative of the country's growing diversity, and believing that the conscientiousness of their voters justifies their position in the queue. The fact that the 2008 Democratic nomination fight went down to the wire may slow the front-loading process to some degree, as states weigh the influence of being first versus the chance to determine the outcome at the end; but the effect will likely be only temporary if close nomination races continue to be the exception and not the rule in the future.

The schedule figured prominently in the 2008 presidential candidate nominations in two ways. First, the Iowa and New Hampshire outcomes mattered: Iowa established Barack Obama's credibility as a candidate by demonstrating that he could win in a predominantly white state, and New Hampshire resuscitated the prospects of both Hillary Clinton and John McCain. Second, Democratic efforts to enforce the preferred schedule created a great deal of uncertainty about the final outcome. The penalties the Democratic National Committee imposed on states that tried to queue jump ahead of Iowa and New Hampshire (that is, Florida and Michigan) would have generated much acrimonious controversy at the Democratic National Convention had Obama not been able finally to lock up the requisite number of contested delegates for the nomination in the other states.

The Republicans penalized offending state parties by cutting the size of their delegations to the national convention in half. The Democrats decided on the more drastic punishment of not seating any of their delegates. The Republican solution did not stop candidates from competing in the rogue states, but it also did not engender the same degree of hard feeling from Michigan and Florida as the Democratic solution did. In normal times, with nominations determined by a large margin before most of the states even weighed in, this might have been less important. But in 2008, the exclusion of Michigan and Florida delegates favored Obama over Clinton. When rulings determine outcome, it is a natural political reflex to question their legitimacy. But changing rules that were made before the outcome was known is a prescription for even more controversy.

It was a true dilemma. If the Democratic National Committee, the party's national governing body, had caved in and counted the votes of the penalized states, it would have implicitly punished compliance with the party's rules and rewarded noncompliance, thereby undercutting the party's ability to enforce its primary calendar rules in the future. At the same time, not seating the Michigan and Florida delegates risked dividing the party and adversely affecting the Democrat Party nominee's chances in two critical states in the November election. In the end, the Democratic Party narrowly avoided a messy credentials fight because Obama was able to secure enough pledged delegates, but the primary schedule remains a festering problem which will have to be re-examined before 2012.

A second critical feature of American presidential nominations is the choice between caucuses (selection by simultaneous meetings of mostly party activists across a state) and primary elections (formal elections that vary by state in the rules about which voters can participate). While the general trend since the 1960s has been to adopt primary elections, the Democrats still held 16 caucuses and the Republicans 17. Caucuses are unlikely to disappear entirely, as many smaller states and territories seek to avoid the expense of running formal elections, and their political parties like to use the caucuses as recruitment tools for building their party organizations. As it turned out, the caucuses were critical to Obama's eventual victory. He carried all but two. Hillary Clinton's decision to ignore the caucuses in the small rural states was in retrospect a blunder.

The importance of the caucuses was magnified by the unintended consequences of Howard Dean's earlier decision as chairman of the Democratic Party to pursue a 50-state strategy of party building. Dean's logic, which was hotly debated in Democratic circles, was that the party could not grow if it merely concentrated its resources on large and marginal states. The effect of building up the Democratic Party membership in so-called red (that is, Republican-leaning) states was to mobilize a cadre of activists in the smaller caucus states who were motivated by opposition to the Iraq war. They would prove to be highly receptive to the Obama message, and skeptical of Clinton because of her prior support for the Iraq war. While it is more than a little ironic that a country that depends so heavily on elections allows caucuses to have such a central role in the presidential selection, it is unlikely that President Obama will lead any effort to eliminate the caucuses.

Last, delegate allocation and selection rules played a central role in determining the winners in both parties. The fact that the Republicans stuck with winner-take-all rules (allocating state delegates to the candidate that gets the most votes) played to McCain's advantage, as he was able to accumulate a large lead in delegates despite winning only pluralities, not majorities, in many states during the first two months of the Republican primary. By contrast, the proportional share rules that the Democrats used helped to prolong their contest, and tilted the results towards Obama. Clinton won the bigger states like New York, California, and Texas, and would have reaped much larger delegate and momentum rewards had the Democrats used the Republican rules. In the end, the prolonged contest had mixed effects for the Democrats: it cost Obama valuable resources and exposed his weaknesses to a greater degree, but on the other hand, it drove up turnout and interest on the Democratic side, and possibly may have made Obama a better candidate.

Another critical rule on the Democratic side was the provision for super-delegates. There are two types of Convention delegates: pledged delegates who are bound by primary and caucus outcomes, and super-delegates who are free to make independent decisions. Super-delegates slots (largely elected and party officials) were expanded in 1982 on the recommendation of the Hunt Commission. The impetus for this was the perception by many that the party had been taken over in the 1970s by grassroots activists whose influence had to be counterbalanced by more pragmatic elected and party officials. Informally, the officials who were eligible to be super-delegates liked it because it was a guaranteed pass to the convention.

Hillary Clinton, the presumed front-runner, secured an early lead in super-delegate commitments, including several from prominent black elected officials. But as the contest grew tighter, many super-delegates refrained from committing to either candidate, which only served to increase uncertainty about the final outcome. In the end, it was a great relief for them that the nomination was resolved by the pledged delegate count, as many super-delegates did not relish the prospect of being the decisive vote in an intensely fought intra-party competition.

The Democratic Party went through a cycle of continuous reform from 1968–82 (Polsby, 1983), but some are now demanding that they reopen the reform issue as a consequence of the 2008 experience. While nothing is likely to be done about caucuses, there will be continued debate about the schedule, and quite possibly the size and role of the super-delegates and the allocation formulae as well. The Republicans are by and large content with their rules, and passed on the opportunity to review them at their nomination convention.

If there is a case for seeing 2008 as an abnormal election, it rests on the rigid cleavages that emerged within both parties during the primaries. As a general rule, presidential primaries are mostly about organization, money, and the candidate. The "media and momentum" conventional wisdom, the dominant narrative since 1968, maintains that winning candidates attract media attention by their grassroots politics and organization, which then generates momentum in the form of more resources and support (Orren and Polsby, 1987). It is a story, in other words, of fluid, largely non-ideological voter decisions based on candidate resources and effort.

The 2008 election did not fit the media and momentum narrative nearly as well. Voter choices proved to be much more rigid on both sides, and partly for that reason, the momentum of early victories did not winnow the field as quickly as in recent presidential elections. On the Republican side, the divide was very much on ideological grounds, with social conservatives supporting Mike Huckabee, fiscal conservatives Mitt Romney, and independents and moderates John McCain and Rudy Guiliani. When Guiliani faltered, and Mitt Romney was unable to consolidate social and fiscal conservatives (partly because of Romney's mixed record on social issues as the governor of Massachusetts, and partly because of his Mormonism), the party establishment quickly fixed on John McCain as the only credible alternative. McCain, who had been the front-runner the year before, was revived by the "success" of the troop surge in Iraq (which he had supported) and a reorganization of staff and tactics to something closer to the leaner grassroots approach he took in 2000. The exit polls showed very little variation in the Republican vote by demographic measures, but strong relationships with ideology and religiosity. As a sign of the strength of this ideological cleavage in the ranks, Mike Huckabee stayed in the race long after it was clear to almost everyone else that McCain would secure the nomination.

The opposite was true of the Democratic primary: voters were more divided by demography than by ideology. The two front-running candidates held virtually identical positions on most issues (although Clinton was more identified with past support for the war in Iraq and Obama was slower to pick up on the change to economic themes). Instead, the historic nature of the candidacies split the party by voter characteristics: women, Catholics, Latinos, and older and working class voters tended to favor Clinton, while well-educated whites, younger voters, independents and African Americans leaned towards Obama. State party rules dictated whether non-party members could vote in a party's primary, and by March, Republicans were crossing over to vote for Clinton (partly as a result of an orchestrated campaign by Rush Limbaugh, the right-wing radio host, but mostly to affect the vote on the margin). The strong cleavage along demographic lines never lessened right up to the end, producing results that were predictable based on the state's composition and location. And since sentiments ran high along gender lines, it was not clear until the convention whether Clinton supporters would rally to Obama's cause even after he secured the requisite number of pledged delegates. In the end, the divisions along identity lines in the Democratic Party may have been a one-off reaction to the historic possibilities of a black or female presidency, whereas the Republican divisions along ideological lines are more likely to reappear in 2012.

The November election campaign

When political consultants and journalists appear on panels with political scientists, the ensuing conversation often reveals stark differences in the way academics and non-academics think about presidential elections. Campaign workers and reporters dwell on the day-to-day tactical and logistical decisions. Campaigns, they believe, are won or lost by such things as a superb advert, a candidate's misstatement, differences in the amount of money raised, the strategy of media buys, and especially the quality of the campaign staff. Political scientists, while acknowledging that these factors can make a marginal difference in a close race, see presidential campaigns as mainly determined by larger political and economic forces. A sub-field within political science in fact predicts elections in the late summer based on various factors that are known before the fall campaign – for example, the state of the economy (especially GDP growth, but sometimes also the rate of inflation or unemployment), the number of terms a given party has been in office (that is, implying that there is a fatigue or decay factor built into party control), the favorability of the sitting president in the late summer, the gap between self-identifying Democrats and Republicans, and whether the country is fighting a war (which rallies votes for the incumbents in the short run, but whittles support away over time). Other models rely on historical benchmarks, or projections from primary votes to the likely vote in November (Campbell, 2008).

While no one model is acclaimed to be best, some of them have done quite well over the years in predicting both the direction and size of the eventual victory. In 2008, most of the important common indicators in these models pointed in a Democratic direction. Perceptions of the economy were weak well before the collapse of the market. Compared with 2004, a majority of Americans believed that the Iraq war was a bad decision and were looking for a way to end it. Presidential popularity was at or near an all-time low throughout the general election campaign. And the gap between voters who identified with the Democrats as opposed to the Republicans had increased from near equality in 2004 to a 12-point advantage for the Democrats by fall 2008.

Since some of these models have been wrong in the past (most notably in 2000), and the situation in 2008 was unique in several respects, the outcome did not seem certain despite all the disadvantages facing the Republicans. Above all, there was the question of race. No black candidate had ever been nominated before, and given America's racial legacy, no one could be sure whether this would hurt Obama's candidacy enough to allow McCain to win despite conditions favoring the Democrats. At the center of this uncertainty was something called the "Bradley effect." In 1982, Los Angeles mayor Tom Bradley, an African American, ran against George Deukmejian for governor of California. The polls prior to election day indicated that Bradley would win, and when he did not, the final vote pattern suggested that he might have lost because he could not win white conservative Democrat votes. Pollsters speculated that the gap between what white voters said they would do before the election and what they actually did in the election might be distorted if white voters were unwilling to admit that they could not bring themselves to vote for a black candidate. The possibility of a "Bradley effect" in 2008 meant that even though Obama held a steady lead in the polls from the middle of September, no one could be sure whether the lead would stand up in the final tally (Hopkins, 2009).

Race also entered into questions about Obama's character. Because he was an unknown before 2004 and had served in the US Senate for only two years, Obama was not well known to the American public prior to running for the presidency in 2008. Initially, this meant that he was susceptible to rumors that he was a Muslim, like his father. But during the primary, the more salient problem was Obama's affiliation with black pastor Jeremiah Wright. Obama had claimed a close relationship with Wright, but that he had not heard any of Wright's most controversial comments. The Wright issue implicitly raised the question of whether Obama was truly as moderate as he seemed, or whether instead he was an angry black politician with suspect loyalties to the United States. At a minimum, because previous black politicians like Jesse Jackson, Shirley Chisholm, and Al Sharpton had been very liberal, many white voters had to overcome their suspicion, based on a common stereotype of black politicians, that Obama was concealing a radical agenda behind a moderate façade. Obama had addressed these concerns during the primary with a well-received speech on race in America, and while the Republicans never returned to the issue in the fall campaign, the fear was that this stereotype might finally express itself in an election-day Bradley effect.

Aside from the overriding doubts raised by America's racial history about its capacity to elect a black man as president, there were also other reasons to question whether conventional wisdom about political conditions would obtain in this election. Since the sitting vice president, Dick Cheney, had taken himself out of consideration from the start, 2008 was bound to be an unusual election in the sense that the candidate from the incumbent party, John McCain, had not been a member of the administration. Moreover, he could plausibly argue that he had publicly disagreed with Bush on some significant issues, such as the use of harsh interrogation techniques on suspected terrorists. But here the debate between strategy versus conditions as the dominant factor muddles, because McCain nonetheless chose to identify himself more closely with the administration's policies (in part to win over the conservative Republican base), reversing his previous opposition to the Bush tax cuts, and strongly supporting the military surge in Iraq. This important caveat aside, based on his "maverick" image and membership in the gang of 14 (which had brokered a compromise over the use of the filibuster in the Senate in 2005), McCain could plausibly claim to be less tied to the unpopular Bush presidency than anyone from the administration.

Finally, there was the matter of the surge itself. When McCain initially supported President Bush's decision to increase the American troop commitment rather than follow the bipartisan Baker–Hamilton commission's recommendation to begin a phased withdrawal of US troops in Iraq, he immediately lost support. But subsequently, when conditions in Iraq after the surge improved, McCain was able to argue plausibly that he had been vindicated, even though it was impossible to know for sure whether the surge was truly the cause, or other factors as the alliance with the Sunni Awakening or the growing resentment by native Iraqis of foreign Al Qaeda fighters. Even so, McCain's support for the surge became the cornerstone of his claim that he, not Obama, had the better judgment as to how to extricate the United States from Iraq.

If political scientists emphasize the broader electoral context and long-term factors, the *campaign uber alles* camp puts greater weight on the tactical and strategic decisions campaigns and the candidates make. Obama's victory, according to this view, was a product of his eloquent speeches and charismatic style, the steady management of his campaign ("no drama Obama"), the reassuring pick of Senator Joe Biden for his running mate, his better mastery of the economic crisis, and superior performances in the debates.

McCain's defeat, by the same reasoning, was greatly facilitated by his choice of Sarah Palin as a running mate (although it did not seem so initially), his bad gamble to suspend the campaign in order to fly back to Washington to deal with the economic crisis and bailout bill, his weak performances in the debates, and his occasional stumbles and slips on the campaign trail. Topping it all off, Obama had a large advantage in campaign funds, which allowed him to buy more television advertisements across the country. Overall Obama spent $310 million to McCain's $134 million on television advertisements, airing 570,963 spots compared with 272,737 for the Republican candidate. This money disadvantage forced McCain to make strategic retreats early in the fall from states that were expected to be in play (for example, from Wisconsin and Michigan).

But in the end, the broad consensus, even among the consultants and journalists who tend to eschew the big picture for the drama of the campaign, was that the market crash in October was the *coup de grâce* for McCain's prospects, saddling the Republicans as the party in office with retrospective responsibility for the worse economic crisis since the Depression, and discrediting the deregulatory policies pursued during the previous eight years. In this sense, conditions ultimately trumped campaign strategy and tactics in 2008. But could the election have been lost if Obama had made critical mistakes, or if McCain had done better in his vice presidential selection or on the campaign trail? There is of course no way to know for sure, but there were so many factors working against the Republicans in this election that it seems in retrospect as though it would have taken extraordinary actions to reverse the final outcome.

Other lessons of 2008

The 2008 presidential election also demonstrated some important points about the American campaign process generally. First, the public finance system is essentially dead for the foreseeable future. Instituted in the wake of Nixon-era scandals, Congress enacted presidential campaign finance reforms that included public financing in the primary and general election phases. The hitch was that the Supreme Court would only allow the public financing scheme if it was voluntary, ruling that mandatory public financing would violate the First Amendment freedoms of association and speech.

Reformers had hoped that the substitution of public for private money, even if voluntary, would lessen the influence of moneyed interests on American politics. But as the real costs of American elections have continued to rise, the public allocations have not kept pace. Early on, Obama indicated that he would accept the public money, but as it became clearer that he could raise substantially more money by accepting small private donations, he decided against the public finance option. This was a bold decision, not so much because Obama was gambling that he could raise more by private means, but rather because he opened himself up to criticism from reform groups within the Democratic Party (historically the party that has favored campaign finance). McCain, who was already also identified with campaign finance reform, opted for the public money, thereby threatening to pick off some potential Obama supporters on this issue. In the end, however, there is no evidence that this decision hurt Obama politically, and he was able to raise $744 million to McCain's $346 million during the total election cycle.

Obama's choice highlighted a common problem with the public finance system: the court ruled in *Buckley* v *Valeo* (1976) that those who opted in to public financing were restricted in their ability to raise and accept private donations, while those who opted out were not so restricted. As a consequence, strong candidates who can raise more money have little incentive to limit themselves by accepting the public finance option, while weaker candidates often do so. The system for the presidential primary elections matches public money to private funds, and serves to help keep marginal candidates viable for longer than they would be otherwise. The November system is meant to substitute completely public for private funding, but it can only accomplish this if both major party candidates choose to participate. However, unless the public money on the table ($84 million in 2008) is at least equal to or considerably more than what the candidates can raise on their own, there is little incentive to accept public financing in the future. The alternative, which McCain followed, is to accept the public money, but then let political parties and outside groups raise private money and run campaigns on the candidate's behalf. But in an era in which message control is practiced obsessively, candidates strongly prefer to raise and spend the money on their own, as opposed to relying on the judgment and efforts of allies.

Another notable trend in recent American elections is the growing importance of the Internet as an organizational force. Nonprofit groups like Moveon.org and the blogging community generally demonstrated their importance as outside forces affecting US elections in 2004; but the candidates themselves had not progressed much beyond providing webpages until 2008. Obama's campaign took the Internet to another level as both an organizing and fund-raising tool. It allowed him to tap smaller donors and to speak directly to his supporters, including announcing his candidacy and other major decisions by email. Obama's image as technologically aware and a BlackBerry addict consolidated his support among younger voters. By contrast, McCain was not an Internet user, reinforcing the image that he was old and out of touch.

The Internet also figured in the election in other ways. In particular, this was the first presidential election of the YouTube era. Early on, videos of Obama and McCain helped to fashion their images. The Obama-girl video and various hip-hop messages were popular with younger voters. Blunders by McCain (for example, confusing Shiites and Sunnis during a trip to the Middle East) and Sarah Palin's tenuous grasp of national issues (for example, her damaging interviews with Charlie Gibson and Katie Couric), and the *Saturday Night Live* impersonations, were replayed on YouTube and helped to fashion popular images of the candidates. Moments that could have gone unnoticed in the past because they occurred at an obscure event can now become worldwide viewing events thanks to the Web, magnifying mistakes and brilliant moments.

The emerging role of the Internet dovetails with the declining importance of mainstream media. US newspapers in particular are in crisis, raising serious questions about the quality and nature of future campaign coverage. Three forces have converged to undermine the print media's role. First, readership is declining and ad revenues have been siphoned off by Internet competitors such as Craig's List. There is a strong generational component to the readership trend, with many younger Americans preferring online to print venues for information. The online versions of established papers in America are popular, but with a few exceptions, they do not generate much revenue. Finding a viable economic model will be critical to the survival of newspapers. Failing that, there is considerable uncertainty about the nature of political coverage in the future. Television reporters rarely have the skill or freedom to do in-depth investigative reporting. TV stories are limited to three minutes or less, and usually focus on campaigning rather than policy or political analysis. Cable TV and talk radio provide a great deal of "analysis" but minimal amounts of sourced reporting. If newspapers fail, it will leave a serious gap in campaign reporting.

Aside from the diminishing market, a second force undermining the print media is the rise of blogging and the Internet. While many bloggers rely on traditional reporters to give them material for their analyses, a new breed of bloggers, often from academia, have diverted attention from the mainstream media. Those following the 2008 election closely often turned to sites such as Pollster.com, Five-Thirty-Eight, the Princeton Consortium, Real Clear Politics, and the Huffington Post for information and analyses that were often more detailed and expert than those provided by the newspapers. To some degree, the newspapers invited this. Unable to beat the television to breaking news, newspapers increasingly assumed the role that weekly magazines had provided in the past, of giving perspective and analysis to events. For this, they turned to experts. But the Web makes it possible for the experts to blog to the public directly without the filter of the reporter and the limited space allocated in printed publications. In short, newspapers were squeezed by their inability to compete on event coverage with television, and on analysis with the Internet.

That is not to say that the newspapers have no role. Detailed interviews with candidates, the daily observation of campaigns, and leaked inside information still largely emanated from print reporters who traveled with the campaigns and established relationships with campaign staff. But information of this sort comes with a lot of spin, and the public has become somewhat skeptical of reporters' abilities to cut through the spin without revealing bias. It is one thing to report what candidates actually said or did, but it is another to speculate about their true motives. The more reporters do the latter, the more they run the risk of being perceived as biased, a characterization of the media that campaigns themselves promote when it is to their advantage to do so.

The third force undermining the media is the growing trend for candidates to bypass press intermediaries and communicate with voters directly. If candidates can cheaply and directly send their messages to voters through the Internet and reach the less interested voters with 30-second spots, they can give voters the messages they want them to hear without the trouble of trying to shape the message through reporters. It remains to be seen whether this strategy will work for less salient and charismatic candidates than Obama. There is a virtual flood of information on the Web, making the competition for voters' attention increasingly intense. Established reporters or newspapers provide reliable filters in the sense that readers count on reporters who know the beat to tell them what is important as well as what is going on.

But of course, the main problem with this development is that it leaves readers the task of cutting through the spin themselves or relying on bloggers to do so for them. The question of whether the press is biased or neutral has been hotly debated in America, with conservatives in particular believing that the press is biased against them. Still, mainstream print reporters are held to professional norms, such as checking sources, attempting to balance divergent opinions, and investigating facts. The absence of this type of reporting leaves the checking function to those on the other side of the partisan or interest-group divide: in other words, it relies more on adversarial reporting. It is hard to predict with any certainty what this would mean for American politics, but we might plausibly worry that it would raise the temperature of political discourse and public uncertainty about the facts underlying disputes.

Implications for the parties

Looking at the pattern of the 2006 and 2008 elections, there appear to be broader trends in play, even if there is much disagreement over

what they imply for or about the political parties. The Democrats have now made substantial gains in two successive elections. The Obama victory (52.6 percent), while impressive for being the first Democratic victory over 50 percent since 1976, was still not of the magnitude of Lyndon Johnson's 1964 win (61 percent) during the height of the Great Society era. Even if we factor in the five points that racism might have cost Obama in his winning percentage, the victory margin would still be less than it was for the Democrats in the 1960s. The 2008 national swing of about nine points is close to normal since 1980 and about one-third of the 1932 swing (Bartels, 2008). Still, while the presidential election swing between 2004 and 2008 by itself may not rank as an historic high, combined with the congressional swing between the 2004 and 2008 elections, there has been a significant regrowth of Democratic strength.

In recent decades, nationalized congressional elections – elections in which national forces like the state of the economy or presidential popularity produce a significant swing in the party shares of congressional seats – have been rare occurrences. Even at the apex of President Bush's popularity in 2002, the Republicans gained only eight seats in the House and two seats in the Senate. In 2004, it was much the same story even though Bush won the presidency by a larger margin than in 2000: the Republicans picked up three seats in the House and four in the Senate. By contrast, the Democratic gains were substantial in the last two elections, picking up 31 House and five Senate seats in 2006, and 21 House and eight Senate seats in 2008. By 2009, the Democrats had a healthy 257–178 margin in the House and a 57–40 advantage in the Senate, with two independents and a converted Republican (Arlen Specter of Pennsylvania) caucusing with them.

More significant perhaps is the changing geographic distribution of the votes, which is evident in both the presidential and the last two congressional elections. The Democrats have made gains in previously Republican strongholds, shrinking the GOP to a highly regionalized base. Obama was able to flip nine states that Bush had carried in 2004, including three in the west (New Mexico, Nevada, Colorado), three in the Midwest (Ohio, Indiana, Iowa), and three in the mid-Atlantic/south (Virginia, North Carolina, Florida). A glance at the electoral college map in 2008 shows the Republicans based primarily in the rural west/Midwest and the Deep South. A look at where Republican Congressional losses have been since 2004 reinforces this point: the Republicans are now virtually locked out of representing the northeast, and have lost seats in the Midwest, the fast-growing sections of the south and economically hard-hit areas of the Midwest.

The pattern of geographic concentration coincides with some long-term demographic concerns for the Republicans. Latinos are a rapidly growing segment of the American population, and McCain, according to exit polls, lost them by 36 points. The hardline positions that many Republicans have adopted on immigration reform and border control have weakened their support particularly in the Mexican American community (the largest Latino group). Unless reversed, this trend will make it harder for the Republicans to win back the southwestern states they lost in 2008, and could possibly put Arizona in play for 2012. The losses in the fast-growing mid-Atlantic/south areas reflect weak Republican support in the professional and technocratic sectors, critical sectors in the new economy. The economic transformation of the southern New Hampshire and northern Virginia suburbs, for instance, paved the way for the recent dramatic political shifts in those states from Republican to Democratic control.

Hence there were two divergent interpretations coming out of the election. One emphasizes the declining Republican base, the adverse demographic trends, and the failure of key Republican policies such as deregulation and the Bush doctrine (which espoused preemptive military intervention against hostile nations or forces), and argues for party transformation, with more effort to win voters in the middle of the ideological spectrum. The other view holds that self-identified conservatives still outnumber self-identified liberals, and concludes that the country still prefers conservative policies. The Bush administration, they believe, failed because it strayed from conservative principles, expanded government spending, and ran up large deficits on ill-advised programs and badly managed wars. The Democrats will err by increasing government spending, for example through the bailout bill, the stimulus package, and health care reform, by driving up taxes, and making big government bigger. By staying true to their principles, and voting against Obama initiatives, the thinking goes, the Republican Party will be well positioned as the alternative if and when Obama's policies fail. In short, their analyses of the 2008 defeat and their strategic prescriptions are very much intertwined.

In addition, the sociology of defeat reinforces the ideology of opposition. When American parties lose, the first incumbents to go are those who represented more competitive districts. They in turn tend to be more moderate on at least some issues as a matter of survival. As this contingent of moderates dwindles, the conservative or liberal base becomes more predominant. There is correspondingly less opposition to ideological purity inside the party. This spiral away from the center only stops when the party tires of losing. If this logic prevails, the recent Republican losses may only increase the incentives to stick to a conservative path.

The Democrats, though less divided, are also somewhat at odds as to the meaning of their recent victories. It is possible for a US political party to espouse an unpopular ideology but still gain office if the incumbent party makes enough mistakes or economic conditions deteriorate significantly. Nixon was able to win in 1968 even though liberalism was the dominant ideology in the 1960s and early 1970s, and Bill Clinton in the 1990s despite the prevailing conservatism. Typically the out party survives by accepting the protest votes of those unhappy with the status quo and moving closer to the dominant ideology: hence Nixon ended the Vietnam War and adopted important environmental regulation, while Clinton embraced the North American Free Trade Agreement (NAFTA) and welfare reform. Mirroring the Republican uncertainty about whether to alter or change course, the Democratic victory could simply mean that voters rejected the Bush administration, or it could mean the dawn of a new liberal era based on global warming and the green economy, renewed efforts at diplomacy, and a concern for rising inequalities and insecurity in the United States.

American attitudes on specific issues like global warming and health care reform have clearly shifted in recent years, even if there is no discernible trend in the public's preference for ideological labels as yet. If the election was primarily about incumbent rejection, the Obama administration may find that it is hard to get consensus on new programs, and that support for it is fickle. But if the failures of the Bush administration have laid the groundwork for new approaches to policy, then the United States could be on the cusp of another ideological shift.

From election to mandate

Elections in a democracy are supposed to translate voter preferences into policies. Americans have adopted numerous electoral reforms aimed at ensuring full and equal citizen participation, and limiting the distortions of money and influence. But in the end, the question of who gets power is more clearly answered by a US election than the question of what policies the voters want from their elected officials. When George W. Bush won the reelection in 2004 with 50.7 percent of the vote to John Kerry's 48.3 percent, it encouraged him to continue on the path he had set out in Iraq and to launch a bold initiative to replace Social Security with a private savings plan. By the summer of 2005, a majority disapproved of his handling of the war, and the social security privatization plan was dead. His presidential approval numbers would begin their dramatic slide, never to recover for the rest of his term.

There are three critical features of presidential election mandates. First, they are personal and not programmatic. American political parties agree platforms, but the press and the public largely ignore them. The Democratic and Republican parties' positions reflect those of their presidential candidates. To be sure, presidential candidates are not completely at liberty in their choices, constrained as they are by party activists, core interest groups, and strategic considerations. But the image of American parties as less ideological than European parties still holds, even though the realignment of the south has clarified the ideological lines in recent years. Party elites have polarized more than voters (Fiorina, 2005), but when it comes to policy-making, bold electoral promises tend to get whittled away by amendments and compromises, thanks to the interest group permeability of the congressional committee structure and the consensual incentives of the American Senate's cloture rules. Obama's plans for health care or immigration reform will have to survive the legislative gauntlet if they are going to be realized during his administration.

Second, US election mandates are also fragmented. The policy messages a president takes away from his victory might not be the same ones that successful congressional candidates in his party get from theirs. Gaining House and Senate seats is an advantage in that larger legislative majorities have more margin of error. With weaker party discipline than in Europe, a larger majority enables successful legislation even when there are multiple defections. At the same time, as the winning party's coalition expands, the party's diversity increases. Just as there is a tendency for the losing party to become more captured by its base (that is, core voters and supporting interest groups), the winning party's new composition changes its politics as well. The cumulative shift of 52 seats from the Republican to the Democratic side moves both the majority and the minority caucuses to the right. The Republicans are captured by their base, and the Democrats have to accommodate their new members, the so-called Blue Dogs and centrists. The Democrats had success in 2006 and 2008 partly by running centrist candidates who matched their relatively conservative districts. Once elected, the Democratic leadership must protect them from politically fatal votes if it wants to keep its margins in the House and Senate. Compromises in order to hold onto newly acquired majorities will further dilute the electoral mandate.

And third, election mandates are conditional. American voters are often retrospective in judgment, rewarding incumbent politicians for good conditions, and even more strongly, punishing them for bad ones. Good conditions breed popularity and trust, and extend presidential influence. Bad conditions do the opposite. President Obama came into office with a big slate of problems to solve. The crisis has given him leverage to take more risks and to be bolder than normal conditions might otherwise allow, especially with respect to government spending and the deficit. In the end, the 2012 presidential election will hinge much more on the improvement or deterioration of conditions during his time in office than on how well President Obama interpreted the mandate the voters gave him in 2008.

Chapter 4

Political Parties and the New Partisanship

Alan Ware

To someone who last observed American politics closely 40 or 50 years ago, the historic vote in the House of Representatives on September 29, 2008 might have seemed familiar. That day appeared to expose the continuing fragility of party in the United States. On a measure that had been initiated by the Republican president to stave off a worsening financial crisis, two-thirds of the members of George W. Bush's own party in the House voted in opposition to him. The House's Democratic leadership, which was also supporting the financial bailout, was similarly abandoned by many of its members; more than a third of the Democratic Party caucus opposed the leadership's position. The behavior of these politicians might seem to confirm the view that there are strict limits to the role of partisanship in American politics. If party could not be relied on in these sorts of circumstances, then surely it could never bind politicians and their supporters tightly to each other. On this view, parties in America continue to differ from their counterparts in the parliamentary democracies of Europe and elsewhere, in the same ways that they have always appeared unusual.

Nevertheless, such a gloss on events in Congress that day obscures two important points. The first is that in many ways it was partisan politics that accounted for what happened. The second is that the previous two decades had seen a growing level of partisanship in American politics, with much closer competition between the two major parties than had been evident for many decades. This chapter is concerned mainly with examining the latter point, but it is necessary to begin by briefly discussing the former.

George W. Bush and the Republican Party

In any presidential system, there is some tension between the elements of the party that surround the president and the rest of his party; these

50

antagonisms increase towards the end of a term-limited presidency. For everyone in the party, except the president and his immediate advisors, there are the next elections to be fought, and that can mean distancing themselves from those presidential actions and policies that will prove unpopular with voters. With an unpopular president, fear of "retrospective voting" (Fiorina, 1981) will lead the party's politicians to ignore those aspects of the presidential record that are regarded as failures, and to emphasize any presidential successes – and when these are few, the party's general traditions and ideology.

George W. Bush had gone from being an asset for his party to one of the worst liabilities a party has had in the White House. Earlier, in 2002 on the back of national fear over terrorism and while the administration was preparing for war against Iraq, the Republican Party had obtained one of the best ever mid-term results for the party of an incumbent president. Only in 1934 were the election results clearly better for a president's party. The failure of the Iraq invasion to bring about a quick resolution of instability in the region, and later the worsening economic conditions, meant that Bush became an increasing liability for his party during his second term. The Republicans lost control of both houses of Congress in 2006, and by early 2008 most observers were predicting that the likely result of that year's election would be increased Democratic majorities in Congress, combined with Democratic victories in various other elections, which indeed was the eventual outcome.

Bush's initiative on the financial bailout was intended to draw on bipartisan support, and the inclusion of the party leaders in the discussions about the legislation, in the week preceding September 29, was designed for that end. The Democratic leadership had to appear to be acting responsibly, so would have to support a Bush proposal – once some concessions had been made to appease Democrats. However, the leadership was never likely to carry with them those members worried that the compromise proposal did too little to help people whose houses were being repossessed, because of an inability to pay for their mortgages – the events that had triggered the crisis in the first place. Nevertheless, most Democrats could still be expected to support the bill. That most House Republicans did not back their president's proposal was the result of three factors, of which two had a directly partisan component. The one that did not was Bush's personal credibility. Like the child who had "cried wolf" too often and was then devoured by the creature, trust in Bush had been eroded by the evident obfuscations that had been made during the build-up to the Iraq war. Bush had claimed that there were weapons of mass destruction in Iraq, and that there was a link between Saddam Hussein and Al Qaeda; neither was true. Now he was claiming that the stability of the world economy depended on the passage of his proposed legislation, but was this true?

Many Republicans might still have been unswayed by this doubt had there been other reasons for supporting the measure, but there were not. Rather, there were two factors that were to push a majority of them into opposing it.

One factor was the adverse public reaction to the behavior of the finance industry in recent years, and a perception that it was being bailed out at the expense of taxpayers, and with no cost to the industry. The more electorally vulnerable a politician was, the more he or she felt unable to accept the president's plan; to win as partisan politicians, they could not afford to incur public hostility, and they had to adjust their stances accordingly. While electoral vulnerability affected Democrats as well as Republicans, in 2008 there were more Republicans who were in danger of defeat.

The second factor was that the necessary action in the crisis seemed to involve a negation of a core Republican belief: that there should be minimal governmental intervention in the economy. Yet Bush's proposal was one that would lead, at least in the medium term, to government ownership of various economic assets. The party would not merely be going to electoral defeat in 2008; it would be abandoning long-held principles in doing so. The party had to be preserved. Acting as a small catalyst in pushing House Republicans towards partisan behavior directed at their own president was the action of the Democratic Speaker, Nancy Pelosi. As the party's leader in the chamber, her speech on September 29 drew attention to the responsibility of Republicans for the crisis. Some Republicans were to use that speech as further justification for their actions: if the Democrats were going to play partisan politics on this matter, then so would they.

Five days later, of course, the House was to follow the Senate in eventually passing a revised version of the legislation, with both bipartisan support and opposition again apparent in the recorded vote. Yet despite the apparent breaking down of party division during a national crisis, these events really expose just how important party had become in American politics during the course of the previous quarter-century. To understand precisely what changed in that period, it is important to explain first how political scientists understood developments in the period preceding the early 1980s.

The state of the parties in the early 1980s

By the beginning of the Reagan presidency parties were regarded as having become much weaker in a number of separate, though interlinked, respects.

Party identification

Compared with 30 years earlier, by 1980 more people now identified themselves as political independents. It was widely assumed that having proportionately fewer self-identified Democrats and Republicans meant that fewer Americans were voting consistently for one party from one election to another. Consequently, there could be massive swings in support, at least in presidential elections, with an increase in the number of landslide victories. That there were more presidential landslides in this period (in 1964, 1972, and shortly after, in 1984) than at any other time in American history seemed to confirm this conclusion.

Ticket-splitting

Since the 1950s voters had become decreasingly likely to vote consistently for a single party at any given election. They were now more likely to vote for one party for one kind of office, such as the presidency, and for another at other levels – including congressional elections. Thus, not only were voters less consistent over time in their choice of party, many were not loyal in any one election year. Rates of ticket-splitting were continuing to rise, and it was widely assumed that this helped to account for a much greater incidence of divided government. Both the weakening of party identification and the increase in ticket-splitting were seen as evidence of electoral dealignment – with voters using party much less as a cue to voting.

Candidate-centered politics

Few candidates now used their party label in campaign advertising. Extensive use of television, in congressional and statewide elections, enabled candidates to campaign on the basis of their own personalities and ideas, without reference to their party (Wattenberg, 1991). It was a strategy that would increase their chances of surviving the national unpopularity of their party.

Candidate-backing activists

Those drawn into political activity were now likely to work for the campaigns of particular politicians, rather than for the party organization in support of an entire party slate. Indeed, the party organizations themselves had a more restricted role, such as get-out-the-vote drives, rather than placing themselves in competition with their own candidates in other aspects of voter mobilization.

Candidate-centered election funding

Earlier in the twentieth century parties in the northeast and midwest of the country had played a major role in the raising of funds for party-centered general election campaigns. (In the south and west this role had already diminished in the century's first decades.) However, with the rise of television-based campaigning during the mid-century years, the balance between candidates and their parties had changed, so that private funding of campaigns was largely within the control of the candidates themselves. With respect to presidential elections the parties had also ceded much of this role after 1974, when public funds became available for general election campaigns.

Cross-partisan policymaking

At both the federal and state levels there were strict limits on the role party could play. Divided government at the two levels meant that negotiations between legislature and executive would continue to prevent distinctive party agendas emerging in the United States. Furthermore, with incumbents positioning themselves on issues to maximize the chances of their own re-election, there were constraints on how much legislative leaderships – both in Congress and in the state legislatures – could push their own members on issues that would be unpopular with their particular electorates.

The empowerment of individual members of Congress in the 1970s

The reforms of that decade had weakened the power of committee chairs in the House and empowered more junior members by increasing the role of sub-committees. At the same time the reforms had also strengthened the bargaining hand of the majority party's leadership team in the chamber, and for the first few years it was not clear that this latter change would prove to be the more far-reaching in its effects on the parties. In the early part of the 1980s the growing strength of ordinary members of Congress seemed to be as significant as the enhanced powers of the Speaker.

An imbalanced party system

In many respects the party system of the early 1980s did not seem intensely competitive, not because one of the major parties had a clear national majority, but because each of them seemed to be dominant in particular political arenas. The Republicans appeared to be the party of the presidency. Of the nine presidential elections since 1950 (including the 1984 election), six had been won by the Republicans. By contrast, their successes in Congress had been few. They had controlled both chambers between 1952 and 1954, but did not have a majority in the House after that. They did not possess a Senate majority again until after 1980, and were to lose control of the chamber once more in 1986. From the late 1950s the Democrats held a clear majority of other elective offices, from state governorships downwards, and even in years when their presidential candidates did badly, as in 1972, 1980, and 1984, the Republicans could not establish the kind of dominance that the Democrats had hitherto enjoyed.

To observers at the time it was unclear that partisan politics would change that much in the future. Supposedly, this was the era of the individual candidate, of more independent-minded voters, of weak party organizations, of powerful factors limiting the possibility for party unity in Congress, and of two national political majorities (normally a Republican one for the presidency, with a Democratic majority elsewhere (Shafer and Claggett, 1995)). Twenty-five years after this view had become firmly established, much, though not all, of the American political landscape seems to be very different. In various ways parties seem to be stronger than they were then, and party competition seems more intense. The remainder of this chapter explains what has changed, why it has changed, and what might be the forces pushing for further change, in possibly different directions, in the future.

The resurrection of party politics

The voters

Research that had begun during the 1980s started to reveal that party identification in America had not weakened since the 1960s in quite the way that had been thought earlier (Keith et al., 1992). Those in the electorate who now identified themselves as independents, rather than Republicans or Democrats, were not necessarily as detached from parties as had been assumed. There remained a core sector of the potential electorate who knew relatively little about politics, were less likely to vote, and who did not regard themselves as Democratic or Republican identifiers. But the newer type of independent supposedly making choices between the parties, sometimes voting for one, and sometimes for the other, turned out to be largely fictitious. In surveys, when respondents who said they were independents were asked subsequently whether they leaned to one party or the other, it turned out that many did so. Furthermore, these "leaners" behaved much more like strong identifiers with parties than they did weak party identifiers, in voting consistently for the party toward which they leaned.

Not only had earlier changes in party identification been misinterpreted, by the end of the 1980s, one of the voting trends emphasized just a few years earlier, increased ticket-splitting, was now being reversed. In every election between 1956 and 1988 at least one quarter of House districts produced victories for one party in the presidential contest, while there was victory for the other party in the congressional election. The high points were 1972 and 1984, when 44.1 and 45.0 percent respectively of all districts ticket-split in this way. However, after 1984 the trend in ticket-splitting was downwards. In the four elections from 1992, only one (1996) saw ticket-splitting occur in more than a quarter of all districts, while by 2004 it was present in just 13.6 percent of districts. This was the lowest level of ticket-splitting since 1944. As studies were to demonstrate, ticket-splitting earlier had not been the result of voters showing a preference for divided government, but of lack of perceived differences between the parties, and also contests that were unbalanced in terms of the resources available to major party candidates (Burden and Kimball, 2002).

Party organizations and candidates

But what about the party organizations and their relationships with candidates? There could be no return to the days when the parties in the northeast and Midwest of the country were at the center of election campaigns, and when many candidates had not bothered to campaign independently of their parties. It is the candidates who continue to attract, directly or indirectly, much of the private funding for elections, and it is to them that activists and supporters turn when looking for a cause with which to engage. As had become the case by the 1970s, party is still subservient to the candidate; this is one area where party resurgence is not especially evident.

However, some of the more individualistic aspects of politics of the 1960s and 1970s are now less evident. Although candidates rarely use their party label in their television adverts, or elsewhere, both in attacking their opponents and in defending themselves, they are more likely to allude to politics being about "teams." Obviously, in 2008 Barack Obama was going to attempt to link John McCain directly to the unpopular Republican administration in order to maximize his chance of victory. However, Republicans themselves, while in many cases partly seeking to distance themselves from the unpopular George W. Bush, did not rely on just their own personal achievements. Few observers could be in doubt that most Republicans were standing with each other in defense of a party that persisted in promoting low taxation, low levels of government control in the economy, limited government-funded social welfare policies, and conservative stances on matters such as abortion and gay marriages. That was why the financial crisis in September resulted in so many House Republicans voting against the policy of their president. To support that policy risked betraying a key component of what they, individually and collectively, had stood for, thereby undermining the credibility of the team to which they belonged.

Parties and the funding of politics

That parties became somewhat more "team-like" in the electoral arena after the first half of the early 1980s was the result of two factors. One will be discussed shortly: the growing cohesion displayed by the parties in Congress, which had an impact on how they faced each other in electoral contests. The other factor was continuing change in the funding of politics. That elected politicians and candidates had become the main fundraisers contributed initially to an individualistic style of electoral politics, with each raising money for their own campaigns. But already by the 1980s, it was becoming clear that senior politicians (in Congress and state governorships) could raise vast sums that they would not have to spend on themselves, because typically few would have serious challengers. That money could then be used in primary and general election campaigns to support candidates whom they favored. Not only did this create ties of loyalty between the newcomers who were beneficiaries of this and their sponsors, it also could be used as a threat against dissident incumbents. One of the reasons that some skeptical, and moderate, Republicans did not vote against their party in 1998 on the attempt to impeach Bill Clinton, which they regarded as ill-judged and unpopular with the public, was that they knew it was regarded as an acid test of party loyalty. The leadership might subsequently fund primary challengers if they broke rank. Symbolically at least, party, in the form of the National Party Committees, also became more significant in the 1990s as the formal device through which so-called soft money could be channeled in support of candidacies without breaching federal financing laws. Until the passage of the Bipartisan Campaign Reform Act in 2002, these party bodies had become the biggest loophole for party candidates in circumventing restrictions imposed by earlier federal legislation (La Raja, 2008).

Today it is still the candidates themselves who are the main driving force in fundraising. So great is their capacity to generate funds that for the first time in 2008, a presidential candidate of a major party opted not to take public funds for the general election campaign, and instead relied on private donations. Before Barack Obama did so, the only really well-supported candidate to have gone this route was the independently wealthy Ross Perot (in 1992), and he was not the nominee of a major party. It was interesting that it was a Democrat who was the first to do this following the introduction of public funding in 1974: traditionally it was Republicans who had greater access to private money. However, in 2008 Obama outspent McCain easily, squeezing the latter's campaign so that a month before the election he was forced to withdraw active campaigning from some states he earlier had hopes of capturing. Yet while it was a candidate, Obama, who was raising the money, the whole thrust of his campaign was very different from the last time private money domination by one candidate had been evident in a general election. In 1972 Richard Nixon's funding strategy had led to him outspend Democrat George McGovern, and his campaign's activities in this regard were then the trigger for the 1974 campaign finance reforms. However, Nixon had used his money solely to re-elect himself, paying little attention to the fate of fellow Republicans. Thirty-six years later, Obama tied his campaign much more closely to the efforts of other Democrats; the cost of having to work with a Congress controlled by the other party had become all too apparent in the interim.

Parties and Congress

As Bill Clinton had discovered after his party's loss of its congressional majorities in the 1994 midterm elections, dealing with a Congress controlled by the other party had now become increasingly difficult. While it is still disputed whether divided government does inhibit decisive policy-making, there is little doubt that managing divided government became less easy towards the end of the twentieth century. This was because the majority party leadership, especially in the House, had started to operate much more in a mode of opposition to the president of another party than had been the case in the middle of the century. Accompanying this change was the growth of hostility between party members in the Congress itself – the so-called "decline of comity" (Uslaner, 1996). An era in which majority and minority parties tended to cooperate with each other in the organization of business in the chambers, and in their committees, gave way to one in which the majority party attempted to exploit its majority status; personal relations between members of different parties often became antagonistic. A series of events – of which the most high-profile were the Republican Newt Gingrich's successful deposing of Democratic Speaker Jim Wright in 1989, the budget crisis of 1990, the attempt after the 1994 elections by new House Speaker Gingrich to take control of the policy agenda from President Clinton, another budget crisis (in 1996), and the House vote to impeach Clinton in 1998 – all heightened antagonism between the parties. That antagonism continued into the new century.

A key factor in this organized battle between the congressional parties was the growth in control over their parties by the leaderships.

The initial effect of the 1970s reforms, of empowering both more junior members and the leaderships, changed, with the latter becoming increasingly dominant. In this respect, they were aided by the capacity, mentioned earlier, of the more senior members to fundraise. In particular, it was the group surrounding the party leader who increasingly called the shots in the House. Symptomatic of the change was the ability of Gingrich in 1995 to ignore seniority in the selection of committee chairs. Appointments went to those members that Gingrich believed would be effective, and who would enact the "Contract with America" on which most House Republicans had campaigned the previous autumn. The centralization of power in the Republican Party in the House continued during the period of their majority, which ended only with the 2006 elections. If they chose to, House Speakers now had more resources with which to control their party members within the chamber than had any of their predecessors since the deposing of "Tsar" Joseph Cannon in 1910 and the subsequent stripping of powers from that office.

Changes in party competition

Along with this sharpening of "team" lines between the parties, and the growing personal hostility between parties, much closer competition between the parties was to emerge in the 1990s than had been evident for many years. In some respects it is possible to make comparisons between the most recent two decades of highly competitive two-party politics and the American party system of the nineteenth century. However, as a close analysis of Table 4.1 reveals, the present era does not constitute a return to the type of party competition evident in that century; in some ways, and not surprisingly, it has more in common with the period immediately preceding it.

Consider first the share of the vote obtained by the winning party in a presidential election. For most of the twentieth century – that is, from 1900 through the 1986 election – the median share of the vote for the winning party was 54.4 percent, while in the nineteenth century winning electoral margins had normally been much lower, with the winning party typically receiving just 48.6 percent of the total vote. (The data for the nineteenth century begins with the emergence of a strong second party in the 1830s, but it excludes the years of the Civil War and immediately afterwards when competition was severely disrupted.) Since 1988 elections have typically been much closer than in the preceding nine decades, although, at 50.0 percent, the median is not quite as low as it was in the nineteenth century. With House elections, how close each party seems to be to obtaining a majority in the chamber is one of the marked features of contemporary politics. The median share of the seats the winning party takes at an election is

Table 4.1   *Party competition for the presidency and House of Representatives*

	1837–59 plus 1873–97	1898–1987	1988–2009
Presidential elections: median share of total vote obtained by party winning most votes	48.6%	54.4%	50.0%
House of Representatives elections: median share of seats taken by largest party	55.1%	57.5%	53.3%
Number of consecutive years party holds presidency: median in bold, mean in italics	**4** *5.3*	**8** *10.2*	**8** *6.7–9.3**
Percentage of all occasions in which party control of House switches after elections	55.%	15.6%	18.2%

* The value of this mean lies in the range 6.7–9.3; its precise value depends on how much of the Reagan presidency (1980–8) is included with, or excluded from, the succeeding George H. W. Bush presidency (1988–92).

smaller in the contemporary era – compared with *both* the period 1898–1987 and the one before that. Typically, and surprisingly perhaps, there are smaller majorities in the House now than there were in the highly competitive early period. Nevertheless, this is only part of the picture. When we turn to look at how frequently party control of institutions turns over, it becomes evident that the recent period has far more in common with the one immediately before it than with the nineteenth century.

During that century parties usually lost control of the presidency after just one term in office. The median for the number of consecutive years that a party held the presidency was just four, while the mean is 5.3. For most of the twentieth century a party often occupied the White House for much longer, with the median being eight years and with a mean also nearly twice the nineteenth century level at 10.2 years. In the contemporary era too, parties tend to keep hold of the presidency for longer than they did a century and more ago. The median number of years is again eight, while the mean lies somewhere between 6.7 and 9.3, depending on how much of the Reagan presidency (1980–88) is included with, or excluded from, the succeeding George H. W. Bush presidency. But there can be no doubt that this is a markedly different pattern from that observed for the nineteenth century.

A similar finding is evident when looking at how frequently control of Congress switches. In spite of the narrow margins in the contemporary House, control over it has not changed that frequently – doing so only in 1994 and 2006. It has happened on 18.2 percent of all occasions, compared with 15.6 percent in the immediately preceding period and with 55.1 percent in the nineteenth century. In the early period, therefore, intense competition in House elections produced frequent turnover of party control in the chamber, but also fairly large majorities for the winning party. In the modern era, close competition produces narrow margins of victory (in terms of seats), but only occasionally does this result in a change of party control. There are fewer party marginal seats than there were over a hundred years ago, so that the majority party usually has less to fear from a forthcoming election.

What lies behind these differences between these two competitive eras is a difference in the ability of parties to keep their coalitions together in the short term. In the nineteenth century a winning coalition tended to collapse quickly because there was too little patronage to satisfy the demands of those who thought they had some claim on it. It was much easier for a defeated party to keep its electoral coalitions together, in the expectation of rewards on the part of the leading activists, than it was for the victorious party to appease those it had disappointed. As patronage declined as the principal source of "political glue" keeping coalitions together, so this changed; in the twentieth and twenty-first centuries the increased power of incumbency helped keep office-holders in office, and that has reduced the rate of turnover in party control of the presidency, Congress, and other offices.

Why parties and inter-party conflicts have become more important

Several factors help explain the emergence of this more partisan American polity, of which two are particularly important. First, is the 1981 tax cut that Congress enacted at the beginning of the Reagan administration. Before then cross-party cooperation had been facilitated by the use of funds to support pet projects favored by members of Congress whose votes might be needed to get a bill passed. Being in the Republican minority did not preclude the legislator from having influence, and this was one of the reasons that a form of cooperative opposition to the Democrats was favored by a succession of House minority leaders. The tax cut created a massive federal budget deficit, which in turn made it impossible for new programs to be funded without eliminating older ones. Reduced funds had two consequences on congressional politics. It provided an incentive, under divided government, for the majority party in Congress to develop its own budget and spending priorities in opposition to those of the president. This hardened party lines in the chamber, with party positions becoming clearer-cut, and it led to three budgetary standoffs (in 1990, 1995, and 1995–96) between the two branches of government. In the 1980s it also acted as a catalyst for younger Republicans to challenge the older mode of constructive opposition to the Democrats. Newt Gingrich's successful campaign to discredit Democrat Speaker Jim Wright propelled him to the House leadership, and he brought in a far more aggressive and partisan approach to the work of the chamber. Republican and Democratic hostility to each other spiraled in the 1990s, perhaps reaching its zenith in the House's impeachment of Clinton, but the spirit of ill-feeling between the parties continued after that. This greater emphasis on the party "team" spilled over into electoral politics, where voters were now confronted with candidates who might not emphasize their own party label, but who were certainly willing to use their opponent's association with the other "team" as a stick with which to beat them. Faced with more partisan-looking contests, the electorate tended to respond by voting more on "team" lines than they had previously.

The second factor involved the working-through of the long-term electoral realignment in the south. Republican penetration of the south had started as early as the 1950s, when "Eisenhower Republicans" helped to break the Democratic monopoly there, though only in the outer south, and only in presidential contests. Over the next few decades Republican strength in the entire region gradually increased, with the party becoming more competitive at both the congressional level and in state politics. While the south now tended to vote Republican in presidential contests, many southerners continued to split their tickets, and one consequence of this was that the Democrats' overall advantage in Congress and in state government persisted. By the later 1980s, and culminating in the mid-term elections of 1994, the long-term change in the south was concluded – leaving the Republicans as normally the larger party in the region. This loss of their southern base was one of the main reasons that the Democrats could no longer dominate Congress, and the balance that it left between the parties nationally was of two evenly sized opponents. Close elections, from the national perspective at least, between a Red (Republican) and a Blue

(Democratic) America were the culmination of a long-term process by which a one-party south became fully integrated into the entire American political system.

Nevertheless, it is important to recognize that the tendency towards the creation of a Red and Blue America was not simply the product of southern realignment. If the south had been the only factor in the equation, then why would the Republicans have not retained their dominance in the presidential arena? That they have not can be revealed in the following way. In the ten presidential elections between 1952 and 1988 the mean share of the total vote taken by the Republicans was 52.1 percent, while the median was 52.3; the corresponding figures for the last five elections are 47.5 and 48.8, with the best performance (in 2004) being only 50.7 percent. While the Republicans were increasing their strength in the south, they were also losing some support among some social groups that had been traditionally Republican. The social conservatism and the fierce anti-government ideology that were reinforced by the party's move into the south did not play that well among more affluent groups in the suburbs surrounding the large metropolises outside the south. The gradual shift of the "moneyed classes" away from the Republicans was one of the reasons that Barack Obama's fundraising efforts could be so successful. The "Wall Street" component of the old Republican coalition was no longer as solid as it had been. The events of September and October 2008 were to reveal this in a pronounced way, with the "Main Street" representatives of the party in Congress, many from southern and interior-western districts, willing to place taxpayer interests ahead of loyalty to their president or their traditional alliance with the financial sector.

Furthermore, if the two parties were more *clearly divided* from each other than they had been, this did not mean that ideologically they were actually *further apart*. They were not. The Republican Party had indeed shifted more to the right since the 1960s, in that it was now stridently conservative on social issues in addition to its continuing support for an unfettered free market economy and a small state. (The standard-bearer of American conservatism in the late 1950s and 1960s, Barry Goldwater was the staunchest advocate of the latter, but he never reconciled himself to the social agenda with which the party was to become associated in later decades.) However, while the Democratic Party lost most of its southern, conservative wing, its erstwhile liberals were replaced by those of more moderate views, especially on matters relating to the economy and social redistribution. In a real sense, what defined the Democrats by the end of the twentieth century was what they were not: they were not conservatives, and that was what united them. The more liberal agenda of the northern wing of the party in the 1950s and 1960s had largely disappeared.

While there is widespread agreement that there is a clearer division among American political elites than 30 years ago, there is considerable dispute over whether this reflects increased polarization among voters. Some scholars (Fiorina, 2005) argue that the division between Blue and Red America derives from the undue influence of political activists, whereas most voters have remained centrists. On this view, institutional factors, such as electoral gerrymandering, have been a contributory factor. Others provide evidence demonstrating that there has been a partisan "sorting" among the electorate, so that Democratic and Republican voters are now distinctive in the views they hold (Abramowitz and Saunders, 2005). Among the causes of this might be long-term changes in the overall composition of the electorate, including a larger Latino population.

Will the new partisanship endure?

Once parties in a two-party system are in intense competition with each other, there is a tendency for that competition to endure. Because of what is known in game theory as the position of being a focal arbiter (Schelling, 1960; Cox, 1997; Ware, 2009), opposition to one major party is normally channeled through the other. Those on one side of the divide tend to keep voting, for fear that the other party will win, and indeed overall voting turnout may increase, as it did in 2000 and 2004, reversing a trend evident since the 1960s. This does not mean, though, that elections decided by just a few votes, or a few seats in a legislature, will remain the pattern over a long period. Indeed, in American history while we find close elections often clustered together, these periods are broken up by years when the party coalitions are less evenly matched. The rise of both slavery and nativism as divisive issues in the 1850s ushered in a period of two decades when contests were less close than they had been. Then in the early to mid-1890s there was a similar disruption to a highly competitive regime, with the voting alliances of the 1880s not being fully restored until 1910 (Ware, 2002). In the twentieth century two periods when the parties were moving into tight competition with each other (1910–18, and 1940–56) similarly gave way to years when, nationally, the parties were not so evenly matched. It might be argued that the 2008 election, which saw the largest popular vote for the winning presidential candidate since 1988 and the largest majorities in both houses of Congress since the 103rd Congress (1993–95), heralds the end of the latest era of close party competition. On the other hand, 2008 might just prove to be a short-term deviation within a continuing competitive era.

That the tendency towards close competition does not last long is the result of forces external to the party system which make it difficult for all the elements of a party's coalition to cohere. One possible scenario for the future is that the financial crisis of 2008 may generate problems for the Republicans in keeping the Main Street and Wall Street wings of their party together. But if the Republican coalition starts to partially unravel, this could also put strains on a Democratic party, much of whose unity has depended on their being in opposition to a coherent and broad-ranging conservative party. Moreover, if economic turbulence persists, incumbent presidents may become more vulnerable, leading to a transformation in the form of competition evident in recent years, where contests have been decided by narrow victories but the impact of incumbency has been to limit frequent alternations in power. The reverse remains possible.

It might be expected too that the recent conflictual politics of Congress will endure, as those whose current experience of the institution has been one of hostility will continue to act in the ways that they have previously. This is precisely what was evident in early 2009. But here again we should not necessarily expect that by, say, 2018 interparty and interpersonal relations in the legislature will be similar to those that dominated the years around the turn of the century. Either frequent alternations in control of Congress, or national dominance by one party, could make way for more cooperative behavior between the parties, though probably not in the short term. That a relatively small number of politicians – presidential candidates and senior members of Congress – mainly dominate fundraising would also come into play here. As we have seen, in recent years they have had an incentive to direct the funds that they raise in ways that help promote party causes and party cohesion. But the incentive for them to do this would weaken, were there to be less cohesion among the parties in Congress, and if the ideological divisions between the two parties became less clear-cut. We might then see a return, at least in part, to the politician–party relationship that had developed by the beginning of the 1980s.

One conclusion can be made definitively, however. American parties will remain rather different from their European counterparts, because of two factors that will not change. The parties were in their origins highly decentralized, so that power could never rest in a central organization at the federal level. An elected presidency – a feature replicated in the form of the governor at the state level – provides for tensions between legislative and executive wings that cannot be overcome, given both the origins of the parties and the internal structures they have introduced subsequently, such as direct primaries. That having been said, what is interesting about parties in the United States is how much they have varied over time with respect to their cohesion and "team-like" characteristics. They will surely continue to change, but within parameters set by their origins and the separation of powers, and it is entirely possible that future generations will refer to the era around the beginning of the twenty-first century as "the party period." After all, this is the term that later writers were to use to refer to the nineteenth century, and to some extent it is a term that is appropriate to the years around the beginning of the current century as well (McCormick, 1986).

Chapter 5

Interest Groups

Dorie E. Apollonio

Although political scientists have studied the role of interest groups in policymaking for decades, the way that interest groups seek to influence political decision-making only occasionally becomes popularly relevant. While interest groups are often viewed with suspicion in popular culture, classic empirical research in political science suggests that the competition between interest groups makes it difficult for any single type of group to control government (Dahl, 1961; Polsby, 1980). In late 2008, however, troubles in the US financial and housing markets led to increasing resentment of wealthy interest groups in American politics, and there was a widespread perception that the government was promoting the good of the financial industry over the public interest (Johnson, 2009).

In late 2008 and early 2009 news spread that the insurance company AIG, which had recently received over $150 billion in rescue funds from the US government, would be offering its executives bonus payments totaling $450 million. As ordinary Americans were suffering increased unemployment, an unprecedented decline in housing values, and huge losses in retirement accounts, their discovery that the banking industry expected to continue business as usual after its bailout sparked a wave of popular resentment. The bonus scandal tapped a deep reservoir of cynicism about the role of interest groups in American politics, encapsulated in Mark Twain's statement that "we have the best government that money can buy."

This chapter reviews key contemporary questions that have arisen in the study of interest group activities, as the United States has been forced to deal with financial crises. It does this against the background of an ideologically charged presidential election, which presages a reconsideration of the relative responsibilities and trustworthiness of government and private interests. Debate about the appropriate role of interest groups in American politics reflects fundamental tensions between concerns about freedom – which have led to constitutional protection of political speech and campaign spending – and about equality – which have inspired frustration about the perceived political dominance of wealthy interest groups. These tensions continue to shape debates about the place of interest groups in American politics.

The role of interest groups in the United States

American political culture has been characterized by its reluctance to accept powerful centralized government, and relatively high levels of trust in the private sector. However, the recession that began in 2007 drew new attention to the role of private-sector interest groups in American politics. In late 2008, the US government launched the Troubled Asset Relief Program (TARP), and began purchasing assets from the American financial industry. TARP was proposed as a way to deal with the subprime mortgage crisis that began in 2007, which left banks that had loaned money for home purchases struggling to survive when declining home prices and increasing monthly payments led homeowners to default at unprecedented rates. With hindsight, it became clear that the reduced regulation demanded by the financial industry in the early twenty-first century was implicated in the crisis. As a result, initial efforts to bail out banks, rather than homeowners, were extremely unpopular.

Shortly after the passage of TARP, in November 2008, representatives of three major automobile manufacturers in the United States, known as the "Big Three," also appeared before the federal government to seek bailout funds. This appearance was remarkably politically tone-deaf; the Big Three CEOs each flew in private jets to the hearings, despite their awareness of political disaffection with financial industry bailouts and the popular perception that their troubles were created by their own wasteful business practices. As a consequence, their proposals faced severe scrutiny, and the new Obama presidential administration indicated that it was not necessarily averse to seeing one company go bankrupt. By summer 2009, two of the Big Three automakers seeking assistance had filed for bankruptcy.

The fear that interest groups could capture government for their own benefits has a long pedigree in American politics. When the United States was forming, James Madison inveighed against what he termed "the mischief of faction." The factions he feared were political parties and interest groups, but despite his advocacy, both eventually became institutionalized in American governance. However, while Americans as individuals often identify with political parties, they rarely identify with interest groups. The most commonly used terms for interest groups in the United States are pejorative: they are often referred to as pressure groups, special interest groups, or lobby groups. Despite the fact that many interest groups have individual members, and may claim large memberships as grounds for expecting government to meet their demands, these individual members may have limited interest in the political agendas of the organizations they join. Members of the American Automobile Association (AAA), for example, focus more on free rescue if their cars break down than they do on the organization's lobbying for new roads.

In general, interest groups have a much greater role in government than they do outside government. Researchers agree that throughout the twentieth century, interest groups in the United States increased in both number and influence (Schlozman and Tierney, 1986). The relative weakness of American political parties makes interest groups comparatively powerful, despite the negative popular perceptions of them. Candidates for office in the United States are largely self-selected and privately financed, and as a result, become primarily committed to the groups that support them. Often they must be wooed into the party fold once they become members of government. Elected officials often display greater loyalty to the interests in their districts than to their parties. Members of Congress may explicitly say that they represent "tobacco states" or "farm states," and form coalitions to secure favorable treatment for local industries.

The increasing effort by interest groups to secure their position has led to massive increases in lobbying over the past few decades, and some groups have been especially successful in capturing government resources. In 2008–09 the financial industry's ability to sell troubled assets at inflated values to the government, after they had been successful in reducing regulation to the point that their business model collapsed, has been referred to as privatizing gains and socializing losses.

This expansion in the role of interest groups in government over time has received limited popular attention, and only rarely led to new regulation. Popular awareness of interest group activities tends to reflect individual scandals, and the issue of group influence attracts little attention in the absence of publicized and egregious instances of corruption. For example, the Watergate scandal, which implicated President Nixon in a range of illegal activities including money laundering, campaign fraud, and illegal wiretapping and break-ins, led to the amendment of the Federal Election Campaign Act (FECA) in 1974 to limit campaign contributions and expenditures, and created an independent agency, the Federal Election Commission (FEC), that would enforce the new regulations. No additional major campaign finance legislation appeared until 2002, when the Bipartisan Campaign Reform Act (BCRA) made unlimited contributions to political parties illegal and imposed new restrictions on political advertising. Yet the role of interest groups in American politics has grown steadily in scope and size throughout all those years. From 1998 to 2008, the reported amount of money spent on lobbying Congress more than doubled, from $1.4 billion to $3.3 billion (Center for Responsive Politics, 2008). Interest groups also contribute money to candidates seeking election and to political parties for their recruitment and party-building activities, develop independent advertising campaigns in support of favored or opposition to hostile candidates, and increasingly seek to recruit sympathetic candidates to run for local and state offices.

All of these activities are legal, and according to many observers, desirable. The American Constitution, through the Bill of Rights, protects the activities of interest groups as a form of free speech protected by the First Amendment. Efforts to lobby Congress are clearly speech, and the Supreme Court has consistently indicated that even direct political spending is a form of protected speech. In *Buckley v Valeo* (1976), the Court struck down limits on campaign expenditures as unconstitutional. Recent efforts to control the effects of private money in congressional races by allowing the opponents of self-financed candidates to collect additional money for their campaigns were also struck down in *FEC v Davis* (2008). As a result, the activities of interest groups remain largely outside legislative control. If interest groups see participating in politics as advantageous, as they have to date, the only real limits on their involvement are their own levels of commitment and the resources available to them. Interest groups' political participation is an expression of democratic values that allows any voice to be heard, even if those voices are unrepresentative.

Whose interests are being represented?

In 1994 the US House of Representatives in Congress was won by Republicans for the first time since 1954. This legislative victory (which came on the heels of President Clinton's Democratic win in 1992) was not only a huge triumph for the GOP, but an opportunity for its traditional interest group allies to achieve policy goals that had been sidelined for decades. One such group was a relatively new organization named Get Government Off Our Back (GGOOB), which campaigned against what it called unnecessary government regulation. GGOOB was a coalition of several conservative groups, ranging from advocates of home schooling to the National Rifle Association (NRA) and taxpayer groups. It drew extensive popular support, demonstrated in multiple state rallies, and this led legislators to pledge support for its causes. Some of GGOOB's policy proposals were inserted verbatim into the Republican Party's promised legislative agenda, the "Contract with America," and, as a result, many of the regulations it opposed were eliminated.

Nearly 15 years later, evidence emerged that GGOOB was not a spontaneous coalition of like-minded groups at all, but instead a carefully orchestrated front group created by a public relations firm and bankrolled by a tobacco company (Apollonio and Bero, 2007). Despite GGOOB's stated agenda to reduce all kinds of onerous and unnecessary government regulation, its primary goal was to prevent specific kinds of regulation: controls on tobacco and the institution of clean indoor air laws. The tobacco company anticipated that this pro-tobacco agenda would be far less popular than a broad anti-regulation message, and viewed funding a coalition that would advocate its goals indirectly as a more successful political strategy than acting alone. Although some of the member groups that joined the coalition were paid outright for participating, others joined the effort without compensation because they supported GGOOB's purported mission. In other words GGOOB was a tobacco industry front group, but a very sophisticated one. Ultimately it fooled not only its target audience, but also some of its own members.

Although research on the use of front groups in the United States is limited, evidence suggests that a range of interest groups, including the tobacco industry, pharmaceutical manufacturers, telecommunications firms, and credit unions, have relied on them. Most recently, casino operators have begun using Native American tribes as front groups for the expansion of gaming (Nelson, 2007). Given current law, only court cases can force lobbyists to reveal these activities. The creation of front groups like GGOOB raises questions which are difficult to answer about whose views are represented by interest groups. In the past, many wealthy interest groups have bankrolled less well-endowed organizations under the table, hoping to capitalize on their credibility when both sets of groups' interests are aligned (Reid, 1980). In most cases, this strategy is invisible to outside observers. As a result, advocacy on policy issues may be substantially skewed toward particular viewpoints without the bias becoming evident.

Participation in policymaking is expensive. Interest groups offer value to policymakers by providing them with something they cannot get themselves. In some cases this is information, either in the form of direct research on issues, or about the extent to which policy positions are supported or opposed in the general population or their own memberships (Wright, 1995). Supplying this information requires the ability to do research and pay staff who can reach decision-makers once relevant information has been collected. In other cases interest groups provide direct financial support to candidates and elected officials through campaign contributions. Researchers have noted that these demands lead to a population of interest groups that is strongly weighted toward wealthy interests (Schlozman and Tierney, 1986). Although some political scientists have proposed theories about how unorganized or underfunded interests could be represented effectively (Denzau and Munger, 1986), nearly every empirical study of interest groups has concluded that the majority of the interest group population is made up of businesses. Although the number of groups representing non-economic interests has increased, the number of groups representing economic interests has increased at the same time.

Americans who opposed the financial and automobile industry bailouts in 2008 may have wondered why these particular interests had managed to arrange government support while less organized constituencies like homeowners were left out. That choice reflected the fact that policymakers make decisions based on the information available to them, and the groups providing information had strong incentives to portray their own rescue as being critical in preventing a deeper recession. Moreover, legislators who had taken campaign contributions from these groups were inclined to view them favorably. One of the Big Three automakers famously claimed in the 1950s that what's good for General Motors is good for America. While this may be true, it is difficult to view this statement as objective when it is made by General Motors. Unfortunately, the nature of interest group politics in the United States makes it difficult to find objective perspectives.

Virtually every study of the interest group population confirms the popular suspicion that the interest group population does not accurately reflect the views of the general public, at least as far as they can be ascertained. This problem is compounded by the fact that interest groups hold private information that could be useful in making policy decisions, and by a system of financing elections that relies largely on interest groups to provide the money for campaigns.

The provision of information

In early 2009 baseball player Michael Tejada was charged with lying to congressional investigators when he claimed ignorance about the use of steroids by other players (Associated Press, 2008). The ability and need to file charges against those who give misleading information to congressional investigators points to a problem faced by political decision-makers at every level of government – they rarely have direct or relevant experience to guide them in their choices. Few have training as researchers, and efforts to train policymakers to systematically collect and evaluate evidence have had limited success (Jewell and Bero, 2008). As a result, policymakers rely on information gathered and presented by others. For obvious reasons, these decision-makers are concerned about whether the information they receive is trustworthy.

Given the means by which the national government considers legislation and regulation, the main source of information for policymakers is interest groups. Although not all legislative and regulatory actions are public, there is an expectation in the United States that much of the business of a democratic government should be visible to the general public. As a result, hearings on proposed policies are often both open and publicized. However, given that most legislators sit on multiple committees and are also obligated to appear for floor votes, hearings and committee meetings are most frequently convened at the seat of government. Regulatory agencies also conduct most of their business in their home offices. Interest groups, which are committed to observing and influencing government, are the most likely to attend and often eager to testify.

Researchers and policymakers agree that interest groups are a key source of information for policy decisions. This is particularly the case in states with part-time legislatures which lack professional staff that can collect information independently. Interest groups often hold private information that can influence proposed policy changes; for example, utility companies are likely to know the true cost of building a nuclear power plant, AARP (formerly the American Association of Retired Persons) is well informed on the amounts seniors pay for prescription drugs, and the NRA knows which areas have the highest concentration of gun owners. Much of this information has policy relevance, and frequently policymakers would like to have access to it in evaluating proposed changes in the law. When such information supports an interest group's preferred policy outcome, the group is also interested in sharing it.

Researchers, policymakers, and interest groups themselves view the provision of specialized information as one of the most important functions of interest groups in American democracy. Interest groups provide information that both assesses the extent of popular support for proposed policy changes, and indicates their costs, benefits, and likely effects. Lobbyists for groups often present themselves as "information service bureaux" for policymakers who can serve as an extension of government research staff.

However interest groups are not necessarily objective; instead, many groups have direct economic interests in particular outcomes. As a result, both policymakers and the general population have persistent concerns about the accuracy of the information provided by organizational lobbyists. The fact that this information is private, and in many cases cannot easily be verified by outsiders, in combination with the knowledge that interest groups are involved in policymaking in the hopes of ensuring outcomes favorable to them, raises the understandable concern that interest groups will misrepresent information to get what they want. Lobbyists themselves argue that they cannot afford to lie because of the risk of exposure and the need to maintain long-term relationships with policymakers. However there is evidence that interest groups have at least occasionally hired lobbyists and public relations firms to deliberately communicate false information to policymakers (Lopipero, Apollonio, and Bero, 2007), suggesting that a reputation for dishonesty may be a surmountable problem for lobbyists.

Despite the fear that interest groups will misrepresent information, policymakers may have little choice but to rely on them. When information is private, the interest group that holds it, even if untrustworthy, may have access to policymakers who prefer biased information to remaining ignorant. Legislators and regulators who hear testimony often seek to identify whether interest groups presenting information are truly credible; decision-makers will demand information about who has funded research or the travel costs of individual witnesses. Yet even when policymakers are aware of bias in the information they are given, that information will nonetheless anchor their expectations and affect the decisions they make (Cialdini, 2009).

Moreover, for lobbyists to provide information to policymakers, they must have access to them. At the most basic level, government responds to groups that have the resources to communicate effectively; both gathering information and presenting it require money. Yet concerns about any resulting bias in lobbying and the provision of information are intractable in American politics. The American Constitution provides ironclad protection for free speech, even if protecting such speech would unfairly advantage interest groups willing to lie about private information or organizations wealthy enough to make sure that their opinions are presented more vehemently than any others. This fundamental tension between the two democratic values, the freedom to express opinions and demand for equal representation, results in enormous suspicion about the role of interest groups in government but no obvious strategy to resolve that suspicion.

The power of money

In early 2006, lobbyist Jack Abramoff pleaded guilty to criminal charges for defrauding multiple American Indian tribes he had taken as clients by arranging lobbying against their interests in order to increase his own fees. In 2008, he was also found guilty of bribing public officials and exchanging gifts for political favors. Mr Abramoff is now a former lobbyist serving a prison sentence, but his case heightened concern about the role of interest group money in American politics.

Candidates for office in the United States rely almost exclusively on private contributions to fund their campaigns, and interest groups provide the majority of these, either directly through Political Action Committees (PACs) or indirectly through bundled individual contributions (Marshall, 1999). Interest groups provide money directly to candidates for their campaigns, spend independently in support of favored candidates or in opposition to candidates they dislike, and sometimes recruit candidates to run for office. They give to political parties in support of particular ideological positions, or in the hope that the party will reflect their interests if it controls the government. They also spend independently in the hopes of swaying public opinion to support their policy goals.

The idea that interest groups make campaign contributions in order to affect policymaking is usually taken as a given, although statements from groups themselves are far more equivocal. Although some contributors argue that making campaign contributions is a civic responsibility, and a few organizations claim they seek only to change electoral results by supporting candidates with strongly held beliefs, most claim that political spending is a way for them to gain access to policymakers and ensure that their interests are not ignored. Overall, there is very little empirical evidence about what campaign contributors hope to achieve with campaign contributions, other than information gathered through interviews with willing lobbyists and interest group representatives, which presumably reflect both limited samples and efforts by respondents to present their activities in a positive light.

Research on campaign finance is equivocal at best about whether contributions can influence policy outcomes. Interest groups and policymakers are reluctant to claim that contributions could affect legislative behavior. Interest group representatives perceive, correctly, that explicitly claiming to buy influence over legislators would be taken as evidence of corruption, as it was with Jack Abramoff. In unusual situations – such as the one detailed in *Montana Right to Life Association v Eddleman* (2003) – certain legislators admit that they tailor policies to respond to the demands of contributors, although these efforts are typically circumspect. When questioned about the effect of campaign contributions on their decision-making, policymakers are quick to argue that they are not influenced by money, although psychological research on the social effects of gifts suggests this is unlikely (Cialdini, 2009).

In contrast, media reports on lobbying and fundraising scandals suggest that corrupt practices are extensive and ongoing: that wealthy interest groups use lobbyists to buy the time and votes of legislators, and that legislators require organizations to "pay to play." Many researchers who study campaign finance, however, believe that policymakers are unlikely to change their behavior when interest groups give them money, because interest groups most often make contributions to legislators who already support their goals. Others disagree, noting that legislators sometimes change their positions on legislation after receiving campaign contributions from interest groups (Langbein and Lotwis, 1990).

Some critics of the role of interest groups in campaign finance point out that the expense of running a competitive electoral campaign results in a pool of candidates biased toward wealthy interests as a result of the exigencies of fundraising, regardless of whether legislators are willing to sell their votes or lobbyists wish to buy them. The American political system's reliance on private financing thus has a troubling systemic implication: that even if individual candidates are not corruptible, the only candidates who can raise enough money to be electorally competitive may be those that support the policy goals of interest groups that can afford to sponsor candidates.

In contrast to the controversy of the effect of money on policy outcomes, nearly every observer agrees that money can buy *access* to policymakers. The Supreme Court has expressed concern about the idea that large contributions can ensure preferential access, and advocates for campaign finance reform find the idea that contributions buy access to policymakers distressing, because it implies non-contributors have less access. However policymakers, interest groups, and the researchers who study them all accept the idea that money buys access, and most find this unremarkable and relatively inoffensive. Business PACs, in particular, have been shown to direct their campaign contributions in order to gain access for their lobbyists.

Members of Congress often solicit interest groups for campaign money, knowing that they will respond to these solicitations rather than risk losing access. The majority of campaign contributions are given at fundraising events attended by interest group lobbyists, and in some cases, when former staffers become lobbyists they openly offer to sell access to legislators in return for contributions (Loomis, 2007). One lobbyist summarized his role in the political process by saying, "I raise money and I give money" (White, 2005).

The general public is far less sanguine about the idea that money can buy access to legislators. The notion that contributions to political candidates, especially sitting legislators, can buy anything at all, even extra consideration, raises the suspicion of corruption, a phenomenon most commonly described as undue influence on officeholders' judgment. One survey found that over half of constituents polled felt it was inappropriate to use money to buy access to legislators (Baldassare et al., 2004). The finding that constituents dislike the idea that contributions buy access to legislators suggests that there is a fairly wide gulf in the perception of what constitutes ethical behavior between legislators and the public. In *Buckley* v *Valeo*, the Supreme Court suggested that the perception of corruption and the existence of corruption were "almost equal" concerns. In the light of this finding, surprisingly little effort over the last 30 years of research on campaign finance has gone into determining what the general public believes constitutes corruption, despite the fact that such findings could have enormous implications for devising regulations on campaign finance that decrease the perception of corruption.

Reforms: existing and possible

Advocates for reforms intended to limit the influence of interest groups have proposed a number of possible regulations, which can be loosely classified into three approaches: (1) increased information, or disclosure, (2) limits on contributions, either in size or scope, and (3) subsides. Each of these approaches has different strengths and weaknesses, but in general they grow more expensive and controversial as their intended goals become broader in scope. Moreover, the extent of potential reforms is constrained by legal decisions that define all lobbying activity and most forms of political spending as protected speech under the First Amendment. These legal protections are an expression of democratic values that support relatively unfettered political speech and participation, and that make changes in the status quo unlikely. Unsurprisingly, most reforms passed in recent years have focused on the least controversial and least expensive policies.

Disclosure

Although there is widespread ideological and partisan disagreement about some proposed reforms, nearly all political actors support increased disclosure. One remaining holdout, however, is the United States Senate, which continues to resist electronic filing (Pierce, 2007). Most disclosure laws are also consistent with the Supreme Court's interpretation that political spending is a form of constitutionally protected speech, a position recently restated in *McConnell* v *FEC* (2003); and disclosure laws are uniformly popular. Despite the nearly universal support for disclosure, increasing the scope of information disclosed about political activities has been difficult. Many details remain unreported, including information about certain kinds of lobbying, and the amounts and distribution of money spent on issue advocacy, a form of political spending where interest groups campaign for particular policy issues without directly discussing candidates or office holders.

The Lobbying Disclosure Act of 1995 required far more lobbyists on the federal level to report their activities than ever before, but the disclosure of lobbying expenditures in particular remained incomplete, with reporting requirements only taking effect after interest groups had spent several thousand dollars. There was also only very limited information on issues that organizational lobbyists pursued. Critics of the bill noted that it also did not require lobbyists to report "bundled" contributions. This phenomenon occurs where individuals are solicited to support a particular candidate by an interest group and these contributions are then handed over to the candidate by an interest group representative, guaranteeing that the candidate knows the interest group raised the money while the general public does not. The Honest Leadership and Open Government Act of 2007, however, introduced the first requirement to report bundling activities. Although empirical research on bundling is understandably limited, estimates suggest the majority of contributions given by individuals are solicited and bundled by organizations (Marshall, 1999).

Both the 1995 and 2007 lobbying laws, however, failed to address the exchange of money between interest groups, such as that used by the tobacco company in its creation of GGOOB. Although amendments were introduced to both bills that would have required organizations lobbying the federal government to disclose the source of their funding, these amendments were removed from the final legislation in the face of vehement interest group opposition. Existing research on public relations notes that media investigation of organizational sponsors has frequently limited the effectiveness of front groups, and notes that requiring industries to disclose all of their political activity would also limit the value of front groups (Lyon and Maxwell, 2004). Unfortunately, recent federal legislation provides even greater incentives for interest groups to form front groups because it is a form of lobbying that does not have to be disclosed to government. At the state level, disclosure of lobbying is even less detailed; many state governments fail to require lobbying disclosure at all, and those that do demand disclosure of interest group lobbying activities frequently provide far less information than the federal government requires.

In contrast, direct contributions by interest groups to candidates and political parties have been reported since the establishment of the FEC in 1974, although not always in a timely or detailed manner. Individuals who make contributions to candidates and political parties often fail to include meaningful background information; for example, large numbers of individual contributors identify their occupations as "lawyer" or "housewife." In addition, contributions made in the final days of an election campaign may not be disclosed until months after the election. In recent years, however, disclosure laws, particularly at the state level, have focused on making reporting more immediate by requiring electronic filing of campaign contributions and spending, allowing the public, the media, and researchers to observe when substantial contributions are given to candidates shortly before elections.

Despite its popularity and increasing use, the implications of requiring increased disclosure are unclear. Disclosure is popular both for practical reasons and because the idea of increasing information is intuitively appealing. But there is very limited research on what the public views as corruption, and no evidence indicating whether disclosure of lobbying activity decreases or increases the perception of corruption, or whether having more information about campaign contributors affects individual voting decisions. There is also little information indicating whether disclosure could deter candidates and interest groups who might otherwise seek to sell votes or buy influence from doing so.

Limits on contributions

Reforms that seek to limit contributions by interest groups, unlike disclosure, can be explicitly linked to perceptions of corruption, and there is also evidence suggesting that more stringent regulation of campaign contributions may influence the conduct of campaigns and the outcome of elections. Contribution limits historically focus on size or scope: government may restrict the amounts any single contributor can give to a single candidate per election, and may also limit the types of contributors and the timing of contributions.

Since the passage of FECA in 1974, most limits on the size of campaign contributions in the United States have been viewed as constitutionally acceptable. Recently, however, the Supreme Court revisited this approach in *Randall* v *Sorrell* (2006), striking down very low contribution limits in Vermont ($200 maximum) as an unacceptable restriction on free speech. The legality of similarly low contribution limits currently in effect in other states has not yet been determined. There is some evidence suggesting that these contribution limits have an effect on candidate behavior; lower limits appear to reduce incumbent spending (Hogan, 2000). However, reducing the amount that interest groups can spend on campaign contributions does not imply that groups give up political spending; groups substitute other political activities for campaign contributions when contribution limits go down (Hogan, 2005), and some organizations seeking to influence politics do not make campaign contributions at all.

Restrictions on the scope of contributions have rarely been accepted by US courts as constitutionally acceptable. Although government can prevent corporations and unions from making contributions to candidates directly from their treasuries, these organizations can still form affiliated political action committees that raise money for contributions by soliciting individuals. Efforts to ban spending by other kinds of contributors, such as PACs or individuals that reside outside legislators' districts, have been ruled unconstitutional, along with efforts to limit the size of incumbent "war chests" and banning loans by candidates to their own campaigns. Similarly, efforts to restrict political advertising by outside organizations in the wake of the Bipartisan Campaign Reform Act (BCRA) passed in 2002 were also unsuccessful. (These organizations are widely known as 527 groups because of the section of the tax code under which many groups are classified.) In 2007, the Supreme Court decided that the efforts by BCRA to limit advertisements that mentioned the names of candidates near election dates were constitutionally unacceptable (Greenhouse and Kirkpatrick, 2007). As a result of court decisions like these, many reforms proposed to limit political advertising by interest groups have devolved into variations on disclosure laws.

Restrictions on the timing of campaign contributions have been far more successful in surviving legal challenges. Several states ban campaign contributions during legislative sessions, and these restrictions successfully survived legal challenge in *North Carolina Right to Life Inc.* v *Bartlett* (1999). Although there is little information regarding the substantive implications of banning contributions during legislative sessions, this limit is one of the few that attempts to address the efforts of interest groups to influence legislators when relevant policies are under consideration. Nonetheless, like the other proposed reforms imposing limits on contributions, it has been difficult to judge whether there is much influence on actual behavior.

Subsidies

Given the difficulty involved in limiting the activities of interest groups, and that the activities that reformers wish to control are protected by the Constitution, some advocates have chosen to focus on encouraging nontraditional interests to participate in the process as a counterweight to established policymakers and interest groups. Subsidies for candidates are designed to increase political competition as well as limiting interest group access to legislators. Subsidies for underrepresented interest groups are intended to provide information that legislators would not otherwise hear (Apollonio, Cain, and Drutman, 2008). Proposed subsidies include partial measures such as free broadcast time for candidates, efforts to increase the contributor base of candidates through tax credits or contribution vouchers given to individuals, and direct monetary support from government, as well as full public financing for candidates or interest groups.

Reformers also hope that having government provide public financing will make elected officials less likely to respond to contributors and more likely to respond to constituents, because they face a credible outside threat in the form of well-funded challengers. Currently, incumbents possess overwhelming electoral advantages over other kinds of candidates: they have greater name recognition among voters, may design districts through redistricting that help protect them from electoral challenge, and perhaps most importantly, find it easier to raise money. In general, subsidy programs have been acceptable to the courts as long as they are voluntary, but their political implications are not clear; and they are both expensive and difficult to establish. Providing free broadcast time for candidates, for example, has been vehemently and successfully opposed by media companies, who find the prospect of having to provide broadcast time worth millions of dollars to candidates without compensation unappealing.

Some states have established partial public financing for campaigns. These programs give money to candidates either directly from government or indirectly though tax credits and contribution vouchers. Such contributions typically constitute a small share of candidate fundraising, which leaves candidates dependent on private campaign contributions. Perhaps in part because they do not eliminate dependence on private fundraising from interest groups, this subsidy appears to have limited effects on electoral competition or political outcomes.

At the federal level, public financing for presidential campaigns has been offered since the 1970s. Yet in recent years this public financing system has almost completely broken down because it is more advantageous to candidates not to participate (Cigler and Loomis, 2007). The indecision expressed by both candidates in the 2008 presidential election about whether to accept public financing suggests that it will not be relevant in future presidential campaigns unless it is radically restructured.

A few states have experimented with a new form of public financing subsidy for candidates by establishing full public financing for all state candidates, known as "clean elections." Two states (Maine and Arizona) began their programs in 2000, and one more (Connecticut) implemented clean elections in 2008. In these programs, candidates collect a number of small contributions (as low as 50 contributions of $5 apiece) to qualify for public funding, at which point the state provides campaign funds equal to average expenditures in past election cycles. Participating candidates may not raise private funds. If a publicly financed candidate faces a privately financed opponent who attempts to spend more than the subsidy, the state provides additional matching funds to the publicly financed candidate to equalize the amount that both candidates can spend, up to two or three times the amount of the original subsidy (Public Campaign, 2002a). Although these programs are voluntary, this escalation clause dramatically reduces the appeal of raising private funds, given that every dollar raised results in an equal contribution to a publicly financed opponent. Full public financing appeals to reformers because participating candidates opt out of receiving campaign contributions entirely, meaning contributions buy neither access nor influence. Practically speaking, full public financing also seems to affect electoral competition; studies suggest the programs have augmented the number of candidates, equalized spending levels (US General Accounting Office, 2003), and decreased incumbent reelection rates (Mayer, Werner, and Williams, 2004).

Because participation in clean elections is voluntary, the spending caps imposed by the system appear consistent with the Supreme Court's decision in *Buckley* v *Valeo* that mandatory spending caps are illegal. And although public financing is generally considered to be unpopular in the United States, given the long-standing desire for smaller government, nearly every state using this system adopted it through the initiative process. In the two states with the most extensive and long-standing clean elections systems, Maine and Arizona, the majority of candidates now choose public financing.

Critics of the system have argued, however, that interest groups are still heavily involved in the candidates' collection of small contributions. In addition, the costs of full public financing are substantial. In the states that provide funding to all candidates for state office, the programs demand millions of dollars annually, with expenses greatly exceeding initial expectations (La Raja, 2003; Public Campaign, 2002b). Furthermore, the states currently offering full public financing have relatively inexpensive races; in other states or at the federal level, the costs of a full public financing system could be even more daunting.

In addition to considerations of cost and effectiveness, the idea of providing subsidies for candidates taps into strong beliefs about the appropriate role of government and private interests. These beliefs are strongly articulated in discussions of full public financing. An advocacy group in favor of public financing claimed that "the role of big money in American politics should make the most cynical lawmaker blush and the average citizen furious. . . . Our democracy is sinking in a cauldron of systematic influence peddling, flagrant abuse of loopholes and political favors granted to wealthy special interests" (Public Campaign, 2002a). On the other hand, a think tank opposing the program argued that public financing makes political campaigns "a wholly owned subsidiary of the state government, giving the government significant power over political speech in the state" (Franciosi, 2001); similarly, one candidate in Arizona described his state's system as "dirty, muckraking, dishonest elections using taxpayer money" (Arizona Daily Star, 2005).

Possibilities for change

The history of reforms intended to affect interest group influence in American politics suggests the difficulty of substantive change. The proposed reforms that are most practical to establish, because they have few costs and generate little controversy, do not appear to be effective. The proposed reforms that seem most likely to limit interest group influence are expensive, ideologically controversial, and thus difficult to enact. As a result, the system rarely changes. Laws affecting interest group activities have largely been instigated by political scandals. In the absence of such scandals, history suggests that changes that might affect the activities of interest groups are unlikely.

Conclusion

Interest groups play a large role in American politics and arguably a greater role than political parties play. They fund elections, may solicit candidates to run for office, and provide much of the information used in policy decision-making. Yet they clearly are not representative of popular interests in the way that elected representatives are intended to be, and there is little evidence that elected representatives can influence their behavior. Efforts to enact reforms in the past have had only limited success, and increasingly encourage interest groups that are wealthy or unrepresentative to hide their activities from scrutiny.

The escalating expenses involved in effective lobbying and campaigning raise continuing popular concern about how to protect the interests of the general public from organizations pursuing their own self-interest. To pass constitutional muster, however, any proposed reform must preserve the right to petition government as the courts have defined it, as well as broadening the representation of interests. Despite popular distaste for interest groups and their perceived influence on government, questions about the extent of interest group influence on American politics are typically viewed as being of low importance. In addition, there is no well-defined constituency that would gain from reform, and many well-established and powerful groups that oppose it.

In early 2009, President Obama established new restrictions that limited the pay of White House employees and prevented administration members from lobbying for two years after leaving government employment, stating that these changes, among others, were intended to reduce the temptation to use public service as an opportunity to advance individual and corporate self-interest. Although these new ethics rules were intended to decrease the influence of lobbyists, like most previous reforms, it remains unclear whether they will be effective in doing so.

Chapter 6

The Media

Jonathan Parker

2008 was a watershed year for the media in the United States. The financial collapse and recession have severely undermined traditional media companies, driving many familiar and established names into bankruptcy. This economic crisis has hastened a process already in motion, the technologically driven shift from older media to newer forms of delivery, particularly the Internet. The most potent symbol of this generational shift from old to new was the presidential election of 2008, in which Barack Obama used the Internet, email, social networking sites, and mobile technology as never before to organize and run an effective insurgent campaign for the Democratic Party's nomination and then repeat the feat to win the general election campaign (Anderson, 2008; Fraser and Dutta, 2008; Huffington, 2008; Stirland, 2008).

Many news headlines and commentators declared after the election that the Internet had won it. However, Obama did not invent the new technologies, and he developed his campaign out of strategies that had shown success in the past, though on a smaller scale. His real genius was to recognize the potential of these newer forms of communication and successfully build a campaign around them in order to utilize their potential. Applying existing technology and techniques, and successfully melding them with traditional campaign tactics, were what led to victory, not the innovation of a brand new form of political communication.

Just as Obama's victory came from wedding the old and new tactics, the shift to new ways of accessing news media does not mean that traditional media content is unpopular. Newspapers, for example, are more successful than ever in terms of readership. The difference between collapsing on the sofa on a Sunday morning with the *New York Times* and reading it on the computer is that the latter undermines the business models that sustain newspapers. People still want all the old media content, but they no longer have to pay for it. Though no one is rejecting the content of the news media, the institutions that create this content are going bankrupt or shutting down at an alarming rate.

The economic downturn has led to two consecutive years of decline in advertising, with another one forecast for 2009, which would constitute the first three-year decline since the Great Depression. These declines have affected all media, but they hit newspapers particularly hard. This short-term decline in advertising revenue was as high as 16 percent for newspapers in 2008, and it comes on top of long-term declines in audience numbers as the explosion in options for audiences fragment the traditional mass media markets (Perez-Peña, 2008). In the case of newspapers, audiences are all declining for traditional print versions of papers, but this drop is usually much smaller than increases in Internet viewers. The problem for newspapers is that the revenue from Internet advertising is a fraction of that for print. The economic downturn has eroded other traditional sources of advertising, particularly from car dealers, who are the largest single source of advertising in newspapers and local television.

New media, particularly the Internet, are not immune to the economic slump, and revenues from online advertising fell rather than grew in 2008 (PEJ, 2009). However, the consistent growth in audience figures for media on the Internet show it is rapidly taking the place of traditional media. In 2008 online news sources gained larger audiences than traditional newspapers for the first time. Television and radio audiences on the Internet continue to rise, and may become as important a share in this sector as is now the case for newspapers.

It is unclear what the media industry will look like in a decade, but it will certainly not resemble the past few decades. The decline in traditional media will have unknown effects on the provision of information to the country. Many local communities now have only one or even no choice of newspapers. Radio stations have been bought by large corporations and centralized to the extent that they provide very little local news any more. Many commentators assume the Internet will fill this gap, but Internet-based media often use stories researched and distributed by the traditional media, so it is unclear who will carry out investigative journalism in the future. The decline in the traditional media also signals a decline in the standards of professional journalism, particularly with regard to factual accuracy and partisan neutrality. The shift towards cable and Internet sources brings a distinct shift to more opinionated, partisan coverage of the news. While these trends have been well documented, what is unknown is what impact these changes in news will have on people's political knowledge, opinions, and behavior.

The decline of traditional media

Media usage has changed rapidly over time, with the development of new forms of communication and means of delivery. The current situation is characterized by a continuing shift from network television news towards more on-demand formats such as cable and the Internet. More importantly, the rapid growth of the Internet has undermined many traditional media formats, including television, newspapers, magazines, and radio.

The decline of traditional media sources such as newspapers and television is a long-term trend. The past century has been characterized by the rise of new forms of media which overtake old ones as they compete for audiences. Mass-market print newspapers have dominated journalism for the past century. Radio developed into a potential rival source for news by the middle of the twentieth century, when it was cited by over a third of people as a primary news source, but it never seriously threatened to overtake newspapers. Television arose as a new medium after the Second World War, reaching 90 percent of US households by 1959. By 1964 it passed newspapers as the most commonly cited source of news for individuals (Mayer, 1993). Though newspapers remain in clear second place as a source of news, they provide much more content than television and wield influence far beyond the daily circulation figures through strong readership among elites. However, television continued to rise as a source of news, cited by 69 percent of respondents by 1992, while newspapers and radio went through a steady decline in this same period, falling to 43 percent and 16 percent respectively (Mayer, 1993). These figures become even more complicated with the rise of cable and Internet sources, so the more fragmented media use of the past two decades will be considered separately.

Television was dominated by the "Big Three" national networks, ABC, CBS, and NBC, throughout the 1960s and 1970s. These compa-

Figure 6.1   *Media listed as primary sources of news, by percentage of respondents, 1959–92*

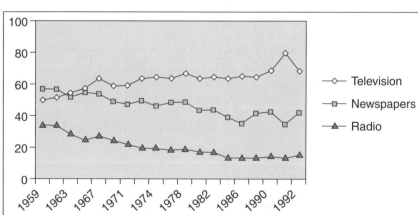

nies provided much of the programming content to their affiliated stations in local areas. As late as 1980 these three networks were watched by 90 percent of viewers in prime time. Cable television accounted for only 6 percent of viewers during this period, largely confined to rural areas out of the reach of broadcasters (Head, Sterling, and Schofield, 1984). The dominant position of these networks made their flagship national news programs highly popular and influential. Roughly one third of all households watched one of the national network news shows on a daily basis throughout the 1960s and 1970s. The national network news provided the stories watched by much of the nation, and just as importantly, carefully monitored by policymakers. However, people's interest in the news mirrors their interest in politics: they think local. Correspondingly, more households watched local news rather than national throughout this period, and this trend remains unchanged (Prior, 2007).

By 2003, broadcast television's overall audience share had dropped by half, from 80 percent of viewing time to 40 percent, as a result of competition from new cable networks, new broadcast networks, and VCR/DVDs. Cable network access grew rapidly from 1980, when it was only 20 percent, to reach 68 percent of homes by 1996. Satellite access grew steadily in the 1990s, to reach 11 percent of households by 2000. Its popularity, aided by smaller dishes and falling costs, rapidly expanded to 29 percent of households by 2008 (Federal Communications Commission, 2006). The growth of these alternatives to broadcast television stations also brought competition in the news.

Cable News Network (CNN) was a television station launched by Ted Turner in 1980 to provide news from around the world 24 hours a day. During the first Gulf War in 1991 it became the news source watched by heads of state, diplomats, and ordinary citizens. CNN reporters were the only television news correspondents in Baghdad, and the network could provide constant updates of events. Dramatic live broadcasts and footage of the bombing raids, many of which were helpfully supplied by the increasingly media-savvy US military, attracted a huge worldwide audience and set the trend for 24-hour news broadcasts. The continued growth of cable television since the 1990s now strongly competes with network broadcasters for viewers, fragmenting the overall audience. There is also more internal competition among cable news stations, with the rise of new networks Fox, MSNBC, and Headline News. People no longer have to watch the national network news broadcasts at set times because of 24-hour news coverage on cable networks.

While national networks still only broadcast one daily flagship news program in the early evening, local stations have adapted to changing lifestyles and the rise of on-demand delivery by expanding the number of local news broadcasts. Stations broadcast in four slots. Morning

news catches people getting ready for work between 5.00 am and
8.00 am. Midday news occurs between noon and 1.00 pm, evening
news between 5.00 pm and 7.00 pm, and late news occurs between
11.00 pm and 11.30 pm (PEJ, 2009).

Not only are there multiple broadcasts of news throughout the day,
but they can also be viewed "on-demand" through recording devices
such as TIVO, or the Internet. These changes in the way the news is
accessed has generated debate over the best way to measure audiences
and gauge the popularity of programs. Traditionally, the Nielsen
Company has measured audiences through individual meters and
diaries. Audiences for each show could be measured through these
meters to provide ratings, which show the percentage of all households
watching, and shares, which show the percentage of the audience
watching television at that time. However, with 24-hour cable news,
people may watch for a few minutes to get the headlines multiple times
each day. Similarly with local news broadcasts, people might watch at
any one of four times per day to get their news. The use of VCRs and
DVRs to record programs means they may be watched at another time.
The Internet allows people to watch news programs at any time. The
rise of this on-demand approach to viewing television means that the
audience for a program at any one particular point in time might be
relatively small. However, the overall number of people who watch
that program at different times might be extremely large.

"Cume," short for cumulative audience, has been developed to
measure the total number of unique viewers who watch a program,
which gives a better indication of the overall "reach" of a program or

Figure 6.2   *Cable and broadcast television news audiences, 2002–08*

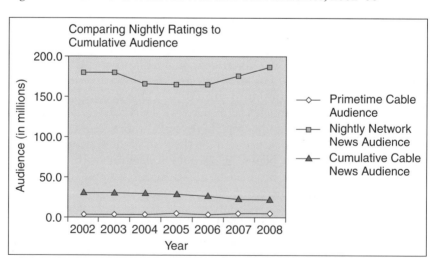

network. For example, CNN might have many fewer viewers for its news during primetime than a national network news broadcast. However, many more people will tune in to CNN for periods throughout the day, so it might actually reach many more people than network news. The same phenomenon occurs with local news, which broadcasts multiple times a day. The weakness of this method is that it does not measure how long people watch, or how closely they pay attention. Further, Cumes do not translate directly into revenue, since advertisers buy particular time slots for their products, so they care far more about traditional ratings.

Public opinion surveys can also gauge long-term audiences for particular types of media. Pew's Project for Excellence in Journalism surveys people, asking them to list their primary sources of news. The problem with such opinion polls is that people notoriously overestimate their attention to news.

Public opinion surveys of people's primary sources of news demonstrate the influence of cumulative audience ratings. News shown multiple times throughout the day, which includes both 24-hour cable news and local television news, is cited much more highly as a source of information. In 2008, local television news was the most common source of news, cited by 52 percent of people. Cable news, with 39 percent, now surpasses the national network news, at 29 percent.

Table 6.1   *Regular news consumption, by source, 1993–2008*

	1993 %	1996 %	1998 %	2000 %	2002 %	2004 %	2006 %	2008 %
(Listened/read yesterday)								
Newspaper	58*	50	48	47	41	42	40	34
Radio news	47*	44	49	43	41	40	36	35
(Regularly watch)								
Cable TV news					33	38	34	39
Local TV news	77	65	64	56	57	59	54	52
Nightly network news	60	42	38	30	32	34	28	29
Network morning news			23	20	22	22	23	22
Online news for 3+ days a week		2**	13	23	25	29	31	37

* from 1994; ** from 1995
Source: compiled by author using data from PEJ (2009).

Figure 6.3   *Network and cable television news audiences, 1980–2008*

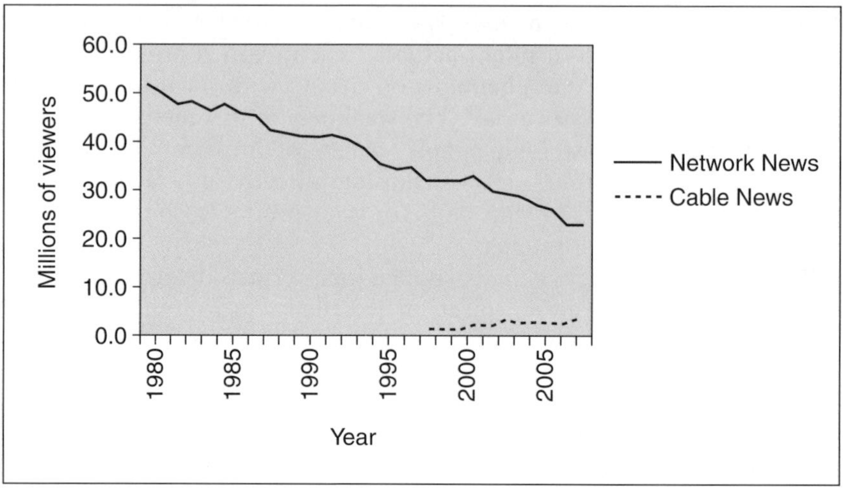

Audience figures show a similarly dramatic decline. The total audience for network news dropped from 41 million in 1993 to 29 million by 2003.

Local news broadcasts have expanded during this same period. Like cable news, these stations broadcast news throughout the day, but people tune in for information not available in national broadcasts, such as weather and sports. While local television news audiences, like those for national network news, have been falling over time, they have fallen more slowly, and local television news is firmly established as the largest single source of news.

The long-term decline in the audience for nightly network news broadcasts also heralds the decline in the standing and influence of the news with the public. The model of the elderly, respected (male) news anchor providing information the nation could trust has eroded over time. Walter Cronkite was news anchor for CBS from 1962 until 1981. He was widely hailed as one of the most trusted men in America, and his distinctive voice is associated with many of the historical events that he covered during his career. When Cronkite reported during the 1968 Tet Offensive that the Vietnam War was unwinnable, President Lyndon Johnson is reported to have replied, "If I've lost Cronkite, I've lost middle America" (Wickert, 1997). Cronkite retired in 1981 and was replaced with Dan Rather. During the presidential election in 2004, Rather broke a story about President Bush's national guard service which was based upon documents that turned out to be fake. Rather had to step down and retire in the furore that followed (Kurtz, 2004).

Changes to the news

2005 proved to be a huge transition year for network news. All three network news anchors retired, igniting a competition to keep current viewers and attract new ones. Two networks responded to their declining and aging audiences by bringing in younger and, they hoped, more appealing anchors. Most prominently Katie Couric, the popular host of the morning news program *Today*, replaced Dan Rather at CBS in 2006. Couric, the first woman to anchor the network news, was expected to attract new, younger viewers from *Today*, but audience figures continued to decline. Worse, CBS news now trails behind both of its rival networks. None of the new anchors have been able to halt the long-term decline in network news audiences, though interest in the election appears to have kept these losses negligible for 2008.

The presidential election also brought some critical success to the network news. Charles Gibson, the ABC News anchor, carried out the first major interview of vice presidential nominee Sarah Palin, and his testy questioning of her fueled the debate over Palin's lack of knowledge and suitability to be Vice President. Those doubts became much more widespread after a series of long interviews with Katie Couric, which exposed a lack of knowledge and experience, and brought much more extensive criticism of Palin's suitability, even among Republicans. The impact of these interviews on the electorate cannot be gauged precisely, but they did have a large effect on the campaign and coverage of the candidates in the media.

Despite network news' prominent role in some key moments in the campaign, the 2008 election demonstrated the declining power and influence of the network news. The overall media coverage demonstrated a continuing shift towards cable news. While the network news still commands the largest audience for primetime, cable stations offer 24-hour coverage. Surveys asking people where they get their news show that cable overtook network news in 2002 and continues to expand this lead. In 2008, 39 percent of people regularly watched cable news as opposed to 29 percent for network news.

The rise of 24-hour cable news is accentuating the importance of minute-by-minute political judgments by journalists. Speed has become an even larger factor in political coverage (PEJ, 2009). The constant coverage of events also reinforces the need for additional means to attract audiences. The use of big personalities and highly opinionated coverage that characterizes much of cable news became more successful and pronounced in the 2008 elections.

Clearly, opinionated coverage is popular with a large segment of viewers, and this more partisan approach to news is challenging the traditionally neutral values of professional journalism that characterize most news reporting in the United States. The most successful cable news station is Fox, which Rupert Murdoch formed in 1996 with the explicit purpose of providing news from a conservative perspective. Fox took the lead in the cable ratings during the invasion of Iraq in 2003, and currently has a clear lead in primetime viewers, with a nightly audience of 668,000 compared with 300,000 for MSNBC and 271,000 for CNN (Carter, 2008). MSNBC, the second most popular cable news, emulates Fox's partisan approach by providing a more left-wing approach. CNN, which encapsulates the traditional ethos of professional journalism, has a strategy of "no bias," but has been struggling for viewers and has even fallen behind its own Headline News station. CNN dismissively claims it is not competing with other "so-called cable news networks. They don't have journalists on in prime time" (Carter, 2008). Instead, it cites cumulative monthly audience figures, which amalgamate all viewers during the day. In those ratings, CNN leads with 74 million viewers compared with 61 million for Fox and 56 million for MSNBC. Though advertisers do not buy on the basis of cumulative audiences, CNN remains a successful and profitable station.

Promoting shows with celebrity hosts with very opinionated views has expanded cable news viewership. Bill O'Reilly, Sean Hannity, and Glenn Beck at Fox, all conservatives, are the most popular personalities in cable news. Keith Olbermann and Rachel Maddow, left-leaning commentators on MSNBC, follow closely behind. Cable news's ability to expand its audience as the network news shrinks indicates the importance of this more opinionated journalism, in contrast with the more traditional values of strict neutrality found on the nightly network news broadcasts.

The shift toward more partisan news coverage follows a trend set by one particular type of media in the United States: talk radio. There is a long history of demagogues on American radio, such as Father Coughlin's radio broadcasts of the 1930s, which were marked by their strong partisan opinions and open anti-Semitism. The contemporary talk radio format developed after the repeal in 1987 of the Fairness Doctrine, which had required broadcasters to equally represent different views. Talk radio relies on charismatic commentators who are usually highly oppositional and conservative. The lead commentator by all accounts is Rush Limbaugh, who leads in audience figures with over 14 million weekly listeners with his barbed political views and openly racist, homophobic, and sexist content (Kurtz, 1997). The next four most popular, and conservative, hosts are Sean Hannity (13 million), Michael Savage (8 million), Laura Schlessinger (8 million), and Glenn Beck (7 million) (PEJ, 2009). Hannity and Beck also host popular cable shows on Fox News.

Like cable news, talk radio has increased its audience. A 2002 poll found that 37 percent of the public listed "regularly" or "sometimes,"

Figure 6.4   *Total newspaper circulation, 1980–2008*

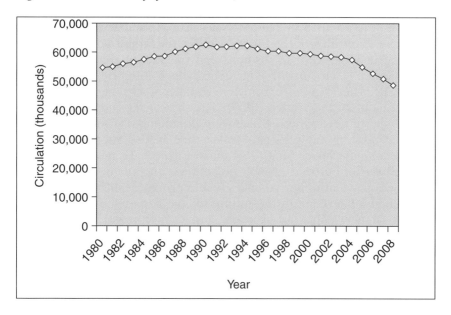

and 17 percent of respondents rely on talk radio for their news. Talk radio listeners, contrary to their characterization as uneducated, disaffected white men, are actually more educated, wealthier than average, and pay attention to the news. While talk radio is most popular with conservatives, its audience is large and includes a wide cross-section of the population, particularly among moderates and independents (Pew, 2002). Its continuing success is important because it provides a ready stream of conservative viewpoints to a politically active and aware segment of the population.

Newspapers, while they have been replaced by television as the most popular news source among the public, still provide much more news content than other media, and have retained strong influence among elites. Similar to the problems facing network news broadcasts, newspapers have also been struggling against long-term declines in their audience. As Table 6.1 indicates, the percentage of respondents claiming to read a newspaper regularly has fallen from 58 percent in 1993 to just 34 percent in 2008. The newspaper industry cannot sustain such steep and continuous declines. Like television news, newspapers have also suffered from an increasing lack of trust by the public and a crisis of conscience over recent scandals and the failure to rigorously scrutinize the Bush administration before the Iraq War.

The economic downturn hit newspapers particularly hard. The business model upon which traditional journalism is built has been undermined over the past few years, and for the newspaper industry it has collapsed. In 2006, total industry advertising was $49.3 billion. By 2008, it was about $38 billion (NAA, 2009), and it should decline further in 2009. Before the financial crisis, the largest companies were engaging in large-scale acquisitions and buyouts of other companies. The recession left them with large debts, which completely undermined their value. The 14 publicly traded newspaper stocks lost 83 percent of their value in 2008 (Mutter, 2009). The shift to the Internet had been noted by most newspapers, which were expanding their online services. Large expansions in web-based advertising helped support the print editions. Online advertising grew an average of 27 percent per year from 2004–07, but that growth became a 2 percent decline in 2008, dashing hopes that online revenues would provide a sufficient and reliable source of revenue in the future. Online ads only account for 12 percent of newspaper ad revenue, and cannot make up for losses elsewhere (NAA, 2009).

Rise of the new media

As audiences for traditional media decline, other sources rise in popularity. The fragmentation of media into many different types of sources and formats means that no one format, network, or program will become as dominant as traditional media in the past, which faced fewer sources of competition. The year 2008 proved a watershed in which the Internet emerged to become a leading source of information, exceeding all other media except television as a source for national and international news. In 2008, 40 percent of people said they get most of their news from the Internet, up from 24 percent in 2007, and out-doing newspapers at 35 percent. Television continues to lead as the main source at 70 percent, though for people aged 18–29 the Internet now ties with television as a source, with 59 percent (PEJ, 2008).

The shift to the Internet has threatened all traditional media formats, though the impact on news is more acute and immediate. People can now listen to music or radio, download podcasts, watch television or movies, and get magazines and news over the Internet. The increased convenience and choice presented by this shift towards an on-demand culture provides great benefits, but it has also encouraged a culture of free content. This assumption that content should be free manifests itself in both illegal actions, such as downloading music, movies, and books without respecting the intellectual rights of their producers, and perfectly legal activities, such as watching television or reading newspapers.

The damage done to traditional media by the Internet is not caused by luring audiences away from traditional content. In fact, the case is

Figure 6.5   *Sources of news, 2001–08*

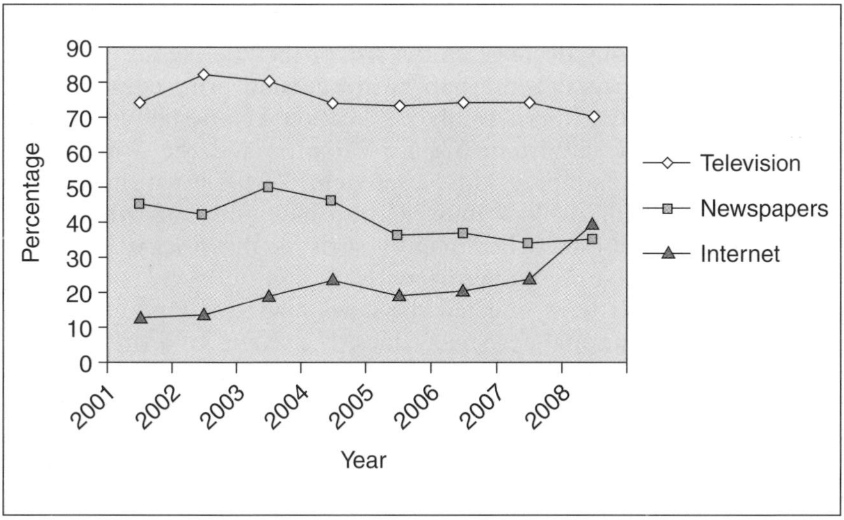

Figure compiled by the author with data from Pew (2008).

more the opposite. The Internet has attracted many more people to seek out traditional news content, particularly newspapers. The problem is that reading newspapers online has expanded at the expense of print editions, which raise subscription and advertising revenue that online ads cannot match. Online sources of news generate a much greater audience for traditional news content, but at the same time they completely undermine the business model that underpins the creation of that content. It is a terrible irony that technology has provided new ways to gain easy and convenient access to news at any time. The use of these formats, combined with a severe economic downturn, is now bankrupting the companies that provide news content.

The Internet has hit certain areas of newspaper revenue particularly hard. Classified advertising is the most prominent loss. The use of Internet sites to advertise jobs and goods for sale, such as Craigs List, quickly undercut this staple of local newspapers. Further, search engines made these Internet listings both cheaper and more effective than print versions. Even real estate and cars can be sold through the Internet. As a result, revenues from classified advertising in newspapers have fallen from $20 billion in 2000 to $10 billion in 2008 (NAA, 2009). Eighty percent of losses in newspaper advertising revenue stem from the collapse of the classified ad market (PEJ, 2009). This decline in ad revenue is likely to decline further in the near future. This continuing loss of income and the crippling debt load carried by many of the news companies have prompted a drastic round of cost-cutting that will severely impact on the quality of the news nationwide.

The physical size of newspapers is shrinking, mainly to save in print costs, with a resulting decrease in the size of the "newshole," or space for news on the pages. Some papers are ceasing print editions altogether and becoming Internet-only publications. Nationally renowned papers such as the *Christian Science Monitor* and the *Seattle Post Intelligencer* have adopted this approach. Well-known newspaper groups such as Sam Zell's Tribune Group have filed for bankruptcy. Finally, many well-established papers such as the *Rocky Mountain News* in Denver have closed permanently.

Similar upheavals have affected the news magazine market as well. One of the three national newsmagazines, *U.S. News & World Report,* is to cease publishing its magazine to concentrate on its college rankings and other catalogue publications. *Newsweek* is seeking to become a more elite, upscale publication with a smaller circulation and higher price. *Time* is now the only weekly mass-market newsmagazine left in the United States (Kurtz, 2009).

Newsroom staff losses have been heavy, with the loss of over 10 percent of staff in just the past year (American Society of News Editors, 2009). Particularly hard hit are state capital beats, with many local papers pulling out of state legislative coverage entirely (Gurwitt, 2009). Similar cutbacks are occurring in Washington and foreign bureaux (PEJ, 2009).

One point of consensus appears to be that reduced print advertising added to Internet advertising will not prove sufficient to sustain newspapers. While this is a controversial issue, many commentators note that journalism needs to find a way to charge for online content. The *New York Times* failed in an attempt to charge for content in 2005, but it will reportedly introduce another scheme in summer 2009 (Koblin, 2009). Specialist publications such as Rupert Murdoch's *Wall Street Journal* successfully charge for content, but more general newspapers such as *The Times* have not been able to run such a scheme successfully. The future of print newspapers may depend upon the development of a scheme.

The 2008 election and new media

The use of the Internet provides many new opportunities, and many of the most successful applications can be put to use in political campaigns. Barack Obama's adept use of the Internet and social networking to win the campaign for the Democrat nomination and then the presidency in 2008 has been hailed in many circles as a victory of the Internet (Anderson, 2008; Lewin, 2008). However, Obama ran a hybrid campaign in which both old and new media played interdependent and complementary roles (Smith, 2009).

Howard Dean pioneered most of these tactics in his unsuccessful run for the Democratic presidential nomination in 2004, particularly the use of the Internet to gather donations and organize a volunteer following. As chair of the Democratic Party he also pioneered the "50-state strategy," which sought to compete in all states rather than just key battlegrounds. Obama adopted the use of the Internet, social networking, and the "50-state strategy" as key foundations of his campaign, and made them work successfully. His use of the Internet and other communication formats to raise funds and organize his campaign volunteers and staff did represent an innovative and effective application of technology. However, these innovative practices were integrated into a campaign that operated in very conventional ways. In particular, the Obama campaign used its large advantage in fundraising to blanket media markets with paid political ads, just as other presidential campaigns do. The use of the Internet was vital to the campaign, but it did not achieve victory in the election alone. In one sense, it simply applied a highly effective method of fundraising to bankroll a traditional campaign. However, fundraising was only half the advantage provided by the campaign's use of the Internet. Social networking gave it an added advantage that was new.

Though Howard Dean pioneered the tactic of using social networks to organize local efforts, the Obama campaign recognized its potential very early and integrated it into the heart of its strategy. The achievement of crafting a successful nationwide social movement was immense, and successfully applying the technology in this way was a monumental innovation by itself. The development of the campaign social networking site MyBarackObama.com (or MyBO) allowed volunteers to actively participate, feel like a valued part of a movement, and channel their energies into practical organizing. By election day volunteers had created 2 million profiles, 200,000 events, 400,000 blog posts, and 35,000 volunteer groups on the site. Through its automated software and contact databases, 70,000 people had raised $30 million for the campaign (Green, 2008). The Internet was used to develop an immense fundraising machine which raised $500 million online (Vargas, 2008).

Beyond simple fundraising, the social networking site and training materials helped volunteers create organized Obama offices throughout all 50 states, and compete in areas in which other campaigns had no substantial presence. These volunteers created, updated, and made use of email lists, walk lists of neighborhood precincts, phone banks, and cell phone banks for SMS, video, and voice calls. These efforts provided continually updated assessments on the candidate's success in local areas to campaign headquarters. These local networks of people bombarded family, friends, and acquaintances with emails during the election. The scope of this effort was immense, but its exact size and impact are unknown because volunteers tapped into their own personal networks to influence people. The emails did not cost the campaign anything, and the total traffic they generated remains uncounted.

The way in which the Internet now encouraged people to generate their own content helped the campaign tap into its volunteers' energy and abilities. Numerous YouTube videos and other messages allowed volunteers to tap into networks previously unknown or unreachable by traditional, paid political marketing firms. Allowing local activists the initiative to produce and distribute their own material can be risky, and centralized campaigns rarely relinquish their tight control over the candidate's message. However, trusting these local volunteers unlocked a wealth of creativity and energy, while making them feel a valued and important part of the campaign, rather than an unimportant part of a machine whose role is to simply follow directions.

The ease of creating and sharing videos has also amplified the influence of gaffes, mistakes, and other embarrassing moments in the campaigns. This easy access to video clips of damaging events affected Obama during the primaries when clips of controversial statements by the Rev. Jeremiah Wright, Obama's pastor, emerged in March 2008 and were viewed over 7 million times on YouTube. Far more damaging was the repeated viewing of video clips of misstatements by Sarah Palin during her interviews with Charles Gibson and Katie Couric. As doubts emerged, even amongst Republicans, about Palin's suitability for the vice presidency, comedians relentlessly mocked her candidacy. The most famous incident involved impersonations of her by Tina Fey on *Saturday Night Live*. The first skit about Ms Palin, on September 13, was viewed 14.3 million times on Hulu and NBC's website, and watched by 10.2 million on television, but was estimated to have been viewed over 35 million times on YouTube (Carter, 2008). These clips were widely talked about and discussed on the news, becoming part of the election agenda and focussing attention away from other topics.

The heated partisanship of the primary and general election campaign led to inevitable charges of bias on the part of the media from all sides of the political spectrum. Clinton supporters charged that the media exhibited misogynistic tendencies in the negative coverage of Clinton, while failing to rigorously examine Obama. The McCain campaign echoed the charge, repeated by many conservatives, that the media gave Obama a "pass" (Goldberg, 2009). Evidence from the Pew Research Center for the People and the Press does indicate that Obama received far more positive press coverage than McCain, though the cause of this coverage was not the partisan bias alleged by conservatives.

Figure 6.6   *Tone of news coverage of presidential candidates, September 8–October 15, 2008*

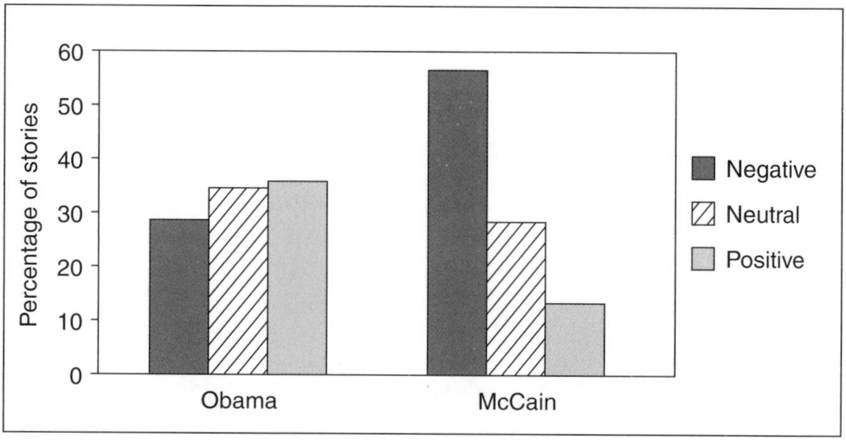

Figure compiled by the author with data from PEJ (2009b).

Figure 6.6 clearly shows that Obama received a much higher percentage of positive stories (36 percent) than McCain (14 percent), while McCain received many more negative stories (57 percent) than Obama (29 percent). The reasons for this stark difference become more evident when the election coverage is broken down by story subject. Commentators have long documented the declining coverage of policy issues in political campaigns. The media now tend to focus on the horse race, going into great detail over who is winning in which state and by how much. The rapid expansion of opinion polling during the election has increased this shift towards horse race coverage by providing new data on a frequent basis for journalists to report. From January 2008 until election day there were 491 polls taken, which gave news organizations an almost daily source of new information (Rosenstiel and Kovach, 2009).

An analysis of news coverage by the Project for Excellence in Journalism (2009a) reveals that horse race coverage dominated all other election topics by a wide margin. Over half of all stories were about the state of the race. Obama led in the opinion polls during this period and appeared to be making substantial inroads on traditional Republican territory, so the news coverage inevitably appeared much more favorable to him. Whoever is winning tends to get better coverage in horse race stories. The media was filled with stories about Obama's lead in the polls, how that lead increased during the financial crisis, and how state after state that McCain had to win appeared to be swinging towards Obama. The continual stream of such stories

Figure 6.7   *Campaign news coverage, by type of frame, January 1–*
November 5, 2008

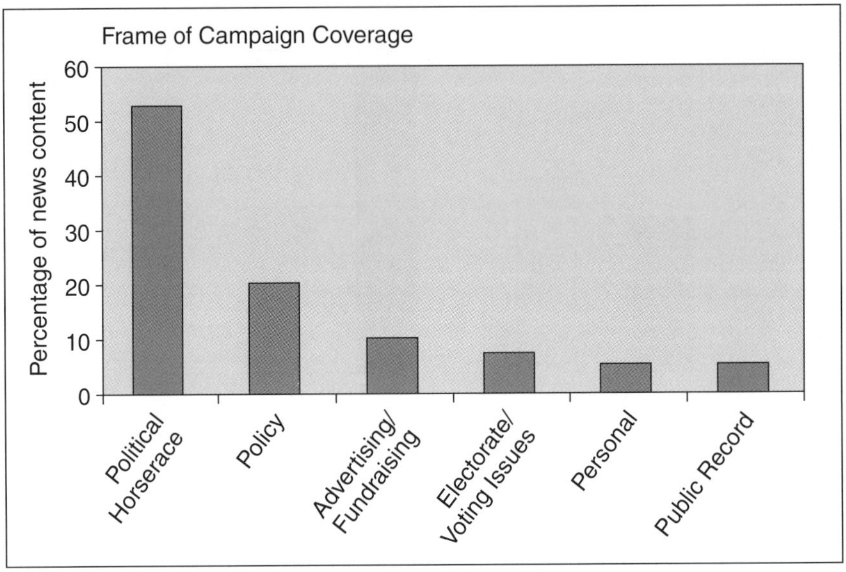

demonstrates why Obama's coverage was so positive while McCain's was so negative. The horse race bias accounts for most of this difference without any effects from partisan bias.

Conclusion

The media is moving towards a new era in which the old business models that supported print journalism and the dominance of the national network news are no longer sustainable. It is a period of transition in which the changes can be observed and charted, but no one can confidently predict what effect these changes will have. The public is shifting towards on-demand access using a new generation of technology that is most firmly embraced by the younger generation of citizens. The content provided by old or traditional media remains more popular than ever, but it is not clear under what conditions it will continue. The financial underpinning for traditional journalism is dying, but a new system has not emerged. Current sources of news are decidedly more partisan and opinionated, which is a challenge to traditional journalism values in the United States. This generational shift in media was symbolized during the election by the death of Tim Russert, one of the best known and respected political pundits in Washington, of a heart attack during the campaign. David Carr of the *New York Times* was covering the Bonnaroo music festival in Tennessee, and the political engagement of the younger audience was evident. Voting organizations and the Obama campaign were present to canvass voters, and comedian Chris Rock and musician Eddie Vedder of Pearl Jam were speaking in support of Obama. When Carr solemnly announced to the press room that Russert had died there was silence until a woman asked, "Wasn't he on TV?" (Carr, 2008).

Chapter 7

The Presidency

Jon Roper

Barack Obama's election as the 44th President of the United States demonstrates how politics, personalities, and events converge every four years to determine the nation's choice of its leader. The Democrat's victory owed much to the popular reaction against the perceived failures of George W. Bush's administration, to the error-prone campaign of the Republican candidate, Senator John McCain, and to the onset of an unprecedented economic crisis, of unknown depth, indeterminate length, and global extent. Obama's campaign mantra, "Change we can believe in," struck a populist chord at a time of waning support for the continuing American military action in Iraq, a war he had opposed. In January 2009, his inauguration as the first African American to hold the office represented a symbolic step across the fault-line of racism that has persisted as the historic legacy of slavery and the Civil War. Yet along with the sense of anticipation and heightened expectation that accompanied his initial months in the White House came an awareness that the new President's political inheritance was the most challenging and complex of modern times.

He succeeded a President widely viewed to have usurped his legitimate sphere of constitutional authority through the aggressive assertion of executive prerogatives, particularly following the 9/11 terrorist attacks. During the campaign and the transition, prior to entering the White House, Obama revealed elements of a leadership style that augured well in terms of his capacity to handle the demands of the office. Nevertheless, from the outset of his presidency, he needed to show an appreciation of the constitutional limits of his position, and to recognize an acceptance of the constraints that inevitably limit his room for political maneuver.

Two of his most celebrated predecessors, Abraham Lincoln and Franklin Roosevelt, with whom he invited comparison even before he took the oath of office, were both able to expand the scope of presidential power relative to that of the legislature during times of national crisis. In this respect, domestically, Obama's framing of his relationship with Congress during his first 100 days in office was a key element in setting the tone for the new administration. The limits of the President's influence were soon exposed during the negotiations surrounding his "stimulus package." Obama's professed hope to build a bipartisan consensus in the legislature proved to have little political traction on Capitol Hill.

The President's power to place his imprimatur on American foreign policy is traditionally the least contested realm of his constitutional authority. However, the change that Obama offered here, and that Hillary Clinton, his Secretary of State, was charged with implementing, was one of style rather than substance: the tempering of the reflexive threat and unilateral use of America's military resources in favor of "smart power," a strategic vision that relies on a range of policy instruments, from force to diplomacy, to further the national interest overseas. Throughout his campaign, Obama made it clear that his worldview was not based upon a radical philosophical or even ideological departure from the core assumptions that have consistently underlined American internationalism. Indeed, despite his opposition to America's invasion of Iraq, he shares the liberal progressive's readiness to use military power if he judges it necessary to achieve foreign policy objectives.

First-term Presidents cross the political road from the campaign to the White House while looking both ways: to the future and to the past. Barack Obama has four years to transcend his predecessor's legacy and build a solid record of achievement. His performance will determine not only his prospects of re-election in 2012 but also where he will rank among those who have held the American presidency.

From the moment of his formal announcement of his intention to run for the presidency in February 2007, Obama's ability to invent himself as a different kind of candidate was allied to his formidable talent as a politician. He revolutionized presidential campaigning. Howard Dean's short-lived bid for the Democratic nomination in 2004 had demonstrated the latent money-raising potential of the Internet, but Obama's use of new technologies and in particular social networking sites enabled him to raise unprecedented funding for a campaign that could then outspend and out-organize its rivals. He also changed the electoral landscape of presidential politics, showing that he could compete – and win – in states the Democrats had hitherto ceded to the Republicans. Aspiring presidential candidates will study Obama's campaign for the White House as a model that they will have to emulate if not surpass.

The problem of presidential power

America's founders had initially seen the presidency as at least co-equal with, if not subservient to, the Congress. They outlined the executive's powers in the second article of the Constitution, after they first established those of the legislature. It took 150 years before Franklin Roosevelt, the architect of the "modern presidency," laid the foundations for the transformation of the institution, cementing the presidency at the apex of the federal government. During the Cold War and after, the President's control of the nation's nuclear arsenal in his role as commander-in-chief ensured that all those who followed Roosevelt into the White House would become, particularly at times of national and international crisis, in Alfred de Grazia's apt phrase: "the focus of the anxious crowd of the age" (1969: 65).

However, if his successors have lived "in the shadow of FDR" (Leuchtenburg, 2001), it is because the expanded potential for the use of presidential power creates tensions within a constitutional system that was explicitly designed to constrain it in order to prevent it from being abused. As Richard Neustadt acutely observed, "Power problems vary with the scope and scale of government, the state of politics, the progress of technology, the pace of world relationships" (1960: 2). In his seminal work on presidential power, therefore, Neustadt focused upon the ways in which the executive could legitimately and constitutionally negotiate its way, at any given time, through the political obstacles that stood in its way, famously concluding that presidential power is "the power to persuade" (1960: 10).

After Roosevelt's death in office, for some of his successors, persuasion was not enough. Presidents could evade accountability for their actions by invoking the need to preserve national security, the issue that came to dominate the American political agenda. Until the Vietnam War and the Watergate scandal revealed the potential consequences of unchecked executive power, in one area of delegated constitutional authority the President remained by and large unchallenged: the definition of his role as the nation's commander-in-chief. Moreover, by annexing the war-making initiative from the legislature, first in Korea and then in Vietnam, the executive effectively circumvented the Constitution. The temptation was for the "imperial presidency" then to assume prerogatives that further undermined the delicate machinery of checks and balances (Schlesinger, 1973). When Richard Nixon's conduct in office was revealed during Watergate, his resignation avoided the inevitability of an impeachment trial. Nevertheless, the executive suffered collateral damage. Nixon's successor, Gerald Ford, at the end of his brief tenure in the office expressed his concern that the presidency was "imperiled."

When the Republicans won back the White House in 1980, therefore, they sought to reclaim some of the political territory abandoned in the retreat from the "imperial presidency." Taking their cue from Alexander Hamilton's assertion in the *Federalist Papers* that "unity" was the principal element necessary for "energy in the executive," lawyers in Ronald Reagan's Office of Legal Counsel (OLC) started to interpret the Constitution in ways that reasserted presidential prerogatives. During Bill Clinton's presidency, the Republican debate over the form and function of the "unitary executive," which presupposed the President to have unlimited authority over the federal government, continued in legal journals. It was not until George W. Bush won back the White House in 2000 that advocates of an increased sphere of executive authority were once more in a position to give practical effect to their views.

The events of 9/11 crystallized their argument. Key members of the Bush administration, including Vice President Dick Cheney, who had pressed for a resurgence of presidential power since his time as Gerald Ford's chief of staff, supported the OLC in its confident opinion that the prerogatives of the "unitary executive" enabled it to act decisively at a time of perceived national crisis. What followed – internment without trial for terrorist suspects at Guantánamo Bay in Cuba, legitimization of torture, "extraordinary rendition," and executive orders sanctioning surveillance of those designated a threat to national security within the United States itself – was the product of the exploitation of the existential fear embedded in the President's unilateral declaration of the "war on terror."

However, as the Bush administration unraveled, the pathology of presidential power that had helped destroy Lyndon Johnson's presidency re-emerged. Like his Texan predecessor, Bush suffered increasingly from a "credibility gap" which contrasted his interpretation of the continuing conflict in Iraq with the popular mood of the moment. As the insurgency gathered momentum, like Vietnam, Iraq became an intractable military and political problem. In turn, this led to criticism that Bush's – and Cheney's – interpretation of presidential power was having a corrosive impact on American constitutionalism (Pfiffner, 2008). In its initial incarnation, the "imperial presidency" had reached its apogee during the Nixon administration, when the President resigned to avoid slipping over the precipice of impeachment. George W. Bush left office having escaped a similar fate, but his conduct presented his successor with a dubious legacy that would haunt the initial months of his presidency.

Leadership style: the "presidential difference" of Barack Obama

Barack Obama entered the White House with the anticipation that he would end the constitutional excesses of his predecessor's administration through adopting a fundamentally different approach to the problem of presidential power. The optimism that surrounded his election and inauguration was based not only upon the assumption that he had a more balanced view of the Constitution than that adopted during the previous eight years. It was also the product of his supporters' belief that, although inexperienced, he had a character and qualities that augured well for his presidency. This potential may be assessed by looking at Obama's abilities in terms of the skills appropriate to the position outlined by Fred Greenstein in *The Presidential Difference* (2000), a perceptive work that examines the leadership styles of each American President since Franklin Roosevelt.

The new President scores highly in Greenstein's first required talent: proficiency as a public communicator. In marked contrast to the strangled syntax and staccato delivery of George W. Bush, on his way to the White House Obama repeatedly demonstrated his talent for public speaking in a manner that suggested he could use Theodore Roosevelt's "bully pulpit" of the presidency to full effect. His professionalism during the debates that punctuated the primary season and the election campaign demonstrated that he could handle the constant pressure of public performance. His sense of humor – at once sharp and on occasions self-deprecatory – added to the impression that the Democrats' candidate had the elusive charisma of a Kennedy.

In both his campaign and in forming his administration, through his capacity for organization – the second of Greenstein's criteria for success – Obama showed that he is willing to innovate and to conciliate. As a former community organizer, he was able to build a grassroots populist movement, buttressed by the use of technology, which relied on engaging the support of those who might hitherto have assumed that they could have little impact on the political process. The campaign exhortation "Yes, we can!" was based on the painstaking construction of a new and formidable political machine which galvanized the Democrat vote nationwide.

During the transition period, Doris Kearns Goodwin's book *Team of Rivals* (2005), for which the President-elect had expressed his admiration, may have seen a boost in sales. It was widely cited as an example of how a great chief executive, Abraham Lincoln, persuaded his political opponents to set aside their ambitions and former differences of opinion, joining him to serve the nation during the Civil War. Key appointments to Obama's cabinet were greeted as examples of the organizational approach taken by his illustrious predecessor, who had also journeyed to the presidency from the Illinois state legislature. While persuading Hillary Clinton to become his Secretary of State was the appointment most reminiscent of Lincoln's gestures towards his former political rivals, Obama's selection of Tim Geithner as Secretary of the Treasury and Robert Gates, who continued as Secretary of Defense, also suggested the new President would encourage debate and accept dissent in his cabinet rather than allow ideological conformity to underpin political consensus. Yet approval for the way in which Obama went about constructing his administration was tempered when some of his high-profile choices – with Tom Daschle, nominated to oversee health care reform, the most prominent among them – failed to survive the intense scrutiny of the confirmation process.

Greenstein's assessment of a President's abilities as a political operator rests upon the extent to which political skill, allied to a policy vision, enables the executive to implement a coherent program of legislative initiatives. Having emerged from the murky world of Chicago city politics, Obama's achievement in reaching the White House only 12 years after his first election to the Illinois State Senate suggests that he understands not only how to play the political game but also (as a poker player) when to gamble in order to win it.

The blueprint for Obama's America was laid out in his second book, *The Audacity of Hope* (2006), published on the eve of his run for the presidency. It is nothing less than a repudiation of the public philosophy of the "Reagan revolution," and represents an attempt to harness once more the power of the federal government to the cause of social justice. While this vision is framed in the Democrat tradition of Franklin Roosevelt's "New Deal" and Lyndon Johnson's "Great Society," wrapped up in the messages of political and generational change, it has been necessarily tempered by the severity of America's prevailing economic recession. However, it still provides Obama's administration with a focus for its political ambitions, among them health care reform, tackling the problem of climate change, and investing in the nation's educational infrastructure.

In terms of his foreign policy vision, during the campaign and the transition, Obama provided enough evidence in his writings, speeches, and appointments to indicate that his broad outlook on America's contemporary place in the world harked back to the mainstream of the traditional bipartisan consensus that had been long established in the nation's foreign policy. If his assumption of American primacy was similar to that articulated by Theodore Roosevelt, Obama's rhetoric was reminiscent of that of Woodrow Wilson: a reworking of the themes of early twentieth-century progressivism that have re-echoed since then in the nation's foreign policy.

Greenstein identifies cognitive style and emotional intelligence as the remaining criteria by which to judge presidential performance. A President must be able to "process the Niagara of advice and information that comes his way" (Greenstein, 2000) when faced with myriad complex problems. Obama's approach to the task, the product of his intellectual curiosity and Harvard law school training, relies upon inviting debate and discussion of conflicting points of view before he reaches his decision. His family background, his sense of the richness of his African and American heritage together with his time spent as a child in Indonesia and as an adolescent in Hawaii, gives him an eclectic reservoir of influences and experiences upon which he can draw.

Coupled with this is the suggestion that Obama possesses the existential aura similar to that which the novelist Norman Mailer, describing the 1960 presidential campaign, saw in John F. Kennedy's "elusive detachment to everything he did" (1976: 22). In the closing stages of the 2008 election it was "no drama Obama" whose conduct in the immediate aftermath of the initial collapse of the nation's financial system appeared presidential, in contrast to the political posturing of John McCain. Such preternatural calm suggests that the new President has sound emotional intelligence, the quality that, for Greenstein, is paramount in establishing a successful leadership style: "in its absence all else may turn to ashes" (2000: 200).

The first 100 days: "Yes we can?"

In his inaugural address, Obama signaled his intent. With his predecessor and members of the outgoing administration looking on, he distanced himself from the perceived excesses of the previous eight years, observing that:

> As for our common defense, we reject as false the choice between our safety and our ideals. Our founding fathers, faced with perils that we can scarcely imagine, drafted a charter to assure the rule of law and the rights of man, a charter expanded by the blood of generations. Those ideals still light the world and we will not give them up for expedience's sake.   (Obama, 2009a)

His initial actions as President were carefully calibrated with symbolic significance. Obama moved swiftly to revoke George W. Bush's executive orders that had limited the public release of the records of former Presidents and sanctioned the continued use of some forms of excessive coercion in the interrogation of terrorist suspects. He also took action to close the detention camp at Guantánamo Bay, while demanding an immediate review of detention policy practices and options. Interspersed with this reversal of the discredited directives that had defined his predecessor's "war on terror," Obama framed a clear code of ethics for those joining his administration.

While executive orders set the tone for the new administration, the first political test of Obama's presidency came when he presented Congress with his "stimulus package" to revive the American economy. He had started lobbying for it even before his inauguration: a proposal that envisaged tax cuts, increased spending on America's infrastructure and other job creation schemes, and which came with a price-tag of over $700 billion. On February 17, 2009, less than a month into his presidency, the President signed the measure into law. In his address to a joint session of the legislature just over a week later, he expressed his gratitude that "this Congress delivered" (Obama, 2009b), and immediately began the process of lobbying for his $3.6 trillion budget.

The aftershocks of the financial earthquake that had impacted during the closing months of George W. Bush's presidency continued to be felt as Obama's administration began to come to terms with the enormity of the economic challenge it faced. Treasury Secretary Tim Geithner faced fierce criticism and early calls for his resignation when the administration appeared powerless to prevent bonuses being paid to executives at the insurance conglomerate AIG, despite the government bailout that had kept it in business. At the same time, Wall Street gave a mixed reception to Geithner's plan to stabilize the banking sector and encourage capital flows by reducing exposure to "toxic debt."

In an interview he gave two months into his administration, when the President was asked if he was "punch drunk" in the face of the economic crisis, he gave an insight into how he was dealing with the pressures of office:

> There's gotta be a little gallows humor to . . . get you through the day. You know, sometimes my team . . . talks about the fact that if . . . if you had said to us a year ago that the least of my problems would be Iraq, which is still a pretty serious problem, I don't think anybody would have believed it.   (CBS, 2009)

His reply encapsulated not only the economic uncertainties he faced in his efforts to bring the country out of recession, but also his awareness of the political complexities that the new administration was inevitably encountering in framing a working relationship with Congress.

It soon became clear that the changes that Obama offered in terms of American foreign policy were of style and focus rather than direction. In keeping with the new administration's foreign policy mantra – "smart power" – on the day after his inauguration, the President ordered a review of America's military strategy in Iraq. Just over a month later, in a speech at Camp Lejeune in North Carolina, he announced the timetable for "a transition to full Iraqi responsibility" in "an Iraq which is sovereign, stable, and self-reliant." He announced that the United States would end its combat mission there by August 31, 2010. Some forces would remain to support the Iraqi government as it took over responsibility for national security, but Obama made a further commitment that by the end of 2011, US troops would return home.

The planned withdrawal of America's military forces was underpinned by the principles of "smart power." Obama argued the case for a "smarter, more sustainable and comprehensive approach" to the Middle East. This involved "refocusing on al Qaeda in Afghanistan and Pakistan" as well as "developing a strategy to use all elements of American power" to halt Iran's ambition to build nuclear weapons and to broker "a lasting peace between Israel and the Arab world" (Obama, 2009c).

Prior to his North Carolina speech, Obama had approved a request to send more troops to Afghanistan. On March 27, in remarks outlining a new strategy for Afghanistan and Pakistan, he continued his recalibration of his predecessor's "war on terror," reiterating the need for "a stronger, smarter, and comprehensive strategy" that would redeploy American forces "to disrupt, dismantle and defeat Al Qaeda" both there and in Pakistan. As the military commitment to Iraq wound down, the President pledged to continue the fight against potential terrorists and the Taliban in the border region that he identified as having become "for the American people ... the most dangerous place in the world." It was also "an international security challenge of the highest order" in which "the safety of people around the world is at stake" (Obama, 2009d). Like his approach to tackling the economic crisis, this military stimulus package to confront the deteriorating situation in Afghanistan and Pakistan was a political gamble with an unpredictable outcome.

Obama's first overseas trip as President thus focused not only on building an international consensus behind his effort to jump-start the global economy, but also on attempting to persuade America's NATO allies to support his new priorities in the continuing fight against terrorism. At the G-20 summit in London the initial differences between America and a number of its European allies were glossed over in what was generally seen as a successful round of public diplomacy to which the President and the First Lady contributed their star quality. Compromise was reached on the emphasis that each nation placed upon coordinating efforts to revive economic growth and international trade, and embracing the demand for a more robust regulatory regime that might address a recurrence of the problems caused when the global economy careened from boom to bust. On the other hand, America's European partners in NATO offered little more than rhetorical support for the President's call for an increased multilateral military commitment in Afghanistan.

Within the United States, the release of documents showing the extent of the complicity of President Bush and senior members of his administration in authorizing the torture of terrorist suspects in the aftermath of 9/11 increased the political pressure on Obama to go beyond his repudiation of such action, and agree to an independent inquiry to investigate the issue. Americans were treated to the ironic spectacle of Dick Cheney – the most influential and secretive Vice President in the nation's history – demanding full disclosure of information that he insisted would vindicate the policies the former administration had pursued.

David Axelrod dismissed the anniversary of Obama's first 100 days as a "hallmark holiday." However, as if to celebrate the occasion, the House of Representatives and the Senate reached agreement on the budget. The President's influence in Congress was also potentially enhanced by the defection of the veteran Republican, Arlen Specter, to the Democrats, raising the possibility of their having a filibuster-proof majority in the Senate. But in a press briefing to mark the traditional first milestone in a new President's administration, Obama made it clear that, unlike George W. Bush, he appreciates that his constitutional power is indeed the power to persuade. Asked what had humbled him during his first months in office, the President replied that it was:

> the fact that the presidency is extraordinarily powerful, but we are just part of a much broader tapestry of American life and there are a lot of different power centers. And so I can't just press a button and suddenly have the bankers do exactly what I want or . . . turn on a switch and suddenly . . . Congress falls in line. And so . . . what you do is to make your best arguments, listen hard to what other people have to say and coax folks in the right direction. (Obama 2009e)

The White House and Capitol Hill

Obama's appreciation that there are constitutional limits to presidential power was reflected in his initial efforts to construct a working and workable relationship between the White House and Capitol Hill. The new President put together "the most Congress-centric administration in modern history" (*New York Times*, 2009). The first chief executive to be elected straight from the legislature since John F. Kennedy in 1960, Obama could draw not only upon his own – albeit relatively brief – experience of the Senate, but also the more substantial knowledge and political networks of his Vice President, Joe Biden, who had represented Delaware there for 36 years. His chief of staff, Rahm Emanuel, formerly the fourth-ranking Democrat in the House of Representatives, assumed a pivotal role in shaping the administration's relations with Congress. Phil Schiliro, who became Director of Legislative Affairs with direct responsibility for congressional liaison, had been a long-serving and well-respected aide, principally to Henry Waxman, the Californian representative who took over as chair of the

House Energy and Commerce Committee and also – briefly – to Tom Daschle in the Senate.

According to Lyndon Johnson,

> There is but one way for a President to deal with the Congress and that is continuously, incessantly and without interruption. . . . If it's really going to work, the relationship between the President and the Congress has got to be almost incestuous. . . . He's got to know them even better than they know themselves. (quoted in Cowger and Markman, 2003)

While Obama's personal style in his dealings with his former Capitol Hill colleagues is very different from "the Johnson treatment" – the persuasive technique that very few in Congress proved able to resist – by the time of the July 4 Independence Day celebrations he was still on course to break LBJ's 1965 record of a 93.1 percent success rate in legislative votes on his administration's policies (*CQ Today*, 2009). Yet although this suggests that during his "honeymoon period" he enjoyed extremely high levels of support in the legislature, particularly among Democrats, the stratospheric statistics also mask some political realities that will continue to impact upon the Obama administration as it pursues its ambitious domestic policy agenda.

The Congressional response to the President's economic stimulus package, the first and critical test of his relationship with the legislature, illustrates the point. Despite Obama's call for a bipartisan consensus around his Keynesian flag, Republicans in the House of Representatives stood to one side and voted unanimously against the measure. Nevertheless, it cleared its first hurdle by a comfortable margin of 63 votes before being submitted to the Senate. It was here that the administration had to compromise, accepting that some of its proposals for immediate spending on education and health care would be sacrificed in order to put together the coalition of Democrats and moderate Republicans that saw the bill pass by a single vote.

Indeed, the President's initial successes in Congress had more to do with Senate moderates realizing the need to respond to the gravity of the economic situation that America faced than it did to the persuasive skills deployed by the combative Emanuel and the more emollient Schiliro in convincing a bare majority to support the President's initiative. Nevertheless, the battle over the stimulus bill set the tone for the administration's approach to Congress. In many ways Obama, whose political agenda promised a reversal of the "Reagan revolution," resembled his Republican predecessor in setting out the broad aims of his policies and allowing Congress to decide on the details.

Up until the July 4 holiday weekend, Obama had staked out an explicit political position in comparatively few floor votes in the legislature. Although this helped to minimize the risk of the President suffering defeats in Congress (two out of 26 in the House and only one out of 37 in the Senate), his apparent willingness to defer to Congress had potential political costs as well as benefits. During the debates on the stimulus package, public support started to fluctuate for what appeared to be a measure being shaped and twisted by a Congress that was far less popular than the new President. There was a threat that the legislation would be derailed. At that point, Obama staked his public prestige on the outcome, and using the advantages of the "bully pulpit," rallied support for what he now emphasized was the President's initiative in well-publicized appearances outside the "Washington bubble" in Indiana and Florida.

While the experience of persuading Congress to pass the stimulus bill suggested that Obama could rely on his party's support in the relatively liberal House of Representatives, the Senate continued to confront him with more complex political challenges. In his press briefing marking the end of his first 100 days in office, the President admitted that he was "under no illusion that suddenly I'm going to have a rubber-stamp Senate" (Obama, 2009e), despite Arlen Specter's defection from the Republican ranks. His remark proved prescient. The Senate's first act of defiance against a presidential proposal came just a few weeks later when, on May 20, it voted against his plan to close the terrorist detention center at Guantánamo Bay. The scale of the Democrat defection was almost complete as, by a vote of 90–6, the Senate refused to fund the relocation of the prison's inmates from Cuba to the United States mainland.

It was a reminder, if Obama needed it, that persuasion remains the fulcrum of presidential power. The new administration proved adept in working with Congress to achieve its early goals, believing that a President who allows its members the opportunity to shape policy outcomes can achieve more than one who presents Capitol Hill with fully drafted legislation and then invites a battle over its details. Nevertheless, as the passage of the stimulus bill demonstrated, there is a time when the chief executive has to take ownership of a particular policy and mobilize the power of public opinion behind it in order to bring maximum leverage to bear on the legislature. This remains the case, particularly in the Senate. Despite the resolution of the protracted recount battle in Minnesota that saw the Democrats inch further towards a filibuster-proof majority, party control there is brittle, and the President's influence is on occasion at its weakest, as the Guantánamo defeat demonstrated. Managing his agenda of change in controversial areas such as health care, energy, and taxation in the period up to the mid-term elections and beyond will press Obama's political skills to their persuasive limits.

Crisis as challenge: "Change we can believe in"?

In November 2008, Rahm Emanuel, in a widely quoted comment, observed that "You never want to let a serious crisis go to waste." The new administration claimed that its daunting inheritance could be the catalyst for fundamental alterations in America's political landscape. Emanuel therefore argued that crisis was an opportunity to deal with hitherto neglected problems. These he prioritized as the issues revolving around health care, energy, the tax regime, education, and financial regulation (*Wall Street Journal*, 2008).

The $787 billion stimulus bill and the $3.6 trillion budget resolution could be presented as necessary and ambitious efforts first to kick-start the stalled economy, then to invest in the development of an infrastructure for renewed growth. Despite the concerns of fiscal conservatives, the passage of both measures through Congress was a reminder that "persuading congressmen to spend public money in their districts doesn't exactly qualify as dark magic" (*New York Times*, 2009). The greater challenge was to convince them to support the need for change in tackling the five domestic problems that Emanuel listed as the administration's main concerns.

As the Obama administration continued in its efforts to translate the potential of campaign rhetoric into the reality of White House performance, it still faced formidable domestic and foreign policy challenges. Levels of public confidence in states such as California, among the worst of those areas affected by the collapse of the housing market, remained low. Many there were left paying mortgages on properties now devalued to such an extent that it seemed likely they would remain in negative equity for the period of the loan. The number of foreclosures, adding to the unsold housing inventory, underlined the problem. The California state government struggled to agree eventually to spending cuts that would tackle a projected $26 billion budget gap in the state's finances. It was an indication of the extent to which the economic recession continued to impact unevenly across the country, making the anticipated pace and timing of recovery unpredictable.

Overseas, Obama's recalibration of his predecessor's "war on terror" away from Iraq focussed attention once more on the problem of Afghanistan. His new approach to the apparently intractable military situation there was signaled by the "surge" in American troops committed to the campaign, coupled with the appointment of General Stanley McChrystal, with his experience in the unconventional warfare waged by Special Forces, to replace General David McKiernan as commander of NATO forces. In taking such action, Obama risked being drawn into the protracted military stalemate of a war that, as it emerges from the long shadow cast by Iraq, could become equally unpopular in the United States. At the same time, the turmoil in Iran that erupted following the contested re-election of President Ahmadinejad was another reminder of the political volatility throughout an area of the world critical to American interests.

Conclusion

Since the whirlwind of presidential activism that characterized Franklin Roosevelt's first 100 days in the White House, his successors have been aware that the public perception of their administrations is often shaped during those critical initial weeks in office. Richard Neustadt's advice to the incoming President John F. Kennedy in 1960 remains relevant: "Nothing would help the new administration more than such a first impression of energy, direction, action, and accomplishment" (2000: 21). Yet as he also later observed, while the changeover in administrations creates such opportunities, there are accompanying risks. "The transition hazards that afflict a President-to-be and his immediate associates are born of haste, hubris, and the unfamiliarity native to newness" (2000: 157). In Kennedy's case, one outcome was the early debacle of the failure of the attempted invasion of Cuba at the Bay of Pigs.

Similarly, Jim Pfiffner has pointed out that new Presidents are under pressure to spend the political capital accumulated from a successful campaign in the relatively short "window of opportunity" that coincides with their early days in office. It is then that public and congressional goodwill towards them is at its height. But this is also a time when:

> The size and complexity of the huge programs and organizations of contemporary U.S. government argue for a more deliberate approach. With time and experience come added competence as the new administration matures and learns how to manipulate the governmental levers of power. (Pfiffner, 1996: 4)

Obama's first 100 days in office demonstrated his ability to negotiate the hazards of the transition and to exploit the political advantages of his historic victory. He defined rapidly the broad parameters of his approach to the presidency. In contrast with Bill Clinton, whose comparative lack of organizational ability resulted in his presidency "hitting the ground walking" (Pfiffner, 1996), Obama entered the White House with key cabinet appointments made and policy initiatives ready to send to Congress. He maintained an image of activism and engagement, taking immediate control of his political agenda and setting a clear sense of purpose for his administration. In part this was a product of his personal style and the need to give substance to his campaign promise of change. But in large measure it was also due to the circumstances of his election and inauguration.

The new President's initial challenge was to restore America's faith in an executive office that under his predecessor had aggressively expanded and then abused its constitutional power. This was coupled with the need to shore up the nation's confidence in an economic system brought to the point of collapse as a result of unregulated speculation and financial mismanagement. Buoyed by a reservoir of national and international goodwill, and helped by Democrat majorities in Congress, Obama began by demonstrating "energy, direction, action, and accomplishment," and achieved some notable successes. According to the Gallup poll tracking the President's popularity, his approval rating stood at 65 percent at the end of his first 100 days in office.

By that time, Obama's strategic approach to Congress had also become clear. Like Lyndon Johnson, he appreciated the need to know personally his potential supporters and opponents on Capitol Hill. Aware that the prestige of the presidency is a valuable political resource, the Obama White House opened its doors to members of Congress: in the first four months of the administration 320 of the 435 House representatives and around 80 of the 100 senators had visited. The Legislative Affairs Office developed a tracking system to monitor the use of what were seen as the "strategic assets" of the White House – the opportunities to spend formal and informal time with the President and his family – in the allocation of invitations (*New York Times*, 2009).

In the face of continuing uncertainties at home and abroad, however, Obama's task remains: to build a record of achievement that will take his party forward into the midterm elections of 2010 and beyond. Bringing the country out of recession is his paramount concern, but the irony may be that, to follow the logic of Rahm Emanuel's analysis, overcoming the economic crisis will undermine the President's opportunity for effecting fundamental political change. For the moment, Americans may be prepared to share Obama's vision of a future in which the United States embraces a public philosophy closer to that which underpins the social democracies of Europe. However, as the American economy recovers, those Republican critics who accuse him of presiding over the "Europeanization" of America may find that the political mood begins to change back in their direction. At the same time, such is the relentless discipline of America's electoral cycle, that it will be the pace of recovery – both of the economy and of the Republican Party after its electoral mauling in 2008 – that will ultimately determine President Obama's own political fortunes and his prospects for a second term.

Chapter 8

Congress

Thomas E. Mann

The 2008 American elections produced the first unified Democratic Party government since 1993–94, the start of the Clinton administration. Those two years of the Clinton administration underscored the reality that controlling both ends of Pennsylvania Avenue is no guarantee of policy and political success by the President. In spite of healthy Democratic margins in the House and Senate, comparable to what Barack Obama enjoyed upon taking office in 2009, President Clinton's miniscule ($16 billion) stimulus package fell prey to a Senate filibuster; his first budget passed by a single vote after many painful months and humiliating opposition from a number of prominent Democrats; and his highest-priority policy initiative – health reform – suffered an ignominious death without even making it to the floor of the House or Senate. What followed was a midterm electoral landslide for the opposition, producing the first House Republican majority in 40 years.

Unified party government under Republican President George W. Bush (interrupted for a year and a half in 2001–02 when Republican Senator Jim Jeffords defected from his party and became an independent, leading to a 50–49 Democratic majority) managed some notable economic and foreign policy victories. Those legislative victories, however, set the stage for painful setbacks in Iraq and a devastating financial and economic collapse which dispatched Republicans from control of government. The George W. Bush years also witnessed the further decline of Congress as the first branch of government. Responsible lawmaking, ethical self-regulation, and effective oversight of the executive were largely sidelined as shared ideological interests jettisoned the institutional competitiveness of the executive and legislative branches, and regular order in Congress became a luxury its leaders could do without (Mann and Ornstein, 2006: 122–91). Public discontent with the performance of Congress and the ethical improprieties of some of its members contributed to the 2006 midterm election landslide that ended the 12-year Republican majority. The ensuing 110th Congress struggled with only modest success to confront its internal problems and restore some measure of public trust (Binder et al., 2009).

So in spite of the most impressive electoral performance by a new Democratic President since Franklin Roosevelt – easily outpacing John F. Kennedy, Jimmy Carter, and Bill Clinton – analysts were skeptical of what Obama could accomplish working with the Democratic Congress. That skepticism was rooted in more than the traditional understanding of the many obstacles to effective policymaking in the American constitutional system. The deep ideological polarization between the parties in recent decades left its mark on Congress in ways that diminished its comparative advantages and weakened governing arrangements more broadly. This chapter, after first reviewing the most striking characteristics of the contemporary Congress and assessing whether it changed significantly after Democrats took control of both chambers after the 2006 elections, explores how President Obama and the Democratic Congress fared in their initial months in office, and what this bodes for the operation and performance of the first branch of government in the years ahead.

Characteristics of the contemporary Congress

While the American constitutional system has been remarkably stable, its political institutions undergo constant change. The relative influence of the building blocs of the Congress and its two chambers – individual members, committees, and parties – shifts in response to such factors as changes in the career patterns of elected officials, the infusion of new members, the competitiveness and coalitional bases of the two parties, and challenges from key actors outside Congress. During the course of American history, Congress has experienced weak and strong parties, autonomous and constrained committees, centralization and decentralization of legislative authority, the primacy and marginalization of individual members, and assertiveness and passivity in dealing with the executive. The contemporary Congress is characterized by strong parties, a centralization of authority (particularly in the House), circumscribed committees, a Senate increasingly subject to filibusters, and a highly uneven pattern of engaging with, checking, and overseeing the executive.

Strong parties

While parties in today's Congress do not match the strength and unity of their Westminster-style parliamentary counterparts, they come closer than they have in a century. In both House and Senate, the ideological differences between Democrats and Republicans evident in their roll call voting are strikingly large (Sinclair, 2006: 3–35). The conservative coalition has vanished. Liberal Republicans and conservative Democrats are virtually extinct. No Democrat in either chamber has a voting record consistently more conservative than the most liberal Republican. Party unity scores (the percentage of members voting with a majority of their party on roll call votes on which a majority of one party opposes a majority of the other) – typically above 90 percent – are at a modern-day high.

Congressional party campaign committees strengthen parties by playing a major role in congressional elections. They build large war chests by taxing members representing safe constituencies and operating sophisticated large and small donor fundraising programs. This allows them to be major players in financing marginal seat elections, primarily through independent expenditures not subject to limits on party contributions to candidates. These campaign committees are also increasingly active in recruiting candidates to run in promising seats and favoring those in primary elections thought to have the best chance of winning the general election. Sometimes they must compete with party-aligned but policy-driven interest groups that threaten to oppose the renomination of members who stray too far from the party's ideological pole, but the overall effect is to reinforce ideologically distinctive parties in Congress.

Party caucuses in both House and Senate constitute the major venues for legitimizing the delegation of substantial authority to party leaders, refining legislative priorities and positions, reinforcing and extending party loyalty, and advancing the careers of members. To be sure, there are limits to the primacy of parties in the contemporary Congress. Some members represent districts and states that are not politically hospitable to elements of their party's core agenda, and find it uncomfortable to follow the party position. Certain issues evoke interests that cut across party lines. Individuals can still make a mark in Congress through exemplary committee work or teaming up with a member from the other side of the aisle, especially in the Senate. But political parties are the dominant building blocs in the current Congress.

Centralization

As parties in Congress became more ideologically coherent, members increasingly empowered their leaders to use the full resources of their positions to advance a partisan agenda (Gamm and Smith, 2009). The majoritarian House of Representatives was especially well suited to strong party leadership that rested on a broad policy consensus in the caucus. Speakers Jim Wright, Newt Gingrich, and Dennis Hastert (together with his partners Richard Armey and Tom DeLay) moved aggressively to centralize agenda setting, policy development, and parliamentary procedure. As we shall see, Nancy Pelosi continued this pattern after Democrats captured the majority in the 2006 midterm elections and following Obama's victory in 2008.

The leadership brokered policy agreements outside of normal committee deliberation and dictated the adoption of special rules that suspended regular order in committee, on the floor, and in conference. Committees were given less discretion in crafting legislative language and less deference on the floor relative to party leadership alternatives. Restrictive rules limited floor debate and amendments by individual members and the opposition party. Conference agreements between the House and Senate were reached by a handful of key leaders and outside players, often without any pretence of a full committee mark-up with members of both political parties present. All points of order against conference reports were routinely waived, making it virtually impossible for members to discover what was in each report before voting on it.

Because of the limits on majority rule through the threat of extended debate, the Senate was not as susceptible to centralization as was the House. Individual senators and the opposition party had the resources to frustrate party leaders and prevent majorities from working their will. The two parties in the Senate were as ideologically polarized as in the House, which made parties and their leaders more important players in the Senate than in earlier eras, but this was not sufficient to produce a significant centralization of authority in the institution.

Circumscribed committees

A Congress dominated from the 1930s into the 1970s by relatively autonomous committees with chairs selected exclusively by seniority gave way initially to a more even balance between parties and committees, and eventually to an ascendant role for party leaders (Aldrich and Rohde, 2009). Gingrich was particularly assertive in departing from seniority in selecting committee chairs, influencing bills drafted by committees, and bypassing committees altogether to achieve party goals. In spite of his promise to restore regular order after Gingrich's ignominious departure from the House, Hastert kept the new powers accorded the Speaker and used them to advance Republican party objectives. On issues central to the party's agenda, committees were treated as agents of the party caucus and not as independent decision-making bodies. This change was especially pronounced on the high-prestige Appropriations, Energy and Commerce, and Ways and Means Committees.

The shift of authority from committees to parties was not as pronounced in the Senate, where committees have long been less central to its work than in the House. Nonetheless, deepening partisan conflict in the Senate has altered the relations between parties and committees.

Majority party leaders often intervene in the crafting of legislation in committees, and occasionally develop proposals entirely outside the committee process. And both parties have taken modest steps to constrain or replace committee chairs who appeared to be out of step with the prevailing sentiment of their party caucuses.

Routinization of filibusters

The rules of the Senate relating to extended debate (filibusters) invite their strategic use by individuals and groups of senators to achieve a wide variety of objectives – from killing or modifying legislation to extracting concessions or bargaining chips on unrelated measures. This has long forced the Senate majority leader to negotiate unanimous consent agreements (UCAs) to bring bills to the floor, set limits on amendments that may be offered, and specify a time for the final vote. (In the House, a Speaker supported by a simple majority of members can dictate all of these terms through his or her control of the Rules Committee.)

As Barbara Sinclair has demonstrated, the task of negotiating UCAs has become infinitely more difficult in recent decades (Sinclair, 2009). This can be seen from the increase in the number of filibusters per Congress (from an average of five in the 1960s and 11 in the 1970s to over 30 in the 1990s and early 2000s) and in the number of cloture votes (requiring 60 votes to end debate) in each Congress (from roughly five in the 1960s to over 50 between 1992 and 2006.) As Sinclair (2009) notes, however, visible filibusters are only the tip of the iceberg. Holds by senators, which are effectively threats to object to a UCA, are much more numerous and equally effective. She estimates that the frequency of major measures subject to extended-debate-related problems grew from 8 percent in the 1960s to 27 percent in the 1970s and 1980s to 51 percent from the 1990s to the mid-2000s.

A parliamentary tactic once used infrequently on high-profile legislation such as civil rights, and then embraced by more senators as an attractive tool for advancing their individual interests, now became a routine device the minority party used to frustrate the agenda of the majority. Obstructionism was now the hallmark of the Senate, which increasingly became the graveyard for House-passed bills.

Atrophied checks and balances

As partisan divisions in Congress and the country hardened and competition for control of the Congress increased, the institutional incentives and resources designed by James Madison to produce a system of checks and balances proved inadequate. In this political environment, party and ideology often trumped institutional interests and responsibilities when one party controlled both ends of Pennsylvania Avenue. During the 40-year reign of the Democrats as the House majority, the ideological diversity of the party and its comfort as the "permanent" majority led to an aggressive and independent stance with Democratic as well as Republican Presidents. Officials in the Carter and Clinton administrations found that a shared party brand did not spare them the wrath of their congressional overseers.

The situation following the 2000 elections was strikingly different (Mann and Ornstein, 2006: 141–61, 216–24). The first unified Republican government since Dwight Eisenhower produced a markedly deferential Congress, whose members and leaders showed little evidence of being part of a separate and independent branch of government. The Republican Congress was passive in the face of the most grandiose assertion of executive power in American history, and indifferent to the Bush administration's aversion to sharing information with Congress and the public. A flood of presidential signing statements declaring unconstitutional entire sections of bills enacted by Congress and signed by the President went unchallenged by the majority in Congress. During the critical months leading up to the military strike against Iraq, no serious effort was made to garner the necessary information and raise the critical questions essential to make an informed decision about waging a preemptive war.

Most telling was the precipitous drop in the amount of congressional oversight of the executive. From homeland security to the conduct of the war in Iraq, from the use of torture initially uncovered by the Abu Ghraib revelations to the performance of the IRS, Congress mostly ignored its responsibilities to see that laws are faithfully executed. Fear of harming the political reputation of the administration led Congress to largely abandon one of its most essential tasks.

A return to divided party government in 2007 created a strong partisan incentive for more vigorous engagement with, and oversight of, the executive; but it was not at all obvious what would happen in 2009 when Democrats regained control of both ends of Pennsylvania Avenue.

The aftermath of the 2006 elections

A review of the performance of the 110th Congress underscores the limited extent to which the new Democratic majority was able to reverse the policy commitments of President Bush or the institutional dynamics that have shaped congressional behavior in recent years (Binder et al., 2009). Nor is there compelling evidence that Congress was able to respond effectively to the most serious financial and economic crisis since the Great Depression. The 2006 election produced a clear agenda change in Washington, some mid-level policy reversals, increased congressional oversight of the executive, a strengthening of ethics standards and procedures, and a modest rebalancing of power between Congress and the White House. But divided government, the continuing ideological polarization of the parties, and the bipartisan proclivity for blame avoidance frustrated efforts to deal with the central challenges facing the country. Meanwhile, the venomous partisan atmosphere, routine suspension of regular order, filibuster politics, and demise of deliberation continued unabated.

Legislative productivity

Unlike their counterparts following the 1994 Republican landslide, who promised to deliver a dramatic "Contract with America" but were largely foiled by Senate inaction, presidential vetoes, and a government shutdown, the new Democratic majority in the 110th Congress aimed lower in their "New Direction Agenda," and managed to get most of it enacted into law. Their legislative harvest included a number of long-stalled proposals, including higher fuel-efficiency standards for motor vehicles, a minimum wage increase, and a restructuring and expansion of college student assistance. Confronting a recession and financial meltdown in 2008, the Democratic-led Congress passed and President Bush signed a stimulus package, a housing rescue bill, and a Wall Street bailout.

At the same time, stalemates over the State Children's Health Insurance Program, climate change, the alternative minimum tax, the Colombian free-trade agreement, the war in Iraq, and the automobile industry bailout attest to the difficulty of legislating in periods of divided government. Moreover, the troubled response of Congress to the financial crisis demonstrated more weakness than strength, with its huge delegation of authority to the executive and failure to grapple seriously with the full dimension of the economic challenge.

Oversight

What was most striking about the 110th Congress was the dramatic increase in the amount and scope of its oversight of the executive following years of relative inattention and deference under the Republican majority. Much of the oversight was devoted to the war in Iraq, the dominant public concern, which had been largely neglected in the previous Congress. But oversight activity ranged across diverse subjects, was mostly serious in its approach, and often had real consequences for policy and administration. Examples include the departure of many political appointees at the Justice Department following revelations about the firing of several US attorneys; changes in resources and administrative arrangements following investigations of neglect and abuse in the treatment of injured veterans from Iraq and Afghanistan; and new provisions governing contracting arrangements, from Blackwater to Halliburton.

One important change was the revitalization of the authorization process. The decline of regular authorizations, which traditionally entails a serious examination of programs and agencies, seriously weakened one of the most effective forms of oversight. Authorizations increased in number, quality, and content in the 110th Congress, as did the number of authorization hearings.

Divided party government was actually conducive to reviving congressional oversight of the executive. Democrats had the political incentive and ability to use committees in both chambers to scrutinize the performance of administration officials and the implementation of policies and programs. And they did so with energy and effectiveness.

Ethics, lobbying, and earmarks

The "culture of corruption" – a term used to describe the toxic stew of scandals associated with former House majority leader Tom DeLay (R-Tex.), Jack Abramoff, and others that erupted in and around Congress in 2005 and 2006 – was a powerful argument Democrats used to propel themselves back into power on Capitol Hill. Not surprisingly, ethics, lobbying, and earmark reform became a priority for the new majority at the beginning of 2007. Incoming House Speaker Nancy Pelosi announced an ambitious reform agenda for the coming year, including a moratorium on earmarks (designations of funding for specific constituency-based projects), a promise to toughen lobbying and contribution disclosure rules, and the creation of an independent office to conduct preliminary investigations of potential ethics violations by members and staff. The formal Democratic Party rules package unveiled and adopted by the House on the day the new Congress convened contained some ethics provisions that were far-reaching and not widely popular among lawmakers. These included restricting the use of corporate jets, a ban on gifts and meals paid for by lobbyists, restrictions on privately financed travel, disclosure of the campaign finance bundling activities of lobbyists, and earmark transparency.

The Senate two weeks later passed its own version of ethics and lobbying reform; the House followed with its own bill in May, complementing and codifying in law the changes approved as part of the rules package. Finally, the House in 2008 approved the creation of an independent Office of Congressional Ethics, a major step toward revitalizing a long-moribund ethics process.

The explosion of earmarks during the 108th and 109th Congresses – the number peaked in 2005 with 13,492 projects totaling almost

$19 billion – became a rallying cry for Democratic candidates in the 2006 election. Generous funding for an Alaskan "bridge to nowhere" was widely portrayed as a typical earmark: an outrageous misuse and waste of taxpayer dollars. Congressional leaders pledged to increase the transparency of earmark requests by members, and to reduce their funding by 50 percent below the level approved in the 109th Congress. Progress was made on both pledges, but implementation has been difficult and incomplete. Most members of both parties in Congress are reluctant to weaken their institutional power of the purse, and are perfectly willing to publicize projects they succeed in steering to their constituencies. Nonetheless, the new rules are likely to constrain some funds directed to private entities in implicit return for campaign contributions and/or personal benefits to members.

Checks and balances

The 110th Congress under Democratic control was more aggressive in challenging the Bush administration's far-reaching assertions of executive power. It held wide-ranging hearings on abuses of power, and challenged several of the White House's positions on sensitive issues including electronic surveillance, allegations of perjury and obstruction of justice in the so-called Valerie Plame affair, and misbehavior in the Justice Department over the firing of US attorneys. But souring public opinion and intervention by the federal courts were at least as consequential as steps taken by the Congress to begin to restore an appropriate balance between the branches.

The main tug of war between the President and Congress in 2007–08 came over the issue of warrantless surveillance. In 2005 the *New York Times* reported that the Bush administration had conducted wiretaps of electronic conversations without warrants from the Foreign Intelligence Surveillance Act (FISA) court. The administration argued that it was not bound to use the FISA court to conduct foreign intelligence electronic surveillance, a position challenged by two judges in secret rulings by the FISA court. Democratic leaders in the 110th Congress pledged to rein in this behavior by explicitly expanding court oversight of domestic-based surveillance and denying immunity to the telecommunications companies that cooperated with the administration's disputed surveillance activities. They struggled unsuccessfully throughout 2007 to deliver on that promise, but finally concluded intensive negotiations with the White House and congressional Republicans to reassert some measure of control over electronic surveillance.

As part of its investigations of alleged abuses of executive power, congressional efforts to compel testimony by White House staff and the submission of key documents to Congress proved largely unsuccessful. Similarly, a series of hearings and proposed bills on presidential signing statements designed to limit their scope, challenge their constitutionality, and shed public light on their intent failed to alter the President's behavior or the prevalence of signing statements claiming unfettered presidential power.

Partisanship and regular order

Democratic leaders in 2007 quickly concluded that the implacable opposition to their agenda by President Bush and the Republican congressional leadership, combined with the 60-vote hurdle in the Senate, made it virtually impossible to return to regular order in committee, on the floor, and in conference and still advance their legislative agenda. In this intensely competitive, partisan environment, facing high expectations to set a new policy direction following the decisive 2006 election, they opted for action and product over process. Their pledge to curb the procedural abuses of the previous Republican majority would for the most part have to be set aside. The choice was not surprising. The new Republican leadership in 1995 came to the same conclusion despite years in the minority decrying the tactics of House Democratic majorities. Still, it exacerbated partisan tensions in Congress and further fouled the toxic atmosphere enveloping Washington.

The session saw some pockets of cooperation and civil engagement between the parties, mainly in committees such as Financial Services and among some individual party leaders and rank-and-file members. Speaker Pelosi and her office, like their predecessors, were deeply involved in setting the agenda and drafting legislation central to it. Pelosi, however, loosened the reins a bit on committees and gave them more room to operate. But as the Congress progressed and the agenda became more controversial, opposition tactics in the House and frustrations with the Senate led the House Democratic leadership to embrace many of the same unorthodox means (circumventing standing committees, writing closed rules, using the suspension calendar, waiving layover requirements, avoiding the conference process) that Republicans had employed to advance their agenda (Sinclair, 2007). The number and percentage of restrictive rules used by Democratic leaders to control debate and amending activity on the House floor exceeded the degree of control and departure from regular order exercised by their Republican predecessors. Democrats were at least as willing to forgo committee deliberations and bring unreported bills directly to the floor under special rules as their Republican counterparts. And after pledging to make the conference process (in which different House and Senate versions of bills are reconciled with one another) more open and inclusive, Democratic leaders almost banished conference committees altogether in the second session of the 110th Congress. A pattern of tighter, more centralized control – which began more than two decades ago under Democratic rule and then intensified under Republican majorities, especially after the 2000 election – continued unabated.

Senate filibusters

The award for the most arresting statistic in the 110th Congress goes to the Senate, where 142 cloture motions were filed – an all-time Senate high. This compares with 71 cloture motions in the previous Congress. More than once a week, on average, senators resorted to the chamber's cloture rule in an effort to limit debate and bring the chamber to a vote. Not surprisingly, given the Senate's slim majority and polarized parties, Senate leaders succeeded less than half the time in securing the necessary 60 votes to invoke cloture. Sinclair's measure of extended-debate-related problems on major measures in the Senate jumped from roughly a quarter in the 1970s to 1980s, and a half in the 1990s to mid-2000s, to almost three-quarters in 2007 (Sinclair, 2009: 11).

Roughly half of the cloture motions were aimed at bringing the Senate to a vote on Democratic policy priorities, including repeated efforts to force a change in the course of the war in Iraq. But not the entire rise in cloture is due to deep partisan differences. Sometimes it was used by senators of both parties to rein in maverick Republicans such as Senators Tom Coburn (Okla.) and Jim DeMint (S.C.) pursuing their own individual agendas.

Although the Senate's record of 142 cloture motions is remarkable, the chamber's reliance on 60-vote thresholds is even more common than a count of cloture votes suggests. On numerous occasions, Senate leaders negotiated UCAs that required amendments or bills to secure 60 votes for passage. In other words, counting cloture votes under-states the power of the Senate minority to block majority will.

Congress under unified Democratic Party control

In spite of the shortcomings of the new Democratic majority in Congress and its low approval ratings during the two years following their 2006 electoral success, the public in 2008 directed its unhappiness with the direction of the country against the party of outgoing President Bush. By strengthening Democratic majorities in the House and Senate while decisively electing Barack Obama to the White House, voters invested in governing arrangements heavily dependent on party accountability across the executive and legislative branches. This was in spite of the fact that those same voters found distasteful the deep and often bitter partisanship characteristic of recent politics and policymaking.

Illinois state Senator Obama had catapulted to national public attention in his keynote speech to the 2004 Democratic Convention by
denying the polarization of the country into red states and blue states,
a liberal America and a conservative America. We are, he asserted
forcefully, "the United States of America." Candidate Obama repeatedly called for moving beyond the stale debates and partisan warfare
to a new post-partisan politics. And yet his election was very much a
Democratic Party victory, one that reinforced the sharp partisan divide
between and within states. Republican losses in the House and Senate
further diminished the moderate ranks of the opposition party and
moved their caucuses to the right. Moreover, much of the agenda
Obama championed during the campaign – health care and energy,
taxes and government regulation, redefining and reshaping the war on
terrorism – was passionately contested by the two parties. Under these
conditions, how likely is President Obama to govern effectively and
Congress to restore its luster as a serious, deliberative, and independent
branch of government?

Policy inheritance

Obama took the oath of office on January 20 facing the most daunting
set of policy challenges since the Great Depression. A global financial
meltdown and severe recession threatened to deteriorate into deflation
and depression. Massive global trade and investment imbalances and
huge inherited budget deficits complicated emergency economic policymaking, and threatened to derail promised efforts to tackle widely
acknowledged problems with health care, energy security, climate
change, and education. The foreign policy landscape was littered with
dangers: a withdrawal of US military forces from a far from stable
Iraq, deteriorating conditions in Afghanistan and Pakistan, Iran apparently moving closer to achieving a nuclear weapons capacity, a mori-
bund Middle East peace process, a bellicose Russia, a rising China not
integrated into global economic and security systems, and Mexico
threatened by criminal cartels selling drugs and buying arms in the
United States. The list goes on.

Obama identified stabilizing the financial markets and shortening the
recession as his highest initial priorities. His early efforts to ensure the
release of $350 billion in Troubled Assets Relief Program (TARP)
funds, pass a large ($787 billion) economic stimulus bill, and develop a
revised strategy for dealing with the troubled banking system reflected
those priorities. But he insisted on linking his economic management to
reform of health policy, energy, and education. This led to the inclusion in the stimulus package of substantial funding for health information technology, renewable energy, and education. He also encouraged
Congress to move ahead on big-ticket reforms as essential parts of a

long-term strategy to foster economic security and prosperity by controlling health care costs, making the transition to a green economy, and improving educational performance from pre-kindergarten through college.

Approaches to Congress

Unlike his immediate predecessor, Obama is respectful of the constitutional standing of Congress as the first branch of government, and solicitous of the views of its members on both sides of the partisan divide. While careful not to compromise what he considers to be legitimate presidential prerogatives (including presidential signing statements), Obama has pulled back from the Bush administration's expansive assertions of the inherent powers of the presidency – although not fully enough to mollify some critics. In his first six months, he appears to have had personal meetings in the White House and on Capitol Hill with more members of Congress of both parties than Bush did during his eight years in office. His White House team – including most prominently himself, Vice President Joe Biden and chief of staff Rahm Emanuel, but including dozens of others – is steeped in the personalities and folkways of Congress, and acutely attuned to the politics of the major issues with which they are grappling.

The President's comfort with Congress taking the lead in drafting legislative language, and his respect for the independent role of Congress and its leaders, Speaker Pelosi and Senate majority leader Harry Reid, reflect his considered judgment of how he can be most effective in advancing his agenda. Republican critics see in these approaches to Congress signs of passivity and partisanship. The first charge is obviously inaccurate. The impressive legislative harvest during his first months in office has been overwhelmingly consistent with his own blueprint, reflecting both shared values with congressional Democrats and skillful White House dealings with Congress.

It is undeniable, however, that the parties in Congress remained deeply polarized during 2009. Obama's overtures to the opposition party have been unsuccessful to date, primarily because Republicans reject the central components of his agenda, including his economic recovery program. In less polarized times, the seriousness of the crisis and the decisive nature of the 2008 election would have produced a significant number of Republican votes for the fiscal stimulus. But not a single Republican in the House and only three in the Senate voted for the stimulus; most have since gone on record supporting a repeal of the stimulus, a freeze on federal spending, and a massive, permanent, across-the-board tax cut – because those are the policies in which they believe. This leaves little room for reaching common ground.

To be sure, Obama is likely to continue overtures to the Republicans on a wide range of domestic and foreign policy proposals, and to court constituencies with high stakes in these policies that have traditionally aligned with the Republican Party. The public already gives him credit for reaching out to Republicans, and blames the latter for failing to cooperate; in April 2009, 66 percent of respondents in a USA Today/Gallup poll said that Obama was making a sincere effort to work with Republicans, but only 38 percent believed the Republicans were reciprocating (Jones, 2009). These overtures could eventually pay dividends notably absent during his first months of office. But the reality is that Obama perforce will rely heavily on his own party in moving policy changes through Congress. With fewer Republican moderates but a more unified Democratic party than Clinton faced 16 years ago, winning coalitions on divisive issues will depend primarily on maintaining support within the majority party.

Whither the broken branch?

Does this partisan formula for presidential success suggest that the Democratic majority under Obama will operate much like the Republican majority under Bush? In one respect, the answer is yes. Regular order in the legislative process continues to be viewed by congressional leaders as an unaffordable luxury. The more the Republicans assume the position of an aggressive, ideologically extreme opposition seeking only to delay or embarrass the President and his party, the more Speaker Pelosi will bypass normal processes in committee, on the floor, and in conference to advance the Democratic agenda. In the Senate, Reid's moves during the first months of 2009 to give Republicans ample opportunity to debate and amend proposals coming to the Senate floor will give way to much tougher steps to achieve 60 votes for cloture (made possible, though not at all easy, with Arlen Specter's defection to the Democratic Party and Al Franken's election after an eight-month contest), and to use the budget reconciliation process to allow a simple majority to adopt major substantive policy reforms.

In most other respects, however, this Democratic Congress looks very different from its Republican counterpart. House and Senate committees have been actively engaged in brokering interests and drafting legislative language, from the stimulus package to health reform, cap and trade, and financial regulation. Congressional oversight of the executive has not waned with the arrival of unified party government. For example, Democratic committee and sub-committee chairs have investigated contracting abuses in the Defense Department and challenged the President's positions on the need for indefinite detention of some Guantánamo prisoners and the desirability of a commission to examine abuses of power in the Bush administration. Speaker Pelosi and majority leader Reid have warned the Obama team to respect the institutional independence of their respective chambers. In the early months of the new administration, there are signs of cooperation between the two branches based on shared political and policy interests, as well as a measure of institutional patriotism at both ends of Pennsylvania Avenue.

The willingness of Congress to police the ethical behavior of its members will test the mettle of the 111th Congress. A number of prominent Democrats have been accused of egregious abuses of the earmark process. The new Office of Congressional Ethics and the long-standing ethics committees in the two chambers will appropriately be judged by their ability to deal responsibly with these cases.

What seems clear, however, is that the ideological polarization of the parties will continue to shape the organization and behavior of Congress – sharpening the bitter partisan tone of policy debates, diminishing the quality of deliberation, and making it difficult to build broad coalitions in support of policies on the biggest problems confronting the country. Democrats will have difficulty holding their moderates in line on difficult votes on taxes and regulation in the face of unified Republican opposition. For example, Democrats representing high coal producing and consuming states and districts will be reluctant to support any cap and trade schemes to curb carbon emissions without a broader agreement being reached with the affected interests and at least some Republicans. The same is likely to be true with financial regulation, immigration, tax reform, and efforts to deal with the projected long-term fiscal imbalance.

Obama's success or failure in changing the broader political dynamic in the country will determine in large part whether the prominent characteristics of the contemporary Congress are reinforced, or begin to shift in a direction more conducive to a deliberative and productive policy process.

Chapter 9

The Supreme Court

Paul Martin

Introduction

For all its appearance of stability, the American Supreme Court is an institution subject to substantial, if subtle, change. The period since 2006 is an especially interesting one, marked as it is by three key developments in its internal operation and its relation to the wider political system. First, this period witnessed the achievement of an authentically conservative majority on the Court. Second, these years saw a major constitutional struggle, which in some ways continues, concerning the war on terror. Finally, there has been major change in the political balance and in the constellation of institutions that shape the Court's agenda and its responses. The contemporary period is thus a potential turning point for the Court, as after a long period of conservative appointments which have had relatively limited conservative policy outcomes, it has to live in a very different political environment from the one that shaped it.

Before beginning that discussion, it is important to set out why and how the Court can seem to be an important political actor. Its power is that of judicial review: it can review the actions and orders of the president to check their legality, as well as reviewing the laws themselves to check their constitutionality. These are fundamental umpiring powers: the Court gets to decide what the rules of the political game are, and whether the players are following them.

Since the cases that are appealed to the Supreme Court are inherently controversial and political, and since they are not usually clear-cut, the Court is both a locus of political attention and something more than simply a legal interpreter (Segal and Spaeth, 2002). While there is a case for the role of law in what the Court does (Friedman, 2006), ultimately it is a political institution with tremendous and robust support from mass public opinion (Kritzer, 2001).

But the Court does not simply dictate the terms of politics. For example, the Supreme Court has been heavily involved in responding to the Bush administration's aggressive agenda-setting on constitutional issues. Assisted by their argument that the Constitution set up a "unitary executive" (Calabresi and Yoo, 2008) – roughly the idea that the president, and thus the executive branch, could not be constrained in their core executive function by laws passed by Congress – the administration had fought hard to extend a vision of how to proceed – above all in the so-called war on terror. As Chapter 15 describes in more detail, the administration took an almost extralegal approach to the pursuit of various aspects of this "war." In general, the Supreme Court – or at least a narrow majority thereof – had often opposed the stance the administration had taken, and continued to do so after 2006. But in many ways later events showed the weaknesses of the Court in tackling determined opposition from the executive branch, especially where aided by Congress, as with the passage of the Military Commissions Act 2006, and where the executive was able to work on the basis of its own legal interpretations.

Clearly, in the period under review, the Court has played a major role in determining detainee policy. But, these decisions – even *Boumediene* v *Bush* (2008) – have not been final; it has not been the case that the Court has spoken and its view of the case has triumphed. Rather, the issues have been litigated several times, with the Court taking a fairly deferential stance while still refusing to go along with much of what the administration, and Congress, has decided. Each Court decision has been followed by institutional redesign of the detainee process, which has itself resulted in further litigation leading to Supreme Court review. This process is not yet complete. There are more detainees at places such as the Bagram Air base in Afghanistan, and outstanding complex issues concerning the eventual disposition of prisoners if and when the Guantánamo complex eventually closes. All of these issues are likely to see extensive further litigation.

An authentically conservative majority: appointees, biography, and the selection process

Appointments and luck

Justices of the Supreme Court are nominated by presidents and confirmed by the Senate. Since justices serve until they die or choose to retire, there are element of both strategic retirement and pure luck in such appointments. The 40 years from January 1969 to January 2009 have seen almost all that luck favor Republican appointments. The Republicans held the presidency for 28 of those 40 years, to the Democrats' 12 years of presidential control. We might therefore expect the Republicans to have been able to make just about 2.3 times as many appointments to the Supreme Court. However, the effect of retirements – luck – was to give Republicans many more opportunities to shape the Court's membership. Thus Republican presidents in this period of 40 years collectively made 12 appointments to the Court, and appointed two chief justices; Democratic presidents by contrast made only two appointments, and no appointment to the position of chief justice. On average, Republican presidents made almost two appointments per presidential term, Democrats fewer than one. The Court in 2009 was only partly the product of 40 years of Republican dominance of the presidency to a greater degree, it was the product of the timing of retirements, which has significantly favored Republicans.

This partisan differential would not, of course, matter much if weak party ties, and the disconnect between the judicial and political worlds, had meant that nominations were not ideological. But judicial appointments are now highly ideological and political; since the late 1960s, conservatives in particular have made their opposition to liberal judges a major feature of politics and political campaigning. As the liberal justices of the Warren era retired, they were replaced by conservative Nixon, Reagan, and Bush appointees, pushing the Court significantly rightwards. Only the replacement of the moderate Justice White by the more liberal Justice Ginsburg, in 1993, has bucked this trend. In particular, the Court has found itself absolutely central in the so-called "Culture Wars" concerning gender equality, abortion, and sexuality issues (Teles, 2008).

Conservatism's critical moment

For many conservatives, however, the outcome of Republican dominance of the appointments process has been disappointing. A Court shaped by Republican presidents has failed to overturn decisions such as the *Roe v Wade* (1973) abortion decision, and has even discovered new liberal rights in cases such as *Lawrence v Texas* (2003), which in 2003 struck down a Texas law prohibiting sodomy. Conservatives, especially social conservatives, have been left unhappy as liberal results had been defended, and extended, often with 5–4 majorities. In these circumstances it was evident that George W. Bush's court appointments would be crucial to the future direction of the Court. Replacing Chief Justice Rehnquist with Chief Justice Roberts was expected to have limited effect – while Chief Justice Roberts is in some ways a rather more modern figure than Chief Justice Rehnquist was, both were staunch movement conservatives who generated only very occasional surprises in their approach to legal issues. But replacing Sandra Day O'Connor with Samuel Alito did make a significant change in the Court's membership. Although Justice O'Connor had been, at the time of her appointment in 1981 one of the Court's most conservative justices, the retirement of justices more liberal and replacement with those more conservative had left her roughly in the middle of the Court ideologically and strategically. As a result she was responsible in many cases for holding back, or even defeating, the other conservative justices on the Court. In her opinions in gender-related cases such as *Planned Parenthood* v *Casey* (1992), which dealt with abortion, and in her dissent in *Ragsdale* v *Wolverine World Wide Inc.* (2002), which dealt with unpaid leave, O'Connor developed a particularly marked reputation for moderation. By contrast Justice Alito is a movement conservative who is not publicly enthusiastic about gender equality: the *New York Times* in 2005 reported his membership of an organization opposed to coeducation at his alma mater, Princeton University.

Thus, for conservatives, the latter part of the first decade of the twenty-first century was a crucial moment. Earlier liberal-leaning decisions, which had had 5–4 majority support, seemed particularly vulnerable to reversal by a conservative court. On the other hand, after the 2006 midterm elections there was a Democratic majority in Congress, which was inclined to resist the Court's interpretation of its statutes, and after the 2008 elections, a president who would not veto those attempts. So, in terms of understanding the behavior of the Court after 2006, the key issue was whether those 5–4 liberal decisions would flip to 5–4 conservative decisions, and with what consequences. Two major cases show the effect of this change.

The Roberts Court's new conservatism

Lily Ledbetter's unequal pay

One case that underlined the new character of the Court and highlighted its changing relationship with the other branches concerned equal pay. Lily Ledbetter had worked for nearly 20 years at Goodyear Tire and Rubber Company. When she retired in 1998 she was being paid less than male employees doing the same job at the same plant, as a result of supervisors' annual evaluations of her performance over the whole of her time there. At her retirement, the worst-paid male equivalent employee was paid 15 percent more, and the best-paid 40 percent more, than Ledbetter. She brought a case to the Equal Employment Opportunity Commission under Title VII of the Civil Rights Act of 1964, alleging that her lower salary was a result of sex discrimination. Each time she had had a poor evaluation as a result of sex discrimination, her salary had fallen onto a slightly lower path, such that even if she had been treated equally after the evaluation, she would have continued to lose out as a result of the earlier discrimination. By the end of her career she was earning significantly less than men in the same position; contractually, however, she was not supposed to discuss pay with colleagues, and she only discovered the pay differential from an anonymous tip-off. At trial, the jury found in her favor and she was awarded back pay and damages.

On appeal, however, Ledbetter lost to a new argument from Goodyear. The Civil Rights Act requires a complaint to be brought within 180 days of the discrimination occurring. Ledbetter had argued that, since she was being discriminated against each time she was paid up to her retirement, and complained within 180 days of that, she had met the deadline. But the Court of Appeals for the 11th Circuit held that each individual year's review of her salary constituted the discriminatory act: Ledbetter should have complained within 180 days of each annual review. Once that initial period had passed, even if she continued to be discriminated against, the discrimination could not be challenged. Since, in her last 180 days at Goodyear, she had not had an annual review and her pay had not been altered, there was no discrimination that could be addressed by the Civil Rights Act.

When Ledbetter appealed to the Supreme Court in *Ledbetter* v *Goodyear Tire and Rubber Co.* (2007), she lost again, in a 5–4 decision upholding the Appeals Court ruling. Like the Appeals Court, the majority held that the discriminatory act that Ledbetter complained about had to involve discriminatory intent, which was present only at the discriminatory annual reviews and not in the continued payment of lower salary long afterwards. As very frequently has been the case with conservative 5–4 decisions, Justice Alito, who wrote the opinion, was joined by Chief Justice Roberts and Justices Scalia, Kennedy, and Thomas. Justice Ginsburg, writing a dissent joined by Justices Stephens, Souter, and Breyer, took the unusual step of reading it in its entirety from the Supreme Court bench – usually a signal of particularly intense dissatisfaction by the minority with the majority decision. Justice Ginsburg – by this stage the only woman on the Court – argued that the Court had essentially ignored how payments worked. Often employers would keep pay differentials secret from employees, making it almost impossible to bring complaints of discrimination within 180 days. Equally, large differentials in salary could, over time, result from repeated small differences in salary increases, as had been the case with Ledbetter's salary, with each small annual difference being difficult to bring a complaint about. Justice Ginsburg argued that employees in Ledbetter's situation would essentially be unable to bring complaints about pay discrimination, given the majority's ruling. She also noted that the Civil Rights Act limited back pay to two years for each complaint – which, she argued, was hard to square with the idea that the complaint must be made within a quarter of that time.

In conclusion, Justice Ginsburg's dissent made a very pointed reference to a much earlier case concerning the same act: *Wards Cover*

Packing Co. v *Antonio* (1989). In that case a conservative majority had overturned a liberal precedent, *Griggs* v *Duke Power Co.* (1971), interpreting the Civil Rights Act, with the effect of making it much harder to prove that unlawful discrimination had occurred. Congress had reacted to this, and several other contemporary decisions interpreting the 1964 Act, with something close to outrage. After passing a bill in 1990 which was vetoed by President George H. W. Bush, Congress passed and Bush signed the Civil Rights Act 1991, which reinstated the older interpretations that the Supreme Court had just overturned. Ginsburg noted the possibility that this history might be repeated.

That repetition seemed particularly likely in 2007 given that Democrats had just retaken the Congress, and indeed there was a remarkably rapid reaction. The Court had issued the decision on May 29; on June 22, Rep. George Miller (D-Calif.) and 93 co-sponsors introduced into the House a bill to amend existing anti-discrimination legislation to clarify that it dealt with ongoing discrimination which would reset every time a pay check was issued, rather than merely with the original discriminatory act. The bill comfortably passed the House on a largely party-line vote; but in the Senate a cloture vote failed, with 56 votes, again largely on party lines with some Republicans crossing over to support it.

With the parties roughly lined up behind opposing sides on the Court, Ledbetter's case became a major public and political issue, and Ledbetter herself became a minor celebrity, lobbying Congress, speaking to the Democratic National Convention, endorsing Barack Obama for president, and then appearing in a series of adverts for him. Her case was also used by liberal interest groups targeting vulnerable Republican senators such as now-former Senator John Sununu (R-N.H.). Sununu was attacked for his votes to confirm Justice Alito and Chief Justice Roberts, and for the shift to the right on the Court which they represented and which had led to the Ledbetter decision.

In light of the Democrats' enthusiastic use of her case in the 2008 campaign, and their overwhelming victories in presidential, Senate, and Congressional races, it was perhaps not surprising that the 111th Congress returned to the issue very quickly. Senator Barbara Mikulski (D-Md.) introduced a bill, which passed the Senate 61–36 on January 22, and passed the House 250–177 on January 27, largely on party lines. This became law as the Lily Ledbetter Fair Pay Act of 2009 when Obama signed it on January 29; symbolically, this was the first law the new President had signed. Within nine days of the new administration's arrival, the Supreme Court's decision in 2007 had been rendered moot, and – as with *Wards Cove* a generation earlier – a major conservative step in civil rights law had been rather quickly overturned by the political response. Indeed, the use of the Ledbetter case in campaigning by the Democrats implied that it had actually assisted them – that the

Supreme Court's decision had helped bring about a Congress that would overturn it.

Again, the issue showed that the Court does not stand alone, especially in statutory interpretation; there is interplay between the politics of other institutions and the decisions of the Court, which collectively results in particular outcomes. But given the basic conservatism of the Roberts court, it is quite possible that they will again, in the near future, interpret civil rights and anti-discrimination legislation in ways that are unacceptable to congressional majorities, especially if they overturn settled understandings or seem as procedurally unfair as the Ledbetter decision.

Establishing new rights in Heller

A major feature of the liberal Supreme Courts that dominated the mid to late twentieth century was that they made, or found, new readings of the Constitution that granted new liberal rights for the first time – for example, the right to representation by an attorney in court, the right to silence, the right to contraception and abortion. Indeed, quite sweeping new, liberal rights were established as recently as in *Lawrence* v *Texas* (2003). What has been rather less common is the manufacture, or discovery, of rights favored by conservatives rather than liberals.

One such right is the right to bear arms. In popular culture, such a right has often been associated with the Second Amendment, which states that a "well regulated militia, being necessary to the security of a free state, the right of the people to keep and bear arms, shall not be infringed." The contingent phrasing and complex history of the Amendment had not led the courts to identify a clear individual, personal right to keep and bear arms on that basis. Indeed very few Supreme Court cases had dealt with the Amendment, and none had established that right. *US* v *Cruickshank* (1875) found that private actors who violently (indeed murderously) disarmed others did not breach the Second Amendment, which was binding only on the Federal Government; in *Presser* v *Illinois* (1886), the Amendment was found not to be breached by a state law banning private militia drills and parades; in *US* v *Miller* (1939), the National Firearms Act, which required registration of certain types of weapon, was found not to conflict with the Amendment, because the relevant weapons were unconnected with the "well regulated militia" mentioned in the Amendment.

For decades after *Miller*, even as gun-control issues became highly politically salient, it was widely accepted that the Second Amendment did not pose a significant constraint on gun-control laws. The main pro-gun lobby, the National Rifle Association (NRA), was predominantly focused on electoral politics, in which it became extremely successful, at the expense of the sort of litigation strategy that the National Association for the Advancement of Colored People (NAACP) had adopted from the 1930s onwards to counter segregation. Indeed, the NRA opposed the litigation strategy that would, in 2008, bring about a sea-change in the law relating to the possession of weapons.

The first indication that the status quo might be under threat came in *Printz* v *US* (1997). The case concerned the use of state law enforcement officials to enforce the Brady gun control act; portions of the act were found to be unconstitutional for reasons of federalism. But Justice Thomas wrote a separate concurrence suggesting that he thought the Second Amendment might itself convey a personal right to keep and bear arms – even though neither party to the case had raised the Second Amendment issue. He suggested that the Court might in future consider that issue – essentially inviting potential litigants to find and bring gun control cases to the Court. While Justice Thomas's phrases were noncommittal, the meaning of his concurrence was clear: there was at least one vote on the Court for a personal right to keep and bear arms which would seriously constrain gun control legislation.

District of Columbia v *Heller* (2008) arose when a libertarian lawyer, Robert Levy, looked for individuals who could challenge the District's extremely strict gun laws in response to Justice Thomas's invitation. These DC laws made it both a crime to carry an unregistered gun, and impossible to register a handgun; they also required legal firearms to be kept in a nonfunctional state using a trigger-lock. Levy found among others Dick Heller, who tried to register a handgun he wished to keep at home and was refused. He then sued the District in the Federal District Court, arguing that both the ban on handguns and the trigger-lock requirements were contrary to the Second Amendment. Heller lost in the District Court, but the Court of Appeals for the District of Columbia reversed and found in Heller's favor. So, in 2008, did the Supreme Court, in a 5–4 decision. Justice Scalia's majority opinion found both the handgun ban, and the trigger-lock requirement, unconstitutional. Dissents by Justices Breyer and Stevens criticized both the outcome and the nature of the ruling, which left unspecified, in large part, much of the question of how the Second Amendment would now be interpreted. Justice Scalia, defending his ruling, noted that *Heller* was the Court's first serious examination of the Second Amendment in detail; further exploration would, he implied, need to wait for other cases.

The *Heller* decision was a major step: it provided a new account, supported by a narrow majority on the Court, of the Second Amendment's meaning. It provided a personal right to keep and bear arms, which at least some gun control laws contravene. But the DC gun control laws were a special case – they were extremely strict – so it remains unclear how and to what extent other gun control laws are affected. Indeed, there are two unclear issues here. The first issue is how far gun ownership and use can be regulated under the Second Amendment, as the majority on the Court understands it. On this question there has been considerable litigation, since *Heller*, in lower courts; in almost all the cases decided in the first year after *Heller*, other gun laws have been upheld. As these cases are appealed and work their way up to the Supreme Court, the majority will have to decide how they want to rule when the gun control laws are more nuanced than those overturned in *Heller*.

The second issue is whether the Amendment constrains only *federal* gun laws, or whether it also applies to state and local laws and regulations. The doctrine of incorporation has been applied to most of the Bill of Rights – that is, the rights are held to apply not only to the Federal Government, but also to state and local government. But incorporation is not automatic; the Supreme Court might decide to limit its new Second Amendment jurisprudence only to the federal level. The Court will certainly have opportunities to do so; in *Nordyke* v *King* (2009), the Ninth Circuit Court of Appeal decided that the Second Amendment is incorporated, and this or a similar decision is very likely to be appealed.

This case, then, represents a tantalizing but incomplete view of conservative judicial policymaking on the Court. The Court was willing to reconsider the meaning of the Second Amendment to reach a wholly new result (albeit one which, the majority claims, is contained within the original meaning of the text of the Amendment). But as ever, the Court is not an unconstrained policymaker. To reach this point it has been dependent on organized Second Amendment litigation, originally encouraged by Justice Thomas in the *Printz* decision; and for extension and development of the right it will be highly dependent on the explosion of new Second Amendment litigation that the *Heller* decision has brought about. It has also, and importantly, been dependent on scholarship: as the Court has moved from a "militia" to a "personal" right reading of the amendment, it has followed (and its arguments have depended on) recent scholarship that has moved along the same lines (Bogus, 2000). As the historical meaning of the Second Amendment has been brought into question, so originalist-minded justices like Antonin Scalia have found encouragement for a novel application of the Amendment to contemporary politics. However, in achieving conservative political aims through finding novel rights in the constitution, the conservatives on the court have opened themselves to vigorous criticism as "activists" from some conservative legal scholars and judges (Wilkinson, 2009).

Limits on the new conservatism: 'Ledbetter' and 'Heller' in context

So can conservatives be satisfied with these major cases of the new conservative era? The answer is mixed. On the positive side, these are very significant steps for conservatives. The *Ledbetter* opinion was written by Alito, but it is unlikely that it would have been joined by O'Connor, whom he had replaced. The tactic that the court used – blunting anti-discrimination lawsuits by reinterpreting the use of time limits – as well as the precedent itself was swiftly used by lower courts to reject cases concerning age discrimination and racial discrimination in employment, gender discrimination in education, and disability discrimination in housing. Although the tactic might appear to be a legal technicality, in practice its use implied a major setback for liberal-inspired anti-discrimination legislation.

Heller is, if anything, even more of a dramatic step forward for conservatives. It had been widely accepted for many decades that the Court had no interest in finding a Second Amendment right for individuals to bear arms, and almost no cases had been brought before the Court. The five justices from the Ledbetter decision here joined to find a right that had barely ever been litigated before – a piece of judicial creativity or activism on a par with the much-criticized liberal Supreme Courts of the 1950s and 1960s.

From the conservative movement's point of view, these are decisions which are clear, novel, and major. But just as liberals were ultimately unsatisfied with the Court as a source of social change when they held a significant majority on it (Rosenberg, 2008), so conservatives now face the limitations on what the Court can achieve. These limitations apply in different ways in the two cases.

In *Ledbetter* and similar cases, a liberal president and Congress can, and did, simply overturn the Court's decision by rewriting the legislation. Indeed a backlash against such a decision as *Ledbetter* may make a liberal president and Congress more likely to take the initiative. In *Heller*, on the other hand, the conservatives face some basic problems of judicial activism. First, they have opened up a novel question (a fundamental individual right to bear arms) of great complexity concerning both the incorporation doctrine and the issue of how far this right goes. Exactly what rights to arms do Americans have? Second, they face the problem of keeping the conservative coalition together: while there was a bare majority for the conservatives in *Heller*, the case was relatively straightforward. By American standards, the laws that were overturned were exceptionally strict. But when the court comes to decide about the constitutionality of the firearms laws in other jurisdictions – laws that are more widespread, more popular, and more limited in reach – there is no guarantee that the five will stick together and view those cases in the same way. If they do not do so, *Heller* will not have been the foundation of a meaningful new right.

In other words: the Court has power, and an ideological majority can capture it, as a liberal majority did during the Warren Court era and a conservative majority has done under the Roberts Court. But they then must try to exercise that power in interplay with the other governing institutions of American politics, and will in turn often find themselves divided by increasingly difficult questions about the consequences of their decisions.

A conservative trend? An overview of the Court's other recent decisions

The Court has, of course, not simply confined itself to two major areas of policymaking. Across the board, and in a range of different issue areas, there have been major cases that have shown a significant (thought not wholly uniform) move to the right.

Affirmative action

Towards the end of the Rehnquist court, two affirmative action cases concerning the University of Michigan were decided. In *Gratz* v *Bollinger* (2003), a points-based system of undergraduate admissions that granted extra points to members of underrepresented racial groups was held to be unconstitutional, by six votes to three. *Grutter* v *Bollinger* (2003) found a more holistic system, in which race was taken into account in a less mechanical way than through points, to be constitutional – although marginally so – and did so by five votes to four. The *Grutter* decision – in which Justice O'Connor joined the four most liberal justices to make the majority – appeared to be vulnerable to being overturned when Justice O'Connor was replaced by the markedly more conservative Justice Alito in 2006.

The Court has not, however, yet returned to the issue of race in university admissions; but in two cases – *Parents* v *Seattle* (2007) and *Meredith* v *Jefferson County Board of Education* (2007) – it has significantly changed the law on race and desegregation in schools. Both cases were decided by 5–4 majorities – the four in the minority in *Grutter*, plus Justice Alito. In the new conservative majority, Kennedy appears to be the marginal justice, having joined only part of the majority opinion and writing concurrences (and indeed partial dissents). These cases arose in states that had previously had racially identifiable schools (Seattle) or legal segregation (in Jefferson County, which is in Louisville, Kentucky). The school boards had, in different ways, used race as part of the process of assigning students to schools, in order to prevent "resegregation." In both cases, the Court found these policies to be unconstitutional, but did not overturn the *Grutter* precedent because of Justice Kennedy's qualms. While in principle this seemed to leave some space for so-called "race-conscious" policies aimed at ensuring racial diversity in schools, in practice the constitutionality of affirmative action programmes in education appears to have been very significantly limited. Justice Kennedy himself was in the minority in *Grutter*; future cases on the issue will surely turn on his views.

Outside of education, the Court's majority seems even less sympathetic to affirmative action. In *Ricci* v *DeStefano* (2009), for example, the Court held by a 5–4 majority that the New Haven Fire Department could not decide to discard the results of tests used to determine promotion chances when those tests were found to discriminate against minority firefighters.

Abortion rights

The Rehnquist Court decided *Stenberg* v *Carhart* in 2000, finding by 5–4 that a Nebraska abortion statute was unconstitutional. The statute had banned a particular medical procedure, which abortion opponents call "partial birth" abortion (and which medically is referred to as "D & X" or "D & E" abortion) – a method used in relatively late abortions which were nevertheless protected under the *Roe* v *Wade* (1973) and *Planned Parenthood* v *Casey* (1992) precedents. O'Connor joined the four more liberal justices to produce the *Stenberg* majority. In 2003 Congress passed, and President Bush signed, the Partial-Birth Abortion Ban Act, which banned the same procedure as the Nebraska statute that had been declared unconstitutional. This federal statute was appealed to the Supreme Court in *Gonzales* v *Carhart* (2007). Again, Justice Alito's vote proved crucial – he joined the other four conservative justices to uphold the constitutionality of the federal statute, with the four more liberal justices in dissent. The majority did not overrule *Stenberg*, arguing that the Nebraska statute had been more vague than the federal statute, but would allow a ban on specific medical procedures that did not have a health exemption as had previously been required.

It seems unlikely that Justice Kennedy, who was in the majority in both *Planned Parenthood* v *Casey* and *Gonzales* v *Carhart*, would vote to overturn the *Casey* decision and abandon the constitutional right to an abortion altogether – although the other four conservatives almost certainly would. However, he is clearly willing to allow much more intrusive regulation of abortion than previously, when Justice O'Connor was the decisive vote.

First Amendment rights

The Court recently decided one well-known free speech case in *Morse* v *Frederick* (2007). The case concerned a high school student who had been suspended for displaying the phrase "BONG HiTS 4 JESUS" on a banner when his school turned out to watch the Olympic Torch Relay for the 2002 Winter Olympics. By a 5–4 vote along conservative–liberal lines (with Justice Breyer making some parts of the opinion 6–3), the Court decided that it was constitutional for the student to be punished for displaying a banner that promoted illegal drugs, notwithstanding the First Amendment's protection of free speech.

Another particularly important free speech case to reach the Court concerned the Bipartisan Campaign Reform Act of 2002, which (among other things) set limits on political advertising by third parties (unions, corporations, and others) in the period immediately before an election. These limits had been upheld as constitutional in *McConnell* v *FEC* (2003) by a 5–4 vote, with the four more liberal justices joined by Justice O'Connor. The issue arose again in *FEC* v *Wisconsin Right to Life* (2007), where a 5–4 conservative majority, including Justice Alito, ruled that the limits were unconstitutional in most cases. As with the *Carhart* abortion cases, though, the conservative majority did not explicitly overrule the prior case. Again, the switch from Justice O'Connor to Justice Alito appeared to have flipped the conservative side from minority to majority, at some expense in legal consistency.

Voting rights

One striking case that did not fit the usual ideological division on the Court was *Northwest Austin* v *Holder* (2009). This case arose out of the Voting Rights Act of 1965, Section 5 of which requires federal pre-clearance – that is, permission from a federal court or the Department of Justices – for changes to voting procedures in a number of states, towns, and counties. Those states, towns, and counties had engaged in substantial racial discrimination prior to the Voting Rights Act in order to keep African Americans from exercising voting rights, and were thus singled out for ongoing supervision both in 1965 and when the Act was renewed, most recently in 2006. The Northwest Austin Municipal Utility District, a governmental body with an elected board, was covered under Section 5 because it was located in Texas, even though the district itself appeared not to have a history of electoral discrimination. The district sued, arguing that either it should be released from the preclearance requirements, or if this was not possible, that Section 5 was unconstitutional.

All the justices apart from Thomas signed up to the chief justice's opinion, which held that the district could be released from pre-clearance.

However, the opinion also raised deep constitutional concerns with Section 5, and the decision has been widely interpreted as a request to Congress to amend the Voting Rights Act. The implicit threat is that in a future case a majority of the Court might simply declare Section 5 to be unconstitutional, as Thomas had argued in dissent in this case.

Death penalty

In recent years the Court has tinkered with the machinery of the death penalty, in response to the vast number of appeals in death penalty cases that it receives. This it has done almost constantly since *Gregg* v *Georgia* (1976) refined the criteria that states had to meet to make the death penalty constitutional. Of particular importance are two cases – *Hill* v *McDonough* (2006) and *Baze* v *Rees* (2008) – where the court considered the lethal injection procedure through which most death penalties are carried out, eventually deciding that it was constitutional.

Although the death penalty had been applied for crimes including robbery, rape, assault, and kidnapping as late as the 1960s, since then it has been used only in cases of murder. This trend was underlined when the Supreme Court decided, in *Coker* v *Georgia* (1977), that use of the death penalty to punish the rapist of a 16-year-old was unconstitutional, because it was disproportionate to the offence. But the existence of horrific crimes that are not murder does occasionally raise the issue in politics. In 1995, the Louisiana legislature amended its death penalty statute to cover the crime of rape of a child, and five other states have done so. In *Kennedy* v *Louisiana* (2008) the Court decided by a 5–4 vote that this was unconstitutional. It appears likely that, without further conservative justices being appointed to replace some of the moderate/liberal wing, the death penalty henceforth will be limited to murder cases.

The environment

The Court has recently decided two important environmental law cases, which provide some evidence of the limits to the conservative trend on the Court in at least this area. In *Rapanos* v *US* (2006), which concerned wetlands protection, the court was almost exactly divided down the middle. Four conservative justices voted radically to limit the protection of wetlands; four more liberal justices voted for expansive protection of the sort the Environmental Protection Agency (EPA) and the US Army Corps of Engineers had been pursuing. Justice Kennedy voted to decide the case on as narrow a basis as possible, agreeing with the conservatives that the EPA had gone too far in this particular case, but generally agreeing with the EPA view that the liberals had supported. However, when environmental groups sued to prevent the Army Corps of Engineers giving permits to mining polluters in Alaska, in *Coeur Alaska* v *Southeast Alaska Conservation Council*, all five conservatives plus Justice Breyer voted to allow the permits to go ahead.

In *Massachusetts* v *EPA* (2007), the Court considered the question of greenhouse gases: several states and cities sued to force the EPA to start regulating CO_2 and other greenhouse gases. By 5–4, with Justice Kennedy joining the four more liberal justices, the Court supported the states, and the EPA was required to begin planning the regulation of greenhouse gas emissions as an air pollutant.

The Court and Obama

As a number of the preceding cases show, the replacement of Justice O'Connor, usually the most moderate of the conservative justices, with Justice Alito, who is substantially more conservative, has had a significant and perhaps lasting effect on the Court's jurisprudence. In that sense, the Court's long and unsteady march to the right, begun over 40 years ago, had reached a significant destination by the time Obama took office in January 2009.

Justice Kennedy is often the decisive vote, being now the most moderate of the conservatives; but he is also significantly more conservative than Justice O'Connor was. Decisions are nearly always being made by Kennedy joining either the four more conservative justices, with a conservative outcome, or the four more liberal justices, with what is usually a moderate rather than a liberal outcome. But it is worth noting that the Court, although it now leans rightward on many highly controversial issues, is much more united in many less overtly political cases. In particular, it is much more friendly to business interests, often unanimously or by a large majority, than the Warren Court ever was. It is also inclined to be skeptical about government domestic powers. Although, on the controversial issues that tend to attract great attention, the Court is quite narrowly balanced, on many other issues it represents the presidents who appointed nearly all its members – that is, it represents an era of Republican domination and Democratic moderation. At a political moment when Republican domination seems to be in serious question, and when Democratic liberals seem to be recovering some confidence, the Court may be in danger of lagging behind a change in public mood towards the role of government. That the Court lags behind political change is implicit in its institutional design, but this can render it unpopular (as in the 1930s and 1970s) or irrelevant.

President Obama, Justice Sotomayor, and the future

How will the Court develop? Predicting the future of the Court in this context depends on two things. First, it depends on which of the existing justices retires: only if one of the five most conservative justices departs will Obama have a major chance to change the shape of the Court and its jurisprudence. Second, it depends on what kind of court appointments President Obama seeks.

The President's two Democratic predecessors arrived in office with reputations for ideological moderation; not since 1960 had a northern liberal been elected president. While President Clinton was not a conservative in the sense of a previous generation of Arkansas Democrats, he was not entirely comfortable with liberal politics and was, in many issue areas, careful to demonstrate political moderation. His Supreme Court nominees fit that mould: neither Justice Ginsburg nor Justice Breyer is particularly liberal in many respects. Both are punctiliously liberal on identity and equality issues, but neither is strongly pro-union, and Breyer in particular has a pro-business and somewhat anti-regulation stance, sometimes joining the conservatives in cases concerning free speech, environmental regulation, and other controversial issues. Both are also relatively moderate on criminal procedure issues. Their moderation is somewhat mitigated by general social trends – for example, the Supreme Court on which they serve has done more for gay rights than any of its predecessors, largely as a result of broader social trends. In sum, like the president who appointed them, Clinton's nominees are moderate, pragmatic liberals.

President Obama did, however, arrive in office as a northern liberal; and moreover, as a former constitutional law professor, someone with both an interest in the subject matter of the Court and a politics to the left of any of his recent predecessors. Thus the President's biography and apparent personal ideology seemed possibly to indicate that he would make more liberal appointments than Clinton.

The first vacancy Obama faced answered the first question: Justice Souter, who announced his retirement in May 2009, was one of the Court's more liberal justices. Although appointed by President George H. W. Bush, and widely supposed to be a "stealth conservative," he had turned out to have more in common with Justices Ginsburg, Breyer, and Stevens than any of the other Reagan or Bush appointees. In replacing Justice Souter, Obama would not be able to shift the five more conservative justices. But would he put on the court a more liberal voice – a "liberal Scalia?"

In the short term, the answer appears to be no. His nominee, Justice Sotomayor, follows broadly the pattern of Clinton's nominees: she is a highly experienced sitting appeals court judge, who attracts considerable approval from conservative lawyers such as Kenneth Starr, a former Republican solicitor general and the Whitewater special prosecutor. Indeed she had originally been appointed as a federal judge by President George H. W. Bush. Sotomayor is the first Hispanic justice, and like Clinton's first nomination represents a doubling of the number of women sitting on the Court; but there is little evidence that she is ideologically very liberal. Like Clinton's nominees, she has been on the liberal side in equality cases, controversially including an affirmative action case, which the Supreme Court later overturned. But she appears to be quite conservative on criminal law issues, as a former federal prosecutor, and may indeed be to the right of Justice Souter, whom she replaces.

If any of the Court's conservatives were to retire and be replaced by President Obama with a justice more like Justices Breyer, Ginsburg, or Sotomayor, then there would be a shift in the Court's jurisprudence. The four remaining conservatives would have to find an ally from the moderates and liberals – perhaps most likely Justice Breyer – to forge a majority, and in practice some of the post-2006 cases would be ripe for overruling or limiting. That said, at the time of writing the more likely retirements would seem to be from the Court's liberal wing, with Justice Stevens (who has clearly indicated that he will leave the Court by October 2010) and Justice Ginsburg, who has had serious health problems, most likely to retire in Obama's term of office.

Conclusion: the Supreme Court as a place to exercise power

While Justice Sotomayor's jurisprudence has yet to be fully revealed, there is then little evidence that she will represent a major shift on the Court. There is also little evidence that President Obama wishes for or thinks possible such a shift: arguably the modern Democratic party has largely given up the project of the mid-twentieth century, in which courts could play a significant role in liberal social reform.

There are two recurrent themes in this chapter. First, conservatives are now more engaged than liberals in using the federal courts to achieve political outcomes, and are indeed in a position to use their dominance of the Supreme Court to achieve some major changes. But in doing so they face the second theme: that the Supreme Court is not an autonomous umpire, capable of radically shifting the rules, but rather one institution among many, and not necessarily a dominant or particularly powerful one.

There is no guarantee that the Supreme Court will be a major player in a given policy area, even one that raises basic issues of rights, equality and constitutional law. For example, several states have been forced, by state courts interpreting state constitutions' guarantees of equality, to permit gay marriage. But this has caused remarkably little "backlash"; challenges to these decisions have had mixed effects, and while states like California have narrowly overturned court decisions by popular vote, other states, such as Massachusetts, have let the decisions stand, and since then further states, such as Maine and Vermont, have amended their marriage statutes through the normal legislative process without court intervention. Other states have moved, through court and legislative action, towards an intermediate step of permitting civil unions. This has been, in other words, an apparently successful – albeit far from complete – program of civil rights reform brought about by litigation. But the federal judiciary has remained almost entirely uninvolved, and the Supreme Court entirely so.

Chapter 10

American Federalism in the Twenty-First Century

Tim Conlan

During the first decade of the twenty-first century, American federalism was subject to a renewed burst of governmental activism, the latest in a long but episodic and irregular trend that has gradually increased the power, authority, and resources of the national government. Under the presidency of George W. Bush, grants in aid to state and local governments reached historic levels, several new and intrusive federal mandates were adopted, federal preemption of state authority quickened, and federal involvement in education, health care, and the financial sector expanded. Many of these trends accelerated in the early months of the Obama administration, with record increases in federal grant spending, dramatic interventions in the financial and automobile industries, and proposals for comprehensive health care reform and climate change legislation.

Such developments were largely unexpected on the eve of George W. Bush's inauguration in 2001. On the contrary, many anticipated a strong movement toward decentralization and smaller government under the new President. Significant efforts at devolution had been made under Ronald Reagan and Bill Clinton, including federal tax and spending cuts, the enactment of welfare reform and other new block grants, a string of Supreme Court decisions imposing limits on Congress's powers under the Constitution, and a burst of renewed state activism. Although promises of devolution often advanced far beyond actual results – even welfare reform had significant centralizing as well as decentralizing elements – new devolutionary momentum seemed a plausible expectation with the inauguration of a conservative former governor and Republican majorities in both houses of Congress.

Instead, President Bush actively sought or readily accepted the rapid acceleration of intergovernmental spending, the enactment of an expensive new health care entitlement program, extraordinary levels of federal intervention into traditional state-local functions, and continued federal preemption of state authority. Such policies resulted partly from factors beyond the President's control, such as the 9/11 terrorist attacks and economic globalization. But they also reflected a transformation of conservative ideology in the United States – a transformation that has important implications for the future of American federalism. Traditional conservatism once formed a political bulwark for decentralized governance and "states' rights" in American politics. Such conservatism was animated by a reverence for established institutions and social norms, and it was reinforced by the institutionalized power of southern segregationists in Congress and the dominant political role of big-city mayors and state governors in the machinery of party politics. These last two pillars of political decentralization eroded dramatically in the late twentieth century, and they were joined finally by changes in American conservatism as well. As more assertive strains of economic and social conservatism replaced traditional, institutional conservatism, the linkage between ideology and decentralized governance was altered. Issues of federalism were made contingent upon other, often centralizing, ideological and policy goals, from gay marriage to deregulation. Thus, while contemporary liberals and conservatives may pursue very different ends, they now share a common willingness to employ instruments of national action to attain their policy objectives.

The Bush-era tilt toward Washington DC is continuing in the Obama administration. More than one-third of President Obama's first major policy initiative, the American Recovery and Reinvestment Act (ARRA), provided grants to state and local governments, and additional increases in grant spending were proposed in his initial budget request to Congress. Other initiatives of President Obama – including health care reform, financial regulatory reform, and climate change policy – are likely to place additional strains on the intergovernmental system, given the close interactions between federal and state spending programs and regulatory authority in all three fields. With or without health care and these other reforms, the projected increases in federal deficits in the years ahead are likely to place growing constraints on federal grants to state and local governments within the decade. Future intergovernmental conflict is sure to follow.

Fiscal federalism under George W. Bush

Expenditures

Levels of federal aid provided to state and local governments are the traditional yardstick for measuring fiscal concentration in American federalism. Such federal grants grew rapidly in George W. Bush's first term, continuing a trend that emerged in Bill Clinton's second term. As Figure 10.1 shows, grant spending totaled $461 billion in fiscal year (FY) 2008, and this figure will rise to approximately $652 billion in FY2010 once President Obama's economic stimulus funding is factored in (OMB, 2009: 89). In nominal dollars, grants almost doubled in the decade from 1998 and 2008, increasing from $234 billion to $461 billion, and they grew from $318 to $407 billion in George W. Bush's first term alone. In constant dollars, grants grew by 41 percent during the decade preceding 2008. Areas of particularly rapid growth were education, including large additions to funding as part of No Child Left Behind (NCLB), homeland security, election reform, and health care – especially Medicaid (the joint federal–state program of medical assistance to the poor) and the State Children's Health Insurance Program (SCHIP).

In relative terms, grants as a percentage of total federal outlays totaled 18 percent in 2003, the highest level ever recorded by OMB up to that point. The previous high was 17 percent under Jimmy Carter in

Figure 10.1   *Federal grants to state and local government, 1980–2010*

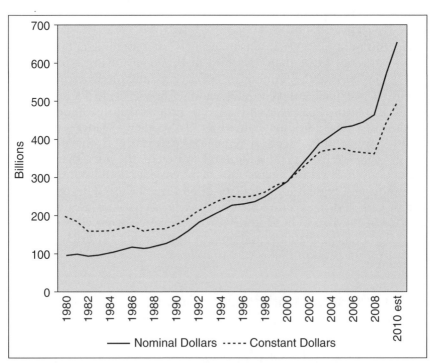

Source: US Office of Management and Budget, *Budget of the United States, FY 2010*, Historical Tables.

1978 (OMB, 2009). Although this percentage declined in subsequent years as the growth of grants slowed and defense spending and other elements of the budget increased, it remained at historically high levels throughout the Bush administration. It will return to an estimated 18.2 percent in FY2010 once spending from President Obama's economic stimulus package is factored in. Similarly, grants-in-aid reached a ten-year high as a percentage of state-local spending in 2004 (US Census Bureau, 2009).

In addition to aid to state and local governments, the Bush administration also left a permanent legacy of direct federal spending with the enactment of the Medicare Modernization Act of 2003, which provides prescription drug coverage for Medicare recipients. Medicare is a federally funded and administered health insurance program for the elderly. At an estimated cost of $362 billion during its first five years, Medicare part D represented the largest new federal entitlement program since Lyndon Johnson's Great Society. In a unique twist to the normal pattern of grants in aid, states were obligated to pay the federal government approximately $48 billion of this total amount, part of a federal "clawback" provision intended to take back state savings on "dual eligible" Medicaid patients (the elderly poor) whose prescription costs would now be underwritten by the federal Medicare program (Derthick, 2007).

Tax policy

Revenues as well as expenditures have intergovernmental consequences, and the Bush administration's tax policies also had important implications for American federalism. One of the principal domestic policy achievements of President Bush was legislation substantially reducing federal individual, corporate, and estate taxes. The enactment of large tax-cut packages in 2001 and 2003 set the stage for future deficits, which ultimately can place pressure on domestic intergovernmental spending. Such federal tax cuts could have been designed to systematically reduce federal policy influence, by simplifying the tax code and eliminating tax expenditures designed to alter private behavior. However, the Bush tax cuts did the opposite, adding complexity to the tax code by providing multiple new tax credits and deductions for married couples, families with children, small businesses, investors, and other favored interests.

Moreover, because of their design, Bush's tax cuts depressed state and local tax receipts. The gradual reduction and elimination of the federal estate tax reduced state revenues by $9 billion annually, because many state tax systems coordinate their provisions with the federal code (Posner, 2007). Yet such intergovernmental revenue effects were never seriously considered by administration officials or by

Republican leaders in Congress. Congress, with administration support, also enacted a prohibition on states seeking to tax access to the Internet, and it refused to cooperate with state efforts to promote the collection of state sales and use taxes on online purchases. Given the rapid growth of Internet sales, the long-term fiscal implications for state sales tax revenues are daunting (Schappach and Shafroth, 2008).

Regulatory federalism in the Bush administration

Intergovernmental relations in the United States were once concerned almost exclusively with grants and subsidies. In recent decades, however, mandates and regulations have become equally important policy tools. Here too, the Bush administration was surprisingly active, in ways that lent credence to libertarian complaints that George W. Bush was a "big government" conservative (Tanner, 2007).

Federal mandates

Major new mandates were adopted during the Bush administration in education, homeland security, election administration, and other fields that traditionally have been the principal responsibility of state and local governments. The most prominent of these was NCLB, which was the signature domestic initiative of George W. Bush. Originally passed in 2002, the Act provided substantial new funding for education but also inserted federal influence into aspects of elementary and secondary education that were long considered the preserve of states and localities. Specifically, the law mandated annual testing of students in grades one through eight, required mandatory corrective actions for individual schools and school districts that failed to meet their testing targets, and promoted the fundamental restructuring of education service delivery, including state takeovers of problematic local schools, publicly funded private tutoring services, statewide curriculum changes, and expanded use of charter schools. As one education scholar has argued, NCLB's prescriptive mandates "reach into every major area of education policy and will require states and districts to fundamentally change the way they run their public schools" (McGuinn, 2006: 182). In a country that has long valued local control of elementary and secondary education, this constituted a breathtaking change in policy direction.

The Help America Vote Act was another Bush-era measure, which set standards for state and local voting systems and mandated that states establish statewide voter databases. The law required that voters be allowed to correct voter registration errors and to cast provisional ballots when mistakes are found. By specifying new requirements for statewide voter databases and uniform voter definitions, the law entailed significant new centralization of the registration and election processes at the state level (Liebschutz and Palazzolo, 2005). Although Congress provided $3 billion in funding for implementing the new law – to help pay for modernizing voting technology – federal funds fell well short of the actual costs (Congressional Research Service, 2004). In addition, some of the new voting systems that states and localities purchased shortly after passage of the law proved to be seriously flawed, requiring some states to expend additional funds to upgrade their systems yet again.

Homeland security was another field that witnessed new federal directives in the wake of the 9/11 attacks. A sprawling Department of Homeland Security was established in Washington, and it began to develop new national standards for emergency preparedness, communications, and response. Many of these functions are primarily carried out by local police, fire, and ambulance services, which will be required to implement the national standards. In addition, the so-called Real ID act established new standards for issuing state drivers licenses, with document validation requirements that imposed an estimated $11 billion in compliance costs on state motor vehicle departments (NGA, NCSL, and AAMVA, 2006). Finally, as noted earlier, unilateral federal actions in tax policy, particularly the elimination of the federal estate tax and changes in federal rules governing depreciation and dividends, had major fiscal implications for states that couple their tax systems to federal tax law.

Presidents should be measured by their proposals as well as their accomplishments, so it is worth noting that President Bush advocated important mandates and constraints on state policymaking that were ultimately not enacted. The President supported congressional Republican efforts to move into federal court the case of Terri Schaivo, a comatose woman in Florida whose husband sought to remove her feeding tube. He also challenged Oregon's statute allowing physician-assisted suicide. Finally, President Bush supported a constitutional amendment to ban gay marriage, which would block efforts in certain states to legalize marriage between homosexual couples.

Preemption

Federal preemption of state authority also increased during the Bush administration. Preemption occurs when the national government claims constitutional authority to fully or partially regulate a field of policy hitherto left to the states. According to data compiled by Joseph Zimmerman, a total of 64 new preemptions were adopted in the first five years of the Bush administration (Zimmerman, 2007). Although many of these were relatively modest restrictions of state authority, a handful of others substantially restricted state authority to raise revenues or regulate behavior, such as the limitation on state taxation of Internet access and the removal from state courts of liability lawsuits against firearms manufacturers. Moreover, the Bush administration vigorously sought but failed to pass legislation preempting state authority over medical malpractice lawsuits.

From an institutional and historical perspective, the most important development was an increase in the velocity of federal preemption during the Bush administration. An average of 12.8 new preemptions were adopted annually during the first five years of the Bush administration. This was a higher adoption rate than under Ronald Reagan, George H. W. Bush, or Bill Clinton (Zimmerman, 2007: 434, 435). Moreover, a downward trend from Reagan to Clinton in the rate of annual preemption adoptions was reversed under George W. Bush and the Republican Congress. Although all preemptions cannot be weighted equally, few would have predicted such an active pace of federal preemption or mandating during the first period of Republican control of the White House and Congress in almost 50 years.

Block grants and waiver authority

Centralization is rarely a consistent and unidirectional process, and policies were proposed or implemented during the Bush years that pointed in a devolutionary direction. Yet even here, results were often limited. Two particular techniques of intergovernmental policy that are commonly viewed as instruments of devolution, block grants and program waivers, proved to have contradictory characteristics.

For example, the 1996 Welfare Reform Act was hailed – and attacked – as an unprecedented effort to devolve authority over welfare services. In many respects it did. It converted an individual entitlement program into a fixed block grant to states, the Temporary Assistance to Needy Families (TANF) program, and it granted states more flexibility to determine eligibility and benefits under the law. On the other hand, it also imposed strict federal time limits on the payment of welfare benefits, eliminated additional benefits for new family members, and imposed significant new work requirements for welfare beneficiaries. When welfare reform came up for renewal in 2002, the Bush administration insisted on tightening these work requirements even further, mandating new targets that states must meet in order to avoid fiscal sanctions under the law. After several years of debate and conflict, such provisions were included when TANF was finally reauthorized in 2006 (Allard, 2007).

Similarly, Bush expanded the use of waiver authority in the Medicaid program, building upon previous practices in the Clinton and George H. W. Bush administrations. Their use of administrative waivers in the

Aid to Families with Dependent Children (AFDC) program allowed certain states to experiment with many of the policy innovations that later were included in the TANF program. George W. Bush's administration sought to make equally aggressive use of experimental waivers in the Medicaid program. But in doing so, it demonstrated that waivers permit the expression of national policy goals even as they grant states additional flexibility. This was because the Bush administration was highly selective in its allowance of Medicaid waivers, permitting Florida to experiment with market-oriented reforms to the program while denying more progressive health care reforms proposed by other states (Weissert and Weissert, 2008).

Judicial federalism

One of the most important developments affecting US federalism during the 1980s and 1990s was the Rehnquist Court's attempt to develop new judicial doctrines restricting Congress's powers under the Constitution and carving out a protected sphere of state sovereignty. Led by Chief Justice Rehnquist and Justice Sandra Day O'Connor, the Court delivered decisions in the 1990s that expanded state authority to restrict abortion, limited citizens' ability to sue state governments, prohibited Congress's ability to "commandeer" the administrative machinery of state and local governments, and held that Congress had exceeded the scope of its power to regulate interstate commerce for first time since the 1930s. Virtually all of these cases were decided by a five to four margin, however, so the winner of the 2000 presidential election was expected to have opportunities to shape the future of the Court.

Bush had such opportunities, and he appointed two judicial conservatives to replace Justices O'Connor and Rehnquist. But the momentum toward a judicial "new federalism" was slowed. Neither the new Chief Justice, John Roberts, nor Samuel Alito appears to be as dedicated to the new federalist project as were Justices O'Connor and Rehnquist. Though conservative, both men appear to be more similar to other judicial conservatives, including Justices Antonin Scalia and Clarence Thomas, in their willingness to support federal preemption of state regulations that impinge on interstate commerce, for example (Banks and Blakeman, 2008). The Bush administration has tended to do the same in its briefs to the Court (Conlan and Dinan, 2007). To date there has been no judicial revolution, and there likely will not be one with the ascendance of Barack Obama to the presidency.

State policy initiatives

No review of federalism developments would be complete without considering state and local policy initiatives during the past decade.

Federalism after all is shaped from below as well as from above. This is particularly true in the US system, which provides states with significant autonomy to raise their own revenues and pursue a broad array of policy initiatives.

As Richard Nathan has observed, state policymaking is often counter-cyclical. That is, it tends to counter the prevailing ideological tendency at the national level, as political activists seek to find an alternative avenue for their policy ambitions (Nathan, 2008). When conservative Republicans control Washington, as was the case under George Bush and the Republican Congress, liberals may find that they have more opportunities to pursue progressive policies at the state and local levels, just as conservatives previously favored state rights when Democrats dominated the national government.

This counter-cyclical tendency was abundantly evident in several policy fields during the Bush era, as federal government policies turned in a sharply conservative direction. For example, advocates of gay marriage, seeing little prospect of success at the federal level, have focused their efforts on state courts and legislatures. This has not only given rise to the legalization of some form of gay marriage in Massachusetts, Vermont, and Iowa, but spawned conservative efforts in Congress, as well as the states, to try to constrain this trend, through national legislation or constitutional amendment, if necessary. Similarly, President Bush's executive order limiting the use of federal funds in stem cell research prompted efforts in states like California to support such research with state funds.

Climate change policy is another area where the lack of federal policy initiative, including the Senate's unwillingness to ratify the Kyoto treaty under Bill Clinton as well as the Bush administration's skepticism about the problem, led numerous states to take initiative for addressing the problem. Half of the states have now adopted "renewable portfolio standards" – policies requiring state regulated electric utilities to provide a certain percentage of electric power from renewable forms of energy by specified dates. Other states, notably California and the northeastern states, which established the Regional Greenhouse Gas Initiative, are attempting to establish cap and trade policies for regulating carbon emissions. Still other states, such as Massachusetts, have devised plans for universal health insurance coverage. (See Chapter 11 for more discussion of environmental policy.)

Such state initiatives are constrained by interstate competition and collective action problems, which tend to limit the effectiveness of many state-level initiatives. This has been especially evident in regional climate change initiatives, where states fear that costly regulations will place them at an economic disadvantage (Rabe, 2008). Interstate competition has also been a factor in both promoting and limiting the Streamlined Sales Tax project, which seeks to increase the collection of state sales and use taxes in online sales by establishing a common set of tax rates and taxable goods. Moreover, when such state initiatives are successful, they often become the basis for national legislation applying a uniform policy response to the issue (Posner and Conlan, 2008).

Federalism and the Obama administration

Explicit debate about issues of federalism and federalism reform was largely absent in the 2008 presidential election campaign. This is not surprising, perhaps, given the centrality of economic and foreign policy concerns. Yet neither was it inevitable. Federalism reform and restructuring were central elements of the campaigns and administrations of Richard Nixon and Ronald Reagan, and federalist themes underlay much of the "Republican Revolution" of the mid-1990s (Conlan, 1998). But only one contender for the Republican nomination, former Senator Fred Thompson, made the restoration of traditional federal roles a salient part of his campaign, and he bowed out early for lack of support. The eventual Republican nominee, John McCain, did pay homage to the Tenth Amendment in his speeches, and the Republican Party platform had platitudes about respecting "the limits imposed upon [Congress] by the Tenth Amendment," but federalism and devolution were not treated as central themes by either McCain or Obama.

Despite this, issues of federalism and intergovernmental relations were implicit in many of the policy proposals made by both candidates. The roles of the federal and state governments in financing and implementing health care reform is one obvious example. So too was candidate Obama's pledge to rebuild the nation's infrastructure, much of which would be carried out by state and local governments with financial assistance from federal grants. Whether the federal government should preempt state efforts to recognize gay marriage or civil unions was one of several social issues with important intergovernmental implications.

Stimulating the economy

This implicit intergovernmental agenda came quickly to the fore once President Obama assumed office. The second piece of legislation signed by the new President, in only his second week in office, was a $32 billion expansion of SCHIP. This expansion, which was twice vetoed by President Bush, extended health insurance coverage to 4.1 million children in working families with incomes too high to qualify for Medicaid (Armstrong, 2009).

Intergovernmental relations were even more prominent in ARRA, the so-called economic stimulus bill. Grants to state and local governments comprised approximately $275 billion, or 35 percent of the total stimulus package of $787 billion – a sum roughly comparable to the much-debated tax cuts in the legislation. Increased funding was provided in the stimulus bill for nearly a hundred separate grant programs, delivered in three basic forms. One form was relatively flexible funding for Medicaid and education. For Medicaid, ARRA temporarily increased the federal matching rate for state Medicaid expenditures, allowing recession-weakened states to serve an influx of needy clients with less of their own money. The Recovery Act provided an additional $87 billion in federal Medicaid payments for this purpose. Flexible funding for education was provided in the form of the State Fiscal Stabilization Fund. This $40 billion fund can be used by states and school systems for any purpose allowed by a range of existing federal education grant programs, from NCLB and special education to adult education and student loans.

Another grant funding format in the ARRA was categorical aid for over 75 specific programmatic initiatives, both new and established. Approximately $100 billion was earmarked for such purposes as grants to expand broadband Internet access to rural and underserved areas ($7.2 billion), grants supporting the development of high-speed rail ($9 billion), highway transportation and other infrastructure grants ($26.6 billion), weatherization and state energy grants ($11.3 billion), and various public safety programs ($3.7 billion). Finally, about $40 billion of additional grant funding was provided in the Recovery Act for intergovernmental social safety net programs like extended unemployment benefits and food stamps.

As a result of this influx of new funding, the curve of federal grant spending turned sharply upward again under President Obama (see Figure 10.1). The temporary stimulus spending is reinforced by other spending requests contained in the regular budget. For fiscal year 2010, President Obama requested additional funding to "support ... extend, and expand the down payments made in the Recovery Act" (OMB, 2009: 19). This included creation of a new National Infrastructure Bank, additional funding for high-speed rail, community drinking water systems, port security, early childhood education, and health care reform initiatives.

Transparency

The federalism implications of President Obama's early policy initiatives extend beyond their fiscal impacts. In order to maximize the economic stimulus provided by the ARRA – and to minimize the inflationary risks of recovery funds being spent after strong economic growth has resumed – both federal agencies and the recipients of stimulus funds were put under great pressure to spend their monies quickly. Three-quarters of the $787 billion total was intended to be spent within 18 months of the legislation's enactment. Yet such speed exacerbates the potential for waste and misuse of funds. It reduces the time available for careful planning and prioritizing, it overloads agencies with hurriedly prepared funding requests while accelerating the review and approval processes, and it limits the time available for hiring and training personnel.

The Obama administration's response has been a heightened focus on accountability and transparency. Two new federal websites, Recovery.gov and FederalReporting.gov, were established to publicly identify grant and other recipients of stimulus funding, track their specific projects and funding levels, and report on the use of funds. These government websites have been duplicated by a number of private efforts to do the same, though often with a commercial or ideological bent.

In addition to such transparency efforts, the President launched a series of accountability efforts. The Office of Management and Budget (OMB) published 62 pages of guidance for agencies and funding recipients within a week of ARRA's passage, detailing the additional reporting, monitoring, and evaluation requirements of the Act. This was followed in April 2009 by a 172-page "updated" memorandum of guidance designed to "supplement, amend, and clarify" the original instructions, and an additional 39 pages of guidance in June 2009 about how to report back on how the federal funds were spent. Hundreds of millions of additional dollars were also provided for oversight of stimulus funds, to support additional staff and activities by executive branch inspectors-general and the Government Accountability Office. As a result, Paul Posner argues that the Obama administration's new accountability and transparency agenda raises the potential for additional policy centralization, as state and local governments adopt federal priorities to avoid penalties and second-guessing:

> State and local governments will be on the hot seat as never before. The stimulus legislation is accompanied by an unprecedented wave of new accountability requirements and provisions. While geared toward promoting public trust and confidence, and motivating those on the front lines to improve the efficiency and quality of services, the new information could generate a wave of second-guessing and blame shifting, with state and local officials as the possible target. (Posner, 2009)

Other initiatives

Beyond the economic stimulus plan, many other policy initiatives of the early Obama administration promise to have important intergovernmental consequences, depending on the ultimate design and enactment of legislation. These include health care reform, climate change legislation, financial regulatory reform, education legislation, and homeland security policy.

As President Obama's top domestic priority, health care reform may be the most important. Current health care policy in the United States is characterized by a complex mixture of federal, state, and private responsibilities which reflects the intricacies of the US federal system overall. Medicaid, as noted earlier, provides medical care for the poor and for many elderly and disabled patients in long-term care. It is jointly funded by federal, state, and, in some states, local governments, and administered by states and some localities. Medicare, which provides health insurance for the elderly, is financed and administered entirely by the national government. Public health services are funded and jointly administered by all three levels of government. States license doctors, nurses, and hospitals, and the federal government and the states each play roles in the regulation of private health insurance.

Thus, any form of comprehensive health care reform that seeks to rationalize this complex system and extend health insurance coverage to all citizens will have intergovernmental consequences. For example, many Democrats support using Medicaid to provide health coverage to low-income individuals above the poverty line. This makes sense administratively, but could result in billions of dollars in additional health care spending by states. Similarly, states are expected to play a role in establishing new health insurance markets for individuals and small employers, and the creation of national standards for patient care and private health insurance coverage will preempt state authority in these areas.

Federal legislation to create a cap and trade system to lower CO_2 emissions also impacts state and local governments. Building codes in the United States are promulgated by local governments, so national efforts to promote "green building" standards may preempt existing state and local authority. The same is true of national standards for renewable energy production, since state governments largely perform utility regulation. A national cap and trade system would also eclipse state efforts to adopt such systems on a regional basis, and it would have very different economic effects in different regions of the country.

These reforms, along with those proposed for banking and finance, are centralizing in their effects on the US federal system, by expanding the national government's role, preempting state and local authority, imposing minimum or uniform national standards, and potentially imposing increased costs on state and local governments. On the other hand, some other early initiatives by the Obama administration suggest a loosening of Bush-era policies. The new administration has supported some relaxation of the Real ID act, which imposed costly new standards for state drivers licenses. There is also strong support in Congress and the White House for providing more flexibility in the implementation of the NCLB education program. And the administration has signaled a willingness to be more flexible in the design of certain homeland security mandates. Taken together, however, these actions do not compensate for the overall drift toward centralization in public finance, health care, energy, and financial regulation.

State policy initiatives

State policy initiatives since the inauguration of President Obama have been dominated by responses to the economic recession. The economic downturn has dramatically eroded state and local revenues. For only the second time in history, state revenues are projected to decline for two consecutive years. At the same time, demands for state services have gone up, as more people collect unemployment benefits and qualify for welfare and other low-income assistance. Consequently, a majority of states have suffered major budgetary crises. Collectively, the 50 states face a shortfall of $230 billion between 2009–11, and most states have made multiple rounds of budget cuts and tax increases in order to meet their balanced budget requirements (NGA and NASBO, 2009). In California alone, the 2009–10 budget shortfall was estimated to be $26 billion in July 2009 (McKinley, 2009). Without agreement on a plan to cut spending and raise revenues, the state government was forced to furlough state employees and issue IOUs to vendors and taxpayers.

Given their budgetary challenges, many state initiatives have focused on issues with modest or positive fiscal implications. Since 2004, courts or legislatures in nine states have legalized gay marriage or domestic partnerships, including six in 2009 alone: Maine, New Hampshire, Vermont, Iowa, Nevada, and Washington State (Stateline, 2009). Seven states closed prisons in 2009 to save money, and others have undertaken legal reforms to reduce prison populations. New Mexico joined 14 other states that prohibit the death penalty, and ten additional states considered legislation to restrict or abolish the death penalty.

Conservative social policies have also advanced in many states. For example, six states adopted some form of limitation on abortions or established new legal recognition for fetuses in 2009. In recent years, conservatives have also had success defeating restrictions on the use of firearms and passing "right to carry" gun laws. Given the counter-cyclical tendency for the party out of power in Washington to seek opportunities to advance its agenda in the states, we may see more conservative policies emerging from the states in future years. Indeed, several Republican governors with presidential ambitions made a public show of rejecting portions of the economic stimulus package, although most of their actions were overridden by state legislatures desperate to close their state budget gaps.

Conclusion

Whether we look at federal aid trends, fiscal policy more generally, or regulatory mandates and preemption, a spike of intergovernmental growth and policy centralization occurred in the first decade of the twenty-first century. Yet such a development was not widely anticipated in the 1990s, when the United States was in the throes of a "Republican revolution" and the dual forces of globalization and localism appeared to be undermining the role of central governments worldwide. Thus, understanding the factors contributing to this trend both illuminates the political dynamics of American federalism and hints at its future trajectory.

In fact, many of the drivers historically associated with governmental growth and centralization have contributed to the current state of American federalism (ACIR, 1981). Historically, wars have been one such driver, and the so-called war on terrorism and the wars in Iraq and Afghanistan have played that role in the Bush and early Obama administrations. Not only did these conflicts accelerate the growth of federal defense spending and shift the policy agenda toward national and international affairs, but new and expanded homeland security initiatives have greatly enhanced the federal role in local law enforcement, fire, and emergency response functions, which traditionally have been among the most local of public functions in the United States.

Similarly, economic crises have stimulated federal activism since the 1930s. Thus, it is no surprise that the 2008–09 financial meltdown and recession sparked federal spending growth as automatic stabilizers kicked in and unemployed citizens, overburdened service providers, and revenue-starved state and local governments sought federal assistance. The size, scope, and speed of the federal policy response was astonishing, however. It included appropriations of $1.5 trillion for the Troubled Asset Relief Program (TARP) and the economic stimulus package, as well as other costly and aggressive policies by the Federal Reserve Board, the Federal Deposit Insurance Corporation, and the Treasury Department to address the problems of failing banks, insurance and automobile companies, and efforts by Congress to establish a new financial regulatory framework. To the extent that the economic recession also provided the political opening to enact comprehensive health care and energy reform, it will have been by far the most significant crisis – in terms of intergovernmental, political, and economic effects – since the Great Depression.

Long-term economic and demographic changes have also lent political force to intergovernmental change. Just as industrialization laid the foundation for the New Deal and post-war affluence for the Great Society, so too are economic globalization and societal aging driving long-term trends in governmental finance. Globalization and technology are eroding the future revenue streams of state and local governments, by accelerating the mobility of labor and capital, and by expanding electronic commerce. They are also driving demands for new financial and environmental regulatory frameworks adapted to a global economy. An aging society will drive long-term spending on health care and retirement programs, accelerating the growth of Medicaid in state budgets and likely crowding out discretionary spending at both the federal and state levels.

Finally, underlying political change has contributed significantly to recent intergovernmental trends. The role that state and local political parties once played as a structural check on national policy ambitions – by controlling congressional and presidential nominations, organizing the electorate, and delivering the vote – is a thing of the past (Grodzins, 1965). National political parties, leaders, interest groups, and the media all play more important roles in their stead.

Perhaps most important for understanding Bush administration policies has been the demise of conservative ideology as a principled check on the central government. Traditional institutional conservatism is a spent force. Few politicians take principled stands on federalism issues, and few voters reward them if they do. Rather, the energy within the conservative movement now resides in its social, economic, and foreign policy wings. For each of these, federalism matters only as an instrumental value. If a "state rights" stance is useful in pursuing a particular policy objective, federalist rhetoric will be embraced. If a national policy orientation is more likely to accomplish the policy goal, federalism is treated as an obstacle to progress.

This conservative transformation was emergent as early as the Reagan administration, but its ascendance was solidified under George W. Bush. This was true on a broad range of social issues. From national legislation to deal with the case of a single disabled individual, Terri Schaivo, to broad policies dealing with the medical use of marijuana, gay marriage, and physician-assisted suicide, social conservatives consistently sought preemptive national legislation over state policy autonomy during the Bush years. So too did economic conservatives prefer national solutions to state policy diversity on a broad range of economic issues, from national limitations on state taxing authority, to the federal preemption of state medical malpractice awards, to federal limitations on state environmental and consumer regulations (Greve, 2007).

Thus American conservatism has evolved, with important implications for federalism and other governing institutions. But despite current trends, federalism rarely evolves in a single, steady direction (Bowman and Krause, 2003). By definition, federal systems are polycentric and dynamic, and they rarely achieve a permanent stable balance between levels of government. In the US case, both fiscal and political challenges are likely to constrain the new centralization. In particular, long-term fiscal trends will pose daunting challenges, which are likely to be accelerated rather than solved by comprehensive health care reform. The projected growth of entitlement programs will squeeze future discretionary funding, including and perhaps especially non-Medicaid federal grants (GAO, 2007).

An overt political reaction to the growing size and influence of the federal government is also likely. With control of both Congress and the White House, Democrats will almost certainly overplay their hand. Even if they do not, unified government provides almost no bipartisan cover for unpopular decisions that will be required to rein in entitlement growth or raise revenues to finance a considerably larger government. Even in the short term, President Obama's transparency agenda will make it easier for the media and his political opponents to place a spotlight on inevitable waste and misuse of stimulus funds. However much people support programmatic activism, small-government themes still resonate with broad sectors of the American populace.

There is therefore every reason to believe that conservatives will regain power in the future, with a policy agenda that is likely to emphasize smaller government and lower taxes. But it will not be the conservatism of Eisenhower, Nixon, or Sandra Day O'Connor. Governance, politics, and public philosophy all suggest that the status of federalism in contemporary conservative ideology has been altered forever.

Chapter 11

Environmental Politics and Policy

Christopher J. Bailey

Barack Obama signaled his intention to break decisively with the policies of his predecessor and give environmental issues, particularly energy reform and climate change, a high priority in his new administration when he announced on December 15, 2008 that Nobel laureate Steven Chu would be his Energy Secretary, Lisa Jackson would lead the Environmental Protection Agency (EPA), Nancy Sutley would head the President's Council on Environmental Quality (CEQ), and Carol Browner would become "climate tsarina" with responsibility for coordinating government action on climate change. All four had strong credentials as proponents of government action to protect the environment, and stood in stark contrast to the officials of the Bush administration who were often skeptical of the need for further regulation. Obama returned to the need for action on environmental issues in his Inaugural Address on 20 January 2009 when he mentioned the threat that America's energy usage posed to the planet, referred to the "specter of a warming planet," and spoke of an ambition to "harness the sun and the winds and the soil to fuel our cars and run our factories." Presidential orders issued within days of taking office reversed a number of Bush policies on the environment, and the "New Energy for America" plan announced on January 26, 2009 included a target for substantial reductions in greenhouse gas emissions by 2050, and a promise to make the United States a leader in dealing with climate change.

Three factors explain Obama's determination to break with the environmental policy of the Bush administration. First, a growing scientific consensus about the extent and causes of global warming generated a new sense of urgency about the issue. Reports warning that rising sea levels would flood much of Florida and coastal cities such as New York and Boston, and that rising temperatures would exacerbate water shortages in the southern and western United States and threaten agricultural production in the Midwest, gained media coverage and increased public awareness of the dangers of global warming. Photographs of polar bears adrift on ice floes added to the mood of foreboding. Second, warnings about the national security threat posed by the pattern of America's energy usage and climate change gained currency. Identified threats included not only immediate concerns about the dangers of relying upon imported oil and the possibility of disruption to supplies, but also fears that climate change would increase global insecurity in the medium to long term by causing population movements, economic chaos, and conflict over resources. Finally, decisive action on environmental issues offered Obama an opportunity to show Americans that "change has come to America." In remarks about jobs, energy independence, and climate change made on January 26, 2009, Obama argued that:

> Year after year, decade after decade, we've chosen delay over decisive action. Rigid ideology has overruled sound science. Special interests have overshadowed common sense. . . . For the sake of our security, our economy and our planet, we must have the courage and commitment to change.

The challenge of engineering significant and coherent change in environmental policy is considerable. Not only are environmental problems usually complex, "unbounded," and bitterly contested, but public opinion is volatile, the policymaking arena is crowded with vested interests, and government structures act as a brake on change. Only two significant environmental statutes have been enacted since the Clean Air Act (1990), the federal government and states have been in conflict over various environmental issues, and presidential orders, bureaucratic regulations, and court rulings have produced a smorgasbord of policies that lack coherence (Klyza and Sousa, 2008). A reluctance to cede authority to international organizations and undermine national sovereignty, combined with skepticism about the intentions and actions of other countries, add further complications to the task of tackling global environmental issues.

Old and new problems

In a burst of legislative activity between 1964 and 1980, labeled the "golden era" of environmental lawmaking by some commentators, the US Congress enacted 22 major statutes to control pollution, protect wildlife, and regulate land use (Klyza and Sousa, 2008: 1, 36–7). These laws, including the Clean Air Act (1970), the Federal Water Pollution Control Act (1972), the Endangered Species Act (1973), the Resource Conservation and Recovery Act (1976), the Toxic Substances Control Act (1976), and the Comprehensive Environmental Response, Compensation, and Liability Act (1980), have produced some significant improvements in the quality of America's environment (EPA, 2008; Rosenbaum, 2007). Reductions in ambient levels of carbon monoxide, sulfur oxides, nitrogen oxides, and particulates, together with the virtual elimination of lead and formaldehyde, have resulted in much cleaner air across most of the United States. Controls on chemical discharges and improved sewage treatment works have produced cleaner rivers and lakes. Over 1000 of the country's worst polluted sites have been cleaned up under the Superfund program. A Chemical Assessment and Management Program (ChAMP) has enhanced the screening of new chemicals for health and environmental impacts. Improved protection of wildlife has allowed several endangered species, including the gray wolf, the alligator, grizzly bear, and bald eagle, to recover (FWS, 2009). Some action has even been taken to address global environmental issues.

Despite these achievements, environmental degradation remains widespread in the United States. Old problems that the "golden era" laws have failed to solve, and new problems that policymakers have failed to address, have undermined improvements elsewhere in environmental quality. The Clean Air Act has produced clear improvements in air quality, but in 2007 158.5 million Americans still lived in counties where ambient levels of "criteria pollutants," notably ozone and particulates, exceeded national air quality standards (EPA, 2009). Virtually no progress has been made in reducing non-point water pollution, particularly from agricultural or urban runoff. One in four Americans still lives within four miles of a polluted hazardous waste site. New environmental problems such as climate change pose further challenges. Reports have suggested that global warming will not only lead to rising sea levels which will threaten America's coastal cities, but also melt the snow pack in the Rocky Mountains that provides most of the water of the American west. Even the most optimistic climate models for the second half of the twenty-first century suggest that 30–70 percent of the snowpack will disappear (Gertner, 2007). Rainfall is also predicted to decrease in the western United States by 20 percent between 2040 and 2060. In the Midwest and east, climate change and the spread of non-native plant and insect pests will threaten American agriculture (Revkin, 2008).

Part of the explanation for the persistence of old problems is the complexity of the problems themselves. Problems such as non-point water pollution defy easy solutions. Agricultural runoff and similar problems cannot be resolved simply by putting controls on the end of a waste pipe. Environmental problems that involve "us" (drivers of old cars, farmers, runoff from city streets, dry cleaners) pose different challenges than those that involve "them" (factory smokestacks) (Klyza and Sousa, 2008: 31). Another part of the explanation for the persistence of these problems lies in the choice of policy instruments by the "golden era" lawmakers. Virtually all "golden era" laws rely upon command and control regulatory instruments that mandate standards or changes in behavior and punish non-compliance with penalties (fines, imprisonment). Although such regulatory methods have the advantage of directness and a simple logic, they have been criticized as rigid, costly, and inefficient. Many environmentalists, as a result, argue that greater use of market incentives, pollution prevention, and risk management should be employed in a "next generation" of environmental laws (Chertow and Esty, 1997; Graham, 1999; Kettl, 2002; Durant, Fiorino, and O'Leary, 2004). Prime examples include "cap and trade" schemes that allow individual polluters to trade permits to pollute within an overall limit on emissions.

With the exception of an emissions trading scheme for sulfur dioxide and nitrogen oxide included in the Clean Air Act (1990), no "next generation" proposals have found their way into federal law. One reason for this is that many lawmakers view policy instruments such as cap and trade schemes with considerable wariness. Trading schemes that allow polluters to buy permits to continue polluting appear counter-intuitive, difficult to explain to constituents, and may not stop factories from polluting their local environment. Another reason is that environmental lawmaking has been gridlocked at the federal level since the passage of the Clean Air Act. The only significant environmental statutes enacted during the last two decades have been the California Desert Protection Act (1994) and the Food Quality Protection Act (1996).

Numerous factors explain this gridlock, some related specifically to environmental issues, others a consequence of more general developments in congressional politics (Klyza and Sousa, 2008). First, past environmental laws have created a "green state" composed of institutions and vested bureaucratic interests that constrain change. These "tenacious organizations of power" (Skowronek, 1982) protect old values and resist reform. Second, the environmental policy arena is thick with political organizations that compete fiercely over proposed changes to laws. Myriad environmental groups, business organizations, and a grassroots "green backlash" movement protect their interests and make reform difficult. Finally, the intense partisanship that has characterized congressional politics in general over this period is also evident in environmental politics. The deregulation impulse that has dominated the Republican Party since the Reagan era has driven a wedge between Republicans and Democrats on environmental issues, and made agreement on reform difficult to achieve.

The factors that have stymied efforts to address old problems have also frustrated attempts to address new problems such as global warming. Institutional rigidities, conflicting interests, and a partisan divide have produced legislative stalemate on the question of what, if anything, the United States should do to reduce emissions of greenhouse gases. The international dimension to climate change adds a further complication to policymaking. Although the United States produces approximately 20 per cent of the world's carbon dioxide (it was overtaken by China as the largest producer in 2006), business groups and their supporters argue that American action will be meaningless unless other countries, particularly developing countries such as China and India, agree to similar reductions. In 1997, for example, the Senate passed a resolution notifying President Clinton that it would not ratify any treaty that imposed mandatory reductions in greenhouse gas emissions on the United States without imposing similar reductions on developing nations. China and India have resisted agreeing to such terms.

Who cares about the environment?

The environmental laws of the 1960s and 1970s were enacted against a backdrop of overwhelming public support and general bipartisan agreement. For example, the National Environmental Policy Act (1969) passed both the Senate and the House of Representatives by voice vote with no roll call vote needed, the Federal Water Pollution Control Act (1972) passed the Senate 74–0 and the House 336–11, and the Endangered Species Act (1973) passed the Senate unanimously and only four representatives voted against its passage in the House. Although public support for environmental protection remained high in subsequent decades, the saliency of the issue varied considerably, and partisan divisions began to emerge in Congress which destroyed the consensus of the "golden era" of environmental lawmaking. Part of this increased partisan polarization on environmental issues stemmed from broader developments in legislative politics, but the willingness of the Republican Party to listen to the demands of business and anti-green backlash groups for regulatory relief also contributed to the partisan divide (Klyza and Sousa, 2008: 22).

Opinion poll data reveals considerable stability in public attitudes toward the environment over the last decade. The proportion of Americans who identified themselves as active participants in the environmental movement, or sympathetic towards its goals, hovered around the 70 per cent mark throughout the 2000s, while only 5 percent or so regarded themselves as unsympathetic (see Figure 11.1). No significant differences in attitudes towards the environment between different social, racial, or ethnic groups have been found, while partisan and ideological differences account for only small variations in concern (Guber, 2003). This has led a number of scholars to conclude that concern for the environment is a "core American value"

Figure 11.1   *Public attitudes towards the environmental movement 2000–08*

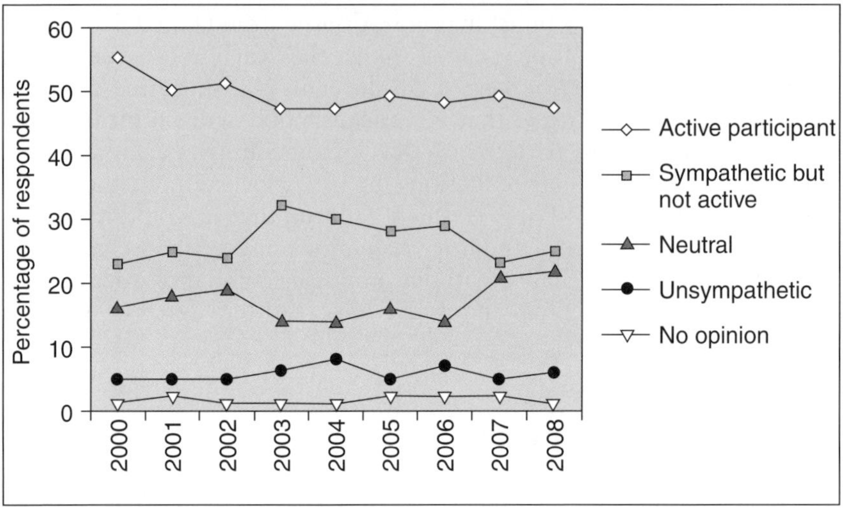

Source: compiled from Gallup Poll Data, www.gallup.com/poll/1615/Environment.
aspx.

shared by the vast majority of the population (Kempton, Boster, and
Hartley, 1995; Ladd and Bowman, 1996; Guber, 2003; Xiao and
Dunlap, 2007). Less certain are the depth, intensity, and even meaning
of the public's concern for the environment. Environmental issues
rarely arouse intense or sustained concern among the American public.
Opinion polls typically show that only 1–2 percent of Americans spon-
taneously mention the environment or pollution when asked to name
the top one or two problems they wish the government to address.
Polls that ask people to rank a number of issues by importance reveal
considerable changes in the saliency of environment concern (see
Figure 11.2). The environment is a powerful latent concern among
Americans, but usually lacks the saliency of issues such as the
economy, terror, or war. There is also little evidence that Americans
use environmental issues to evaluate government performance or
candidates for office (Guber, 2003).

The broad consensus about environmental protection evident among
the general public has disappeared among political elites. Over the last
30 years deep divisions over environmental issues have become
apparent between Republicans and Democrats in Congress (Shipan
and Lowry, 2001). In the mid-2000s the difference between mean
Republican and Democrat League of Conservation Voters (LCV)
scores (a measure of voting on environmental issues) was approximately 60 percentage points compared with 20 percentage points in
the early 1970s (see Figure 11.3). To a certain extent this partisan

Figure 11.2   *Saliency of key issues*

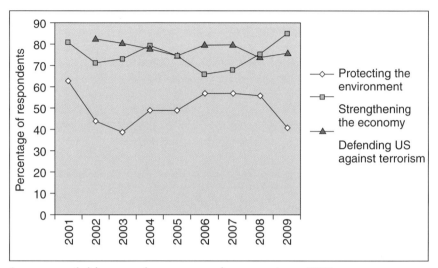

Source: compiled from new data, www.people-press.org/report/485/economy-top-policy-priority.

divide on environmental issues can be seen as part of the deep general divisions that have demarcated the parties during this period. Conflict has become commonplace over a wide range of issues. The deregulation impulse that has dominated the Republican Party since the late 1970s, however, has contributed significantly to partisan polarization on environmental issues. Most Republicans regard the "green state" created by the "golden era" laws as a prime example of big government run wild. Former House majority leader Thomas Delay (R-Tex.) even likened the EPA to the Gestapo in one comment (Gerstenzang, 2003). Requests for regulatory relief from business and anti-green interest groups have consequently found a receptive audience among Republicans.

The number and range of interest groups populating the environmental policy arena is vast. Over the last 30 years the environmental movement has grown in size and diversity, with one study estimating that there may be as many as 10,000 environmental groups operating at the national, state, and local levels (Brulle, 2000). These groups cover a wide ideological and organizational spectrum (Bosso, 2005). Mainstream groups such as the Sierra Club and the National Wildlife Federation advocate pragmatic reform, while groups such as Greenpeace and the Sea Shepherd Society often advocate nonviolent direct action. Business interests and a diverse grassroots "green backlash" movement have mobilized to challenge the environmental movement. The financial resources of business interests have allowed them

Figure 11.3   *Divergence between Democrats and Republicans on voting on environmental issues*

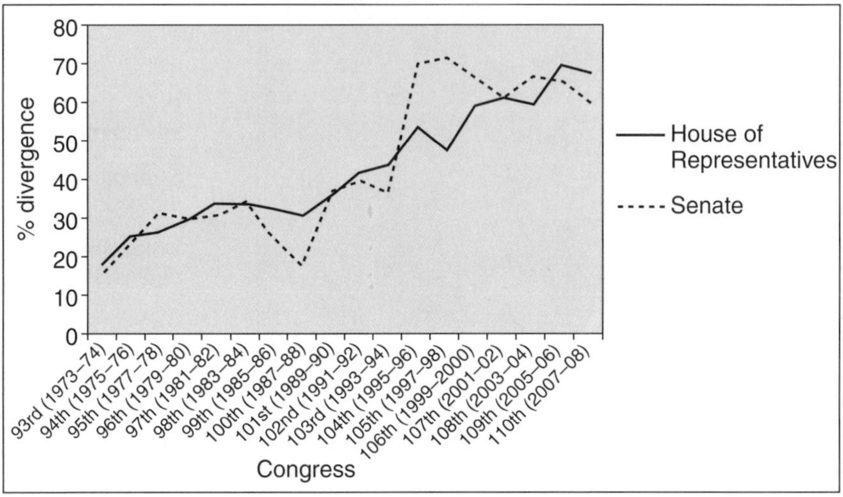

Source: compiled from LCV dats, "Past National Environmental Scorecards"
http://lcv.org/scorecard/past-scorecards/

to compete with the environmental movement. In the 2007–08 election cycle, for example, energy and natural resources industries contributed $78.4 million to federal candidates while environmental groups contributed only $4.4 million (Opensecrets, 2009). A grassroots "green backlash" movement composed of ranchers, farmers, property rights activists, outdoor recreationalists, and other similar concerns also campaigns against environmental protection (Switzer, 1997). These groups have not enjoyed much success in reversing environmental laws, but they have succeeded in highlighting the costs associated with environmental protection (Klyza and Sousa, 2008: 29).

The intense mobilization of competing interests in the environmental policy arena has contributed to legislative gridlock. Neither the environmental movement nor their opponents have proved powerful enough to advance their agendas in Congress, and each has been able to block initiatives with which they disagree. Strong public support for environmental protection has helped the environmental movement counter legislative challenges to the "green state," but the lack of saliency of environmental issues has not helped them persuade lawmakers to reform environmental statutes. This legislative gridlock has meant that the focus of environmental policymaking has shifted to the executive branch, the courts, and the states.

The Bush legacy

In January 2009 the White House published a document that commemorated the achievements of President Bush's years in office (White House, 2009). The document claimed that "Throughout his Administration, President Bush made protecting the environment for future generations a top priority" (p. 27). Improvements in air quality, forestry protection, wetlands conservation, and marine protection were cited as major achievements. The document further claimed that "President Bush worked to confront climate change through a rational and balanced approach" (p. 28). A different White House report, *The Record of the Bush Presidency 2001–2009*, told a similar story (Thiesen, 2009). In a section titled "Environment and Conservation" the report listed a number of successes that had been achieved during the Bush administration (pp. 111–14). Bush's actions on ocean conservation received the most attention, but claims were also made about his efforts to clean up abandoned and polluted industrial sites (brownfields), reduce air pollution, and conserve wildlife.

Environmental groups vehemently disputed the White House's version of history. In a review of the environmental record of the Bush administration's first term, the Natural Resources Defense Council (NRDC) declared:

> After four years in office, the George W. Bush administration has compiled an environmental record that is taking our nation in a new and dangerous direction. . . . Over the course of this first term, this administration led the most thorough and destructive campaign against America's environmental safeguards in the past 40 years. (NRDC, 2005)

The NRDC claimed that the Bush administration had attempted to weaken the Clean Air Act, narrow the scope of the Clean Water Act, undermine the Endangered Species Act, and had ignored new environmental challenges. Four years later Josh Dorner, a spokesman for the Sierra Club, claimed that "[Bush] has undone decades if not a century of progress on the environment" (quoted in Goldenberg, 2009). He argued that the Bush administration had launched an unprecedented assault on the environment that involved efforts to weaken existing laws, open public lands to mining and energy interests, and undermine science. Only Bush's designation of four Marine National Monuments in the Pacific (the Northwestern Hawaiian Islands, the Marianas Trench, the Pacific Remote Islands, and the Rose Atoll) received credit from environmentalists. "We and others in the environmental community have been at odds with this administration on a lot of things, but if one looks at this one event it is a significant conservation event" noted Joshua Reichert, managing director of the Pew Environment Group (quoted in Goldenberg, 2009).

Two general charges underpin the environmental movement's indictment of the actions of the Bush administration. First, critics argue that President Bush used his executive powers to undermine environmental statutes in a way largely hidden from the public gaze (Barcott, 2004). Executive orders, discretionary authority, and rulemaking powers have long been used by presidents to engineer change in environmental policy, but their use has increased significantly in recent years as gridlock in Congress has made it very difficult to amend environmental statutes. President Clinton used his rulemaking powers, for example, to protect nearly 60 million acres of roadless national forests from future development, tighten wetlands regulation, and adopt stricter air quality standards for ozone and particulates. The charge against Bush is not that he used these means to change policy, but that he sought to undermine laws that enjoyed popular support in an underhand way. Second, critics claim that President Bush deliberately subverted science for political reasons (Mooney, 2006). The charge is that the Bush administration engaged in a systematic effort to manipulate the membership of scientific advisory bodies, censor the findings of government scientists, and mislead the public across a wide range of policy areas, but particularly about climate change. The intention was to introduce uncertainty into discussions about global warming and minimize the importance of the issue.

President Bush indicated his willingness to use executive powers to undermine environmental protection on his first day in office, when he placed a moratorium on all environmental rules issued by his predecessor that had not yet taken effect. Two months later the White House signaled a further retreat from the policies of the Clinton administration when a spokesperson declared that the Bush administration had "no interest in implementing the Kyoto Protocol" (a treaty signed in 1997 that sought to reduce emissions of greenhouse gases).

Subsequent orders and rules sought to weaken the capacity of government agencies such as the EPA, undermine key provisions of key environmental statutes such as the Clean Air Act, the Clean Water Act, and the Endangered Species Act, and make it easier for timber, energy, and mining companies to exploit public lands. Prominent among efforts to weaken the Clean Air Act were rule changes that exempted old power stations and factories from meeting some pollution control standards (New Source Review standards), removed carbon dioxide from the list of pollutants regulated by the EPA, downgraded the regulation of mercury, and weakened controls on some air toxins. Provisions of the Clean Water Act were undermined by rule changes that allowed waste treatment plants to release treated and untreated sewage, and weakened the regulation of waste from factory farms.

Rule changes that removed a requirement for the EPA to consult with the Fish and Wildlife Service about the harmful effects of pesticides on wildlife undermined the Endangered Species Act. Further rule changes allowed timber companies greater scope to log trees in national forests, opened millions of acres of public land in the Rocky Mountains and Alaska to gas and oil drilling, and allowed mining companies greater access to protected areas. In his last weeks in office President Bush issued new rules that allowed oil companies to drill within sight of Arches National Park in Utah, removed a requirement for federal agencies to consult government wildlife experts when opening up new areas for logging or road construction, and prohibited the EPA from investigating the effects of climate change on protected species.

Administration officials claimed that President Bush used his rule-making powers to make changes in environmental policy because new laws were not needed, and involving Congress would be unnecessarily complicated (Brinkley, 2004). Critics argued that the real reason was to initiate change "below the radar," as overt attacks on environmental protections had little support among the public, and would have had little chance of passing Congress (Barcott, 2004). Opinion polls have consistently revealed little public support for weakening environmental laws in the United States. Gallup polls conducted throughout the 2000s show that the public overwhelmingly wanted stronger enforcement of federal environment regulations, higher auto emission standards for automobiles, higher emission standards for industry, and mandatory controls on carbon dioxide emissions and other greenhouse gases. Opinion was more evenly divided on the issue of allowing oil drilling in the Arctic National Wildlife Refuge in Alaska, but a majority still opposed the idea (see Table 11.1). Whereas President Clinton used his executive authority to initiate change supported by the public, President Bush employed the same powers in an effort to hide changes from an unsupportive public.

A key criticism of President Bush is that he sought to manipulate science in order to undermine public confidence in knowledge about environmental problems in general, and global warming in particular. Although all politicians employ facts selectively to achieve their ends, the charge against President Bush is that he interfered inappropriately in the work of federal scientists and the dissemination of their findings. The origins of this strategy can be traced to conservative think tanks such as the American Enterprise Institute (AEI), the Cato Institute, and the Heritage Foundation, which realized in the 1990s that they needed to challenge public thinking about global warming if they were to succeed in blocking further environmental regulation (McCright and Dunlap, 2003). To persuade policymakers and the public that global warming did not constitute a problem worthy of government action, they vigorously promoted the ideas of climate change skeptics in

Table 11.1 *Public support for specific environmental proposals (percentages)*

	Open Arctic National Wildlife Refuse for oil exploration		More strongly enforce federal environmental regulations		Set higher auto emission standards		Set higher emission standards for industry		Impose mandatory controls on carbon dioxide emissions	
	Favor	*Oppose*	*Favor*	*Oppose*	*Favor*	*Oppose*	*Favor*	*Oppose*	*Favor*	*Oppose*
2001	44	51	77	20	75	23	81	17		
2002	40	56	78	19	72	26	83	16		
2003	41	55	75	21	73	24	80	19	75	22
2006	49	47	79	20	73	25	77	22	75	23
2007	41	57	82	15	79	18	84	15	79	19

Source: compiled by author from data obtained from:www.gallup.com/poll/1615/Environment.aspx.

congressional hearings and the mass media. Environmentalists claim that when President Bush assumed office he was able to develop this strategy further. In a systematic effort to manipulate public under-standing of environmental issues, he used his powers to appoint scien-tists sympathetic to his views to scientific advisory bodies, censored the findings of government scientists, and misled the public. Surveys of federal scientists conducted by the Union of Concerned Scientists (UCS) between 2005 and 2007 provide an indication of the alleged extent of this political manipulation of science (UCS, 2009). Some care needs to be taken when interpreting the results of these surveys as it would be naïve to ignore the fact that the UCS, and the scientists sur-veyed, have their own agenda in highlighting interference in the work of scientists, but the surveys nonetheless suggest extensive political interference in scientific work, the selective use of data by political appointees to justify a regulatory outcome, scientists' fear of speaking openly about their findings, and a general sense that the work of scientists was being compromised.

Environmental groups argue that the manipulation of climate change science was at the forefront of the Bush administration's efforts to undermine scientific processes. President Bush signaled his willingness to challenge the scientific consensus on the issue when he cited scien-tific uncertainty as a reason for withdrawing from the Kyoto Protocol. In a speech on June 11, 2001 Bush stated that he would not accept emissions targets that are "arbitrary and not based on science" (Bush, 2001). A year later Bush dismissed a report prepared by EPA scientists (*US Climate Action Report: 2002*) which claimed that human activity contributed to global warming with the throwaway remark that "I've read the report put out by the bureaucracy" (quoted in Kennedy, 2003).

Evidence that the Bush administration systematically interfered with the work of climate control scientists began to emerge at this time. In September 2002, for example, officials in the White House removed an entire section on climate change from the EPA's annual report on air pollution (*Latest Findings on National Air Quality: 2002 Status and Trends*). Two years later James Hansen, a NASA scientist, publicly accused the Bush administration of trying to block the release of data that showed acceleration in global warming. UCS surveys of federal climate change scientists revealed that almost half the respondents had been pressured to remove words such as "climate change" or "global warming" from documents, and a similar number believed that officials had made inappropriate changes to their work (Mooney, 2008).

The Bush administration's failure to act on global warming, com-bined with its widespread efforts to weaken environmental protection, had the unintended consequence of galvanizing a number of states into action. State governments not only proved willing to challenge the administration's rule changes in the courts, but also launched policy initiatives of their own to fill the vacuum left by federal inaction. Lawsuits brought by individual states, or groups of states, succeeded in blocking many of the rule changes proposed by the administration (Klyza and Sousa, 2008). Court decisions delayed, or voided, changes to the rules governing New Source Review standards and other air quality regulations, pesticides, the Endangered Species Act, and the use of public lands.

The states also acted to address the problem of global warming using a two-pronged strategy that involved using litigation to force the federal government to take action, as well as launching their own policy initiatives. Prominent among the lawsuits brought by the states was a successful effort to compel the EPA to treat carbon dioxide and other greenhouse gases as pollutants (*Massachusetts* v *EPA*, 2007). Two significant policy initiatives supplemented the litigation strategy. First, states began to develop renewable portfolio standards (RPSs) that required utility companies to generate a specific amount of electricity from renewable sources (Rabe, 2004). In January 2009, 33 states had RPSs. Second, states began forming regional pacts, often involving Canadian provinces, to reduce emissions of greenhouse gases. In 2005 seven northeastern states signed the Regional Greenhouse Gas Initiative (RGGI) to cut emissions to 1990 levels by 2010 and to achieve a level 10 percent below 1990 levels by 2020. In February 2007 the governors of Arizona, California, New Mexico, Oregon, and Washington state formed the Western Climate Initiative (WCI) to tackle global warming. Utah, Montana, and the Canadian provinces of British Columbia, Manitoba, Quebec, and Ontario subsequently joined the WCI. A further regional pact was formed in November 2007 when nine Midwestern governors and the premier of Manitoba signed the Midwest GHG Reduction Accord to reduce carbon emissions and set up a trading system to meet reduction targets (Broder, 2007.

President Bush's environmental legacy is complex. An emphasis on deregulation rather than improving environmental protection undermined existing laws, and meant that old problems remained unresolved, and new problems were not addressed by the federal government. Rule changes lacked popular legitimacy, generated legal challenges, and pulled environmental policy in different directions, with the courts upholding some proposals but rejecting others. Increased tensions between the federal and state governments became evident, as the states pursued initiatives to fill the policy vacuum left by the federal government. Many environmentalists believe that the systematic denigration of science, however, is the most significant legacy left by the Bush administration. "Certainly the most destructive part of the Bush environmental legacy is not only his failure to act on global climate change, but his administration's covert attempt to silence the science alerting us to the urgency of the problem," noted Jonathan Dorn of the Earth Policy Institute (Goldenberg, 2009).

President Obama and the environment

Environmental issues came to prominence in the 2008 presidential campaign in October 2007, when Al Gore won the Nobel Peace Prize for work highlighting the threat posed by climate change. While Democratic candidates hurried to praise Gore and emphasized their party's initiatives on the issue, Republican candidates sought to distance themselves from the Bush administration's environmental record (Santora, 2007). This repudiation of Bush's approach to climate change, and environmental protection in general, continued in the general election. Both Barack Obama and John McCain concurred that global warming was a serious problem, believed in the need for federal action to reduce greenhouse gas emissions, and agreed that a cap and trade system was the best way to achieve such reductions. The main difference between the two candidates centered on the size and speed of required cuts in emissions of greenhouse gases. Obama proposed cutting emissions of carbon dioxide to 80 percent of their 1990 level by 2050, while McCain proposed a 60 percent cut. Both candidates also supported ocean drilling, opposed drilling in the Arctic National Wildlife Refuge, and stated that they would reverse a Bush administration decision not to grant California permission to regulate carbon dioxide emissions from cars. Environmental interest groups and the public, however, believed that Obama offered the best way forward on environmental issues. He received the endorsement of all mainstream environmental groups, and opinion polls consistently showed that the public thought he had the best ideas on energy and the environment (Garber, 2008).

Obama confirmed his willingness to take a new approach to environmental issues when he announced his key energy and environmental appointments on December 15, 2008. He appointed Steven Chu, a Nobel laureate and director of the Lawrence Berkeley National Laboratory (one of the federal government's most prestigious research facilities) as energy secretary. Not only did Chu have impeccable credentials as a scientist, he also had a reputation as a campaigner for action on climate change. "[Chu's] appointment should signal to all that my administration will value science," Obama stated in a direct, if partisan, rebuke of his predecessor, "We will make decisions based on facts" (quoted in Goldenberg, 2009). Obama's decision to appoint Carol Browner, a former administrator of the EPA during the Clinton administration, to a newly created post of White House coordinator for energy and environment ("climate tsarina") also signaled a new determination to take climate change more seriously. Browner had the task of coordinating government action on energy and climate change. Gene Karpinski, head of the League of Conservation Voters, claimed that Chu and Browner constituted "a green dream team" (quoted in Goldenberg, 2009). Obama also appointed Lisa Jackson, New Jersey's commissioner of environmental protection, as administrator of the EPA, and Nancy Sutley, deputy mayor of Los Angeles for energy and environment, as head of the Council on Environmental Quality.

Action on environmental issues came early in the new administration. On January 26, 2009 President Obama announced a "New Energy for America" plan that promised $150 billion investment in alternative and renewable energy sources, reductions in greenhouse gas emissions, and American leadership on climate change. In his remarks introducing the plan, President Obama explicitly criticized key aspects of President Bush's environmental legacy. First, he argued that "the federal government must work with, not against, states to reduce greenhouse gas emissions." Second, he promised that "my administration will not deny the facts, we will be guided by them." And finally, he declared that "we will make it clear to the world that America is ready to lead" on climate change. Obama subsequently signed presidential memoranda that required the EPA to reconsider a waiver requested by California and 13 other states allowing them to set stricter standards on car emissions, directed the Department of Transport to finalize interim regulations requiring the car industry to increase national fuel efficiency standards, and instructed federal departments and agencies to save energy and be more environmentally friendly. Environmentalists welcomed these initiatives. Frances Beinecke, president of the Natural Resources Defense Council, claimed that "Just days into office, President Obama is showing America and the world that he will lead our country in a bold new direction to protect the environment and fight global warming" (quoted in Maynard, 2009).

President Obama's order requiring the EPA to reconsider California's waiver request signified a sharp reversal of Bush administration policy, and fulfilled a campaign pledge. California enacted a law in 2002 requiring car manufacturers to reduce emissions of carbon dioxide and other greenhouse gases, and in 2004 set standards for these emission reductions. Under the terms of the Clean Air Act (1990), California is given unique authority to set stricter emission standards than required by federal law (which other states may adopt) provided the EPA issues a waiver to do so. The Bush administration refused California's request for a waiver in 2007, claiming that it was unnecessary and would result in a chaotic patchwork of environmental law, where some states adhered to one set of emission standards and others conformed to another. The EPA finally granted the waiver in June 2009. Other action to reverse rule changes made by President Bush included stopping drilling in national parks, and requiring government agencies to consult with the Fish and Wildlife Service on whether new developments posed a threat to endangered species. The EPA also issued an important finding in April 2009 that defined greenhouse gases as air pollutants that may endanger public health or welfare. This finding opened the way for the future regulation of gases such as carbon dioxide.

Efforts to enact legislation requiring reductions in greenhouse gas emissions have proved a challenge. In his address to a joint session of Congress on February 24, 2009 President Obama called for "legislation that places a market-based cap on carbon pollution." Four months later the House of Representatives passed the American Clean Energy and Security (ACES) Act, otherwise known as the Waxman–Markey bill, which contained a cap and trade system that would bind the United States to phased reductions in greenhouse gas emissions. Other provisions included initiatives to promote renewable energy sources and support energy efficiency programs. Although passage of this bill was lauded as a significant achievement and hailed as signaling a new willingness to address climate change, the negotiations and compromises necessary to secure votes in the House of Representatives diluted many of the environmental targets contained in earlier versions of the legislation (Broder, 2009). Greenhouse gas emissions targets were weakened, emissions permits were given free to polluting industries, and renewable energy targets were watered down. Demands for similar compromises also characterized initial discussion in the Senate of companion legislation.

President Obama acknowledged the political difficulties of securing agreement for meaningful greenhouse gas reductions when he told leaders at the G8 Summit in L'Aquila on 9 July 2009 that he had to "wrestle with these issues politically in my own country." Awareness of the fragility of support for action on climate change in the US Congress also shaped Obama's response to demands for action at the G8 Summit. Although he took the symbolically important step of agreeing that countries should take action to ensure that global temperatures should not rise by more than 2 °C on pre-industrial levels, and committed the United States to a goal of cutting greenhouse gas emissions by 80 percent by 2050, he refused to accept interim targets for emission reductions by 2020 because he believed this would undermine congressional support for the ACES Act. He also insisted that no agreement to tackle climate change would be effective without developing countries accepting the need for reductions in their emissions. "We also agree that developed countries, like my own, have a historic responsibility to take the lead," he told the G8 Summit on 9 July 2009,

"Yet, with most of the growth in projected emissions coming from these [developing] countries, their active participation is a prerequisite for a solution."

Conclusion

President Obama's early use of his executive power to reverse many of the rule changes made by the Bush administration is testimony to both his commitment to change the direction of American environmental policy, and the ease with which presidents can nullify decisions made by their predecessors. While environmentalists have praised Obama's actions, the problem is that the use of executive power to produce change can lead to wild swings in policy. Just as Obama reversed decisions made by his predecessor, so a future president may reverse decisions made by Obama. Legislation is needed to bring stability to environmental policy. Enacting new environmental laws, however, is difficult to achieve. Not only are the parties polarized on environmental issues, there are also significant divisions within the Democratic Party. Democrats representing coal-producing Midwest states, for example, have different interests than their colleagues from elsewhere. "Green/brown" divisions in the Democratic Party, in other words, may complicate environmental lawmaking as much as the "red/blue" divide between the two parties (Bomberg and Super, 2009). Overcoming such obstacles will not be easy in a period of recession when legislators are hypersensitized to the economic well-being of their constituents. President Obama's engagement with environmental issues certainly marks a change from his predecessor, but does not signal the beginning of a new "golden age" of environmental policymaking.

Chapter 12

The American Economy in Crisis

George A. (Sandy) Mackenzie

Introduction

The Obama administration took office at a point when the American economy was confronting its most profound crisis since the Great Depression. That crisis, which to a large extent had its origins in the US sub-prime mortgage market, obviously constrained Obama's early policy priorities and meant that his political prospects would be dependent on the strength and speed of American economic recovery. The sheer scale of the crisis, which was global in its reach and threatened the stability of the international economic order, meant that Obama and his economic team were in wholly new territory and that there could be little confidence that the economic and financial measures available to them would work.

The severity of the crisis that overtook the American and the world economies from the middle of 2007 should not be allowed to mask the fact that the United States had already experienced a period of economic turbulence. Indeed George W. Bush had himself inherited a gloomy economic situation when he took office in 2001. Unlike President Clinton, who took office when the American economy was coming out of a recession and presided over the dot.com boom, President George W. Bush took office when the American economy had already slipped into recession in the wake of the collapse of the boom. The terrorist attacks of 9/11 in 2001 worsened the overall economic situation by shaking the confidence of consumers and business investors alike. However, and in part because of the Federal Reserve's policy of aggressive interest rate cutting, the economy began to recover in 2003, and enjoyed robust growth until 2007. Inflation, which reached historical lows in 2002, was pushed up by the rise in energy prices in 2005–07, but core inflation – inflation adjusted for the impact of food and energy prices – remained low. Unemployment, which had risen as high as 6.3 percent of the labor force in 2003, fell below 5 percent by the end of 2005. Overall, therefore, macroeconomic performance, if it is gauged by the standard indicators of GDP growth, inflation, and unemployment, was reasonably good for most of President Bush's two terms.

The standard indicators could not tell the whole story of an economy with serious vulnerabilities that would shortly precipitate a severe recession and contribute to the global financial and economic crisis that erupted in the fall of 2008. As this chapter will explain, the low interest rates that marked the Bush administration contributed to an unsustainable boom in housing prices and encouraged financial institutions to take risky bets to increase their rate of return. Even during the good years, the country's social safety net was beginning to fray, and the recession has worsened the situation.

In more normal times, this chapter would survey American economic developments and federal government economic policy during the eight years of the Bush administration as a prelude to the analysis of the economic policy issues facing his successor. Because of the momentous consequences of the global economic and financial crisis, the chapter is instead largely devoted to explaining its causes and consequences for the American economy. To set the stage for this analysis, the chapter briefly reviews economic developments during the Bush administration, provides some background on the institutions of fiscal and monetary policy, and briefly summarizes the President's budget for Fiscal Year (FY) 2010. It then turns to its main subject and to a discussion of some basic structural issues that have long predated the crisis, and notably the financial imbalances of Social Security and Medicare/Medicaid.

Developments prior to the emergence of the crisis

The recovery of the American economy from the recession of 2001–03 was sustained by the accommodating interest rate policy already noted and by an expansionary fiscal policy. The federal funds rate, which, as is explained below is the standard instrument of monetary policy, had been lowered from 6.5 percent at the end of 2000 in a series of steps to 1.0 percent by June 2004. This aggressive policy of monetary easing had been partly motivated by the fear that the economy might experience what economists call deflation, when prices are actually falling, or close to falling. The stagnation of the Japanese economy during the deflationary decade of the 1990s heightened the concerns of the Federal Reserve and other central banks that the United States and other economies might become mired in a similar plight. Although in retrospect it appears that deflation was less likely than it appeared to be at the time, the rate of inflation had already fallen to low levels, and would have fallen further had recovery not set in.

The Federal Reserve's policy of low interest rates was undoubtedly abetted by the willingness of the rest of the world to finance the large and sustained deficit on the external current account (roughly, the difference between what the United States buys and what it sells abroad, minus net income and transfers from abroad) that marked these years. Normally, low interest rates might have caused the dollar to depreciate excessively. However, the demand by non-residents for US dollar securities was so strong that this did not happen. The counterpart to these deficits was a substantial increase in the reserves of creditor countries, mainly China and other Asian countries. Economists assume as a rule that large current account deficits are not sustainable indefinitely, essentially because surplus countries lose their appetite for the debt that is issued to finance them. At the time, however, arguments were advanced that this pattern might be quasi-permanent (Morris, 2008: 91–5).

Whatever their rationale in macroeconomic policy terms, the low interest rates of 2001–04 contributed to a boom in asset prices, and notably in the price of housing. When interest rates on bonds and similar assets decline, the return on other assets becomes relatively more attractive. Rising house prices in turn spurred a boom in new residential construction, and made it easier for homeowners to borrow on the strength of the equity in their homes (the sales value of their home minus the principal value of mortgage and home equity loans). Personal consumption was the mainstay of aggregate demand during this period and later years, in large part because of the increased collateral that a buoyant housing market permitted. Of course, although high prices benefit homeowners, they pose a barrier to would-be homeowners. The subprime mortgage crisis was fueled in part by homebuyers desperate for a mortgage on terms that they could, or thought they could, afford. The consequences of easy mortgage money are picked up again in the section on the origins of the financial crisis.

One striking feature of financial markets in the years leading up to the crisis was the narrow spread between both long-term rates and short-term rates (for example, the difference between ten-year Treasury bonds and three-month Treasury bills), and very high-quality and less high-quality debt. Low spreads mean low profit margins. Their persistence prompted investors to increase their leverage – the ratio of borrowed funds to equity or their own funds in the financing of an investment – in an effort to restore them. (An example may illustrate how increasing leverage works. Suppose that an institution with assets of $500 billion, deposits and other liabilities of $400 billion, and net worth of $100 billion, paid 5 percent per annum on its liabilities and earned 10 percent on its assets. The institution would have net earnings of $30 billion per year, or 30 percent of capital. With more leverage, specifically with liabilities of $900 billion and assets of $1 trillion and the same capital base, it would earn $55 billion, or 55 percent of capital. Leverage is risky. If the rate of earnings on assets dropped to 3 percent, the institution would incur losses. Losses with less leverage are $5 billion, but with increased leverage they rise to $15 billion.)

Low spreads also prompted the creation and widespread use of complex new financial instruments that would squeeze extra yield out of a given investment. This phenomenon, which came to be known as the hunt for yield, was a risky strategy, essentially because it was based on very high rates of leverage. With high leverage, even moderate declines in the value of the assets the leveraged equity finances can erase investor equity.

In the light of the recovery and the increase in oil prices that began in 2004, the Federal Reserve began to increase interest rates in June 2004. The federal funds rate was increased in a series of steps, reaching a high of $5\frac{1}{4}$ percent in July 2006. In spite of the increase in short-term rates, overall credit conditions remained relatively easy. The stance of fiscal policy, which had been greatly relaxed – that is, made more stimulative – in 2001–03 by two successive tax cuts, and the increase in military expenditures for the wars in Iraq and Afghanistan, remained more or less neutral – unchanged – until 2008, when the rescue programs for the financial sector caused the deficit to balloon.

Contrary to the impression given by the conservative media, the domestic discretionary expenditure programs of the federal government were not out of control. The much-publicized practice of earmarking, in which expenditure projects favored by particular congressmen are tacked on to a spending bill, has not had significant macroeconomic consequences. In 2005 for example, earmarks were estimated to amount to $27.3 billion or 0.2 percent of GDP, about double but only 0.1 percent of GDP higher than they were in 2000 (Bartlett, 2006: 213).

By late 2007, the support for economic growth from household consumption was beginning to flag. The economy officially entered a recession in the fourth quarter of 2007, mainly because of a huge drop in new housing construction together with a slowdown in the growth of personal consumption and business investment. Aggregate demand growth fell significantly. The housing market was already in serious trouble at this point. Nationwide housing prices had started to decline in 2006, and the level of residential construction had been falling for several quarters. By the second half of 2008, the combination of declining house prices and stock market values had drastically reduced households' net worth, and household real incomes were lowered by a huge increase in the price of gasoline. The price of regular gasoline topped $4.00 per gallon in July.

The combination of this negative wealth effect and concerns over the security of jobs and incomes in retirement led households to cut their expenditure. Monthly job losses, which averaged about 80,000 at the beginning of the year, increased to average about 640,000 in the last two months. High job losses continued in the first four months of 2009, and real GDP is estimated to have declined by 6.1 percent at an annual rate in the first quarter. Although many observers claimed there were some signs that the recession had bottomed out, the outlook for the American economy in the summer of 2009 was quite uncertain.

The budget and fiscal policy

In any country, changing the direction of fiscal policy is akin to changing the direction of an ocean liner: neither budgets nor big ships can turn on a dime. In no industrial country is this truer than in the United States. The American budgetary process is exceptionally complex. Its complexity derives from the two basic characteristics of a republican system of government: the considerable independence normally enjoyed by the legislative branch, and the substantial power of the Senate. Although many parliamentary democracies have a bicameral system, the American Senate has far more power than upper chambers in other countries. Consequently, in the United States, budgetary process entails two different negotiations: one between the executive and legislative branches, and one within the legislative branch between the House and the Senate. The comparative bargaining position of the legislature is enhanced by its access to the studies and analyses of budgetary and fiscal issues prepared by the Congressional Budget Office (CBO). This agency, which was established in 1974, has a large and expert staff and enjoys a well-deserved reputation on Capitol Hill for impartial and high-quality analysis. Its website is a source of countless informative studies of US fiscal policy and related topics.

Budget preparation and approval

The federal government's fiscal year begins in October – so that FY2009 runs from October 2008 to September 2009 – and the budgetary process begins about 18 months earlier (in the spring of the previous calendar year) with the preparation of the President's budget. The Office of Management and Budget (OMB), which is part of the White House, takes the lead in this effort, which includes preparing spending authorizations for all the federal government's departments and agencies. The preparation of the budget is a laborious task which entails discussions between the OMB and all the government's departments and agencies. Once this work is done, the President's budget is presented to Congress in early February, about eight months before the start of the fiscal year.

The President's budget goes to the budget committees of the House and the Senate. Unlike the case in many countries, neither House nor Senate is required to accept the budgetary projection for expenditure, its components, or the projections for revenue. The House and Senate budget committees, having studied the budget, may propose their own estimates for total revenues, total expenditure, and their major components. The CBO assists them with the technical aspects of this work. Its outcome is known as the *concurrent budget resolution* (or simply the budget resolution), which has to be approved by the budget committees and then by the full House and Senate. As a resolution, it lacks the force of law. Instead, it serves as a disciplining fiscal framework for the ensuing deliberations.

The budget resolution lacks the detail of the President's budget. Its purpose is to guide the work of the 13 appropriations sub-committees in the House and the Senate, each of which is given an expenditure ceiling for their particular area. Congress is supposed to approve the budget resolution by April 15, but this deadline is not always observed.

The budget resolution may contain a *reconciliation directive* which requires tax measures or changes to entitlement programs to achieve an overall target for the deficit. These proposed measures are taken up by the regular House and Senate authorizing committees to change permanent laws affecting both receipts and outlays. Directives specify dollar amounts for each authorizing committee, and not the measures to be taken to achieve the monetary targets. The budget committees' reports can discuss specific measures, however. The implementing legislation that is drafted by the committees subject to reconciliation directives is combined in a (single) omnibus budget reconciliation act. Senate debate on these bills is conducted under expedited procedures which limit total debate.

The appropriations process starts in the House, with House appropriation committees preparing appropriation bills for their particular area. Once the bills receive the approval of the House, they are forwarded to the Senate and the corresponding Senate appropriations committee. If necessary a conference committee resolves any differences. Once both houses have approved a bill, it is sent to the President for his approval. The President may veto an entire bill, but not some parts of a bill and not others. The budgetary process may be said to be completed when all the appropriations bills have been passed. No vote takes place on the budget as a whole.

About 60 per cent of the federal government's expenditure – mainly the expenditure of the entitlements programs and interest on the national debt – does not have to be approved by Congress unless changes are being made to the programs. In practice, Congress will sometimes make changes to certain entitlement programs to offset the impact of revisions to the total of expenditure appropriations.

When an appropriations bill is not enacted by the beginning of the fiscal year, Congress usually enacts a joint resolution called a *continuing resolution*, which is an interim appropriations bill. Presidents can veto a continuing resolution if they find some of its provisions unacceptable. The operations covered by the bill are then required to shut down (with the exception of some activities). Brief shutdowns of parts of the government did take place during the Clinton administration. They are not a common occurrence.

The standard discussion of the efficacy of fiscal policymaking that is found in an intermediate macroeconomics textbook essentially ignores these institutional complexities, usually noting only that there is a lag between the perception of a problem, like sagging aggregate demand and rising unemployment, and the implementation of a revised budget to deal with it. This chapter's brief description makes clear that the federal budget as such cannot be a nimble instrument of macroeconomic management. That said, it is possible to pass what are effectively supplementary budgets relatively quickly. The American Recovery and Reinvestment Act (ARRA) of 2009, which included stimulus measures totaling about $800 billion – most of which would take effect in 2009–12 – took about two months from conception to passage by the House and Senate.

The federal nature of American government in and of itself is not an impediment to activist fiscal policy. Although the federal government's expenditure and revenue are each about two-thirds of general government expenditure and revenue, the comparatively broad base of the federal income tax and the size of its expenditure programs mean that the federal government can in principle inject or withdraw a sizeable fiscal stimulus if the executive and legislative branches can agree on a package.

The FY2010 budget

The drafters of the new administration's first budget faced daunting challenges. The budget had to balance the urgent need for short-run stimulation of the economy with President Obama's ambitious reform agenda and the compelling need to prevent runaway growth in the deficits and the debt of the federal government. Although huge deficits were unavoidable in the first two years of the new administration given the state of the economy, the government's borrowing requirement would have to be reined in sharply in later years.

The FY2010 budget makes projections over a ten-year period, although Congress will ultimately approve a one-year budget. On the expenditure side, declining outlays under ARRA and an assumed substantial decline in outlays for the Middle East conflicts reduce the ratio of expenditure to GDP to 22.2 percent by 2012, although it remains above its historical rate.

On the revenue side of the budget, the ratio gradually increases from the low point it reached in FY2009, aided by an assumed recovery of profits and personal income growth. The budget includes proposed cuts in tax for 95 percent of the taxpaying population. The impact of these cuts on revenues is offset by a limitation on itemized deductions, a phase-out of the personal exemption, increased capital gains tax rates, and an increase in the top bracket applying to taxpayers earning more than $250,000 if married (and more than $200,000 if single), as well as various measures to close loopholes, with an average annual yield of about 0.2 percent of GDP. Some of these measures will undoubtedly meet with resistance in Congress, because they challenge various special interests. No general tax increase is included in the budget, although this could be necessary if expenditure is not brought under control or the projected deficits cannot be financed.

Every budget is built around a macroeconomic framework, which is a consistent set of projections of the national accounts and other key macroeconomic aggregates such as the unemployment rate, consumer price inflation, and interest rates. The FY2010 budget's framework makes optimistic assumptions about the economy's recovery from what nearly all observers believe will be a deep recession. After a projected decline of 1.2 percent in calendar year 2009, real GDP is projected to grow by 3.2 percent in 2010. The projected growth rate increases further, reaching 4.6 percent in 2012 before declining to the more sustainable rate of 2.6 percent in the out years.

The deficit remains close to or above 3 percent throughout the ten-year projection period, and the ratio of federal debt held by the public to GDP does not decline below 65 percent. Despite the increase in debt, the budget assumes that interest rates will increase from their current low levels but remain moderate in both real and nominal terms by historical standards. This is a key assumption of the macroeconomic framework, which could prove to be unrealistic if the dollar comes under downward pressure and the Federal Reserve is forced to intervene and push interest rates up to stem its decline.

Much of the summary budget document is given over to the cost of health care reform, and the scope for cost reductions. However, projections of the impact of reform are not actually incorporated in the budgetary estimates. The document notes the considerable scope for cost savings. It is particularly telling that the same medical procedures can have vastly different price tags in different parts of the country, without any apparent difference in patients' health outcomes. (See Chapter 13 on social policy, which discusses the issue of health care reform in some detail.)

Monetary policy

In contrast with fiscal policy, the stance of monetary policy – as reflected in the level of short-term interest rates – can be altered very quickly. This difference reflects the more technocratic nature of the monetary policy process as well as the instruments with which monetary policy is conducted. Changes in the monetary stance do not require the approval of either the executive or the legislative branches, and the policymaking apparatus of the Federal Reserve, America's central bank, is designed expressly to allow it to make speedy decisions. Specifically, the Federal Open Market Committee normally meets ten times a year – and can meet more often than that.

The outcome of these meetings determines whether the Fed will act to move interest rates up or down, or leave them unchanged, and the communiqué that is issued at the conclusion of each meeting is intended to give a signal about the future direction of monetary policy. Its language has often been criticized for its opacity, but in the light of the uncertain future that any policymaker confronts, precise language about future policy changes may not be called for. The current chairman, Ben Bernanke, who succeeded Alan Greenspan in February 2006, comes from an extremely distinguished academic background, and his approach to communication is considered more direct than that of his predecessor.

Notwithstanding the greater flexibility that monetary policy enjoys, the Fed is not in a position to determine the full range of interest rates from very short to long maturities (the yield curve, in more technical parlance). This became apparent in the run-up of short-term rates that the Fed oversaw in 2004–06, which did not result in much change in long-term rates, which have more of an impact than short-term rates on expenditure decisions. This said, the enormous prestige of the Fed means that markets avidly absorb and analyze its views on the economic outlook. The monetary policy tools that the Fed normally wields are well suited to an essentially stable economy. However, as the section on the origins of the financial crisis explains, they proved insufficient to deal with the panicky financial environment that developed in the fall of 2008.

Origins of the financial crisis

The financial crisis originated with the unsustainable increase in American housing prices that began in 2000, the negligent lending practices of financial institutions in the housing market, and the inadequate regulation of that sector. Its effects were magnified by the use of complex and unregulated financial instruments called derivatives, which effectively spread the risk far beyond the original lender, and even beyond the United States itself.

American housing prices had been rising since the mid-1990s, but between 2000 and 2006 they almost doubled, fueled in part by the very expansionary monetary policy stance adopted by the Federal Reserve in the wake of the terrorist attacks, which it was feared would aggravate the recession then underway. From the perspective of traditional monetary policy, the measure of inflation that needs to be controlled is a measure of the cost of currently produced goods and services, like the retail or consumer price indexes. Asset price inflation – increases in the price of the housing stock and other assets – was also a concern, because rising wealth would indirectly lead to an increase in consumer price inflation as consumption demand increased, but also because of the potentially disruptive effects of a bursting asset price bubble. At the time, however, both the Federal Reserve and most other central banks deemed the risk that asset price inflation posed to be less than the risk of deflation. The deflation that plagued Japan in the 1990s was the sequel to the bursting of that country's asset bubble.

An expansionary monetary policy can have a particularly stimulating effect on the housing market, if it lowers long-term interest rates, since lower rates will substantially reduce the cost of carrying a mortgage of a given principal amount. Expansionary monetary policy was not the only source of the increase in housing prices, however.

The 2002–06 period saw a substantial increase in the share of the so-called subprime mortgage market. In principle, the subprime market is simply a market for borrowers who are less creditworthy than the average borrower. Subprime mortgages would as a result carry both a higher rate of return on average and be subject to a higher than average risk of default, in the same way that interest rates on corporate debt exceed rates on government debt, which is deemed to be risk-free. However, the market was excessively stimulated by the role played by Fannie Mae and Freddy Mac, the two giant "government-sponsored enterprises" established in the 1930s to promote home ownership, which offered a kind of insurance to mortgage holders that proved to be underpriced, by predatory lending practices that saddled financially naïve would-be homeowners with properties they simply could not afford, and by lax regulation.

A common feature of subprime loans (and of many prime market loans) is a low starting interest rate (the so-called teaser rate), which can be hiked up after only a few months. Many borrowers either failed to understand this crucial feature of their loan, or assumed mistakenly that if they could no longer afford to carry the home they would at least enjoy rising resale values. After 2006, this was no longer generally correct.

A further development stimulating house prices was the growth of the market for mortgage-backed securities (MBS). MBS are created when a financial institution buys up a large number of mortgages and creates a new security backed by the mortgages. The securities thus created were sold to other financial institutions in the United States and abroad, and to other investors as well. The pooling of income that a MBS entails should also pool risk. A crucial feature of this "originate to distribute" model is that the initial appraiser and lender sell the mortgage shortly after approving it. Compared with traditional lenders, mortgage brokers have less incentive to perform due diligence during the approval process.

The growth of the MBS market helped in turn to stimulate the growth of the market for complex derivative securities, and notably credit default swaps (CDS). CDS offer a kind of insurance to holders of debt. (A derivative is so called because its price depends on (is derived from) the price of other securities. Credit default swaps, which entail an obligation to insure holders of debt against default, lose value when the risk of the debt's defaulting increases, lowering its price.) In return for a part of the income stream of the debt instruments, the issuer of the CDS agrees to insure the debt holder against default. Investments in derivative investments became very highly leveraged, meaning that small price movements could wipe the investor out. With the benefit of hindsight, it is clear that the riskiness of these new instruments and the degree to which investments in them were leveraged were not well understood. In particular, the extent to which defaults or declining values of one type of debt might be correlated with another type was not adequately appreciated.

Housing prices tend to move cyclically in any country, and the housing price boom in the United States was to some extent part of a global phenomenon. Perhaps because of this, and because rising rates of home ownership are a tenet of American politics, both Republican and Democrat, relatively few voices were raised to sound an alarm.

The first financial institutions to find themselves in deep trouble were those most heavily involved in the mortgage market. Bear Sterns, an investment bank that was heavily exposed to the market for MBS, was forced to merge with JP Morgan in March 2008 (Morris, 2008: xiii). In the fall of 2008, the government took over Freddie Mac and Fanny Mae. These enterprises earned most of their income from the fees on the guarantees they offered on the MBS they sold. In addition to being exposed to the difficulties of the MBS market, both institutions were heavily leveraged. This made them especially vulnerable to the declining housing market. Two other giant private mortgage lenders, Countrywide and Washington Mutual, were also forced to merge or be sold.

As the difficulties of the mortgage-lending institutions spread to the rest of the financial sector, the Federal Reserve and the Treasury had to wrestle with the agonizingly difficult question of whether a particular institution was too big to fail. The government encouraged the Bear Sterns merger, but when the venerable investment-banking firm Lehman Brothers was on the brink of collapse (having delayed finding a source of additional capital), it was allowed to go bankrupt. This decision was severely criticized by the financial industry, on the grounds that Lehman Brothers really was too big to fail – its role in the derivatives market meant that it was part of the basic wiring of the system, and not just another financial institution. The subsequent behavior of the derivatives market suggested the financial industry was right. Following Lehman's collapse, AIG, the giant insurance company with a huge exposure to the collateralized debt obligation market, did receive the support it sought.

As many observers have pointed out, the word "credit" comes from the Latin *credo* (meaning: I trust). Lending, in other words, requires some degree of basic trust by both lender and borrower. Lending between financial institutions essentially dried up in late 2008 because the necessary degree of trust was no longer present.

The bailout

In the fall of 2008, when the outlook was particularly troubled, Congress passed on a second try the Bush administration's Troubled Assets Relief Program (TARP). TARP allocated some $700 billion to provide relief to financial institutions by taking their troubled assets off their books. The program came under almost immediate fire from financial economists and other observers, who argued that its objectives were misconceived, and that the taxpayer would be stuck with a huge bill if the assets could not be resold at a fair price. Many in Congress faulted the program for not stimulating fresh lending, and not holding financial institutions sufficiently accountable for the funds they received. More generally, it was argued that TARP should concentrate on recapitalizing the banking system. These early difficulties led to a change in the use of TARP's funds. They were now to be used to recapitalize the banks.

A basic political difficulty with any bank bailout is giving it a satisfactory social rationale. That rationale would be based on the axiom that the financial sector, or a big part of it, is a kind of utility, and as such cannot be allowed to go bankrupt, because its bankruptcy would bring down the rest of the economy. In a typical bank rescue program, there is considerable consolidation of the industry, with many banks being wound up and others merged. However, rescues do typically involve the recapitalization, with public money, of loss-making private institutions. The combination of private profits and socialized losses is hard for the typical voter to take, especially if he (or she) has just lost a job.

In light of the difficulties initially experienced with TARP, the new administration was under enormous pressure to come up with a program that would really work. In March 2009, Timothy Geithner, the new Secretary of the Treasury, announced a program of asset purchases that would be based on private-sector participation, known as the Public Private Investment Program (PPIP). Unlike programs that other countries dealing with systemic bank crises have implemented, in which the whole operation was carried out by a public-sector agency, the PPIP invites private-sector investors to bid for the distressed assets of financial institutions The government's role is to provide additional equity and provide or guarantee additional financing.

The participation of the private sector was a potentially strong selling point in the United States. In countries where the banking system itself was largely in public hands, it would seem natural to leave the bailout entirely in the government's hands. Nonetheless, the proposal immediately attracted strong criticism from a number of prominent economists. Their basic objection was that the terms of the program saddled the government with any losses, but gave away the bulk of the gains to the private sector. On the whole, however, the program was initially well received.

The role of monetary policy during the crisis

The Federal Reserve allowed short-term interest rates to drop to close to zero in the fall of 2008 in an effort to revive the economy. It became apparent, however, that the standard instruments of monetary policy would not be effective in this kind of crisis. Consequently, the Fed adopted a far more aggressive approach. It started to operate at the long end of the market, meaning that it bought up long-term securities in an attempt to influence their price more directly. The Fed also bought troubled assets from a number of financial institutions. To the extent that these operations had a subsidy element to them, they were quasi-fiscal operations – operations of a basically fiscal nature carried out by a public financial institution. However, they would not be subject to the same degree of congressional scrutiny.

Structural issues

Long-run fiscal trends

The unified budget balance of the federal government, which incorporates the current financial operations of Social Security and Medicare/Medicaid, was in surplus at the outset of the Bush administration. The combination of recession, two rounds of tax cuts, and the Iraq war pushed it into deficit. By 2007, the deficit had stabilized and declined as a percentage of GDP, in part because of the impact of growing inequality of personal incomes on the yield of the personal income tax. (The share in total income of more wealthy Americans has increased, and the progressive nature of the income tax implies that the ratio of tax revenues to income should increase as a result.)

Even if the expenditures of the ARRA are non-recurring, the deficit can be expected to worsen substantially without major reforms. An end to hostilities in Iraq and Afghanistan would improve the short-run picture, but have little impact on the underlying trend, which will have been worsened by the extra interest payments on the recently issued public debt.

The worsening budgetary trend is partly caused by an aging population, which is gradually reducing the surplus of the social security system, and contributing to the increase in Medicare and Medicaid expenditure. The latest intermediate (neither particularly optimistic nor pessimistic) projections of the Old Age Survivors' and Disability Insurance (OASDI) program trustees has the balance of Social Security declining from a surplus of 0.6 percent of GDP in 2008 to a deficit of 1.2 percent in 2045 (SSA, 2008a: 179). Growing deficits are a feature of nearly all the world's public pension systems, and reflect the fact that with the retirement of the baby boom generation the number of pensioners is growing more rapidly than the number of workers who finance the pensions with the payroll taxes they and their employers pay. Increasing life spans also contribute.

The finances of Medicare and Medicaid pose an even more serious problem, one that was exacerbated by the passage of the bill to subsidize the cost of pharmaceuticals to older Americans – Medicare Part D – which took effect in 2006. Population aging is again a contributing factor, but the basic reason is the increase in the cost of treatments and diagnostic tests. Technical progress in medical care is usually not of the cost-reducing variety, like the continued large falls in the cost of computing power. Instead, medical progress usually takes the form of ever more sophisticated equipment that makes possible treatments for conditions previously untreatable (Aaron and Schwartz, 2005: 1). These innovations are marvelous, but they are very expensive. There is no central authority in the United States, unlike most industrial countries, to ration the use of resources devoted to health care high-tech medicine. The Medicare program is less generous than most private-sector health insurance policies, but it still pays a substantial share of doctors' fees, which means that the incentive to choose more economical treatments is blunted. For whatever reason, the annual increase in the cost of medical services always exceeds consumer price inflation by a substantial margin.

Social Security reform

A solution to the deteriorating finances of Social Security does not pose a technical challenge. In principle, the actuarial imbalance could be eliminated in a stroke by a 1.7 percentage point increase in the payroll tax (SSA, 2008b: 3). Revenues could also be increased by increasing or even eliminating the cap of $106,300 on the annual salary subject to the payroll tax. Expenditures could be reduced in various ways: for example, by a further increase in the full retirement age, or by a change in the method of indexation of a worker's wages used to calculate pension benefits. The practice of indexing the pensions of current retirees to the consumer price index might also be modified, on the grounds that the consumer price index has an upward bias and over-states inflation.

It is likely that if there is a technical fix of Social Security it will involve a number of measures on both the revenue and expenditure sides of the system. It is very unlikely that current retirees or workers close to retirement would be affected by the measures ultimately chosen. The generation of current retirees is represented by powerful lobbies, and can always argue that with an average monthly pension of $1,100, below the poverty guideline for a family of two, Social Security is not particularly generous. Moreover, the benefit accounts for about 70 percent of the income of the bottom 40 percent of Americans over 65, so that any significant reduction in it could cause considerable hardship to some older people. The representatives of labor would oppose an increase in the payroll tax rate on the grounds that it was regressive.

The Bush administration did not consider seriously a conventional reform of Social Security along these lines. Instead, in 2004 it appointed a commission that recommended the introduction of individual accounts, possibly combined with more conventional measures. The reform would have entailed the diversion of 2 percentage points of the payroll tax of 12.4 percent to an individual investment account, and a corresponding reduction in the regular Social Security pension. Democrats were almost uniformly opposed to the reform, in part because of their concerns over the investment risk that account holders would incur, and in part because they viewed it as a Trojan horse for the wholesale dismantlement of Social Security.

Despite the long and often acrimonious debate that took place in Washington's think tanks on the merits of individual accounts (or privatization), the administration's proposal died a quiet death. Individual accounts have proven to be most popular with the American public when the stock market was buoyant, as in the late 1990s. The bursting of the dot.com bubble in 2000–01 must have cooled the attraction of individual accounts for many. More recent developments have pounded the last nail into the proposal's coffin. It should be noted in any case that an individual accounts reform cannot be painless if it is to be effective. Simply diverting 2 percent of the payroll tax into individual accounts will not address the financial imbalances of the system unless it somehow causes or is accompanied by expenditure economies.

The public–private safety net

In comparison with other industrial countries, the United States does not provide its citizens with a particularly generous safety net. Social Security has near universal coverage, and provides low to middle-income workers with a long work history with a pension that replaces a substantial share of average career income. The replacement rate (the ratio of the value of the benefit to a measure of income during working life) drops off fairly sharply as incomes rise, however. Social Security provides a disability pension, and surviving family members and spouses of contributing workers can also draw benefits. Public expenditure on health is focused on the elderly (Medicare) and the poor (Medicaid), and the majority of Americans obtain health insurance through their employer. The important role played by employer-provided health insurance goes back to the Second World War, when employers were first allowed to deduct 100 percent of their insurance costs without limit from taxable profits. The states and the federal government together finance the unemployment insurance program, and the federal government finances targeted social assistance programs.

Two ongoing developments are threatening the economic security of the average American family. First, the 401(k) pension plan, a defined contribution plan, has been increasing its share of the 50 percent of American workers who have an employer-provided pension of some kind at the expense of the traditional defined benefit plan. The traditional pension is usually a specified fraction of final income that increases with the number of years worked. Workers who participated long enough in a defined benefits plan would typically be able to draw a substantial pension at retirement for life. With 401(k) plans, the actual rate of saving is optional up to the plan maximum, the worker is responsible for investment decisions regardless of his or her degree of financial expertise, and the balance of the fund at retirement is typically not converted into an annuity (that is, a permanent stream of income). This means that the typical 401(k) plan member does not have the same amount of longevity insurance (insurance against outliving one's resources) that a long-time member of a defined benefit plan would have, and is at greater risk of penury in extreme old age. Second, increases in the cost of health insurance are increasingly obliging employers to cut back on benefits. Consequently, it is not only the uninsured that worry about the cost of medical care.

The financing of unemployment insurance at the state level has also come under strain, given the rapid increase in the number of unemployed and the pro-cyclical nature of states' budgets – the decline in incomes reduces their revenues, and their balanced budget rule forces them to look for areas to cut back. It was for this reason that the ARRA included increased transfers to the states to finance unemployment insurance.

One of the measures included in the FY2010 budget would partially address the inadequacies of the current pension system, and notably the large number of uncovered workers. This is the proposal to require employers to offer their employees a type of low-cost personal retirement account, in which they would be automatically enrolled, but from which they could choose to opt out. What is known as the default setting has a powerful influence on the choices people make (Thaler and Sunstein, 2008). Requiring employees to opt out of an employer benefits program rather than the other way around has been shown to increase take-up markedly. If this proposal meets with Congress's approval, the coverage of the employer-provided pension system could increase substantially.

Conclusion

The severity of the economic downturn and the state of the balance sheets of financial institutions have prompted comparisons of the current period with the 1930s, as well as comparisons of the Obama and Roosevelt administrations. There are undoubtedly parallels, but there are important differences as well. Franklin Roosevelt came to power in 1933 when the Depression had already ravaged the American economy; it was too late for him to undo the mistakes made by the Federal Reserve in tightening credit conditions when the opposite was desperately needed. The initial steps taken by the Obama administration do not appear to have misfired. However, the United States is more dependent on what happens in the rest of the world than it was in the 1930s. Its economy is more open (trade is a larger share of GDP), and its financial markets are more exposed to what happens elsewhere.

The Depression increased the role of government in the economy in a few short years, and bequeathed to subsequent generations a major piece of the social safety net and a durable regulatory framework. It is natural to ask whether the new administration will transform the social and economic landscape of the United States in a similar way. As far as regulation is concerned, it is a reasonable bet that financial institutions will be scrutinized much more closely than they have been. The era of light-touch regulation is over. The April 2009 meeting at the

White House between the President and representatives of the credit card industry sent a clear signal that financial transparency, if not outright intervention in the terms applying to consumer credit, is high on the Administration's list of priorities. Whether the regulatory framework in other areas (food and drugs, worker safety, transportation) will change greatly is not so clear.

Conservative spokespersons are already decrying the huge intervention by the new Administration in the economy. If the degree of intervention were gauged by the increase in the share of expenditure in GDP that will take place in 2009 and 2010, there would be some justice to the claim. It appears, however, that most of the expenditure will be one-off, as the budget implies it is. Thoroughgoing health care reform along the lines that the Obama campaign proposed would undoubtedly entail considerable intervention in the provision or financing of health services, however.

Health care reform, or reform in any other area, is in practice going to depend on economic recovery. This in turn will depend on economy recovery abroad, but will also require that the administration make difficult choices about programs in other areas and general revenue increases. The legislative proposals to reduce cost are good ones, but how much exactly they will save is highly uncertain. However, should these cost savings prove substantial and a durable recovery take hold, a major reform of the way health care is provided and financed in the United States could be feasible, and become the Administration's greatest legacy.

Finally, it is tempting to try to assign responsibility for the financial debacle. The temptation should probably be resisted to some degree. After all, the severity of the financial collapse and economic downturn surprised almost all informed observers. The housing price bubble should, however, have raised a red flag. Housing prices were bound to fall sooner or later, and the risk of a major decline in the housing market should have been evident. More concern with the consequences of asset price inflation would have led the Fed to tighten monetary policy sooner, and perhaps take some of the steam out of the bubble. We have, however, noted that dealing with asset price inflation raises challenges of its own.

The Bush administration can fairly be blamed for the lack of adequate regulation of both the American housing market and the derivatives market – although it was not the only country to neglect to strengthen its regulatory apparatus. Moreover, senior officials from the Clinton administration were generally in sympathy with deregulation. It is not possible to blame America's economic problems on Republicans and absolve Democrats.

As for the federal government's fiscal deficit, President Obama is right in claiming that he inherited a deficit in excess of $1 trillion.

However, it is unlikely that had he and his team been in office in 2008 they would have adopted a fiscal stance much different from that of his predecessor. With the economy seemingly nosediving and panic in the air, fiscal austerity would not have been the right policy.

It is impossible to know with any certainty whether the financial crisis would have been less acute under a different administration. Arguably, mortgage market regulation would have been less lax, which would have reduced the size of the bubble, at least to some degree. That in turn would have tempered the crisis. Whether Obama's economic strategy is sufficient to restore American economic prosperity remains to be seen.

Chapter 13

American Social Policy: The Possibilities for Reform

B. Guy Peters

The American welfare state is, compared with other industrialized democracies, rather meager but there are still some important social programs that provide support for significant segments of the population. In particular the retirement system provided through Social Security helps over 35 million Americans in their retirement, and its disability benefits support another 7 million. There are also a number of means-tested benefits that support the less affluent in society, although not to the extent common in most European countries, and often with a large number of regulations that control the availability of benefits and which continue to "regulate the poor" (Piven and Cloward, 1997).

The most obvious deficiency in the array of programs available is the limited public involvement in providing health care. Although the elderly are covered through Medicare, the indigent are provided some coverage through Medicaid, and many children are covered through State Children's Health Insurance Program (SCHIPS), the majority of the public must use private health insurance. The costs of this private insurance have resulted in almost 50 million Americans not having health insurance. Further, many of those who are covered have minimal protection and have to pay a substantial amount out of pocket if they become sick or injured.

Health policy was a central element of the Democratic campaign in 2008. The candidates advanced a variety of different proposals for universal coverage, but were agreed on the need for fundamental change in the system. In addition, a number of the states have already launched their own programs for health coverage which can serve as models for a national program (Leichter, 1997). The problems of limited access to health insurance are compounded by high costs and declining quality, and health policy will continue to be central to policy and political debates. The ability to address these policy needs will, however, be restrained by the economic crisis and the huge amounts of public money going to fund the economic recovery.

The most important social program that does exist, pensions provided through the Social Security program, remains very popular with voters, but faces severe economic challenges if there is no major overhaul of the program. The administration of George W. Bush sought to utilize market principles to reform the system, but met widespread opposition in Congress and skepticism from the public. Although there is far from agreement on the best options for reform, it is clear to many policymakers and experts that some sort of change is needed given demographic trends that will impose increasing costs with declining income. Further, the disability component of Social Security is under constant attack for its excessively rigid criteria for providing benefits, especially when compared with other public programs such as those in the Department of Veterans Affairs (VA). The VA, for example, assigns percentage disabilities while the Social Security system requires proving full disability of gainful employment. Finally, high levels of unemployment are straining the unemployment compensation system (DeParle, 2009). There is a welfare state in the United States, but it is under serious threat and those threats are likely to become more severe.

This chapter focuses on the needs for reforming social policy, and especially health policy, and the likelihood of those reforms being implemented by the Obama administration. There is little doubt that there is public support for change, as well as public support for maintaining many elements of the existing system. These demands for change confront limited, and perhaps increasingly limited, financial resources. Therefore, this chapter also focuses on the continuing role of private solutions to social policy questions, including the "faith-based" programs advocated by the religious right. Again, with the fiscal problems facing the public sector, leveraging private resources may be essential if there is to be any significant change in social policy.

Existing social programs

While the usual characterization of the United States as a welfare laggard implies that the public sector actually has very limited involvement with social policy, when we begin to detail the programs that are in place, that characterization appears suspect. Indeed, even with the large defense expenditures, over half of total federal expenditure goes to social policies. If we add the social policy effects of tax policy – for example, tax sheltering of contributions to private pensions – and the role of state and local governments in providing social policy, then there is a large welfare state affecting many sectors of the population.

Distinctiveness of American social policy

Although there is a substantial set of social programs, these programs are somewhat different than those found in other industrialized democracies. In the first instance, means-tested benefits are a more important component of the total array of benefits than in most other systems. The "workfare" program that is the successor to the "welfare" program is available to those with little or no income, and then only for a limited period of time. The current program providing support to the indigent is Temporary Assistance to Needy Families (TANF), replacing Aid to Families with Dependent Children (AFDC). Further, in addition to the support for the elderly supplied through Social Security pensions, a significant number of less affluent senior citizens receive assistance through Supplemental Security Income (SSI). And, as already mentioned, the Medicaid program only provides benefits to those who are medically indigent, with each state being able to define medical indigence.

In addition to the relatively large dependence on means-tested benefits, a major feature of the American version of the welfare state is the involvement of state governments in the programs. First, although the federal government supplies much of the money for the major means-tested support program for indigent families, the program is actually administered by the states and localities, and each state provides different levels of benefit (see Table 13.1). The states are also responsible for the children's health insurance program, and some have been creative in finding ways to make the program available to other member of the family as well (National Conference of State Legislatures, 2009). Finally, and perhaps most importantly, the states have been engaged in a number of important experiments in providing health coverage for their own citizens. For example, Massachusetts requires citizens to have health insurance. If employers do not provide the benefit, then individuals are required to purchase at least minimal coverage at a subsidized rate. These state programs have been important for their citizens, but also impose significant costs on the states, which have less buoyant revenues than the federal government.

As well as involving the state governments, the American version of the welfare state also involves a large element of private provision, although these programs tend to create a welfare state for the middle class (Howard, 1997). Individuals with good jobs receive health benefits, private pensions, and a variety of additional benefits that help insure against some of the problems of the market. Further, this middle-class welfare system is supported by the tax system, so that many real social supports subsidized through the public sector are effectively hidden from other citizens. Most of the social benefits provided from employers are not taxable, or are only taxed after the

Table 13.1 *Expenditures per recipient, by state (2005)*

Lowest		Highest	
South Carolina	$82.92	Wyoming	5,249.66
Tennessee	103.54	New York	1,039.92
Arkansas	154.75	Idaho	1,014.92
Indiana	199.55	Illinois	918.50
Kentucky	209.39	Virginia	863.40

Source: Department of Health and Human Services, Administration for Families and Children.

individual retires, so that the public sector is subsidizing the middle-class lifestyle, especially in retirement.

In addition to the middle-class welfare program provided privately, albeit with tax support, there is a very large voluntary sector in the United States that provides assistance for the indigent through private means. While the concept of "charity" is sometimes taken to be demeaning by theorists of the welfare state, the voluntary sector continues to play a major role in providing services for the needy in the United States. This role was emphasized in the idea of "faith-based" programs in the Bush administration, an idea that has been retained in the Obama administration (Christian Science Monitor, 2009). Further, private social programs are often more effective than public programs in dealing with populations such as illegal immigrants who do not want to become involved with official programs because of the fear of deportation. Even many citizens not faced with deportation prefer to avoid the rigidities and perceived indifference of many public social programs if possible.

Public education has been the one area of American social policy that has been fully developed. Free public education was adopted early in the history of the country, and has been considered essential for economic development, integrating the numerous waves of immigrants, and for citizenship. This emphasis on education reflects cultural values emphasizing equality of opportunity as opposed to equality of outcomes. Although public education at all levels has been important for American government, the early expansion of mass higher education was the most exceptional aspect of this policy area.

Education has been primarily a state and local government activity, although the federal government now provides a good deal of financial assistance (approximately 10 percent of all funding) for elementary and secondary education, and intervened more directly during the administration of George W. Bush with the "No Child Left Behind" mandates. Public higher education has also been a state-level service, although the federal government began early (the Morrill Act in 1863) to support higher education, and more recently has become a major source of funding for student grants and loans for higher education.

Public education has been a crucial social program for the United States but there are a number of problems in contemporary education. American students do not perform well when set against those of other nations in international comparisons. Also, there are major inequalities in educational performance by race as well as across states, in part because local education is financed primarily by local property taxes so that more affluent areas can easily provide more money for education. The Obama administration has made some initial attempts to improve educational performance and financing, but this is one of many problems that the administration must confront.

The principal programs

Social insurance

Although I have mentioned that one of the characteristics of American social policy is that it relies more on means-tested benefits than do many other social policy systems, the bulk of the money spent in social programs is spent through social insurance programs. The largest single program is the pension program in Social Security, covering almost all the working population. This program was a product of President Franklin Roosevelt's New Deal, and has become the "third rail" of American politics: something that no politician will dare to touch. President George W. Bush did attempt to privatize the program, at least in part, but soon had to back down when the depth of public commitment to the program became apparent.

As well as providing pensions for retired workers, the Social Security program also provides support for widows and orphans, and disability benefits for people who cannot work because of illness or other incapacity. It is important to note that all these benefits are based on contributions, and having contributed through social insurance taxes while working. Those who have not made those contributions receive no benefits, and are thrown back to reliance on the means-tested programs. This same emphasis on employment can be seen in the current version of the means-tested benefit program, given that these programs now emphasize benefits being offered in exchange for preparing for employment and then getting a job.

The Medicare program providing medical insurance for the elderly is associated with the Social Security program. Individuals who have paid into the program are eligible for medical insurance at age 65, and Medicare now provides benefits for over 45 million older Americans. The coverage is not totally free, however, and there are annual fees and deductibles, designed in part to deter consumption and in part to help fund a program that is increasingly expensive. In the early twenty-first century a prescription drug program was added to the Medicare program, albeit one with limited coverage and benefits. Further, the large number of gaps in Medicare coverage has created an industry in private "Medigap" insurance, which enables individuals to cover those holes in the public program.

In addition to the federal programs the states also administer two important social insurance programs. First, although much of the money comes from the federal government, the states administer unemployment insurance. They provide different levels of benefit, but with a national minimum. As the economic crisis has deepened, the length of time that individuals are eligible for benefits has been increased, but a large number of individuals have exhausted their eligibility. The other social insurance program run by the states is Workmen's Compensation, which provides benefits for individuals who are injured at work. Again, there are marked differences in benefits and eligibility requirements across the states.

Means-tested benefits

The principal means-tested benefit is "welfare," which principally provides benefits for families with dependent children who have little or no income. This program underwent significant reform during the Clinton administration, creating both a requirement for work or training for the recipients, and time limits on the eligibility of individuals for the benefits. Because of these restrictions the number of people receiving "workfare" benefits has tended to decline, although the economic crisis has been forcing more people onto the program. Supplemental security income also provides benefits for certain types of individuals, for example, the elderly or disabled, who have insufficient income from other programs. Also, the Food Stamp program administered through the Department of Agriculture provides food assistance to low-income families.

The war on poverty during the 1960s has left several residual programs that continue to provide assistance for low-income citizens. For example Head Start provides pre-school programs for several million low-income students so that they can be more prepared for entering elementary school. The Head Start program has been evaluated any number of times, and has also been the subject of extensive ideological argument, as indeed has the concept of fighting poverty through public programs. That said, however, until the beginning of the Bush administration the poverty rate had been declining and the residual elements of the poverty programs were perceived to be less valuable.

In addition to means-tested financial benefits the states also provide medical care for the indigent through Medicaid and SCHIPs. Again, the states provide different levels of benefits and impose different eligibility requirements, but the bulk of the funding comes from the federal government. These criteria are generally expressed in terms of percentages of the poverty level. While these health programs do provide medical care for the poorest members of society, the "working poor" are often not covered. These are people who have an income greater than the poverty level, but whose employers do not provide benefits, and who are not capable of paying for the insurance themselves. As noted above, SCHIPs has tended to increase the level of eligibility, but there are still many people who remain outside the limits for coverage.

The prospects for reform

The social policies of the United States now face pressures for reform in at least seemingly contradictory directions. The most obvious direction of change is to spread the social safety net further and to provide benefits for people who are not now covered. As already noted, this direction of change is especially important in health care. Enhancing coverage of health care and other social programs is important not only for humane reasons, but also for economic ones. One of the factors undermining the competitiveness of the automobile industry, for example, is that these firms have large bills for their employees while their competitors in other countries do not, because there are socially provided medical insurance programs.

The other direction for reform is reducing some of the existing benefits because of demographic and financial pressures. Although the population of the United States is on average younger than most other industrialized democracies, it is still aging (see Table 13.2). As the "baby boomers" born just after the end of the Second World War are beginning to retire in large numbers, the pressures on Social Security and especially on Medicare will become intense. These pressures are exacerbated by the success of medical care, and lifestyle changes, in keeping people alive longer. While the average person receiving Social Security when the program was initiated could expect to live a few months on its benefits, the average person now retiring can expect to live at least one decade. With more elderly program recipients and a relatively smaller working-age population, the financial structure of Social Security is precarious, with numerous reports of the impending "bankruptcy" of the program. In this context bankruptcy would mean that the Social Security Trust Fund was exhausted and current receipts

Table 13.2   *Projections of population aging in the United States, 2010–50 (in percentages)*

	2010	2015	2020	2030	2040	2050
Population over 65	13.0	14.4	16.1	18.0	18.8	20.2
Population over 75	6.0	6.1	6.6	8.2	8.9	11.0

Source: US Census Bureau (2008a).

from payroll taxes were insufficient to cover payments to the recipients of benefits.

The pressures on Social Security have produced a certain amount of schizophrenia among the American public about this program. On the one hand the program remains very popular with the public, especially those receiving benefits and those who have parents receiving the benefits. Social security is also the touchstone program for the largest pressure group in the United States, the American Association of Retired Persons (AARP). Politicians who attempt reforms in the system find that many Americans consider most reforms as attempts to undermine the program. After the collapse of the stock market from 2008, the public are especially reluctant to consider privatizing the system.

On the other hand, however, many younger Americans believe that they will receive little or nothing from Social Security when they retire. They have heard all the dire predictions concerning Social Security and have begun to believe them. For example, in a *Washington Post* poll taken in early 2009, only slightly more than one-third of the public had any confidence that they would receive the full benefits they had been paying for when they retired. That lack of confidence may be well grounded, given that the Social Security Administration's own website says that beginning in 2037 it will not be able to pay full benefits without a change in the law, so that people 40 years of age or under in 2009 might not expect to receive the level of benefits that current retirees now do.

Creating national health care

Beginning with President Roosevelt – Theodore, not Franklin – there have been a number of efforts to create some form of national health program in the United States. The most famous failure in these attempts was that at the beginning of the Clinton administration, led by Hillary Rodham Clinton. Although the public then, and now, has said that it wants some form of public program that ensures health care for all citizens, the program foundered because of its complexity and clever political opposition. The SCHIPs program was adopted at this time but the attempt to create a comprehensive plan failed without even a vote on the entire program in Congress.

President Obama campaigned on a platform of creating such a program, and even in the midst of the economic crisis has attempted to move toward adopting such a plan (see Collins et al., 2008). As his administration attempts to formulate concrete proposals, it faces decisions about a number of components that will have major impacts both on the success of the program if adopted, and on the political chances of having it adopted. And as is often the case, the plans that are best in a technical sense might not be the most palatable politically.

Cost is the principal problem facing any attempt at creating a national health insurance program. American health care is the most expensive in the world, accounting for approximately 14 percent of GDP. Of that total expenditure, approximately 46 percent is already paid by the public sector, but any major reform of health care would mean its assuming the 8 percent of GDP that is paid through private health insurance programs. With a deficit already well over $1 trillion, and the costs of economy recovery likely to persist for some time, it is not clear where the extra money for health care will come from.

That said, however, involving the public sector more directly might reduce total health care costs. First, although those 50 million Americans do not have health insurance, they do consume medical care, and they often consume very expensive medical care, for example by visiting hospital emergency rooms once they are very ill rather than having preventive care from primary care physicians. Providing these citizens with basic health insurance would tend to lower costs. That would be especially true given that after some initial catching-up with untreated conditions, with the availability of insurance and the associated preventive care, their general health might improve and they would incur lower total health costs.

In addition to potentially reducing direct medical expenses, there could be further savings. The administrative cost of the current mixed public–private system, with multiple competitive private insurers, is much higher than are existing public programs in other comparable countries. The campaigners against public involvement raise the specter of "bureaucracy," but the existing system is already extremely bureaucratic, and indeed has multiple bureaucracies. Although the calculations vary, almost all analysts believe that a single-payer public plan could save billions in administrative costs.

In addition to cost concerns, there is political and ideological resistance to moving to greater public involvement in medical care. The insurance industry has lobbied extensively against a larger public role, arguing that citizens' capacity to make their own choice of doctors and hospitals would be eliminated in a bureaucratic system. This argument is, of course, somewhat disingenuous given that most existing private health insurance programs do not provide free choices, but restrict patients to providers who are members of a "network." Further, the image of long waiting times and queuing for services in Canada and the United Kingdom has made some citizens reluctant to support public health insurance, even if they agree that the current system is expensive and inequitable. As in many instances, public opinion appears to be internally contradictory, and pollsters can produce support for any position depending upon how the questions are worded.

Even if there is agreement that the United States should move toward a program of comprehensive public insurance, it is not clear what that program should look like. There are several possible models for change, all of which have their strengths and weaknesses. It is clear that the type of complex hybrid system advocated by the Clinton administration is not likely to be a major alternative, but any plan will produce some specific objections, in addition to the general objections of conservatives and the insurers. Indeed, as debates over reform have progressed, it seems more likely that any emerging system will have a number of options for both the insurers and the insured.

The plan adopted by Massachusetts has been an early favorite in the Obama administration. The idea is to require citizens to have health insurance, whether provided by their employer or not. If health insurance is not provided by the employer, then the individual has to purchase at least minimal coverage in the market. The market, however, is subsidized by contributions from employers who choose not to provide insurance themselves, as well as by general tax revenues. This is a variant of the so-called "play or pay" approach to health insurance, requiring employers either to provide insurance or to pay into a fund that covers those who would not otherwise be insured.

The evaluations of the Massachusetts plan have been mixed. It is clear that many people in the state have at least a modest level of insurance for health care. Further, citizens with incomes less than the poverty level receive health insurance that is subsidized or paid for entirely by the public sector. For the citizens in the program, however, access has not necessarily improved. Although cost is no longer the barrier it was, many more patients are now using the same number of physicians and hospitals, meaning that waiting times have increased. This might be short term, and once a backlog of medical problems have been treated the access issues will stabilize, but at least in the short term there are problems.

Another option for creating a national health insurance program is to simply extend the existing programs to cover the remainder of the population, either gradually or all at once. To some extent this has already been happening, as some states provide coverage under SCHIPs for full-time students up to age 25. Likewise, Medicare covers people under 65 who have certain chronic medical conditions such as renal disease. The administrative machinery for running Medicare, Medicaid, and SCHIPs is already in place, so it would involve only the (relatively) simple task of adding more people to the existing programs.

As the negotiations over health care continued in the summer of 2009, one of the necessary elements of any option was a low-cost public plan that would at once provide competition to private insurance providers and provide many citizens with an alternative that was superior to being uninsured or to many private plans. This public plan would require a good deal of public involvement in the health care system, but perhaps no more than the control exercised by private insurers under existing private programs. The political question therefore becomes which source of control is likely to be more accountable and more acceptable to the public.

As might be expected, the politics of moving in the direction of any form of national insurance program have mobilized a large number of interest groups, some directly concerned with health care and others more concerned with the economic consequences of reform. The principal opposition to changing the current private health system is provided by the insurance industry, allied with the hospitals. Both of these industries have been able to extract large "profits" from the existing private arrangements (even though many are nominally not-for-profit organizations), and would be threatened by larger public involvement. In addition to the insurance industry, many conservative organizations are actively opposing any shifts toward larger public involvement, making the now familiar arguments concerning socialized medicine.

On the other side of the argument have been a number of more liberal interest groups, including the unions. There are, however, two groups that might not have been expected. The medical professions have become actively involved in promoting some form of public health insurance, after having actively opposed it in the past. In addition, many segments of big business have become active in promoting public health insurance, so that they can escape the large payments they are now making to cover their employees. Smaller businesses, however, are adamantly opposed to public health insurance because under most plans they would have to bear some of the costs of their employees' insurance.

The politics of making these decisions is, however, more than just balancing the two sets of interests. It is clear that the president and the Democratic Party are now committed to producing some form of change, supported by strong pressures from the public. The difficulty, however, is in moving from some general commitments to change, to actually producing legislation. The election of a Republican to fill the vacant Senate seat in Massachusetts in January 2010 makes reform harder because the Democrats no longer have a veto-proof majority. The president called a health care summit in May 2009, and attempted to extract some minimal commitment for cost-restraint from providers, with a view to slowing the rapid cost changes that would make transition to a public system more difficult. That is, however, only a small beginning toward finding a way to finance medical insurance for all Americans.

President Obama has sought to push health care legislation through Congress, but has encountered a number of roadblocks to what he had thought might be relatively quick adoption of a plan. One of the barriers has been that Congress is a real legislative body and wants a significant impact on the shape of the final legislation, and indeed both Houses of Congress may develop their own approach. The weak support from some parts of the Democratic Party, notably the fiscally conservative "Blue Dogs," has meant that the Republicans have been able to have much more influence over the proposals than might have been expected when the Democrats have 60 senators and a significant majority in the House of Representatives. The plan has also been delayed by estimates from the Congressional Budget Office that the plan would add much more to the deficit than had been estimated previously.

The political problems for President Obama's health reforms were increased in the summer of 2009 when members of Congress returned to their districts for "town hall meetings" about the program. The congressmen were met with a number of vociferous opponents of the program, some expressing genuine concerns about costs and clinical freedom, and others enraged by false rumors about euthanasia. While it was clear that some of the agitation about the reforms had been fomented by the right wing, some of it also represented real concerns about the impacts and costs of the proposed reforms.

As with the attempts to create national health insurance during the Clinton administration, the delays in adopting the health care legislation have allowed the opposition to the program to mobilize. Many of the groups attempting to prevent adoption of the program represent the firms that have been benefiting from the existing medical care system (Mundy and Meckler, 2009). Other groups have been motivated more by their ideological opposition to public health care, or by fears about increased taxation.

Reforming Social Security

Whereas reforming health care will involve the injection of large amounts of public money, reforming Social Security is directed primarily at finding ways of reducing the amount of public liability for spending in the near future. The nature of the Social Security program makes the appearance of bankruptcy relatively easy to create, given that by law the program is funded only by dedicated payroll taxes. This decision was made at the time of the adoption of the program, to create the image that this program was not welfare, but rather was a form of annuity, just like those purchased in the private market. The program had been designed initially to function like a private annuity, with funds being invested for each participant, but it was soon changed to a pay as you go basis. This was done so that reasonable pensions could begin to be paid within a few years of beginning the program.

Over the past several decades there has been a surplus of income over expenditures, so that a reserve has been built up in the fund. By about 2012 there will be more expenditures than revenues, and the trust fund will gradually be depleted. As the baby boomers begin to retire, however, and the size of the labor force stabilizes or declines, the number of working-age people supporting each retiree is declining. For example, in 1960 there were 5.1 workers per beneficiary, by 2007 there were 3.3 workers per beneficiary, and by 2032 there will be only 2.1 (Social Security Administration, 2009).

Options for reform

Most Americans are in favor of maintaining the Social Security program, although many younger people do not believe they will ever receive any substantial benefits – they think the system will be bankrupt. The specter of bankruptcy has been discussed for decades, but Congress has only done minor tinkering with the system. The question in 2009, amid many questions about the political economy, is whether tinkering will be sufficient to address the basic problems within Social Security, or whether more drastic solutions will be needed. Reforming Social Security is not as immediate a question politically as dealing with health care, but government has avoided the issue for several decades already, and ultimately will have to face the potential crisis.

The administration of George W. Bush had proposed more radical surgery on Social Security. It had argued that citizens would be better off if they could invest the tax money they and their employers put into Social Security in the private equities market. This would, it was argued, provide them with higher returns and a higher income on retirement. Under the current arrangements money in the Social Security Trust Fund is invested in US government bonds. These are very safe, but have a low yield. Further, bonds have limited possibilities for growth, as do stocks. The Bush administration's plan was for younger employees to be able to choose to put some portion of their "contributions" into private investments. That possibility seemed attractive to some people before the economic meltdown of 2008–09, but after that, the plan appeared rather unrealistic. Many conservatives continue to advocate fundamental reforms of this type, but there is little popular support.

There is much more support for gradual changes within the Social Security system. A number of reforms have been implemented already. Some of these changes have addressed inequalities in the system, including the treatment of widows, and have sought to provide more opportunities for retired people to supplement their earnings without heavy penalties (see Peters, 2009). Also, the age for receiving full benefits has gradually been raised, both to save money and to reflect changing life expectancy. With the slowdown of the economy more workers are likely to postpone retirement, thereby saving the system some money at least in the short term.

There have also been some reforms that have sought to slow the financial problems facing the retirement system. For example, the retirement age has been moved up gradually since the late 1990s, so that for people born after 1960 the age is 67. The proportion of the benefit that is taxable for people with other sources of income has also been increased. The continuing indexation of the level at which payroll taxation is not taken has helped to increase revenues, but benefits are also indexed, so expenditures continue to increase. Those reforms have helped to slow the erosion of the Trust Fund, but are not nearly enough to produce the savings needed to preserve the program.

One of the proposed reforms of Social Security is to reduce benefits, or to make them means-tested. Simply reducing benefits might be the easiest solution to the problem, but would impose hardship on lower-income recipients without other sources of retirement income. For millions of Americans Social Security is the only significant source of retirement income, so any reductions would have a major effect. Raising the official retirement age for receiving full benefits would have something of the same effect, reducing the total benefits that retirees would receive if they were to retire at what is now the official age.

Making Social Security means-tested, however, would violate the implicit, and to some extent explicit, premise that it is not a welfare program but an analog of buying a private annuity. While many citizens have already come to realize that the program is an inter-generational transfer, the symbolism of not being on welfare remains important in a culture that stresses individual responsibility. Like almost any policy issue of consequence, reforming Social Security involves making difficult trade-offs among values in order to find our collective way and improve policy design.

An analogous reform for Social Security is to increase the income that is received into the system. One way is to eliminate the ceiling on the income level at which the tax – technically a contribution – is charged. This reform would make the tax at least proportional, rather than being regressive as it now is. Under current law someone earning up to $106,800 (2009) pays 7.65 percent of their income into Social Security, while someone earning $200,000 pays only 4.1 percent of their income. Also, the payroll tax is just that and does not apply to earnings from investments, again favoring the more affluent. Applying the payroll tax to all income would, however, undermine the conception that Social Security is different from other social programs, and thus destroy some of its legitimacy.

Another way to increase income is to increase the rate at which Social Security tax is collected. This tax rate has remained constant since it was set in 1990, with only the amount of income on which the tax is collected changing. Raising the tax rate would certainly produce more income for the program, but it would also impose a major burden on younger workers still in the labor force, and if it was also imposed on employers, the tax could reduce job creation at a time at which this might be especially undesirable. Politically, of course, any increase in tax rates is more difficult than simply continuing to raise the amount of income on which the tax is charged.

There also have been suggestions to fund Social Security through a national value-added tax (Montgomery, 2009), similar to that used in all European Union countries (albeit not just for social insurance programs). This change would make the financing of retirement benefits less visible to employees and would not have any significant effects on job creation. It would, like several of the other proposals for reform, end the convenient fiction that it is a self-financing program providing benefits like a private program. In the end, however, one or more of these changes may be necessary if the inter-generational agreement to provide a reasonable level of income in retirement is to be maintained.

Conclusion

The American welfare state is more developed than many of its critics believe, and also less developed than those critics and many other citizens believe it should be. Unlike most European social systems, American political culture has stressed self-reliance, although that commitment to individual responsibility has not extended to the middle class and the tax subsidies available for their pensions and health care. In part because of that emphasis on self-reliance, the American welfare state also has many more means-tested programs than do other welfare systems, and the benefits are in general less generous. Most obviously, there is no comprehensive access to health care guaranteed by the public sector.

Although they are perhaps ungenerous, Americans are committed to the programs that do exist, and most would like some extension to cover health care. There is substantial disagreement on what that extension of health coverage might look like, but the basic concept of providing some form of affordable coverage for all Americans is now widely accepted. Like so many other areas of American politics, health care reform has become the focus of large-scale mobilization of affected interests, as well as of ideologies. These groups create a lively debate, but they also make reaching any workable consensus on change very difficult.

Chapter 14

American Foreign Policy in the 2010s

Timothy Lynch

The inauguration of President Barack Obama in January 2009 was widely seen as a decisive repudiation of the outgoing administration of George W. Bush. American foreign policy would now be reclaimed, and, in an image popular during the euphoria of the Obama victory, the "reset button" pressed in some of the relations Bush had allegedly crashed or frozen. The war on terror would be renamed. America would be more careful in its public diplomacy toward Arabs and Muslims. Obama would reinstate a golden age of American multilateralism. Climate change would be taken seriously as a national security issue. Guantánamo Bay would be closed. The wars in Afghanistan and Iraq would be brought to a reasonable conclusion and American troops sent home. The expectations riding on Obama's shoulders were very high indeed. At almost every foreign policy turn he was expected to be the anti-Bush President and to reverse the purported failures of the 2001–08 years. And this is before we consider the great pressures foisted on him by a global economic recession.

The prospects of an Obama counter-revolution are assessed in this chapter and are, on balance, judged as unrealistic. While the new administration has altered much of the style and tone of US foreign policy, the fundamental structure of the international system – with its many threats to and opportunities for American power – has endured and will endure into the 2010s. This means Obama, in terms of foreign policy substance, will more resemble Bush than repudiate him. Despite his Nobel Prize (awarded in October 2009), Obama has found international peace as hard to achieve as his predecessor.

Context: the Obama inheritance

What kind of world was President Obama obliged to confront? There are several features of international relations that have framed

American foreign policy since the early 1990s, and arguably before. Obama inherited them, just as did his immediate predecessors. Even if he wanted to, his capacity to change them is heavily circumscribed; they come with the job.

Primacy

The first feature to note is American primacy. Primacy means that the United States, despite competition, faces no rival with anything approaching comparable power and influence, especially militarily. During the Cold War, America found itself balanced by the Soviet Union. From the 1940s to the 1980s, the United States faced a series of struggles against an enemy defined in antithesis to it. In 1956 Nikita Khrushchev, the Soviet premier, predicted he would "bury" the United States. In 1991, "without so much as a press release, the Soviet Union simply gave up and disappeared" (Krauthammer, 2004: 1). The United States has enjoyed primacy in the international system ever since. A former French foreign minister, speaking in 1999, acknowledged this:

> The United States of America today predominates on the economic level, on the monetary level, on the military level, and on the technological level, and in the cultural area in the broadest sense of the word. It is not comparable, in terms of power and influence, to anything known in modern history.   (Vedrine in Lieber, 2007: 16)

America enjoys unrivalled military supremacy by spending only 4.5 percent of its national wealth (or GDP) on its armed forces. China, for example, spends more, in proportional terms (about 7 per cent), but remains far behind the United States in terms of global power projection and technological sophistication. America spends close to $800 billion annually on defense. The EU, China, Russia and India *together* spend less than half this figure. This has afforded the United States unique opportunities to craft an international system consistent with its interests and values, but has also exposed the limits of American ambitions and the world's receptivity to them (see Lieber, 2007: 15–25). For example, starting with the invasion of Panama in December 1989, the United States has led an intervention overseas about every 18 months. It has intervened militarily in Kuwait (1990–91), Haiti (1994–95), Bosnia (1994–95), Kosovo (1999), Afghanistan (since 2001), and Iraq (since 1991). In the latter two cases, the American military has been obliged to fight energy-sapping campaigns to realize the fruits of initial success. Clinton's wars in the Balkans, whilst they led indirectly to regime change in Serbia and the creation of an ethnically Islamic state in Kosovo, did little to appease Islamists who continue to plot against American interests. As 9/11 demonstrated, American military primacy did not mean American homeland security. American economic dominance, by the same token, did not insulate it from the sub-prime mortgage crisis and the banking collapse that followed.

Unipolarity

The second feature of the current world order is unipolarity. Whereas the Cold War was characterized by a global competition for power between two nation states – hence bipolarity – after the collapse of Soviet communism only one, the United States, was left standing – hence unipolarity. Scholars writing from a realist perspective argued that such a state of affairs could not long endure (see Mearsheimer, 1990 and 2002; Walt, 2005). And yet American unipolarity has proved a remarkably durable form of global order. Despite predictions of a rising Chinese competitor (considered below) to replace the USSR, China seems more content to join a US-led system than to challenge it. Beijing fears the failure of American capitalism, and the decline of the huge market it represents for Chinese exports, far more than its success. States, again contra the predictions of realists, did not rush to balance against American power when the Soviet Union died but sought instead to join the American imperium. Brazil, Russia, India, and China (the so-called BRIC nations) have moved toward the American model rather than away. During the Bush years, US–India relations, for example, were significantly strengthened. America's pole attracts governments to it. This does not make American power supreme. Nor does it make states, especially the BRICs, subservient to American demands. What unipolarity does do is afford the American government a powerful voice in an international system largely dependent on the success of American capitalism. With the exception of a few outliers, no reasonable foreign leader connects American decline to their own nation's economic success. We are all, to some extent, American now. This calculation was true under George W. Bush and remains so after him.

Global terrorism and nuclear proliferation

The third feature of the contemporary world is the rise of global terrorism and the proliferation of weapons once the exclusive preserve of the United States alone. For some, the predictable "blowback" of American primacy and unipolarity was the rise not of challenger states but of non-state actors, the more high-profile of which have used terrorism to advance their agenda and establish their identity. The attacks of 9/11 (killing 2,975 people), were a dramatic illustration of this new threat. However, 9/11 was merely the largest in a series of terrorist attacks against American interests around the world since the end of the Cold War. Global terrorism did not begin on 9/11 nor should it been seen as a specifically anti-Bush phenomenon. In February 1993, in the second month of the Bill Clinton presidency, the nephew of a key architect of the later 9/11 attacks nearly succeeded in toppling one tower of the World Trade Center onto the other. From then until the present, Islamist terrorism – primarily organized by Al Qaeda and its leader Osama bin Laden or inspired by their example – has manifested itself across the globe, from Bali to Glasgow.

Whilst the capacity of such terrorists may have deteriorated as a consequence of the American response to 9/11 (the academic debate surrounding this assertion is fierce; see Lynch and Singh, 2008: 84–146), their intent to harm American interests and take American lives endures, and the search for weapons of mass destruction remains a central concern of the Obama administration, which stands committed to a war on terror in substance if not in style. In his inauguration address President Obama adapted rather than rejected Bush's termi-nology. Bush spoke of a single "axis of evil, arming to threaten the peace of the world" (Bush, 2002). Obama described "a far-reaching network of violence and hatred" (Obama, 2009f). The latter did not indict the former for seeing enemies all and everywhere, but for failing to see them – in Afghanistan/Pakistan or "Af-Pak" in contemporary diplomatic parlance – where they existed in their most ominous form. Pakistan has become central to Obama's national security strategy because of the potentially catastrophic nexus of terrorism and nuclear technology that this failing state portends. Pakistan has had an offensive nuclear capacity since 1998. The possible capture of the state by the Taliban, who provided a base in neighboring Afghanistan for the 9/11 operation, makes the issue of nuclear terrorism an acute one for the current American administration. Despite adopting a more aggressive approach to Pakistan, Obama has, to date, continued the Bush strategy of subsidizing the Pakistan government (providing $10 billion since 2001) in the hope that it will eradicate the Taliban challenge. As of late 2009, Obama was spending one dollar in Pakistan for every $30 in Afghanistan. This imbalance seems unsustainable. Whereas Bush orchestrated a military "surge" in Iraq, Obama has begun a surge in Afghanistan that will almost certainly expand into Pakistan. "Af-Pak" is likely to become the defining conflict of his time in office.

Limits of international institutions

The fourth feature of contemporary international relations is the limited utility of international law and institutions to meet the security problems posed by the preceding three. Despite the best intentions of more liberal Presidents, such as Bill Clinton, American foreign policy has rarely relied on UN resolutions to advance its security interests. The irony here, of course, is that the creation of many international legal mechanisms and indeed of the United Nations itself was a direct result of American diplomacy in the aftermath of the Second World War. But when the American government has chosen to act aggressively overseas, recourse to the United Nations has been the exception rather than the rule. Vietnam, the interventions of the Reagan years, Clinton's attack on Serbia in 1999, and the 2003 war in Iraq all took place without UN support. The war in Afghanistan since 2001 has been NATO-led.

Despite the concerted action necessary to counter climate change, the United States has shown itself wary of internationally agreed rules on carbon emissions. This resistance was not unique to George W. Bush. Bill Clinton, despite negotiating the Kyoto Protocol, refused to expend political capital in what would have been a doomed attempt to get the Senate to ratify it. American Presidents are understandably cautious about international laws which limit their own room for maneuver or, in the case of climate change, oblige an American compliance greater than that demanded of industrializing nations, like India and China. Obama believes climate change to be a serious global problem, a position Bush never embraced, but like Bush and terrorism will he be prepared to act unilaterally in the absence of concerted international action?

Given these features of international relations, how can we estimate the difference the Obama administration has made and will make to them? We can offer some possible answers to this question by aggregating contemporary US foreign policy into three areas: its rhetoric, its diplomacy, and its grand strategy.

Rhetoric: does the return of syntax to the White House matter?

George W. Bush became notorious for his sometimes-garbled syntax. "Our enemies are innovative and resourceful," Bush once said, "and so are we. They never stop thinking about new ways to harm our country and our people, and neither do we" (Bush, 2004). Opponents variously cited such "Bushisms" as evidence of the President's intellectual failings. When Bush spoke with clarity, however, this confirmed for many his essentially Manichean worldview. The consequence, according to several critics, was a foreign policy devoid of subtly and nuance. His replacement by Barack Obama, a great rhetorician, portended a return to wise diplomacy. However, whilst President Bush often spoke in assertively binary terms when outlining his response to terrorism – bin Laden was wanted "dead or alive;"

"Either you are with us or you are with the terrorists" (Bush, 2001a) – the rhetoric of his successor has not been markedly different. Consider the following:

> These terrorists . . . are the heirs of all the murderous ideologies of the twentieth century. By sacrificing human life to serve their radical visions, by abandoning every value except the will to power, they follow in the path of fascism, Nazism and totalitarianism. And they will follow that path all the way to where it ends: in history's unmarked grave of discarded lies.   (Bush, 2001a)

> We will not apologize for our way of life nor will we waver in its defense. And for those who seek to advance their aims by inducing terror and slaughtering innocents, we say to you now that, "our spirit is stronger and cannot be broken. You cannot outlast us, and we will defeat you."   (Obama, 2009f)

We should expect different levels of rhetorical skill from each occupant of the Oval Office. However, the conceptualizations of the enemy offered by both men are sufficiently similar to suggest that Obama will not fundamentally alter the methods by which it is countered. Indeed, his speeches are a clear indication that he intends to meet the enemy more effectively.

Diplomacy: a return to multilateralism?

The Obama administration's new emphasis on multilateralism can be assessed in several of America's bilateral relationships. Importantly, it allows us to examine more fully assertions that unilateralism was the default position of the Bush administration, requiring correction under Obama. Some important case studies present themselves.

Iran

The central issue America faces in Iran, and arguably in the wider region, is whether the Islamic Rrepublic will develop a nuclear weapons capacity. Iran poses a fundamental test of the rationale behind the war on terror: that no hostile state can ever be allowed to make a usable nuclear weapon available to anti-American terrorists. The supposed novelty of President Obama offering to restart US–Iran relations via a YouTube message, as he did in March 2009, with formal, if faltering, talks beginning six months later, is lessened when we consider that diplomatic engagement, of varying quality and commitment, has been basic in the western approach to Tehran for several years. George W.

Bush, despite including the regime as part of an "axis of evil" (alongside Iraq and North Korea), made Iran the subject not of American threats but of European blandishments. The EU-3 process – made up of negotiators from Britain, France, and Germany and afforded lukewarm support by the Bush administration – was designed to reward Iran for nuclear compliance rather than punish it for non-compliance.

Under the terms of the Nuclear Non-Proliferation Treaty (NPT), states may develop civilian nuclear power – for the purpose of domestic energy needs – but not nuclear weapons. Iran has consistently claimed it is engaged only with the former and is thus not in violation of the NPT. Despite sitting on a huge reserve of natural gas – second in size only to Russia's – the Iranian regime has asserted a right to nuclear power, intensifying fears in Washington, Europe, and across the Middle East, that Tehran is seeking a nuclear warhead to sit atop its already tested Shahab-3 missiles. A nuclear Iran poses a threat to American interests because of the fractious nature of Iranian governance. The possession of nuclear weapons by an undemocratic and unstable state – as frighteningly illustrated by the reaction to President Ahmadinejad's dubious reelection in June 2009 – is more problematic than that posed by a highly centralized and coordinated opponent such as the USSR. And, as Obama has warned, the consequences of a Middle Eastern arms race that Iran would provoke make a solution short of nuclear weaponization as vital as it is difficult.

Thus, while both Bush and Obama, up to the time of writing, have relied on a combination of multilateralism and international law to forestall the development of a nuclear-armed Iran, neither forswore military action. As early as 2007, candidate Obama asserted that "Iran and North Korea could trigger regional arms races, creating dangerous nuclear flashpoints in the Middle East and East Asia. In confronting these threats, I will not take the military option off the table" (Obama 2007). As president, Obama reassured the American Israel Public Affairs Committee (AIPAC), the lobby in the United States most concerned with the consequences for Israeli security of an Iranian bomb, that he would "do everything in my power to prevent Iran from obtaining a nuclear weapon. . . . We cannot unconditionally rule out an approach that could prevent Iran from obtaining a nuclear weapon" (Obama, 2008a). In May 2009, he reassured Israel's president Benjamin Netanyahu that talks with Iran would not last "forever." Thus, while Obama has attempted dialogue, a consistent refrain for each President since the Iranian revolution of 1979, he has recognized this may not be sufficient to block Iranian ambitions. UN sanctions seem increasingly unworkable, given the economic interests that states like France and Russia have in Iran. The prospect of an Iranian nuclear bomb is unthinkable, to Israel especially. It is difficult to avoid the conclusion that military action against Iran's nuclear facilities, in which the United States is either the primary actor or a strong backer of Israeli action, is increasingly likely.

Israel/Palestine

George W. Bush was the first American President to make the creation of a viable Palestinian state official American policy (see Bush, 2002a). The so-called "two-state solution," with Israel and Palestine existing side-by-side within the borders of Israel as currently constituted, commands a significant consensus among the key players. The problem for Bush, as for Obama, has been its implementation. Palestinians, and their fractured leadership, want greater autonomy and geographical contiguity, while Hamas, the Palestinian faction in control of the Gaza Strip, continues to seek the destruction of the Israeli state itself. Israel, for its part, refuses a solution that would compromise its hard-won security and empower Hamas (and by implication Iran, its key backer). These intractable tensions have been the inheritance of every American President since the 1960s. Bush's diplomacy on the issue was obscured by his response to 9/11, which made Afghanistan and Iraq his priorities. Unlike Bill Clinton, Bush did not expend much energy on Israel–Palestine. Indeed, an unintended consequence of his broader democratization strategy in the Middle East was arguably the election of the anti-western, anti-American and anti-Israeli Hamas in Gaza. The recurrent firing of missiles by Hamas into Israel led to a controversial invasion of the territory by Israeli troops in the final weeks of the Bush administration.

President Obama thus inherited not so much a peace process as an Israel–Palestine war. His attempt to revive the former drew directly on the American experience in Northern Ireland. Through the 1990s, Bill Clinton cannily used American intercession and mediation to help broker a peace deal between the warring factions in Northern Ireland (see Lynch, 2004). His key peacemaker in that process, George Mitchell, was appointed by Obama as his new envoy to the Middle East in 2009. This reworking of a soft-power strategy with a proven track record seems common sense. However, the Northern Ireland model is a problematic one. In part, its success depended on the empowerment of the extremes at the expense of the middle ground. The two parties that now dominate Northern Ireland politics – the Democratic Unionists and Sinn Féin – represent the limits of democratic acceptability. How might Obama adapt this for Middle East consumption? Would he destroy the center ground and thus assure the electoral supremacy of Likud, Yisrael Beiteinu, and Hamas, while driving Kadima, Labour, and Fatah to the margins? It is not yet clear how greater dialogue with those most wedded to political violence will empower the forces of moderation and pragmatism.

Russia

The state left behind by the collapse of the Soviet Union has been an irritation to American foreign policymakers without ever presenting itself as an obvious threat. Through the 1990s, Bill Clinton pumped billions of American dollars into the supposedly democratizing Russian state only for George W. Bush to witness a reversion to Russian authoritarianism under Vladimir Putin. Two alternative scenarios present themselves. The first depends on Russia posing no significant threat to the United States and its interests. Russia, according to this scenario, will continue to fade as a major power. The World Bank (2009) predicted that the Russian economy would contract by 4.5 percent in the early 2010s, with unemployment rising above 12 per cent. There are over 500,000 fewer Russians each year simply because of its falling birth rate; more Russian pregnancies end in abortion than in live birth. Male life expectancy is a mere 60.4 years compared with 74.5 in the European Union and United States. Military power is an important reflection of demographics, and Russia is in marked and possibly irreversible demographic decline. Russian energy resources, according to this interpretation, give it influence over its neighbors, who need cheap gas, but not power (see Freedman, 2009). It follows that Russia can exasperate America but not substantially obstruct it as it did in the Cold War.

The second scenario is less reassuring. It concedes that Russia is in long-term decline but posits that this is likely to make the Russian government more of a problem for American interests and allies rather than less. Some commentators even see a new Cold War emerging (Lucas, 2008). The Kremlin fears NATO encirclement. Since the collapse of the Soviet Union, several of its former satellite states have joined the American-led alliance. In the summer of 2008, Putin's forces occupied Georgia in what was clearly a warning to Washington that Russia would not allow that tiny state to cement its westernization by joining NATO. Neither Bush nor Obama showed themselves willing to test Russian resolve. Indeed, a wary realism has increasingly shaped American attitudes toward Russia.

National Missile Defense (NMD) has been a central pillar of American national security strategy since the Reagan administration. However, in September 2009, Obama shelved plans for a 'missile shield' to be deployed in the Czech Republic and Poland. Bush had viewed the shield as a means of protecting America from intercontinental missiles fired from the Middle East; Russia sees it as a means of projecting western offensive military power into its backyard and into Russia itself. Obama, to considerable criticism from conservative commentators, accepted the Russian position and initiated a sea-based system instead. Again, this conforms to a popular conception of his new diplomatic approach as grounded in reasonableness and compromise. It ignores the bilateralism of the Bush–Putin relationship: strong, especially in the immediate aftermath of 9/11, though never fully realized. This failed not for lack of talking but for lack of shared interests, especially in the Middle East. An increasingly autocratic Russia has no long-term interest in the democratization of states like Iran and Syria (see Kagan, 2008). Obama, in the hope that the Kremlin might use its influence to persuade Tehran out of its nuclear ambitions, abandoned the US missile shield in Eastern Europe. The success of this quid pro quo is yet to be seen.

Hitting the "reset" button in US–Russian relations, then, is not as straightforward as it seems. Obama can change some of the style and tone in which that relationship is managed, but not its underlying substance. As one Russia analyst observed, "What happens when you press the reset button on a computer? It goes dark, and then after a while the same screen comes back again" (Ignatius, 2009). Or, as another skeptic of Obama's Russian policy pointed out, "A reset, no matter how often, doesn't change the reality inside a computer. The operating system remains the same" (Joffe, 2009).

China

America's relationship with the People's Republic of China (PRC), complex since its creation in 1949, has been substantially marked in recent years by the economics of global recession. It is through this prism that Obama's Chinese diplomacy should be viewed. The Bush approach to China, pursued in far more tranquil economic times, was a study in ambivalence. In contrast to his strongly ideological approach in the Middle East, in which democratization was presented as a cure to decades of Arab misrule, ideology played a negligible role in how Bush approached China. The country invokes considerable passion within American domestic politics but the lobbies, both for and against further engagement with Beijing, are bipartisan. Portions of the Republican Party favor further economic integration, while other Republicans condemn China's human rights record. The same is true of the Democratic Party. Its labor unions fear the impact of Chinese imports on American manufacturers. Economic liberals insist trade will eventually bring about political reform in China. As a consequence, no American President experiences a consistent pressure operating on his Chinese diplomacy. The Bush solution was to tread a delicate path, which sought to neither appease nor antagonize the Chinese government. The result was a highly pragmatic China policy.

Obama signaled the importance of Southeast Asia in general and China in particular by making the region the focus of his secretary of state's first overseas trip. Obama himself spent several years as a child in Indonesia, which shaped his conceptualization of international relations and China's shadow over them. Like Bush, he has not goaded China on its human rights record, one of the world's worse according to Amnesty International. He has not tried to revitalize the Taiwanese independence movement – China has claimed the island since 1949. He has been mute on the ongoing Chinese penetration of Africa and its support for some of that continent's worse human rights violators, such as Zimbabwe and Sudan. Economic pragmatism has dictated and will continue to dictate much of the content of US–PRC relations for as long as the world remains in recession. The economic co-dependency is hard to overstate. As James Fallows illustrates:

> every person in the (rich) United States has over the past 10 years or so borrowed about $4,000 from someone in the (poor) People's Republic of China. Like so many imbalances in economics, this one can't go on indefinitely, and therefore won't.   (Fallows, 2008)

The Chinese government is America's largest single creditor. It has an interest in protecting America's ability to finance this debt; America has an interest in retaining Chinese credit. Obama cannot change this fundamental economic truth.

Europe

Robert Kagan popularized the concept of a growing EU–US divide in his much-debated *Paradise and Power* (2003). Its central thesis was that Americans and Europeans were destined to grow increasingly divided on matters of international security, with the United States enabled, and thus prepared, to counter threats militarily, and the European Union unable and thus unprepared to use force. The United States would continue to countenance war because it has the means to wage it; Europe would insist first and last on diplomatic solutions as its military capacity declines. "Americans are from Mars and Europeans are from Venus: They agree on little and understand one another less and less" (Kagan, 2003: 3).

Donald Rumsfeld, Secretary of Defense from 2001–06, went further than Kagan and divided the continent into "old" and "new" Europe. According to his crude stereotype, the newly democratized nations of Eastern Europe understood the moral imperatives of the US war in Iraq, whereas France and Germany did not. This, of course, obscured the fact that parts of "old" Europe stood with the United States in Iraq (such as the United Kingdom, Spain – at least initially – and Italy), and even France and Germany have committed troops to the NATO-led war in Afghanistan – though in insufficient numbers. Obama enjoyed at least partial success in convincing the United Kingdom, France, and

Germany to commit more troops to this fight, though their missions remain heavily circumscribed and well below what EU nations are capable of. France, for example, in 2010, was providing only 3000 troops when it could sustain three times that number. President Sarkozy was adamant that "France will not send one more soldier" to Afghanistan (in Samuel, 2009). The more cooperative emphasis of Obama's European diplomacy has borne small fruit. Whether the European Union's initial enthusiasm for an Obama presidency has been and can be equaled by its concessions to it, especially in the Af-Pak theater, remains an open question.

Latin America

During the Cold War, successive American Presidents construed Latin America as a back door for communist infiltration, and developed both overt and covert means to close it. This concern essentially vanished through the 1990s. The transition of several Latin American states from right-wing dictatorships into putative liberal democracies, the seeming durability of a Washington consensus on free-market capitalism, and the failure of Cuba to export its model absent its Russian sponsor, led Washington into a policy of benign neglect. However, Obama inherited not a quiescent Latin America proceeding uniformly toward a liberal democratic future, but a continent increasingly divided on economic, political, and social lines. States such as Bolivia, Ecuador, and Venezuela have developed leftist economic models at variance with the Washington consensus. Each regime has sought to rekindle anti-Americanism as a way of effecting domestic legitimacy, Venezuela's Hugo Chávez especially so. This so-called "pink tide" threatens to revive antagonisms between north and south, which have damaged intra-American diplomacy since the nineteenth century.

How well placed is Obama to resist a reawakened leftism? Some liberal commentators have urged him to adapt his Latin American policy to domestic political developments, much as Franklin Roosevelt did in the 1930s. Instead of heightening tension by meddling, Obama's diplomacy should acquiesce in the leftward shift (see Grandin, 2009). This prescription ascribes Latin America's problems to American imperialism, an analysis that had some credence during the Cold War. However, since the end of that conflict, Latin America has had declining geostrategic salience for the United States. Its purported economic imperialism has not been sufficient to bring Chavez and his allies into line. Trade liberalization across the Americas, a central concern of each post-Cold War US President, still represents the rule of Latin American political economy, with Chavez, Morales, and Castro the exceptions. Washington has formed alliances in the region – such as with Brazil, Chile, and Colombia – which have magnified the regional conflicts between these states but which did not cause them. Obama's diplomacy has not yet showed itself to be markedly different from that of his predecessor. This suggests, for example, that US–Colombia relations will deepen, as they did under Bush, and antagonisms between these partners and Venezuela will increase.

Mexico provides further evidence of the limited impact a new diplomacy might have. Despite his domestic unpopularity, George W. Bush did not lessen the attraction of the United States as a destination for economic migrants crossing the US–Mexican border. Nor did he reduce the "bilateral cooperation" that has marked out US–Mexican relations since the administration of his father (see Domínguez and Fernández de Castro, 2009). In several respects, given his Texan base and governorship, George W. Bush actually affirmed and extended that friendship. It is not immediately obvious why Obama – who, unlike Bush, cannot speak Spanish – will have any greater success with his version of soft power than did Bush. Indeed, candidate Obama's threat to renegotiate the North American Free Trade Agreement (NAFTA) so as to favor American workers would necessarily cause US–Mexico relations to deteriorate (which explains why he moved away from this position early in his presidency). The opening of the Mexican economy since the 1980s represents a near-revolution (see Haber et al., 2008) that Obama is hardly likely to counter. By the same token, Obama has found himself as committed to border security as his Texan predecessor. His continuance of a "drug war" looks more likely than not. Mexico's problems are not ultimately within the power of any American President to solve. Unless the United States took the unlikely step of legalizing cocaine and/or invading its neighbor, the civil strife arising from the illegal drugs trade, which flared in several Mexican cities in 2008, will remain a problem for domestic Mexican governance. Again, this is not to suggest that a fresh approach toward Mexico might not bear more fruit (see Lowenthal, Piccone, and Whitehead, 2009). It is to caution against too great a faith in the capacity of American diplomacy to transform the polities of Mexico and the United States' other southern neighbors.

Bush's grand strategy: what happened to the war on terror?

Barack Obama rejected the "war on terror" as a title for the grand strategy of the United States. However, he continued to wage it. He accepted the end of Bush grand strategy – to stop terrorists acquiring weapons of mass destruction – but disputed the means. Indeed, his foreign policy credentials, in the absence of actual, formal experience, were burnished in the 2008 campaign by his insistence that he could fight America's enemies more effectively than George W. Bush. He did not and has not denied that the enemy exists ("a far reaching network," he called it) or that it seeks a doomsday weapon. Indeed, he is increasing the number of American troops and number of foreign allies – through a more nuanced diplomacy and multilateralism – to improve American counter-terrorism. As he made clear as early as 2007:

> [W]e must confront the most urgent threat to the security of America and the world – the spread of nuclear weapons, material, and technology and the risk that a nuclear device will fall into the hands of terrorists. The explosion of one such device would bring catastrophe, dwarfing the devastation of 9/11 and shaking every corner of the globe.   (Obama, 2007)

There are at least three visions of how his grand strategy will evolve, given Obama's embrace of the strategic necessity of American counter-terrorism. The first posits and hopes for a more liberal approach, the second for a realist one. The third vision, and probably the most likely, is of a grand strategy that adapts and adopts the Bush approach, accepts its logic, but changes its tactics. I will address each in turn.

Liberal grand strategy?

There is much in his presidential record already to suggest the adoption of a liberal grand strategy. Obama's emphasis on dialogue – via letters to Moscow and YouTube broadcasts to Tehran – computes with a basic liberal assumption that most conflicts can be ameliorated through discourse, diplomacy, and engagement. The liberal character of Obama's foreign policy is of course contingent on the definition of "liberal." We can see both a preference for the prescriptions of liberalism as a theory of international relations and a marked liberal record in a more practical, domestic sense.

In terms of liberal international relations theory, Obama's grand strategy seeks to realize American security through a multiplicity of approaches which include diplomacy, international institutions, and a generally friendlier demeanor than George W. Bush was able to present (Obama, 2009g). He has taken multilateralism seriously, to the extent that he has asked Europe for more help in the Afghanistan war. In several respects, he has sought to reclaim the multilateralism of the post-1945 era (see Patrick, 2009). America's capacity to shape world order, according to liberal theorists, was a product of its willingness to devolve power and construct rules that actually bounded Washington's freedom of action (see Ikenberry, 2001). By showing "strategic restraint," in contrast to the purported boldness of the Bush approach, Obama hopes to build a cooperative world order in which the majority of governments become stakeholders.

Obama's domestic, political liberalism – he was the 'most liberal' senator in Congress during his time there (see http://nj.nation-aljournal.com/voteratings/) – suggests a more internationalist approach. His declaration of a personal world citizenship (in Berlin in 2008) fits the stereotype of the domestic liberal as foreign policy leader. The attribution of liberalism to his grand strategy, however, is complicated when the stereotype is unpicked. The Democratic Party is friendly to internationalists but also to protectionists who want greater economic nationalism (in the form of tariffs and trade barriers to protect American jobs), especially during an economic recession.

Similarly, there is little to reassure liberals that Obama's assumed liberalism will make him any less inclined to use military power abroad. As a matter of historical record, it was Democratic commanders-in-chief who fought the great wars of the twentieth century. The First and Second World War, the Cold War, Korea, Vietnam, the Balkans – all were joined by Democratic administrations. Republican-initiated wars are the exception in American history. Bill Clinton had a marked preference for using American troops overseas, doing so over 80 times in his eight years in power (see Herring, 2008: 936). Several of his "liberal hawks" now occupy foreign policy positions in the Obama administration.

Realist grand strategy?

During the 2008 campaign, Obama made frequent references to former Presidents with whom he wanted his term in office compared. Abraham Lincoln and John F. Kennedy featured prominently in this narrative. George Bush Sr was a less obvious choice. Unlike his son, the 41st President has become totemic for realists for his insistence that American national interests should drive American foreign policy. The handling of Iraq by Bush Sr (in 1990–91) and Bush Jr (2003–09) offers several contrasts, the lesson of which for realists is the folly of unrealistic expectations. Bush Sr avoided war on the streets of Baghdad in 1991, reasoning that America had neither the resolve nor the international legitimacy to change the Iraqi regime. Bush Jr, after 9/11, assumed the former and largely discounted the latter. The result, according to several prominent realists (see Scowcroft in Goldberg, 2006; Mearsheimer, 2005) was what Obama labeled a "dumb war" (Obama, 2002). American blood, treasure, and prestige were sacrificed, and according to Obama the realist, the national interest compromised.

Intimations of a return to realism under Obama include his willingness to engage friends and opponents on the basis of interests rather than ideology. His diplomacy toward Syria, Iran, and Uzbekistan – states regarded as "rogue" by Bush Jr. – suggests Obama prizes interests more highly than idealism. Realism discounts the character of foreign regimes and asks only what national interest is served by associating with them. Such reasoning made it possible for George Bush Sr to avoid American intervention in the Balkans as the region descended into bloodshed in the early 1990s. A version of realism in the Clinton administration kept American troops out of Rwanda in 1994. Of what interest was it to the United States whether one African tribe was attempting genocide against another? The place of Israel in advancing American interests in the Middle East has long been the subject of realist skepticism (see Mearsheimer and Walt, 2007).

According to realists, American grand strategy should be tasked with the careful calibration of interests and means so as to realize American security. There are a number of problems with this realist portrait of Barack Obama. He seems prepared, so far, to deal with Arab states irrespective of their nondemocratic character, as realists urge – witness his preference for stability over reform in Egypt. But this will not give him a dispensation from moral questions. The Israeli democracy remains surrounded by Arab dictatorships. Could Obama increase American security by compromising on Israel's? His speech to AIPAC, the largest Israeli lobby in the United States, suggests not (see Obama, 2008a). The dilemma is not restricted to the Middle East. Consider how the first African American President will respond to ethnic conflict in Africa. Will realism be his guiding paradigm and cause him to steer clear? Or will President Obama avoid action not for realist reasons but for liberal ones? Will he make intervention in Darfur contingent on UN approval? Will he leave Kenya's fate – should it return to tribal violence – to international communitarianism? Clinton abandoned Rwanda. Could Obama forsake Congo? Will he dismiss Zimbabweans as a people far away about whom we know nothing? Realists will, of course, insist he do exactly this. Could he? Even his great realist role model, George Bush Sr, invaded Somalia in 1992 because, he said, "no one should have to die at Christmas." How much greater then the pressure on a President Obama to act in the face of genocide and UN obfuscation?

Bush grand strategy – a competent version?

President Obama has resisted easy appropriation by liberals and realists. Instead, his grand strategy has so far sought to navigate between the two approaches. Hillary Clinton referred to "smart power" as the most appropriate tool of American statecraft (Clinton, 2009). The concept is not new (see Nossell, 2004, for example), but appears grounded in a common-sense approach. The question is how far it really departs from the grand strategy of the Bush administration. In important respects the departure is minimal. Obama accepts the imperatives of the war on terror. He has resisted that label and some of the tactics Bush used in its prosecution, but he does not dispute their rationale. The Iraq war, most obviously, was indicted by Obama as a tactical disaster because it risked the longer-term strategy of negating WMD terrorism. The Af-Pak war was and is supported by President Obama because on its success hangs America's security. Guantánamo Bay, extraordinary rendition, and Abu Ghraib appalled him because they undermined America's reputation among the peoples whose cooperation was required to staunch terrorism. His reaction to these issues was moral but also strategic; they did not serve American grand strategy. And in the case of Guantánamo his outrage was not sufficient for him to close the base immediately.

In several respects, then, Obama's objection to Bush was not owed to his conceptualization of American grand strategy but to its prosecution. He has contended he can better blend the soft and hard forms of American power (see Nye, 2002) to better serve the American national interest. While he calls this "smart power," the notion that Bush was invested with a misplaced faith in the efficacy of hard power is overstated. Harder US military power in Iraq in the spring and summer of 2003, for example, might well have established an order on which a protean democratic state might have been built; Bush deployed too little hard power in this theater rather than too much. In matters of soft power too, Bush was hardly a novice. He used soft power in his diplomacy toward Iran and North Korea, relying on the persuasive effort of multilateral coalitions and carrots rather than American sticks – to limited effect, as the pace of both regimes' nuclear programs attest.

Conclusion

How the United States navigates these features of the modern world is necessarily contingent on the character of the American regime itself. American "exceptionalism" is a highly amorphous concept (see Lipset, 1996). As President Obama pointed out, all nations believe in their exceptionality (Obama, 2009f). However, there is much in his public rhetoric and early behavior to suggest he accepts for his nation an exceptional *leadership* role. Obama inherited a range of global commitments that he, like his predecessors, cannot easily evade without sacrificing American values. This does not mean Obama is obliged to support every democracy or every democratic movement. It does suggest his administration will have a conscience about abandoning democrats, from Israel to Iran.

Since 1945, the United States has led an imperfect global struggle to make democracy safe in the world. This pursuit explains many of its successes – like Germany and Japan – and failures – like Vietnam and Iraq. Attempts at more value-neutral approaches, such as Richard Nixon's détente in the 1970s – which sought to accommodate the Soviet Union on the basis of mutual interest – or George Bush Sr's approach to Iraq in the spring of 1991 – when he refused to honor his promise of support to those prepared to resist Saddam Hussein – invariably compromise American power and security, and leave their opponents stronger. For both good and ill, the American polity remains an ideological experiment in the capacity of a people for self-government. The United States' most ferocious wars have been in defense of this principle, from the American Civil War through the Cold War and beyond. Ideological imperatives are not easy to avoid, and we should expect them to explain much of American foreign policy in the years ahead.

It is important to remember that the United States must adapt its foreign policy to its own domestic character and structure. In reality, this means a foreign policy or policies that are especially susceptible to democratic discourse and the values that bound that discourse (see Foley, 2007). For example, it is inconceivable that an American President would ever disavow the free market as a vehicle for American prosperity and security – though President Obama is currently engaged in a reformation of how that market is regulated and the social functions it serves. Israel will remain important in America's approach to the Middle East not because of its oil exports – which are zero – but because the Jewish state is a democracy.

President Obama, therefore, has inherited both an international situation – with many threats and few opportunities – and an American political system – of long duration and ideological character – that he can tinker with but not transform. This is not to deny him agency or to scorn his remarkable personal and political talents. It is to observe the limits that context and structure – foreign and domestic – impose on any US President.

Chapter 15

The American Constitution at the End of the Bush Presidency

Louis Fisher

Eight years of President George W. Bush fundamentally threatened the American constitutional system, converting it from a government of laws (statutes, treaties, court rulings) to one where law was made unilaterally by the executive branch, often in secret. Executive officials would reassure the public that they were following policies that were "lawful," "legal," and "authorized." What they meant was that the policies had been conceived and approved solely within the executive branch, even when in violation of statutes, treaties, and court rulings.

Presidents in the past had invoked the concept of "inherent" power, claiming that they could assert authority over both the domestic and international fields without legislative or judicial checks. The federal judiciary, Congress, and the court of public opinion struck down their initiatives. The assertion of plenary and unchecked power by President Bush was notable for its breadth and the absence of effective restraints.

The terrorist attacks of 9/11 created such an atmosphere of fear in the United States, with apprehension regularly heightened by announcements from the administration, that traditional checks from Congress, the judiciary, and the public fell largely silent. This pattern is seen frequently in time of emergencies and wars. The government identifies an outside enemy (or even an enemy from within) and convinces the public that it needs to surrender certain rights and liberties to promote the national interest. Pushed to the limit, as by Nazi Germany and Soviet Russia, soon the nation is everything and the individual is nothing.

In the United States, when efforts were made in court to challenge actions by the Bush administration, executive officials would advise judges that the President as commander-in-chief had to operate free of restraints from other branches. The subject area was "quintessentially" presidential. In other cases, the administration would advise judges that the subject matter was so delicate (NSA surveillance or extraordinary rendition) that the case could not be further litigated without the risk of disclosing "state secrets." In many lawsuits federal judges regularly accepted the administration's argument. As a result, private plaintiffs who charged illegal and unconstitutional executive actions were unable to obtain or present documents to make their case.

The legal and constitutional abuses after 9/11 originated primarily from the executive branch, but illegal conduct cannot occur and persist without an acquiescent Congress and a compliant judiciary. The framers of the Constitution placed their faith in structural checks, hoping that a vigorous system of checks and balances would limit the damage that can come from concentrated power. Each branch was supposed to have an institutional incentive to fight off encroachments. Those structural checks have operated poorly over the past six decades and especially so after 9/11.

Making emergency actions legal

In previous periods of emergency and threats to national security, the rule of law has often taken a back seat to presidential initiatives and abuses. But at a time of genuine (not contrived) emergency, there are legitimate methods of executive action that are consistent with constitutional government. If an emergency occurs and there is no opportunity for executive officers to seek legislative authority, the executive may take action sometimes in the absence of law and sometimes against it – for the public good. That is called the "Lockean prerogative." John Locke advised that in the event of executive abuse the primary remedy was an "appeal to Heaven."

The American framers devised a more secular and constitutional safeguard. Unilateral presidential measures, taken at a time of an extraordinary crisis, must be followed promptly by going to Congress and obtaining authority. To preserve the constitutional order, two steps are essential: the President must (1) acknowledge that the emergency actions are not legal or constitutional, and (2) for that very reason come to the legislative branch to explain the actions taken, the reasons for the actions, and ask lawmakers to pass a bill making the illegal actions legal. Under Article 48 of the Weimar Constitution, as implemented by the Nazi government, emergency powers were invoked and implemented without ever coming to the legislative body.

The United States has been fortunate to escape the kind of authoritarian regime that emerged in Nazi Germany. Much of the credit goes to Presidents who respected and understood the American Constitution, and to other branches and the public for a willingness to confront executive abuses. The steps and attitudes needed to maintain constitutional legitimacy are seen in the conduct of President Abraham Lincoln after the start of the Civil War. He took actions we are all familiar with: withdrawing funds from the Treasury without an appropriation from Congress, calling up the troops (another constitutional authority of Congress), placing a blockade on the south, and suspending the writ of habeas corpus.

In ordering these emergency actions, Lincoln never claimed to be acting legally or constitutionally. He never argued that Article II of the Constitution or some provision within it, such as the commander-in - chief clause, somehow allowed him to do what he did. Instead, he frankly admitted to exceeding the constitutional boundaries of his office, and for that reason needed Congress to pass legislation to sanction what he had done. He told Congress that his actions, "whether strictly legal or not, were ventured upon under what appeared to be a popular demand and a public necessity, trusting then, as now, that Congress would readily ratify them." He explained that he used not only his Article II powers but the Article I powers of Congress, concluding that his actions were not "beyond the constitutional competency of Congress." Through this process he recognized that the superior lawmaking body was Congress, not the President. When an executive acts in this manner, he invites two possible consequences: either support from the legislative branch, or impeachment and removal from office. Congress, acting with the explicit understanding that Lincoln's actions were illegal, passed legislation retroactively approving and making valid all of his acts, proclamations, and orders (12 Stat. 326 (1861); Fisher, 2004: 47–9).

The danger of "inherent" powers

President Lincoln exercised emergency powers during America's greatest crisis without claiming exclusive or plenary powers. He worked with Congress and accepted statutory constraints, including judicial checks imposed by Congress. After 9/11, President Bush did not follow that model. Although he came to Congress to seek the Authorization for the Use of Military Force (AUMF) for military actions in Afghanistan, the USA Patriot Act, and the Iraq Resolution of 2002, increasingly he invoked powers unilaterally and in some cases in secret, even when violating statutory or treaty law. Among other actions, Bush claimed "inherent" power to create military tribunals and to conduct warrantless surveillance.

Presidents before him claimed inherent powers, provoking sustained battles with Congress and the courts. The problem with inherent powers is that they cannot be defined, either in origin or in scope. Constitutions maintain their integrity by relying on two kinds of powers: express and implied. Express powers are clearly stated in the text; implied powers are those that can be reasonably drawn from express powers. If Congress has the express power to legislate, it has the implied power to investigate and obtain information so that it can legislate in an intelligent fashion. If the President has an express power to see that the laws be faithfully executed, he has an implied power to remove any executive official who attempts to prevent him from discharging that duty.

"Inherent" is sometimes used as synonymous with "implied," but they are fundamentally different. The fifth edition of *Black's Law Dictionary* (1979) defined inherent power as an authority "possessed without its being derived from another." The eighth edition (2004) referred to inherent as a power "that necessarily derives from an office, position, or status." Other dictionaries describe inherent as belonging by nature or habit to something, or intrinsic to it. The purpose of a constitution is to specify and limit governmental powers to protect a realm of individual rights and liberties. That protection disappears when authorities are so open-ended and vague that they cannot be defined or circumscribed. Nebulous words and concepts invite political abuse, endanger individual liberties, and threaten the doctrine of separated powers and the system of checks and balances.

In 1952, the Justice Department argued in court that President Truman possessed inherent authority to seize steel mills to prosecute the war in Korea. It told a district judge that courts were powerless to control the exercise of presidential power when directed toward emergency conditions. According to the Justice Department, only two checks operated on the President: the ballot box and the impeachment process. At a news conference on April 17, 1952, Truman was asked if in addition to steel mills he could seize newspapers and radio stations. He answered that in periods of emergency the President "has to act for whatever is for the best of the country," and at such times he "has very great inherent powers." The district judge repudiated that theory and ruled that the seizure of the steel mills was unconstitutional. In *Youngstown Sheet & Tube Co. v Sawyer* (1952), the Supreme Court upheld that decision.

President Richard Nixon tried his hand at inherent powers. His legal advisers concluded that the President has no obligation to spend money that Congress has appropriated. Under this theory of inherent authority, a President could cut a program in half or zero it out. Presidents in the past had impounded funds but without this sweeping constitutional framework. About 80 cases were litigated and the Nixon administration lost almost all of them. The confrontation came to an end when Congress passed legislation in 1974 to limit the President's power to impound funds. Nixon also claimed inherent authority to conduct warrantless domestic surveillance, a grasp of power struck down both by federal courts and Congress. To set policy for national security wiretaps, Congress passed the Foreign Intelligence Surveillance

Act (FISA) of 1978 to provide statutory limitations on presidential power. The procedures established in the statute set forth the "exclusive means" for such surveillance, thereby rejecting any claims of inherent presidential power (Fisher, 2008: 285–91).

After the terrorist attacks of 9/11, officials in the Bush administration claimed inherent power for the President to create military commissions, designate US citizens as "enemy combatants" and hold them indefinitely without trial or counsel, condone torture as an interrogation technique, engage in "extraordinary rendition" – sending suspects to other countries for interrogation and torture – and conduct warrantless national security eavesdropping. At times the administration cited statutes and court cases to justify those initiatives, but the primary claim of authority consisted of inherent powers said to exist in Article II.

Military tribunals and "enemy combatants"

On November 13, 2001, President Bush issued a military order for the detention, treatment, and trial of noncitizens that belonged to Al Qaeda, engaged in international terrorism, or harbored such individuals. He relied on his authority as commander-in-chief and also the AUMF that Congress enacted to authorize military action in Afghanistan. When challenged in court, the Justice Department argued that Bush "had ample authority" to convene military commissions to try these individuals, and claimed that the Supreme Court "has recognized that courts are not competent to second-guess judgments of the political branches regarding the extent of force necessary to prosecute a war" (Department of Justice, 2006a: 7, 19).

In *Hamdan* v *Rumsfeld* (2006), the Court found those arguments to be without merit. The commissions that Bush created violated various procedures established by Congress in the Uniform Code of Military Justice (UCMJ). The Court therefore disposed of two constitutional questions. First, it rejected the claim that Bush had inherent authority under Article II to create the commissions. Second, it held that Congress had authority under Article I and had exercised that authority through the UCMJ. It was necessary for Bush to come to Congress and request additional authority, which was later passed in the form of the Military Commissions Act of 2006.

US citizens

The military commissions created by Bush applied to any individual "not a United States citizen." A number of suspected alien terrorists were prosecuted in civil courts. Others were designated "enemy combatant" and held incommunicado without access to an attorney. Two US citizens, Yaser Esam Hamdi and Jose Padilla, were treated in that fashion by being placed in military confinement without ever being charged or brought to trial. The Justice Department held that whenever the President designates a US citizen an enemy combatant, federal judges may not interfere with this determination. The department claimed that the Constitution vests the President with exclusive authority to act as commander-in-chief. On June 28, 2004, eight justices of the Supreme Court rejected the administration's central argument that Hamdi's detention was quintessentially a presidential decision beyond the capacity of courts to review and second-guess. Writing for a plurality of four in *Hamdi* v *Rumsfeld*, Justice Sandra Day O'Connor announced that whatever power the US Constitution grants the President in external affairs, "it most assuredly envisions a role for all three branches when individuals' liberties are at stake." On that sentiment four other justices joined her. Shortly after the Court's ruling the administration released Hamdi and sent him to Saudi Arabia (Fisher, 2008: 196).

Padilla, after being designated an enemy combatant, was kept in a Navy brig in Charleston, S.C., without access to an attorney, formal charges, or trial. On the same day that the Supreme Court decided Hamdi's case it ruled in *Rumsfeld* v *Padilla* that Padilla's habeas petition had been filed with the wrong court. His case came back up through the courts and was about to be heard by the Supreme Court, but at that point the government took him out of military detention and tried him in civil court in Florida. On August 16, 2007 a jury convicted him of terrorism conspiracy charges (Fisher, 2008: 208).

The system of military tribunals created by President Bush was praised by administration officials for its capacity to act with greater swiftness than prosecution through federal courts. But a series of legal challenges to the tribunals and the administration's difficulty in agreeing on operating rules slowed the process year after year. By the end of the Bush administration, the system of tribunals at Guantánamo had succeeded in prosecuting only three suspected terrorists over a period of more than seven years.

At the start of his administration, President Barack Obama froze military tribunals until May 30, 2009, giving executive officials an opportunity to review the value of this system of justice. On May 15, he announced his decision to retain tribunals but planned to ask Congress to expand the rights of defendants to challenge charges brought against them. The Senate Armed Services Committee held thoughtful hearings on July 7 to consider improvements in military tribunals. Even with some refinements, these tribunals are likely to be challenged in court and seen throughout the world as a judicial body that offers the accused second-class privileges (Glaberson, 2009: A14).

Guantánamo

During military operations in late 2001 and early 2002, US forces began rounding up thousands of individuals believed to be terrorists associated with the Taliban or Al Qaeda. About 800 were brought to the US naval base at Guantánamo Bay, Cuba. Newspaper stories reported a bounty-hunter system, with members of the Northern Alliance (Tajiks and Uzbeks), Pakistani officials, and other allies given $5,000 if they identified someone as Taliban and $20,000 if they linked the suspect with Al Qaeda. US officials at the naval base recognized that the detainees represented a mix of terrorist suspects and innocent people erroneously swept up. Moazzam Begg, seized in Pakistan in January 2002, was imprisoned for three years at Bagram, Kandahar, and Guantánamo. Initially identified as an "enemy combatant," he was finally released without explanation, apology, or any gesture toward reparation (Begg, 2006). Hundred of detainees would be similarly released.

In the early months of 2002, executive officials debated how to treat detainees at the naval base. In a memo signed on February 7, 2002, President Bush stated that none of the Geneva Conventions regarding the treatment of prisoners of war and civilians should apply to Al Qaeda, although they would apply "to our present conflict with the Taliban." However, he determined that the Taliban detainees were "unlawful combatants" and did not qualify as POWs under Geneva. He further said that "as a matter of policy" (but not of law or treaty obligations) detainees would be treated "humanely and, to the extent appropriate and consistent with military necessity, in a manner consistent with the principle of Geneva" (Fisher, 2008: 217–18). Clearly the administration did not feel legally bound by Geneva.

The torture memos

The administration prepared legal analyses to permit US interrogators to abuse detainees. The memos were highly classified and shared with few executive officials. A key memo, dated August 1, 2002 and signed by Jay Bybee, head of the Office of Legal Counsel in the Justice Department, defined torture to mean "serious physical injury, such as organ failure, impairment of bodily function, or even death." To protect interrogators from prosecution, he explained that the above physical injuries had to be "specifically intended." If causing injury was not the specific intent, but gaining intelligence was, the interrogator could not be prosecuted. Further, Bybee concluded that the President's authority under Article II overrode treaty obligations, such as the Convention Against Torture (CAT). Under this legal analysis, no statute or treaty could interfere with the President's authority as commander-in-chief to order interrogation of enemy combatants to gain intelligence. The legal principles of the Bybee memo were largely adopted by the Bush administration (Fisher, 2008: 221–6).

Two attorneys in the Justice Department, Patrick Philbin and John Yoo, wrote a legal memo concluding that federal courts would probably not have habeas jurisdiction to hear petitions from noncitizens detained at Guantánamo (Fisher, 2008: 219). That theory was upheld in some of the lower courts, partly by relying on a 1950 Supreme Court decision, *Johnson* v *Eisentrager*. On June 28, 2004, in *Rasul* v *Bush*, the Supreme Court denied that *Eisentrager* applied to conditions at the naval base. Unlike the German nationals tried in the 1950 case, the detainees at the naval base were not nationals of countries at war with the United States, had denied being engaged in or plotting acts of aggression against the United States, and were never afforded the procedural protections of the German nationals, who had been charged, given counsel, tried, found guilty, and sentenced. The detainees at the naval base had been held for two years without being charged. Also unlike the 1950 case, the detainees at the naval base were in a territory over which the United States had exercised exclusive jurisdiction and control ever since 1903.

Combatant status review tribunals

The administration responded to *Rasul* by establishing combatant status review tribunals (CSRTs). For the first time, detainees at the naval base would be told why they were being held and given an opportunity to challenge their designation as enemy combatants. However, they could call witnesses only if "reasonably available" and had no right to gain access to classified evidence used to justify their classification as enemy combatant. Congress enacted the Detainee Treatment Act in 2005 to spell out the procedural safeguards. It was uncertain whether President Bush would carry out the law to the letter. In his signing statement, he said his administration "is committed to treating all detainees held by the United States in a manner consistent with our Constitution, laws, and treaty obligations, which reflect the values we hold dear." The operative phrase here is "consistent with" rather than "in compliance with." The first is policy, exercised at the liberty of the administration; the second is binding law.

Detainees at the naval base continued to bring lawsuits against the administration. The Military Commissions Act (MCA) of 2006 had placed restrictions on habeas petitions. According to the statute, no person may invoke the Geneva Conventions or any of its protocols in any habeas action to which the United States "or a current or former officer, employee, member of the Armed Forces, or other agent of the United States is a party as a source of rights in any court of the United States or its States or territories." Any "alien unlawful enemy combatant" was subject to trial by military commission. The Detainee Treatment Act (DTA) of 2005 had also placed restrictions on habeas petitions.

Attorneys representing detainees at the naval base argued that the DTA did not apply to pending cases and did not affect federal court jurisdiction over their habeas actions. Challenges were also brought against the adequacy of the CSRTs used to determine whether a detainee was an enemy combatant. On February 20, 2007 the D.C. Circuit held that the MCA denied jurisdiction to federal courts to consider the habeas petitions filed by detainees at the naval base prior to the date of the statute. A dissenting judge agreed that it was the intent of Congress in passing the MCA to withdraw jurisdiction from federal courts, but held that the statute offended the Suspension clause of the Constitution (prohibiting suspension of the writ of habeas corpus unless required by public safety in cases of rebellion or invasion). Because the statute was void under this reading, it did not deprive federal courts of jurisdiction. The dissent said that the Suspension Clause did not protect only citizens. It covered all persons, citizens and aliens.

The Supreme Court and habeas petitions

At oral argument before the Supreme Court, Seth P. Waxman presented the case for the detainees. He told the justices that the detainees had been confined at the naval base "for almost six years, yet not one has ever had meaningful notice of the factual grounds of detention or a fair opportunity to dispute those grounds before a neutral decision-maker." On June 12, 2008, the Supreme Court held that both the MCA and the DTA operated as an unconstitutional suspension of the writ. Writing for a five to four Court in *Boumediene* v *Bush*, Justice Kennedy took note of the length of time the detainees had been at the naval base. He also observed that they could be held for "the duration of hostilities that may last a generation or more."

Justice Kennedy explained the history and origins of the writ, one of the few safeguards of liberty specified in the Constitution before the addition of the Bill of Rights. While acknowledging the importance of national security in a time of crisis, he pointed out that a crucial value in a system of law is freedom from arbitrary and unlawful restraint: "The laws and Constitution are designed to survive, and remain in force, in extraordinary times. Liberty and security can be reconciled; and in our system they are reconciled within the framework of the law." Habeas corpus "must be a part of that framework, a part of that law." Lakhdar

Boumediene, plaintiff in the case, was flown out of the naval base on May 15, 2009 and taken to France, where he has relatives.

One of President Barack Obama's first actions, on January 22, 2009, was to announce the closure of Guantánamo within a year. Later, on May 21, he explained "the existence of Guantánamo likely created more terrorists around the world than it ever detained." When he took office, about 240 detainees remained at the naval base. The administration hoped to release a large number and appealed to countries around the world to accept them. There were few takers. The administration contemplated prosecuting some of the detainees in federal courts. Others would be brought before a revamped military tribunal. Members of Congress voiced strong opposition to having detainees brought within American prisons in their districts or states. When the administration requested $80 million to begin to close the detention center at the naval base, Congress rebelled. Lawmakers refused to grant the funds unless the administration presented a more specific plan of action (Herszenhorn, 2009: A1).

Interrogation techniques

Legal analysis within the Bush administration concluded that existing statutes and treaties prohibiting torture did not apply to the President's authority as commander-in-chief to detain and interrogate enemy combatants and suspected terrorists. In April 2004, during oral argument before the Supreme Court on the Hamdi and Padilla cases, several justices asked deputy solicitor general Paul Clement how the administration treated detainees. Were they abused? Tortured? Clement assured the justices that the United States honored treaty and statutory prohibitions on torture. Moreover, he said that coerced interrogations did not yield reliable information, and if any soldier violated existing law, they would be prosecuted in a court martial.

That evening, on the CBS News program *60 Minutes*, viewers around the world saw disturbing photos of detainees at the Abu Ghraib prison in Iraq being subjected to degrading and abusive treatment by American soldiers. A report by Major General Antonio M. Taguba described "numerous incidents of sadistic, blatant, and wanton criminal abuses" inflicted on the detainees. He referred to the abuses as "systemic and illegal." Several American soldiers had committed "egregious acts and grave breaches of international law" (Fisher, 2008: 226–8). World condemnation of American practices at Abu Ghraib and other prisons forced the White House to withdraw Bybee's memo. At a press briefing on June 22, 2004, White House counsel Alberto Gonzales told reporters that to the extent that some Justice Department memos regarding interrogations "explored broad legal theories, including legal theories about the scope of the President's power as commander-in-chief, some of their discussion, quite frankly, is irrelevant and unnecessary to support any action taken by the President" (Fisher, 2008: 229–30).

It would be inaccurate to say that the administration repudiated the Bybee memo and prohibited abusive interrogative techniques. As Gonzales explained, some passages of the memo were not necessary and too easy to misread and misinterpret. When reporters probed what he meant and whether his presentation included CIA activities, he said he did not intend "to get into questions related to the CIA." On December 30, 2004, the Justice Department issued a new memo to replace what Bybee had written. But the administration continued to authorize abusive interrogations by the CIA. What the White House had done was to recognize two standards: humane questioning by the Defense Department and harsh techniques employed by the CIA. Senator John McCain added anti-torture language to the Detainee Treatment Act of 2005 but a signing statement by President Bush largely gutted its enforceability. During discussion on the military commission bill in the fall of 2006, the distinction between military and CIA standards was openly discussed (Baker, 2006: A1).

Modifications by Obama

On January 22, 2009, President Obama issued an executive order entitled "Ensuring Lawful Interrogations." The purpose was to improve the effectiveness of human intelligence gathering, promote the safe, lawful, and humane treatment of detainees in American custody, and ensure compliance with the treaty obligations of the United States, including the Geneva Conventions. He revoked all previous executive directives issued by the Bush administration inconsistent with his order, "including but not limited to those issued to or by the Central Intelligence Agency." All interrogations in the future would be conducted in accordance with the *Army Field Manual*, which had been updated in September 2006 to prohibit not only "waterboarding" (simulated drowning) but also the conduct seen at Abu Ghraib (use of military dogs, nakedness, and forcing simulated sex acts).

In April 2009, Obama authorized the release of a number of previously classified Office of Legal Counsel (OLC) memos, some of them dealing with interrogation techniques. Justice Department attorneys wrote detailed memos justifying waterboarding, stress positions, cramped confinement, facial slaps, abdominal slaps, nudity, sleep deprivation, and other methods of questioning detainees (Mazzetti and Shane, 2009: A1). In a major statement on May 21, Obama disagreed that "brutal methods like waterboarding were necessary to keep us safe." He denied that they are "the most effective means of interrogation." Instead, they "undermine the rule of law," alienate the world community, and "serve as a recruitment tool for terrorists."

Extraordinary rendition

The constitutional damage done by inherent presidential power is evident in the area of "extraordinary rendition," a Bush administration policy that sent suspects to other countries for interrogation and torture. It has long been the practice of countries to enter into treaties providing for the extradition to another country of persons charged with serious crimes, such as murder. The purpose of extradition is to bring an individual to court. The Justice Department concluded that Presidents might not send someone abroad under some form of implied, inherent, or extra-constitutional authority. They needed authority granted by either treaty or a law passed by Congress (Fisher, 2008: 321–5). There have also been cases of kidnappings and forcible abduction, where a suspect is captured and taken from one country to another. But here again the purpose is to bring someone to trial with all the procedural safeguards one has in court: to be charged, given counsel, and tried before a neutral magistrate (Fisher, 2008: 326–8).

Officials in the Bush administration defended the practice of interrogating suspected terrorists outside the United States. James L. Pavitt, after retiring from the CIA in August 2004, claimed that the policy of extraordinary rendition had been done only after consultation with the National Security Council and disclosure to the appropriate congressional oversight committees (Priest, 2004: A21). Consultation within the executive branch and touching base with certain congressional committees has nothing to do with acting legally through authority granted by statutes or treaties. Critical stories about extraordinary detention appeared with increasing frequency in the press. Several countries, including Denmark, Germany, Ireland, Italy, Norway, Spain, and Sweden, authorized investigations into the CIA planes that flew regularly over their airspace to carry suspects to interrogation facilities. Prosecutors in Italy filed a formal extradition request for 21 US citizens said to be CIA operatives (Fisher, 2008: 334–6).

Claims by Secretary Rice

In December 2005, secretary of state Condoleezza Rice traveled to Europe to defend American policy. Her detailed statement confused the CIA operations with traditional rendition backed by treaties and due process in court. She claimed that:

> [f]or decades, the United States and other countries have used "ren-
> ditions" to transport terrorist suspects from the country they were
> captured to their home country or to other countries where they
> can be questioned, held, or brought to justice.   (Rice 2005, 1–2)

In cases of forcible abduction, the purpose was to bring drug lords and
other individuals to trial, not for abusive interrogations. She claimed
that rendition "is not unique to the United States, or to the current
administration," pointing to Ramzi Yousef brought to the United
States after being charged with the 1993 bombing of the World Trade
Center, and the terrorist "Carlos the Jackal" captured in Sudan and
brought to France. However, they were not subject to abusive interrogations. They were brought to court to face public charges, trial, con-
viction, and sentencing.

Rice's claim that the United States "does not permit, tolerate, or
condone torture under any circumstances" was contradicted by the
Bybee memo and news reports on the treatment of detainees at Abu
Ghraib, Kandahar, Bagram, and Guantánamo. She said that when the
United States transported suspects to another country it was only after
seeking assurances that "transferred persons will not be tortured." The
Bush administration had no capacity to monitor interrogations to
guarantee that "assurances" were honored. According to Rice, the
United States "complies with its Constitution, its laws, and its treaty
obligations. Acts of physical or mental torture are expressly prohib-
ited." The Bybee memo, as initially endorsed by White House Counsel
Gonzales, denied that statutes and treaties could interfere with the
President's duties as commander-in-chief.

Dick Marty, a Swiss lawyer working for the Council of Europe,
released a report in June 2006 that concluded that at least 13 nations
in Europe and the Mediterranean had cooperated with the CIA on
extraordinary rendition. His report identified the cities where abusive
interrogations were carried out (Whitlock, 2006: A16). After publication of Marty's report, President Bush at a press conference on June 9,
2006 acknowledged that "sometimes renditions take place."

The decision to close down the CIA prisons was prompted in part by
the Supreme Court's decision in *Hamdan v Rumsfeld* (2006). The
Court ruled that detainees must be protected by the Geneva
Conventions, including the provisions of Common Article 3 and its
prohibitions on torture or humiliating, degrading treatment. On
September 6, 2006, President Bush made a lengthy statement about the
CIA rendition program. Fourteen men held in CIA custody would be
transferred to Guantánamo and interrogated in accordance with the
Army Field Manual.

Several individuals subject to extraordinary rendition took their
grievances to court. In each case the Justice Department argued that

their lawsuits could not move forward because they would risk the disclosure of state secrets and encroach upon the President's independent constitutional authority: "The state secrets privilege is based on the President's Article II power to conduct foreign affairs and to provide for the national defense, and therefore has constitutional underpinnings" (US Department of Justice, 2005: 3–4).

Maher Arar

One case involved Maher Arar. He was born in Syria but moved to Canada with his parents and studied at McGill University and the University of Quebec. In September 2002, he was vacationing in Tunis with his wife and two children. Called back to Ottawa for a business meeting, he landed at JFK airport in New York en route to Montreal. At JFK airport he was pulled aside by immigration officials and questioned by the New York Police Department and FBI agents. He told officials not to send him to Syria because he would be tortured. Annual reports by the State Department confirmed that security forces in Syria committed "serious human rights abuses," including electrical shocks, pulling out fingernails, forcing objects into the rectum, beating (sometimes while the victim is suspending from the ceiling), and hyperextending the spine (Fisher, 2008: 346–7).

The Bush administration certified that Arar's removal to Syria was consistent with Article 3 of the Convention Against Torture. He was flown to Jordan and driven to Damascus, Syria, where he was imprisoned at the Palestine Branch of Syrian military intelligence. He was kept in a cell called a "grave" (3 ft wide, 6 ft deep, 7 ft high, with a metal door that prevented light from entering). He was beaten on his palms, wrists, lower back, and hips with a shredded electrical cable. In September 2003 he was flown out of Syria and returned to Canada. An expert who assisted in Canada's investigation of Arar's abduction concluded that his treatment in Syria "constituted torture as understood in international law" (Canada, 2005: 17). Canada produced a three-volume, 822-page judicial report which concluded that Canadian intelligence officials had passed false warnings and information about Arar to the United States. The report found no evidence that he had done anything wrong or was a security threat. The United States refused to cooperate in the inquiry (Struck, 2006: A1; Austen, 2006: A1). The Prime Minister of Canada released a letter of apology to Arar and his family and the Canadian government provided him with $9.75 million in compensation.

On January 22, 2004, Arar filed a civil suit in the United States, seeking money damages and declaratory relief from a number of American officials in their individual and official capacities. On February 16, 2006, a federal district court in *Arar v Ashcroft* held that he lacked standing to bring the case. Any access to remedies, said the court, was foreclosed because of national security and foreign policy considerations. On June 30, 2008, the Second Circuit also dismissed Arar's suit, in part by claiming that he was never technically inside the United States. A dissenting judge called this argument "a legal fiction," concluding that Arar was abducted while attempting to transit to Montreal at the JFK airport (Feuer, 2008: A12). On November 2, 2009 Arar lost again when the Second Circuit sitting en banc confirmed the ruling of the initial panel of three judges.

Khaled El-Masri

Khaled El-Masri, another victim of extraordinary rendition, was born in Kuwait, raised in Lebanon, and later became a German citizen. In 2003 he traveled to Macedonia for a vacation. Because officials thought he was Khalid al-Masri, a suspect from the Al Qaeda Hamburg cell, he was detained in Macedonia and eventually turned over to the CIA and flown to Kabul, Afghanistan. He was held at a secret prison called the "Salt Pit" for five months. Kept in squalid conditions, he was repeatedly refused legal counsel or an opportunity to talk with a representative of the German government. After officials realized they had the wrong person, he was flown to Albania and left alone, at night, on a hill. Three uniformed men took him to the Tirana airport and he boarded a plane to Frankfurt (Fisher, 2008: 352).

On December 6, 2005, El-Masri sued CIA director George Tenet, the airlines used by the CIA, and current and former employees of the agency. The Bush administration invoked the state secrets privilege to block his lawsuit. On May 12, 2006, a federal district court in *El-Masri v Tenet* held that the state secrets privilege had been validly asserted and dismissed his case. Putting the legal issues to the side, the judge said that if El-Masri's allegations were true he "has suffered injuries as a result of our country's mistake and deserves a remedy." The source of that remedy, he said, had to come from the other branches of government, "not the Judicial Branch." There was no reason to expect a remedy from the executive branch, which initiated the rendition and attempted to block any litigation challenging it. Why should Congress have to correct a mistake instead of the courts?

El-Masri lost his appeal to the Fourth Circuit. In *El-Masri v United States*, the appellate court said the case was difficult because "it pits the judiciary's search for truth against the executive's duty to maintain the nation's security." How could the court search for truth if it accepted the government's claim of state secrets and therefore blocked access to documents to inform both the court and the plaintiff? The court also argued that El-Masri's personal interest in pursuing his claim was subordinated "to the collective interest in national security."

What possible collective interest was promoted by the government's mistaken action? On October 9, 2007, the Supreme Court declined to take El-Masri's appeal.

The Jeppesen case

A third case was brought by the American Civil Liberties Union (ACLU) against a private company that assisted the CIA with its extraordinary rendition program. Binyam Mohamed and four other men sued Jeppesen Dataplan, a domestic corporation with its headquarters in San Jose, California. The five men charged that the company, operating through a private contract, provided the CIA with aircraft, flight crews, and the flight and logistical support for hundreds of international flights. According to published reports, Jeppesen knew what it was doing. A former employee of the company told of an internal meeting where a senior Jeppesen official stated: "We do all of the extraordinary rendition flights," calling them "the torture flights." He added: "let's face it, some of these flights end up this way" (Belcher, 2007).

The plaintiffs lost in district court after the Bush administration invoked the state secrets privilege. When the case was argued on appeal before the Ninth Circuit on February 9, 2009, the court asked a Justice Department attorney if the new Obama administration had changed its legal position. The attorney answered: "No, your honor" (Schwartz, 2009: A12; Finn, 2009: A4). From this remark, it appeared that the Obama administration would continue to use the state secrets privilege to block lawsuits against the government. The lead plaintiff, Binyam Mohamed, was released from Guantánamo on February 23, 2009 and flown to London. He spoke openly about the abuse he had experienced while in American custody and accused British officials of being complicit in his "horrors over the past seven years" (Sullivan, 2009: A7).

The Ninth Circuit, on April 28, 2009, reversed the district court and ordered the case to continue (Johnson, 2009: A3). The appellate courts said the plaintiffs in *Mohamed* v *Jeppesen Dataplan* should have "an opportunity to present evidence in support of their allegations." It pointed out that the state secrets privilege could be manipulated to hide executive branch abuse and illegality. "Classified" documents, it said, should not be equated with "secret" documents. Such a practice would "perversely encourage the President to classify politically embarrassing information simply to place it beyond the reach of judicial process."

On May 21 President Obama stated that his administration is rethinking the state secrets privilege and expressed concern that "it has been over-used." As a general principle, he said, "[w]e must not protect information merely because it reveals the violation of a law or embarrassment to the government."

NSA eavesdropping

On December 15, 2005, the *New York Times* reported that, in the months following the 9/11 terrorist attacks, President Bush had secretly authorized the National Security Agency (NSA) to listen to Americans and others inside the United States without a court-approved warrant, a procedure that Congress required in 1978 with the FISA. The next day, President Bush acknowledged that he had authorized the NSA, "consistent with US law and the Constitution, to intercept the international communications of people with known links to Al Qaeda and related terrorist organizations" (*New York Times*, 2005).

Although Bush violated FISA he argued that a separate statute authorized what he had done. At a news conference on December 19 he claimed that as President and commander-in-chief he had the constitutional authority to protect the country. Further, he noted that Congress had passed the AUMF granting him "additional authority to use military force against Al Qaeda" (Bush, 2005: 2). Also on December 19, Attorney General Gonzales claimed, "the President has the inherent authority under the Constitution, as Commander-in-Chief, to engage in this kind of activity" (Gonzales, 2005: 2).

When it passed FISA, Congress stipulated that the warrant process established in the act constituted the "exclusive means" for national security wiretaps. Gonzales would have to argue that the AUMF trumped FISA, but no one during the debate on the AUMF made any reference (express or implied) to national security wiretaps or to any modification of FISA. If Congress wants to amend FISA, as it has done many times, it knows how to bring FISA to the floor, debate the changes contemplated, and enact them. On January 19, 2006, OLC produced a 42-page white paper defending the legality of the NSA program. It concluded that the NSA national security surveillance was supported by the President's "well-recognized inherent constitutional authority as Commander in Chief" (Department of Justice, 2006b: 1). In addition, it pointed to the AUMF as statutory authority for the NSA activity. Yet OLC also argued that the effort by Congress in FISA to establish the "exclusive means" would interfere with the President's Article II authorities. According to that reading, statutory law could not restrict what the President wanted to do under Article II authorities.

Deciding to violate statutory law

When Michael Hayden appeared before the Senate Intelligence Committee on May 18, 2006 to testify on his nomination to be CIA director, he defended the legality of the NSA program on constitutional, not statutory, grounds. He did not attempt to cite the AUMF as legal justification. Recalling his service as NSA director, he told the committee that NSA lawyers "were very comfortable with the Article II arguments and the President's inherent authorities." He repeatedly claimed that the program was "legal" and that the CIA "will obey the laws of the United States and will respond to our treaty obligations." What did Hayden mean by "law"? During the hearing, he treated law as something that flows not from statutes or treaties but from Article II and inherent powers. As he put it: "I had two lawful programs in front of me, one authorized by the President, the other one would have been conducted under FISA as currently crafted and implemented." Hayden made it clear that he was willing to violate statutory law in order to carry out presidential law. CIA director George Tenet had asked Hayden, when he was NSA director, whether he could "do more" to combat terrorism with surveillance. Hayden replied, "Not within current law." He proceeded to implement the NSA eavesdropping program knowing it was illegal under FISA.

Numerous challenges to the legality of the NSA program were taken to court. Many were turned aside by the state secrets privilege (Fisher, 2008: 302–10). Congress passed legislation on July 10, 2008, granting immunity to the telecoms that were being sued for their assistance to the Bush administration in carrying out national security surveillance (Public Law 110–261, sec. 802). However, lawsuits against the government could continue. An interesting case was brought by the Al-Haramain Islamic Foundation. On July 2, 2008, a district court in California held that FISA preempted the state secrets privilege as invoked in the NSA cases. It held that Congress "appears clearly to have intended to – and did – establish the exclusive means for foreign intelligence surveillance activities to be conducted" (In Re National Sec. Agency Telecommunications Rec., 564 F.Supp.2d 1109, 1121). Claims of inherent presidential power did not override the statute. The court gave plaintiffs an opportunity to show whether they are "aggrieved persons" within the meaning of FISA.

Conclusion

Over the eight years of the Bush presidency, the administration came to rely increasingly on the state secrets privilege to prevent litigants from challenging such programs as extraordinary rendition and NSA surveillance. The rule of law is threatened if federal judges accept the standards of "deference" or "utmost deference" when judging the legality of executive actions. When judges fail to assert their independence in these cases, it is possible for an administration to violate statutes, treaties, and the Constitution without any effective challenges in court. Congress has full authority to act legislatively to redress the problem. The House and the Senate held hearings on the state secrets privilege in 2008 and drafted legislation to give federal judges greater independence in reviewing national security claims put forth by executive officials. Those bills were reintroduced in 2009.

Another threat to the rule of law is the extent to which the Bush administration operated on the basis of secret executive orders, memoranda, directives, and legal memos. Congressional and judicial checks cannot function when executive policies are conceived and implemented in secret. If legal memos contain sensitive information, items can be redacted and the balance of the document made public. No plausible case can be made for withholding legal reasoning. Secret policy means that the rule of law is not statute or treaty, enacted in public, but confidential executive policies unknown to citizens and even to members of Congress.

However valuable and useful inter-branch consultation can be, it is never a substitute for legislation that specifically authorizes a presidential action. Lawmaking is the action of the full Congress, not subgroups like the "Gang of Eight" consisting of party leaders in each house and the chair and ranking member of the Intelligence Committees. The decision to make law is assigned to each member of Congress, from the speaker of the House and the Senate majority leader to the newly elected lawmakers. A President and his executive aides should not be able to co-opt a small group of lawmakers into agreeing with a program that flatly violates the law.

The framers of the Constitution did not pin their hopes on the President or federal courts to protect individual rights and liberties. They distrusted human nature and chose to place their faith in a system of checks and balances and separated powers. The rule of law finds protection when political power is not concentrated in a single branch and when all three branches exercise the powers assigned them, including the duty to resist the encroachments of another branch. The rule of law is always at risk when Congress and the judiciary defer to claims and assertions by executive officials, especially in the field of national security. That is the lesson of the last two centuries and particularly of the Bush administration.

To provide assurance to the public and other branches, the Bush administration often announced that what it had done was fully "authorized" and "lawful." Those words implied that the administration was acting in compliance with the rule of law when in fact it was operating squarely against it and doing so in secret. In 1952, Justice Robert Jackson reminded us what is meant by the rule of law: "With all its defects, delays and inconveniences, men have discovered no technique for long preserving free government except that the executive be under the law, and that the law be made by parliamentary deliberation" (*Youngstown Co. v Sawyer*, 343 U.S. 579, 655).

Chapter 16

American Immigration Policy and Politics: An Enduring Controversy

James F. Hollifield

Introduction

Recent debates about immigration policy in the United States can be framed by three events. The first is the passage of Proposition 187 by California voters in November 1994. Known as the "Save our State" or SOS initiative, Proposition 187 was intended to prevent illegal immigrants in California from gaining access to social services, ranging from basic health care to primary and secondary education (K through 12). The measure required local officials to cooperate with federal authorities in the enforcement of immigration law, from the cop on the beat to the teacher in the classroom. State employees were supposed to report anyone suspected of being an illegal immigrant to federal authorities. The measure passed handily by a two to one margin, garnering most support in rural and suburban areas, and among less educated white voters. However, Proposition 187 was never implemented because most of its provisions were deemed unconstitutional. In *League of United Latin American Citizens (Lulac)* v *Wilson* (1995) a district court judge ruled that Proposition 187 violated the long-established "plenary power" doctrine whereby the federal government has sole authority in making and enforcing immigration policy. Proponents of the measure argued that by failing to control the border with Mexico, the federal government had abdicated its responsibility and that power should devolve to the states.

The second event is the terrorist attack of 9/11 which changed the terms of the debate about immigration, shifting it from an almost exclusive focus on the economic and social effects of immigration to a concern over security and protecting the homeland from another terrorist attack. Even greater emphasis was placed on border control, and advocates for a more restrictive immigration policy were given new ammunition with which to make their case. The entire immigration control bureaucracy in the United States was reorganized and given a new mission – to make sure that terrorists would never again be able to slip into the country undetected. In 2001, with the election of two border-state governors as President of the United States (George W. Bush from Texas) and President of Mexico (Vicente Fox from Guanajuato), there were high hopes that an agreement could be reached between the two countries for sweeping immigration reform. But these hopes were dashed by the 9/11 attacks, and immigration reform lost critical momentum. Still, Congress tried unsuccessfully to tackle the immigration issue at the beginning of George W. Bush's second term.

Hence the third event, which helps to frame contemporary debates over US immigration policy, is the passage by the House of Representatives in December 2005 of the Border Protection, Anti-terrorism, and Illegal Immigration Control Act (HR 4437), also known as the Sensenbrenner Bill, after its primary sponsor, Representative James Sensenbrenner (R. Wisc.). The bill contained a number of controversial provisions, such as the construction of a new wall along the US–Mexico border to deter illegal crossings, and it would have made illegal immigration and aiding or assisting illegal immigrants a felony, punishable by stiff fines and imprisonment. Like Proposition 187, the Sensenbrenner Bill was designed to deter illegal immigration. Even though the bill easily passed the House with a vote (239–182) largely along party lines (92 per cent of Republicans in favor and 82 per cent of Democrats opposed), it failed to become law, because the Senate in 2006 opted for a different, more comprehensive approach to immigration reform.

The Senate wanted legislation that included measures for a guest worker program and legalization of the large population of illegal immigrants, estimated at 10–12 million. In the end Congress failed to pass any immigration reform during the presidency of George W. Bush – partly because the terrorist attacks of 9/11 pushed immigration reform off the agenda for several years. Nevertheless the immigration genie was out of the bottle. As is often the case in immigration politics, the reform was initiated by the President, who early in 2005 proposed a comprehensive reform, only to see the issue become highly politicized once Congress took it up. The Sensenbrenner Bill provoked the largest protests in the United States since the civil rights movement of the 1960s. Millions took to the streets in cities across the country, marching to the rallying cry of *hoy marchamos, mañana votamos!* (Today we march, tomorrow we vote!). Cardinal Roger Mahony of Los Angeles led some of the protests and called for civil disobedience, arguing that if the Sensenbrenner Bill became law it would make the most basic provision of charitable and religious assistance to illegal immigrants a crime. Asked if he would obey the law, he said that he would answer to a "higher authority."

The 1996 Illegal Immigration Reform and Immigrant Responsibility Act (IIRIRA) was the last major reform of federal immigration policy. A Republican-controlled Congress passed it in 1996 in part as a response to Proposition 187 and the popular backlash against rising levels of (illegal) immigration. Democratic President Bill Clinton, who vowed to roll back the more severe limitations that the act imposed on the rights of legal and illegal immigrants, signed IIRIRA reluctantly. With the number of illegal immigrants soaring in the first decade of the twentieth century and in the absence of federal action, literally thousands of state and local bills were proposed, with hundreds becoming law. Some of these measures involved Section 287g of the IIRIRA, which authorized local law enforcement agencies to enter into agreements with federal authorities to arrest and detain illegal immigrants. Other laws involved state and local enforcement of sanctions against employers who hire illegal immigrants, penalties for landlords renting to illegals, as well as laws designed to exclude illegals from receiving in-state tuition benefits at state-run colleges and universities, and from getting driver's licenses.

Governor Elliot Spitzer of New York, before his fall from grace in a sex scandal, ignited a firestorm of controversy by proposing a measure that would have made it easier for illegals to obtain New York driver's licenses. In 2009 the Development Relief and Education for Minors (DREAM) Act was introduced in Congress to allow some illegal immigrant students, who were brought to the country as children but graduated from high school in good standing, to gain temporary residency and ultimately a green card, with the proviso that they attend college or serve in the military. As these recent developments in American politics illustrate, immigration is an issue that sharply divides the American electorate, and an enduring controversy (Tichenor, 2002; Zolberg, 2006).

Yet despite the controversy, and unlike in other western democracies where immigration has transformed the political landscape (Norris, 2005), immigration failed to emerge as a "wedge issue" in American national politics. How can we explain this disjuncture between the American public – which, according to opinion polls taken from 1965 to the present, wants illegal immigration stopped, illegals removed, and lower levels of legal immigration (Fetzer, 2000) – and national election outcomes which have stymied major immigration policy reforms? To address this question we need first to put contemporary immigration debates into historical perspective. Second, we need to look more carefully at how immigration has shaped and reshaped American politics and society in recent decades. Third, we need to explore how immigrants and their offspring have become actors on the political stage, thus changing the nature of the electorate and the terms of debate. We will see that public attitudes towards immigration, ethnicity, and race are constantly evolving, and that they are more nuanced than a cursory reading of the headlines (and opinion polls) might lead us to believe.

The historical context: 'e pluribus unum'

In 2004 one of the most respected political scientists of his generation, Samuel P. Huntington of *The Clash of Civilizations* fame, published what would be his final major work, a book entitled *Who Are We? The Challenges to America's National Identity*. In this book Huntington argued that American national identity, and by extension American national interests, are threatened by a growing wave of Hispanic immigration, and that Mexican immigrants in particular are engaged in *la reconquista*, or a retaking of territory lost during the Mexican–American War. This reconquest, he suggested was not through military conquest but through a peaceful "invasion," the result of which has been to undermine Anglo-Protestant (Puritan) values of hard work and loyalty to the "founding principles" of the Constitution, and the rule of law. Huntington decried the wave of illegal immigration of impoverished and poorly educated Mexicans and Central Americans, the rise of dual citizenship, bilingualism, and what he saw as the loss of a clear national identity and purpose – all the result of too much immigration. He began the book by outlining three waves of immigration in American history, first in the mid-nineteenth century with the Irish and Germans and continuing through the late twentieth and early twenty-first centuries with Hispanics and Asians. He omitted the first wave of immigration from the British Isles in the seventeenth and eighteenth centuries, because he viewed this wave as a period of settlement and founding, during which the new American nation was created with a fundamentally Anglo-Puritan outlook.

Huntington's argument underscores the enduring controversy over immigration as a force shaping and reshaping American society (Higham, 1955; King, 2005). His critics accuse him of being a latter-day nativist and "know nothing," echoing the controversy in earlier periods of American history when immigration was seen as a threat to basic "American" values (Tichenor, 2002; King, 2000). In the eighteenth century, for example, Benjamin Franklin was very concerned about German immigration in Pennsylvania, because he thought that the largely illiterate German peasants who were coming from a semi-feudal society had little understanding of what it was like to live in a republic based on the rule of law and individual liberty. Later in his political career Franklin would change his views on German immigration, as German Americans became an increasingly important part of the electorate in Pennsylvania; and less than two centuries later a descendant of those German immigrants, Dwight Eisenhower, was elected President of the United States. It is important to keep in mind that immigration from the colonial period through the Civil War and reconstruction (roughly the first 100 years of American history) was controlled by the individual states, to the extent that it was regulated at all (Zolberg, 2006). Immigration was largely driven by the demand for labor to fuel the engines of industrialization – as in later periods private employers were instrumental in recruiting immigrants – and by westward expansion. It was also driven by a seemingly unlimited supply of labor displaced by the industrial revolution and the concomitant rural exodus in Western Europe.

Models of immigration and citizenship

In *The American Kaleidoscope: Race, Ethnicity, and the Civic Culture* (1990) the historian Lawrence H. Fuchs argues that three ideas have dominated the American approach to immigration and citizenship. They are the Massachusetts and Virginia models, dating from the early colonial period, and the Pennsylvania model, which took shape in the early years of the republic. He admits that these are "ideal types," but he contends that traces of each model can still be found in contemporary debates.

The Massachusetts model most closely conforms to Samuel Huntington's ideal of Anglo-Puritanism (what might be called a White Anglo-Saxon Protestant or WASP view of American national identity). In this view immigrants are to be welcomed if they are willing to assimilate, learn English, and adopt the dominant religion and culture. In colonial Massachusetts that meant conformity to ascetic Puritan ideals, and in the contemporary debates Huntington clearly wanted to make respect for Anglo-Puritan values the basis for selecting and naturalizing immigrants.

The Virginia model revolves around the demand for labor. In the early colonial period (the seventeenth and eighteenth centuries) the Virginia and Carolina planters needed stoop labor to pick tobacco and cotton. They acquired this labor initially through coercion – the forced labor of Native Americans and the enslavement of Africans brought to the New World in bondage. Since both groups were considered to be subhuman, no thought was given to their naturalization and assimilation. Indeed many Europeans were brought to work on the plantations and in shops and factories as indentured servants with limited rights. We hear echoes of the Virginia model in contemporary debates about guest worker programs, whereby foreigners are brought as bonded workers on a temporary basis with no right to settle or naturalize.

Finally, the Pennsylvania model, which Fuchs sees prevailing in the Congressional Act of 1790 establishing a uniform rule of naturalization, calls for equal treatment of all newcomers, welcoming them to settle, live, and worship as they see fit so long as they respect the law and the basic values of the republic. The first President, George Washington, reflected this ideal when he said, "the bosom of America is open to receive not only the Opulent and respectable Stranger, but the oppressed and persecuted of all Nations and Religions; whom we shall welcome to a participation of all our rights and privileges." The Pennsylvania model was reinforced after the Civil War with the ratification in 1868 of the Fourteenth Amendment to the Constitution, which extended citizenship to "all persons born or naturalized in the United States." The Amendment was intended primarily to overturn the *Dred Scott* decision of the Supreme Court (1857) and to grant citizenship to former slaves, but in so doing it created an expansive ideal of citizenship that has had far-reaching implications for immigration policy (Kettner, 1978).

Barely two decades after the end of the Civil War, the Statue of Liberty – a gift from one fledgling republic, France, to another, the United States – was erected in New York harbor (1886); and it would become the most visible symbol of an open and tolerant America, welcoming immigrants from the four corners of the globe. Inside the pedestal of the statue is inscribed the most famous immigration sonnet in American history, *The New Colossus*, by Emma Lazarus, which reads in part:

> Give me your tired, your poor,
> Your huddled masses yearning to breathe free,
> The wretched refuse of your teeming shore.
> Send these, the homeless, tempest-tost to me,
> I lift my lamp beside the golden door!

All three "models" have been present historically in debates over immigration and citizenship, which have followed the unofficial national motto, *e pluribus unum* (out of many, one). At times Americans, like Samuel Huntington, have been more concerned about the "*unum*" and the need to maintain a clear national identity and purpose; at other times Americans have hewed to the Pennsylvania model, showing a greater willingness to accept immigrants and celebrate diversity, the "*pluribus*."

The diversity of American immigration

As mentioned above, we can identify four waves of immigration in American history. The first, from the British Isles before 1820, was made up largely of the English and Scots who came for a variety of religious, political (many of the early English settlers were dissenters), and economic (the promise of land and a new start) reasons. The second wave, beginning around 1840 and running through the Great Depression of the 1870s, was more economic in nature (the Irish were fleeing starvation and deprivation during the potato famine), while other northern and western European groups like the Germans and Scandinavians were mostly farmers and artisans, attracted by land in the vast expanse of the Great Plains. Because many of the newcomers were Roman Catholic, the second wave provoked an anti-Catholic backlash, which found its greatest expression in the "know nothing" movement of the mid-nineteenth century (Higham, 1955). The third wave started in 1880 and continued to 1914, when the Great War brought an end to the transatlantic migrations. This wave proved even more controversial than previous waves, because it was ethnically diverse (King, 2000). Male Chinese laborers were brought into the west to build the transcontinental railroad and to work in the mines; southern and eastern Europeans flooded into eastern cities, and into the Midwest and southwest, increasing the Catholic and Jewish populations in these regions. It was during the third wave that the federal government began to assert control over immigration, starting with the Chinese Exclusion Act of 1882 which, like Proposition 187 over a century later, was the direct result of a nativist backlash in California against a rising tide of immigration and a seemingly complacent federal government.

By the early 1900s political pressure was again building to slow the rate of immigration. The Dillingham Commission was set up by Congress in 1907 to study "the problem" and to recommend new ways of selecting immigrants. The pendulum was swinging back in favor of those concerned about national identity (the *unum*), and the Commission report issued in 1911 concluded that the United States was threatened by the increasing number of immigrants from "non-traditional" source countries. The Commission called for literacy tests, and – relying on the pseudo-science of eugenics widely accepted at the time – argued in favor of a racially based immigration policy (Fuchs, 1990; Smith, 1997; King, 2000). The Commission concluded that immigrants from southern and eastern Europe had more "inborn socially inadequate qualities than northwestern Europeans" (Zeidel, 2004).

After the First World War inflows of immigrants from Europe recovered briefly, but in 1921 Congress enacted the first quantitative restrictions on immigration and in 1924 it passed the National Origins Quota Act, which restricted immigration to northern and western Europeans, essentially locking out all other nationalities. Inflows fell rapidly, and the onset of the Great Depression in 1929 brought a halt to immigration. The foreign population was quite large in the interwar period, but immigration (inflows) would not start again until after the Second World War. The 1924 National Origins Quota Act, which Adolf Hitler in *Mein Kampf* praised as good racial policy, remained in effect until its repeal in 1965. During the turbulent decade of the 1930s through the Second World War avenues for legal immigration were restricted, and the United States had no official refugee policy. Refugee admissions were made purely on an ad hoc basis, and many European Jewish refugees fleeing Nazi persecution were turned away from American shores.

Notwithstanding the wave of nativism and restrictionism in the 1920s, the American political landscape was transformed by the third wave of immigration (King, 2005). Attention shifted from stopping immigration to assimilating immigrants. This was the heyday of Tammany Hall and big-city political machines in places like New York, Boston, and Chicago, where first the Irish, then the Italians, and eventually southern and eastern European Jewish immigrants would come to play a larger role in urban politics. The Democratic Party was the major beneficiary of the support of the newcomers, and Franklin Roosevelt would forge a New Deal coalition between working-class, largely Catholic and Jewish immigrants in the north, and poor whites in the Protestant south. Even though the muscle of the big city machines was not enough to overcome nativist politics in the interwar period, Americans had found a new metaphor to describe the assimilation of immigrants: the "melting pot" was popularized in a play by Israel Zangwill which premiered in 1908. The notion of immigrants from many different cultures melting into a new society would become synonymous with immigration and the "American dream." The protagonist in Zangwill's play proclaims, "Germans and Frenchmen, Irishmen and Englishmen, Jews and Russians – into the crucible with you all! God is making the American!" But all was not love and light in immigration politics following the third wave.

In a dispute in 1930 with a congressman from New York and future mayor of New York City, Fiorella LaGuardia, President Herbert Hoover wrote in a letter to his fellow Republican:

> the Italians are predominantly murderers and bootleggers [and you and your Italian supporters] should go back to where you belong [because] like a lot of other foreign spawn, you do not appreciate this country which supports you and tolerates you. (Baltzell, 1964: 30)

In the presidential election of 1928, Al Smith, the Irish Catholic governor of New York and Democratic candidate, would lose to Republican Herbert Hoover, but by winning the Democratic Party nomination he had broken an important cultural barrier, overcoming anti-Catholic and anti-immigrant sentiments. Thirty-two years later another Irish Catholic politician, the Democrat John Fitzgerald Kennedy, would overcome the final hurdles to the full participation of Catholics in American political life.

Immigration control and rights-based politics

The first cracks in the National Origins Quota policy occurred during and immediately after the Second World War with the repeal of the Chinese Exclusion Act in 1943, the launch of the *Bracero* program in 1942, and the arrival after the war of large numbers of refugees and war brides from Europe and Asia. These groups did not fit within any of the existing quotas (Tichenor, 2002). China was an ally in the war against Japan, and Congress decided that the long-standing ban on immigration and naturalization of Chinese nationals was bad for the war effort. Chinese immigrants living in the United States were allowed to naturalize, but strict quotas on Chinese immigration remained in effect. The United States in the Second World War was leading the fight against fascism and the racist ideology underpinning it. The contradictions of American immigration and refugee policy – not to mention segregation and Jim Crow – were increasingly anomalous and at odds with American foreign policy (Smith, 1997; Dudziak, 2004).

The Second World War also brought new demands for foreign labor. The *Bracero* program was launched to fill gaps in the American labor market resulting from the draft. This guest worker program would have major long-term consequences for US immigration policy. The program allowed for the recruitment of tens of thousands of "temporary" workers from Mexico in the 1940s, first in agriculture and subsequently in the railroad and transportation sectors (Calavita, 1992). It marked the beginning of large-scale immigration from Mexico, which has continued well into the twenty-first century. Attempts were made to reverse the flows with "Operation Wetback" in 1954, in which hundreds of thousands of Mexican workers and their families, including many who were American citizens, were voluntarily repatriated or summarily deported to Mexico. The *Bracero* program remained in effect until its repeal in 1964 and the passage of the Immigration and Nationality Act (INA) of 1965.

Also known as the Hart–Celler Act, the 1965 INA was a landmark piece of legislation, which repealed the National Origins Quota system, thus eliminating race and ethnicity as the principal criteria for selecting immigrants. The pendulum of immigration politics was swinging back in favor of greater diversity (*pluribus*) and tolerance. The 1960s would see the triumph of the Pennsylvania model, and the rise of what I have called "rights-based" politics (Hollifield, 1992). The relationship between individuals, groups, and the state was redefined through a process of political struggle (the civil rights movement) which would sweep away Jim Crow and racial discrimination, and in the process, expand the rights of immigrant and ethnic minorities. A new type of rights-based politics was emerging at every level of the polity, from partisan and interest group politics, to the legislature and executive, and especially in the federal judiciary, which became increasingly active in protecting minority rights and civil liberties. Beginning in the 1960s, the courts would play an important role in immigration policy-making, restraining state and local authorities in their treatment of immigrants, helping to consolidate the rights of immigrants and minorities, and reasserting the plenary power doctrine (Schuck, 1998).

The move away from the Massachusetts and Virginia models in favor of the Pennsylvania model of immigration and citizenship after the Second World War can be attributed to two political developments: the Cold War and the civil rights movement. Public opinion remained suspicious and downright hostile to immigrants and refugees in the 1950s. Congress passed the McCarran–Walter Act in 1952, which made it a felony to "harbor, transport, and conceal illegal immigrants." But, under the *Texas proviso*, those employing illegal immigrants were exempt from the law. Employers, particularly the growers in the southwest, had enough political clout to keep cheap Mexican labor flowing into the US market. McCarran–Walter also loosened racial restrictions on immigration ever so slightly, but without repealing the National Origins Quota system.

Reflecting the fear of communist subversion during the early years of the Cold War, McCarran–Walter contained provisions for screening immigrants to catch communists and subversives, a move which was in keeping with McCarthyism and the new red scare. President Harry Truman vetoed the bill, calling it "un-American;" but Congress overrode his veto. Congressional efforts to placate xenophobic and McCarthyite groups made it difficult for the President to ease restrictions on refugees coming from communist countries (Tichenor, 2002). Immigration and refugee policy were important foreign policy tools, and the President needed a freer hand to accommodate Cold War refugees in particular. Ultimately the civil rights movement, which had as its primary objective to overturn Jim Crow and achieve equal rights for African Americans, swept away the last vestiges of the racist and discriminatory National Origins Quota system, leading to the most radical reform of immigration policy in American history.

The INA of 1965 was passed on the heels of the 1964 Civil Rights Act and the Voting Rights Act of 1965. Immigrants were among the most important beneficiaries of the civil rights movement, as laws designed to end racial discrimination against blacks helped open up

Figure 16.1 *Foreign-born population*

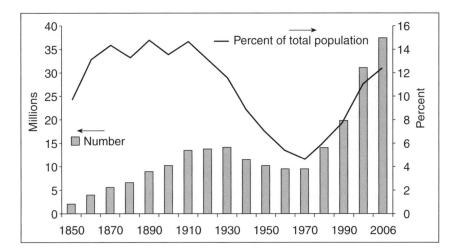

Source: Census Bureau.

new political and legal spaces (rights) for immigrant minorities, setting the stage for the fourth (and largest) wave of immigration in American history.

The fourth wave began slowly in the 1970s, in part because of the severe economic slowdown that was the result of two oil shocks and a steep recession in 1981–82. But as the economy recovered in the 1980s immigration accelerated rapidly, and by the first decade of the twenty-first century the foreign-born population would climb to an all-time high of 35 million. The civil rights movement and the INA of 1965 had laid the political and legal groundwork for a more expansive immigration policy, but it was the soaring American economy in the 1980s and 1990s that propelled immigration to new heights. The free market policies of the Reagan and Clinton administrations made the United States increasingly immigrant-friendly. Demand-pull forces in the American labor market were strong, and there was an unlimited supply of workers in Mexico, Central America, and Asia ready to fill this demand.

Strange bedfellow coalitions of civil rights liberals (northern Democrats, many of them – like Senator Edward Kennedy of Massachusetts – descendants of the second and third-wave immigrants) and business-oriented, Wall Street Republicans helped to pass some of the most expansive immigration laws in American history (Hollifield, Hunt, and Tichenor, 2008). The Refugee Act of 1980 incorporated the 1951 UN Refugee Convention into American law. During most of the Cold War period, American policy favored refugees fleeing persecution in communist countries, whereas the Geneva Convention defined a refugee as *anyone* with a "well founded fear of persecution." Signatories of the Convention were bound by the principle of *non-refoulement*, whereby anyone who met the Geneva standard for asylum could not be returned to the country from which they were fleeing. The 1980 Refugee Act brought the United States in line with international law, giving new impetus to a more rights-based approach to immigration and refugee policy. With the winding down of the Cold War in the late 1980s and 1990s, only Cuba retained its special status as a communist country from which refugees would be accepted with almost no questions asked. However, the Mariel boat lift at the end of the Carter presidency in 1980, in which Fidel Castro opened the Cuban port of Mariel to a massive exodus (125,000 Cubans fled to the United States, including a number of criminals and the mentally ill who were released from prisons and hospitals and allowed to join the exodus) forced America to rethink the blanket asylum policy for Cubans.

In 1979 Congress set up the Select Commission on Immigration and Refugee Policy (SCIRP) under the direction of Lawrence Fuchs – the first such commission since the Dillingham Commission. As the SCIRP went about its work in the early 1980s, holding hearings, gathering data, and conducting research, immigration soared – not only legal immigration, already opened up as a result of the 1965 INA, which made kinship and family ties the primary criterion for admission, but also illegal immigration. The 1965 INA repealed the National Origins Quota system, creating avenues for immigration from non-traditional sources, particularly Latin America (Mexico), Asia, and eventually Africa and the Middle East. The INA also imposed numerical limits on the number of visas, including the first such limits on immigration from the western hemisphere (120,000 annually). These limitations would lead eventually to a big imbalance between the demand for and supply of visas. Rather than waiting in long queues that could last years, many immigrants chose to come illegally, either slipping across land and sea borders, or coming on a tourist visa.   The majority of illegal immigrants were (and are) visa "overstayers," that is, individuals who entered the country on a tourist visa and simply remained in the United States, melding into society, and joining a growing black market for labor. By the time the SCIRP made its recommendations to Congress, illegal immigration was the biggest policy issue; and the foreign-born population, as a percentage of the total population, was rapidly approaching a historic high. By 2008 foreigners constituted 14 percent of the total population – a level not seen since the early twentieth century. Clearly immigration was reshaping American society, and immigrants were coming to play an increasingly important role in the economy.

Continuing policy debates

Policy debates in the 1990s and 2000s would evolve along four lines. First there were economic questions – what are the costs and benefits associated with high levels of immigration, especially illegal immigration? Second, there were social questions – how are the newcomers and their children (the second generation) assimilating or incorporating? Are they learning English and are they succeeding in the labor market? The third dimension of policy debate was political – will the newcomers be good citizens? Will they participate in politics, and if so, how? Will they be Democrats or Republicans, liberals or conservatives? Will they constitute a "swing vote?" And finally there was debate about the relationship between immigration and security: with the terrorist attacks of 9/11, immigration and refugee policy was inevitably in the spotlight. Border enforcement and screening of persons wishing to enter the United States took on a new urgency. How did the terrorists enter the country? Was the attack the result of lax border enforcement and an overly liberal immigration and refugee policy?

It had been easier to stop or slow immigration and roll back the rights of foreigners and immigrants in earlier periods of history. But in the era of rights-based politics, sealing the border, summarily deporting large numbers of immigrants (as happened during Operation Wetback in 1954), stopping family reunification, turning back refugees and asylum seekers, rolling back civil rights (due process and equal protection) for immigrants, and cutting their access to social services, is not so easy – recall the fate of Proposition 187 in California.

Congress attempted to regain control of immigration, especially illegal immigration, in 1986 with the Immigration Reform and Control Act (IRCA). IRCA, also known as the Simpson–Mazzoli Act, was the result of a compromise between "restrictionists," those who wanted to stop illegal immigration, including Republicans led by Senator Alan Simpson of Wyoming, and some southern Democrats, and "admissionists," those who wanted to legalize the large population of illegal immigrants by granting them amnesty, including northern liberal Democrats, led by Senator Edward Kennedy of Massachusetts. In the end a rights–markets coalition formed in the Senate and the House, and a compromise was struck, allowing for the amnesty of illegals in exchange for sanctions (fines and imprisonment for repeat offenders) to be imposed on employers who knowingly hire illegal immigrants (Hollifield et al., 2008). The amnesty succeeded in bringing over 2.7 million illegals out of the shadows. To qualify for amnesty, illegals had to get certification that they were employed and that they had come to the United States prior to 1 January 1982. Critics of the amnesty argued that it created a moral hazard. More people would be willing to take the risk of immigrating illegally on the assumption that they would be amnestied at a later point in time.

Employer sanctions, on the other hand, represented the first attempt by the federal government to pursue an internal control strategy, using labor laws to control immigration. IRCA created the I-9 form, which requires all persons seeking employment to present documentary evidence that they are legal residents. But out of concern that the new law could lead to discrimination against foreign-looking or foreign-sounding job applicants, provisions were inserted in IRCA to ensure that the rights of ethnic minorities would be protected – more evidence of the power of rights-based politics. Under IRCA, employers were not liable for hiring anyone who presented documents that "looked official," and they were not required to verify the authenticity of documents. This loophole made employer sanctions very weak, and it led to the creation of a new black market for false papers, especially social security cards and driver's licenses. Concerns for privacy and civil liberties have prevented Congress from creating a national identification card, which is common in many other democracies. The American Civil Liberties Union (ACLU) is strongly opposed to a national ID.

Agriculture posed a specific regulatory problem, because of the informality and seasonal nature of employment in this sector (Martin, 2009). In the run-up to the passage of IRCA, growers lobbied for a guest worker program (again visions of the Virginia model), but labor unions, especially the United Farm Workers of America (UFW), co-founded by the charismatic labor leader César Chávez, opposed what they considered a system of bonded labor. The result was the creation of a Special Agricultural Worker (SAW) legalization program under which 750,000 mostly Mexican farm workers were amnestied. Finally with respect to the impact of IRCA on overall levels of immigration, it is important to remember that each person covered by the amnesty was able to bring relatives (spouses, parents, brothers, and sisters) into the United States under the family reunification provisions of the 1965 INA.

The IRCA did little to slow the pace of illegal immigration into the United States. Over the course of the 1990s and into the first decade of the twenty-first century, illegal would come to rival legal immigration, setting the stage for a backlash against all immigrants; first came Proposition 187 in California (1994), then the IIRAIRA (1996), which were discussed at the beginning of this chapter, leading to the Sensenbrenner Bill (2005) and contemporary debates over what to do about an illegal population estimated to be somewhere between 10 and 12 million (Passel, 2009). It is important to keep in mind, however, that not all immigration is illegal, and not all is unwanted (unskilled). Illegal immigration dominates the headlines and there are powerful anti-immigration lobbies, like the Federation for American Immigration Reform (FAIR), that seek drastically to reduce immigration; but

Figure 16.2   *Legal versus illegal immigration*

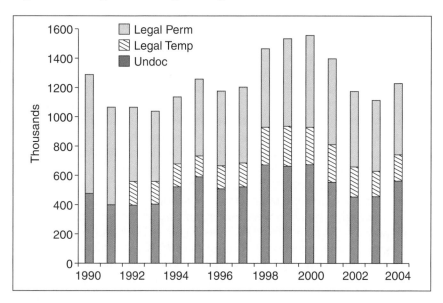

Source: Jeffrey Passel and Roberto Suro, Pew Hispanic.

there are equally powerful pro-immigrant lobbies, some of them, like the Mexican American Legal Defense Fund (MALDEF) and the League of United Latin American Citizens (LULAC), devoted to defending the rights and interests of Latinos. Still others, like the American Chamber of Commerce and various trade associations, represent powerful business interests. Bill Gates, the founder and former head of Microsoft, organized a successful lobbying campaign by high-tech industries to stop Congress from restricting high-skilled immigration at the time of debate (1995–96) over the IIRAIRA.

We might expect Congress to restrict or slow immigration during economic hard times; but at the start of the relatively mild recession of 1990–91, Congress enacted another expansive immigration reform (Hollifield et al., 2008). The Immigration Act of 1990 was designed to reform legal immigration, setting an overall annual ceiling of new immigrants at 675,000. Because of family reunification and the fact that visas not used in one year can be carried over to the next, actual levels of legal immigration are much higher, averaging over 1 million a year throughout the 1990s and into the 2000s. Many illegals are also able to "adjust their status" and become legal permanent residents (LPRs or green card holders), thus adding to the annual totals. The Pew Hispanic Center (Passel, 2009) estimates that over 300,000 people immigrated to the United States illegally each year from 1990 to 2004 (see Figure 16.2).

In fact the US immigration system relies heavily on adjustments of status to deal with enormous backlogs of individuals who find themselves in legal limbo; and this "adjustment of status" system creates a demand for immigration lawyers and other specialists who advise millions of immigrants and potential immigrants, as well as their employers. The American Bar Association (ABA), specifically the American Immigration Lawyers Association (AILA), is among the most important pro-immigration interest groups. Lawyers are essential for the smooth functioning of the system, because they help to adjudicate and manage hundreds of thousands of cases on an annual basis. This gives the American system for managing immigration greater flexibility to deal with admissions on a case by case basis, even though quotas and quantitative caps on the numbers of visas available for specific nationalities and regions make the system cumbersome and inefficient (Cornelius, Martin, and Hollifield, 1994). The highly individualized nature of this regulatory system is consistent with the broader trend in rights-based politics and policy, which began with the civil rights movement of the 1950s and 1960s.

The 1990 Immigration Act created a new category of visas (the H1-B) for highly skilled immigrants, thus adding an important economic and human capital (as opposed to family and humanitarian) dimension to American policy, and generating more work for lawyers who specialize in helping employers recruit individuals with skills that match their company needs. The 1990 Act set an annual cap on H1-Bs of 65,000, but during the high-tech boom of the late 1990s Congress adjusted the cap in response to higher demand for skilled workers and pressure from business groups. The H1-B visa was designed for high-skilled immigrants, and the H2-A and H2-B visas were created for non-agricultural seasonal workers. But the number of job-based green cards, whether for the unskilled (capped at 10,000 a year) or the skilled (capped at 140,000 a year), was too low to accommodate the overall demand for immigrant labor. Throughout the boom years of the 1990s and into the 2000s, the result was the issuance of more temporary visas (over 600,000 in fiscal year (FY) 2005) and rising levels of illegal immigration. It is difficult for Congress to create an employment-based visa system that mirrors the business cycle and perfectly matches the needs of the labor market. With the bursting of the high-tech bubble in 2001, the demand for H1-Bs declined and a binding cap of 65,000 was brought back in 2004, only to see demand rise again in 2004–07. The bursting of the housing bubble in 2008 and the ensuing financial crisis led to declining demand for unskilled immigrant workers, especially in construction, and unemployment reached 10 percent of the labor force as a whole in 2009. Immigration does not follow the business cycle, because of lags between the demand for and supply of visas, the difficulties of quickly adjusting policy, and the rise of rights-based politics (Hollifield et al., 2008).

To combat illegal immigration in the 1990s, the Immigration and Naturalization Service (INS) developed ever more sophisticated strategies for border enforcement (external control), increasing the number of border patrol agents and redeploying them at critical entry points along the US–Mexico border. Operations "Hold the Line" in Texas (1993) and "Gatekeeper" in California (1994) were designed to seal the border in urban areas like El Paso and San Diego, and to force illegal crossings away from the cities into remote, desert areas. These external enforcement policies succeeded in redirecting flows, but levels of illegal immigration continued to rise; and thousands of illegals would die in the deserts of the southwest, leading some to argue that the policies of the Clinton administration were nothing more than symbolic and cynical attempts to show the public that the government was regaining control of the border – an "out of sight, out of mind" approach to immigration control, but with deadly consequences for the migrants themselves (Cornelius, 2001).

The failure of external enforcement policies in the 1990s, combined with the 9/11 terrorist attacks, led to a massive reorganization of border control. In 2003 the INS, formerly an agency of the Department of Justice, was reorganized into two agencies – one for enforcement, Immigration and Customs Enforcement (ICE) and one for services, Citizenship and Immigration Services (CIS) – and placed in the new Department of Homeland Security (DHS). A third agency, Customs and Border Protection (CBP), was created to coordinate border control. All three agencies were tasked with protecting the American homeland from another terrorist attack, as the security function of immigration and refugee policy came to the fore (Rudolph, 2006). The Real ID Act, passed in 2005, established new standards for driver's licenses and non-compulsory state ID cards, to make it more difficult to counterfeit these documents and for individuals to obtain false papers. The law was intended to reinforce checks on individual identity, stopping short of creating a national ID card.

The new emphasis on security made travel and immigration to the United States more difficult, especially for anyone coming from a Muslim country; and the issue of visas in American consulates around the world came under much greater scrutiny, slowing an already cumbersome and inefficient process with elaborate background checks for visa applicants. Overworked Foreign Service officers (the front line of immigration control) were fearful of admitting someone who might carry out another terrorist attack. The 9/11 hijackers entered the United States legally on tourist and student visas, but seven of the 19 had false passports and three were on terrorist watch lists, leading the 9/11 Commission that was set up to investigate the attacks to conclude that better immigration and border enforcement might have prevented the terrorists from entering the country.

Security considerations aside, the debate over immigration reform during the George W. Bush administration (2000–08), as in previous eras, revolved primarily around the economic effects of immigration, especially illegal immigration (Borjas, 1999). In May 2006 Bush proposed "comprehensive immigration reform," to match "willing workers with willing employers," by creating a new guest worker program (a return to the Virginia model) and an "earned legalization" program for the millions of illegals already working in the United States (visions of the Pennsylvania model). Opponents of comprehensive reform charged that it would be a repeat of the IRCA amnesty, creating another situation of moral hazard that would lead to yet higher levels of illegal immigration. The rallying cry of opponents was "fool me once, shame on you; fool me twice, shame on me!" The Sensenbrenner Bill of 2005–06 represented an alternative, "enforcement only" strategy, placing a premium on enforcement of existing laws, reinforced border control, the arrest and deportation of the millions of illegals, and the criminalization of illegal immigration.

But, the collapse of the reform effort in 2006 led many state and local governments to take up the cause of immigration control, further dividing communities and the electorate. It was impossible to resurrect the rights–markets coalitions in Congress that enacted earlier reforms during the Cold War period (Hollifield et al., 2008). The Republican Party in particular was divided between a culturally conservative – if not xenophobic – wing, which refused to compromise, and a more moderate, business-oriented wing (led by future presidential candidate, Senator John McCain), which wanted to give the Grand Old Party (GOP) a more immigrant-friendly face. The fear among many Republicans, like George W. Bush's political "Svengali" Karl Rove, was that demographic changes resulting from high levels of immigration were changing the electorate, and that Hispanics in particular constituted a swing vote in many key states and districts. Some leaders of the GOP did not want to end up once again on the "wrong side of history," as in the 1920s when the Republicans ceded third-wave immigrants to the Democratic Party for the better part of two generations. In the run-up to the 2008 presidential election and flush from their successes in the 2006 midterm elections, Democratic leaders in Congress decided against compromise with moderate Republicans, like Senator John McCain, and the Bush White House, preferring instead to leave the immigration issue open, like a festering wound, and to use it against Republicans in 2008. The question remains to what extent immigration is an issue driving American politics and how the fourth-wave immigrants have altered the course of American political development?

The messy politics of assimilation

Arguments about the assimilation, integration, or incorporation of fourth-wave immigrants abound. Two things are clear, however: the United States is more ethnically diverse than ever before in its history – Latin Americans and Asians have replaced Europeans as the dominant immigrant groups – and immigrants have spread geographically across the country. Rather than concentrating in traditional immigrant cities, like New York, Boston, and Miami on the east coast, Chicago and St Louis in the Midwest, or San Francisco and Los Angeles in the west and Houston in the southwest, immigrants are settling in new "gateway cities" (Dallas-Fort Worth, Atlanta, Phoenix, Washington DC, Charlotte, Nashville, and Las Vegas to name a few) and in states and cities far from the main ports of entry (Singer, Hardwick, and Brettell, 2008). Looking at the last two censuses (1990 and 2000), states with the fastest growing immigrant populations were in the south (North and South Carolina, Georgia, Tennessee, and Arkansas), the west (Nevada, Utah, and Washington), and nontraditional destinations in the east (New Hampshire and Pennsylvania) and Midwest (Iowa and Wisconsin). Overall, immigrants accounted for 30 percent of American population growth from 1980 to 2005. The four biggest immigration states in 2005 were California (10 million foreign born), New York (4 million), and Texas and Florida (over 3 million each). The leading countries of origin in the fourth wave were Mexico (31 percent of the foreign-born), followed by the Philippines, India, China, and Vietnam (Passel, 2009).

The fact that so many of the newcomers are of Latin American and Asian origin has increased the visibility of immigrants across the country, giving greater impetus to debates about assimilation. Mexican and Central American immigrants in particular are predominantly unskilled, many are illegals, and they often speak little or no English (Passel, 2009); hence the concerns expressed by Samuel Huntington and others (Skerry, 1995) for American national identity (the *unum*). Many of these newcomers – much like their counterparts a century earlier – live in ethnic enclaves in large cities. While the first generation may experience significant improvements in their welfare (compared with their situation in the country of origin), their children, the second generation, may experience significant downward mobility – what the sociologist Alejandro Portes termed "segmented assimilation" (Portes and Rumbaut, 1990), which is nonlinear and does not lead to "mainstream" outcomes. The theory purports to explain why many second-generation immigrants engage in deviant or criminal behavior, joining gangs, for example. It is important to note that this is not a new phenomenon – remember the conflicts of *West Side Story*! Apart from debates over assimilation, the cost of educating immigrant children and

Figure 16.3　*Immigrant origins*

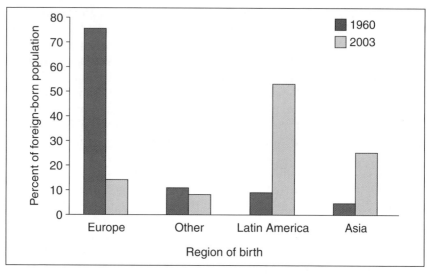

Source: DHS.

providing health care for indigent families have become central features of debates about the fiscal impacts of immigration (Borjas, 1999). But given the rapidly declining percentage of the native-born workforce with less than a high school education (for men this number fell from over 50 percent in 1960 to less than 10 percent in 2004 – a great success of mass-based public education), unskilled immigrants fill a niche at the low end of the labor market (Passel, 2009; Orrenius and Solomon, 2006).

High levels of unskilled and illegal immigration have provoked intense debates among economists over the long-term costs and benefits of immigration, with some (Borjas, 1999) arguing that the service-based, high-tech American economy no longer needs so many unskilled and poorly educated immigrants; while others (Orrenius and Solomon, 2006) point out that key sectors of the economy (agriculture, construction, consumer services such as restaurants and hotels, and health care to name a few) would suffer without access to immigrant labor. Critics counter that without immigrants, wages for native-born workers would rise significantly and the jobs would still get done. This assumes that immigrant workers are substitutes for the native-born, and vice versa, rather than complements, as some would argue. Alan Greenspan, former chair of the Federal Reserve Board, weighed into the debate, arguing that immigration keeps inflation down (by keeping wages and prices in check), and that highly skilled immigrants in particular are a boon for the US economy (*Wall Street Journal*, April 30, 2009).

Not all immigrants are unskilled and illegal, especially those from Asia, who often come with much-needed skills (Filipino nurses and Indian doctors, for example) and high levels of human capital (the foreign-born share of American scientists and engineers is large and increasing). These highly skilled immigrants enter at the top of the labor market, and in a short period of time their earnings rapidly surpass those of natives (Chiswick, 2008). Immigrants also have high levels of entrepreneurial activity, with a willingness to work long hours at low pay, accumulating capital, reinvesting it, and in the process creating new jobs for immigrants and natives alike – a rising tide that lifts all boats. Certain immigrant groups, like the Koreans and Iranians, for example, have exceptionally high levels of self-employment, 28 and 20 percent respectively, which is much higher than among the native-born (13 percent). Clearly fourth-wave immigrants are highly diverse, not only in ethno-cultural terms, but in terms of social class, education, and economic achievement (Passel, 2009).

Not surprisingly, rates of naturalization vary significantly from one group to another. Already in the 1980s there was concern that the new immigrants were not naturalizing, and that the extension of so many rights to immigrants had led to a "devaluation of citizenship" (Schuck and Smith, 1985); but with the political backlash against immigration in the mid-1990s (Proposition 187 and IIRAIRA) and the fact that those amnestied by IRCA in 1987–88 had become eligible for citizenship, the INS was overwhelmed with millions of applications for naturalization, leading the legal scholar Peter Schuck (1998) to announce the "revaluation of citizenship." Naturalization rates are highest among those groups with little prospect of returning to their home country. Refugees, like the Vietnamese and the Iranians, have very high rates of naturalization, a trend that is reinforced by the fact that they tend to be highly educated and in higher income brackets. Mexicans and Central Americans at the other extreme tend to be poorly educated, have a higher propensity to return home, and since 1998 Mexicans are allowed to have dual nationality. All these factors have led to lower rates of naturalization among Hispanic immigrants, but the rates have been going up steadily since the mid-1990s, reaching into the 30 percent range for Mexican LPRs (green card holders) by 2005. Of course these numbers do not take into account the large number of illegals, who are not eligible for naturalization (Skerry, 1995; Jones-Correa, 1998; Pickus, 2005).

Although Hispanics constitute one of the fastest growing demographic groups in US society (46 million strong and 15 percent of the total US population in 2005), they have low rates of naturalization and many are illegal; therefore they are ineligible to vote. Even among those who are eligible and registered to vote, their participation rate has been among the lowest of any major ethnic group (De la Garza and Desipio, 2005; Desipio, 1996). Of those who voted in the 2008 presidential election, whites accounted for 76.3 percent of the electorate, blacks 12.1, Hispanics 7.4, and Asians 2.5. This is the lowest share ever for whites. Yet in 2008 whites had higher participation rates (66.1 percent) than blacks (65.2) or Hispanics (49.9), even though both minority groups voted in higher numbers than ever before, up almost 5 percent for blacks (the Obama effect) and 2.7 percent for Hispanics. The GOP made significant inroads among Hispanic voters in two of the last four presidential elections, jumping from 21 percent for Dole in 1996, to 31 percent for Bush in 2000, and 44 percent for Bush in 2004. But this trend reversed itself in 2008, as John McCain – despite his early support for comprehensive immigration reform – received only 32 percent of the Hispanic vote. The percentage of Hispanics identifying with the GOP, after reaching a high of 28 percent in 2004–06, slipped back to 23 percent in 2007. Hispanics identifying with the Democratic Party, on the other hand, leapt from 49 percent in 2006 to 57 percent in 2007 (Lopez and Taylor, 2009). No doubt some of the decline in Hispanic support for the GOP can be attributed to the divisive effects of the failed immigration reforms of 2005–06, particularly the Sensenbrenner Bill, which provoked large street demonstrations. But the rallying cry of those protests (*hoy marchamos, mañana votamos!*) did not lead to dramatic increases in Hispanic voter registration or turnout in 2008.

It is therefore difficult to argue that immigration has radically transformed American politics. Hispanic voters made a difference in the 2008 presidential elections, especially in swing states that were carried by the Republicans in 2004. The biggest breakthrough came in Florida where in 2008 Obama carried 57 percent of the Hispanic vote, compared with 56 percent for Bush in 2004. Obama also improved the share of the Democratic vote among Hispanics in other swing states, like Colorado, Nevada, and New Mexico, giving the Democrats an edge in the presidential as well as congressional elections. Similar trends can be observed in other important states, like California, New Jersey, and Texas. But immigration as an issue in national elections only affects voting at the margins. The economy – basic pocket-book issues like employment and taxation – dominated the election, followed by war and peace issues, with immigration trailing far behind among the electorate as a whole, except among Hispanic voters in certain swing states and districts. The only presidential candidate who made immigration control the centerpiece of his primary campaign, the Republican Tom Tancredo, got nowhere. If anything Tancredo hurt the Republican ticket (McCain–Palin) in the general elections by alienating Hispanic voters; further, those congressional candidates in 2008 who took a hardline stand on immigration did not fare well, most of them losing by significant margins.

Clearly the biggest immigration issue in American politics going forward (the elephant in the room) is the fate of some 12 million illegal immigrants who contribute their labor to the US economy but pose a challenge to state sovereignty and security (control of borders/territory is a central attribute of sovereignty and vital to security), to the rule of law (it is illegal for employers to hire individuals not authorized to work), and to civil society (large numbers of individuals living in the shadows at the edges of society are detrimental to the social fabric). What to do about this segment of the immigrant population and how to reform immigration policy (how many immigrants should be admitted, from where, and in what status?) are big, unresolved questions that easily could consume the Obama administration and the 111th Congress. The former Democratic speaker of the House of Representatives, Tip O'Neill, when pushed by some of his colleagues to bring the 1986 IRCA to the House floor for a vote, said, "Gentlemen, immigration is political death." O'Neill feared that if you open the issue for debate, everyone will be angry and no one will go away happy. Despite O'Neill's reservations, the 1986 bill did come to the floor, and it narrowly passed. In 2009 immigration is even more controversial and divisive than in 1986, and the Obama administration is likely to tread lightly around the issue.

President Obama is faced with a choice of kicking the can (in this case immigration reform) down the road, or opening a divisive political debate in the midst of the worst economic crisis since the Great Depression. If he does nothing, Obama risks alienating his new Hispanic constituents – during the campaign he promised them that he would propose a comprehensive immigration reform during the first year of his presidency. Since taking office in January 2009, he has vowed to pursue reform that makes immigration orderly and legal, and to find a "pathway to citizenship" for illegal immigrants, but he has avoided specifics, opting instead to convene working groups in the summer of 2009 to "study the issue." At the North American summit in Guadalajara, Mexico in August 2009, President Obama reiterated his commitment to immigration reform, saying that he expected Congress to draft an immigration bill in 2009 – after they have completed legislation on health care, energy, and financial regulation! – which he would work to pass in 2010.

Obama may have bought some time, politically speaking, with Hispanics by naming the first Hispanic American, Judge Sonia Sotomayor, for a seat on the Supreme Court. With the economy in a deep recession, unemployment rising, and other domestic issues (health care, finance, and energy) pressing, it seems unlikely that Congress will tackle comprehensive immigration reform in 2009. Some measures have been taken through executive order to make immigration enforcement less arbitrary and more humane – the highly unpopular worksite raids that were conducted in the last years of the Bush administration, for example, have been stopped – but the new secretary of homeland security and former Arizona governor, Janet Napolitano, has made clear that immigration control and border enforcement will be high-priority items for the Obama administration, and she has shifted the focus of immigration enforcement from arresting and detaining illegal immigrant workers to fining and prosecuting their employers.

Conclusion: the liberal paradox

Like other democracies, the United States is trapped in a "liberal" paradox – in order to maintain economic competitiveness, it must keep its economy open to trade, foreign investment, and immigration. But immigration, unlike trade in goods and services, or the movement of capital, involves greater political risks. The liberal paradox highlights some of the risks and contradictions inherent in American immigration policy. As with any sovereign nation, it is essential for the United States to maintain control of its borders (a degree of political and legal closure); otherwise the government risks undermining the social contract and rule of law, cheapening citizenship, and deepening the political and social divide. The central challenge therefore is to maintain openness while at the same time protecting the rights of individuals – citizens as well as denizens.

In the twenty-first century managing migration is a central function of the modern state, and the state must make strategic choices about how many immigrants to accept, from where, and with what status (Hollifield, 2004). From the end of the Second World War until the recession of 2008, immigration in the United States has been increasing. In 2009, the foreign population stands at a historic high of 36 million (14 percent of the total population) and climbing. The rise in immigration is a function of market forces (demand-pull and supply-push) and kinship (family) networks, which reduce the transaction costs of immigration. Economic and sociological forces are the necessary conditions for immigration to occur, but the sufficient conditions are legal and political. States must be willing to accept immigration and to grant rights to outsiders. How then can a liberal democracy like the United States regulate immigration in the face of economic forces that push it toward greater openness, while security concerns and powerful political forces push it toward closure?

Historically US immigration policy has been driven by three concerns, epitomized by the Massachusetts, Virginia, and Pennsylvania models. The first (Massachusetts) revolves around concerns for national identity, cultural and ideological cohesion (the *unum*). To what extent is the United States a White Anglo-Saxon Protestant nation, and how much diversity (*pluribus*) is acceptable? The second (Virginia model) is primarily concerned about the need for adequate supplies of labor and human capital in a dynamic and fast-growing economy. The third (Pennsylvania model) is open to diversity, tolerant of differences, but stresses respect for the values and ideals of the republic. We continue to see each of these ideas at work in debates over immigration reform.

Guide to Further Reading

Chapter 1   Introduction: The Legacy of the Bush Years

There are now a number of very useful studies of the Bush presidency. See for example Edwards and King (2007), Campbell and Rockman (2004), Campbell, Rockman, and Rudalevige (2008) and Cannon (2008). Aberbach and Peterson (2005) is an excellent overview of the executive branch; Nathan (1975, 1983) provides a useful analysis of the executive presidency model. Greenstein (2004) analyzes presidential character. Rudalevige (2005) is a trenchant analysis of the use of executive power.

The impact of the Bush years on the conservative movement is covered in Tanner (2007) and Edwards (2008).

Chapter 2   A New Political Agenda?

Baumgartner and Jones (1993) and Kingdon (1984) contain useful frameworks for analyzing agenda-setting. Nivola and Brady (2006, 2008) and Fiorina (2005) present different perspectives on the divided nature of American society. Street (2009) has much to say from a left of center viewpoint about Obama's agenda. Eck (1997) and Dionne (2008) provide stimulating discussions of religion. On national identity see Huntington (2004).

Chapter 3   The Electoral System and the Lessons of 2008

Balz and Johnson (2009) gives a vivid account of the election. La Raja (2008) analyses the current debates about money in American elections and campaign reform. Kornblut (2009) looks at the problems facing female candidates. Citrin and Karol (2009) looks at the new dynamics of the nomination process. Polsby and Wildavsky (12th edition, 2007) remains an essential text for the understanding of presidential elections in the United States.

Chapter 4   Political Parties and the New Partisanship

Epstein (1986) remains the best general study of how American parties operate, and especially on the role and functioning of the organizations, while a brief, but contemporary, introduction to the parties can be found in Maisel (2007). An extensive review of the literature on polarization is provided by Hetherington (2009), while Smith (2007) explains how parties work in Congress. On how the current system of campaign financing developed from attempts to control parties, see La Raja (2008).

Chapter 5   Interest Groups

Berry and Wilcox (2008) discuss the role of interest groups in American democracy, and the disproportionate nature of interest group representation is detailed in Schlozman and Tierney (1986). The most complete summary of academic research on interest group activities is provided by Baumgartner and Leech (1998). Information regarding interest group spending, lobbying, and proposed and enacted reforms is regularly updated online at the websites of the Center for Responsive Politics (www.opensecrets.org), which deals with national government, and the National Institute on Money in State Politics (www.followthemoney.org), which deals with state governments.

Chapter 6   The Media

Keeping up with the media and politics can present difficulties in such a fast-changing aspect of society. There are a few classic texts in the area that provide an excellent starting point. Graber (2005), one of best-known experts in the field, provides an excellent overview. A good follow-up is Graber, McQuail, and Norris (2008), which provides a variety of essays on prominent issues by well-known authors. Finally, Bennett (2009) is the other most recognized text on the media. People looking for more pointed media criticism should read McChesney (2004) for one of the best-known critiques of what is wrong with the media today. A less partisan approach can be found in Downie and Kaiser (2002), which discusses how the media operate and how recent changes influence the news you receive. Finally, to get the most up-to date accounts of the media, the Pew Research Center's Project for Excellence in Journalism provides data and evaluations of the press. It can be found at www.journalism.org. This organization is affiliated with the Columbia School of Journalism, whose *Columbia Journalism Review* is another excellent source of information on the media today that can be accessed at www.cjr.org.

Chapter 7   The Presidency

The updated editions of Pfiffner (2007), Edwards and Wayne (2006), and Nelson (2005) are among recent excellent introductions to the American presidency. On presidential power, Neustadt (1960) and subsequent editions remains essential. Schlesinger (1973), Skowronek (1997), and Rudalevige (2005) offer alternative perspectives. Genovese and Han (2006) and Pfiffner (2008) provide trenchant critiques of George W. Bush's use of presidential power, particularly post 9/11. Presidential character is explored by Barber (1992) in the final edition of a classic text. Greenstein (2000) assesses the skills contemporary Presidents bring to the office. The President's relationship with Congress is examined by Wayne (1978) and Bond and Fleisher (1990). Useful insights into how presidential appointees interact with the Washington bureaucracy are provided by Heclo (1977).

Besides publishing *Presidential Studies Quarterly*, the Center for the Study of the Presidency and Congress maintains a website (www.thepresidency.org/). Also online, the Miller Center of Public Affairs, (www.millercenter.org/) and CB Presidential Research Services (presidentsusa.net/) provide useful resources. In keeping with the current administration's adept use of technology and professed desire for transparency, the White House website (www.whitehouse.gov/) is more comprehensive and user-friendly than that of some of Obama's recent predecessors.

Chapter 8   Congress

For further reading, Smith et al. (2009) provide an overview of the procedural and organizational aspects of Congress, and discuss current political developments in the context of congressional procedure. Dodd and Oppenheimer (2009) provide a detailed discussion of the contemporary Congress, with topics ranging from the changing role of committees and parties to the effect of elections on congressional behavior. Mann and Ornstein (2008) present a historical perspective on the development of Congress and a sharp critique of its recent performance. For additional analysis of the polarization of American politics, see Nivola and Brady (2006, 2008). Hamilton (2009) discusses the ways in which Congress today has strayed away from its position as the preeminent branch of American government, and offers some ideas for repairing the broken branch.

OpenCongress is an initiative of the Participatory Politics Foundation and the Sunlight Foundation to make Congress more transparent and encourage civic engagement through the news and blog coverage, social media tools, and background information on Members of Congress and current issues under debate (www.opencongress.org).

Chapter 9   The Supreme Court

Current understandings of the behavior of the Court emphasize the importance of individual justices and their personal political preferences. Segal and Spaeth (2002) provide an essential overview of this approach, while Epstein and Knight (1998) and Maltzman, Spriggs, and Wahlbeck (2000) examine the interplay of those preferences. The importance of the Court's institutional position is covered in Iaryczower, Spiller, and Tommasi (2006) and Frymer (2003). Friedman (2006) addresses the role of legal arguments – that is, the sort of views about judicial behavior that are reflected in legal discussion but which tend to be de-emphasized in modern political science scholarship. There is a further important debate about the power and autonomy of the Supreme Court, which is covered in Rosenberg (2008), and see Dudziak (2004). The effects of the court in major cases such as *Brown* v *Board of Education* are analyzed in Klarman (2004) and Balkin (2001).

Chapter 10   American Federalism in the Twenty-First Century

The American federal system is a complicated and constantly evolving institution. A current and insightful introduction to the system is Stephens and Wikstrom (2007). For a more detailed assessment of the state of US federalism since 2000, including specific policy areas as well as recent fiscal and political developments, see "US federalism and the Bush administration," a special issue of *Publius: The Journal of Federalism*, 37 (Summer 2007). A more theoretically oriented treatment of intergovernmental trends, with detailed chapters on education, welfare, health care, homeland security, and environmental policy, is provided by Conlan and Posner (2008). Finally, an excellent study of state policy innovation and diffusion focussing on environmental issues is that of Rabe (2004).

Chapter 11   Environmental Politics and Policy

Klyza and Sousa (2008) is an excellent account of the state of environmental policymaking in the United States since 1990. The essays in Vig and Kraft (2010) also provide an update on developments in environmental policymaking. Rosenbaum (2007) is a more conventional textbook that gives an account of policy developments in specific areas. Nordhaus and Schellenburger (2007) offers a provocative critique of the environmental movement in the United States. A more sympathetic view of the state of American environmentalism is Bomberg and Schlosberg (2009).

Chapter 12   The American Economy in Crisis

The provision of economic and financial data in the United States is comparatively decentralized. The Bureau of Economic Analysis (www.bea.gov) is the source for national accounts data; the Bureau of Labor Statistics (www.bls.gov) is the source for data on employment, wages and prices, and the Federal Reserve (www.federalreserve.gov) is a basic source for data on interest rates, monetary and credit aggregates, and flow of funds data. Moody's has a website (www.freelunch.com) which is a good source for a range of basic but not detailed data.

The full set of budget documents, including the summary document from which the chapter has drawn, can be downloaded from the website of the Office of Management and Budget (www.whitehouse.gov/omb/). These documents include a great deal of material on the budget, including a concise description of the budgetary process, from which this chapter's account has freely drawn. In addition to the website of the CBO (www.cbo.gov), two excellent sources for analyses of US economic developments, especially fiscal and social economic issues, are the websites of the Urban Institute (www.ui.urban.org) and the Brookings Institution (www.brookings.edu).

Schick (2000) is an excellent source for all aspects of the US budgetary process. Morris (2008) provides an excellent general account of the financial crisis.

Chapter 13   American Social Policy: The Possibilities for Reform

The American welfare state is generally compared unfavorably with those of Europe, and for good reason. That said, Skocpol (1998) provides an important basis for understanding the roots of those differences. Also, Russell (2008) elaborates the contemporary differences and provides an assessment of current trends. Finally, Morris (2008) addresses the role that private provision has played in American social policy and the implications of the collapse of the financial markets.

Chapter 14   American Foreign Policy in the 2010s

Emerging US relations with China and Russia are assessed brilliantly by Kagan (2008). For the argument that Bush foreign policy will and should continue under his successors see Lynch and Singh (2008). Important early assessments of Obama's foreign policy and/or the terrain it must navigate include Bobbitt (2008), Leffler and Legro (2008), Parmar, Miller, and Ledwidge (2009), Renshon (2009), Sanger (2009), and Zakaria (2008).

Chapter 15   The American Constitution at the End of the Bush Presidency

For broad studies on the legal and constitutional issues that developed after 9/11, see Baker (2007), Fisher (2008), and Matheson (2009). For critiques of covert and secret policymaking, see Mayer (2008), Pious (2006), Pyle (2009), and Savage (2007). Bruff (2009) focuses on the quality of the legal memos that led to unconstitutional actions by the Bush administration after 9/11. A good analysis of legal disputes under President George W. Bush was released by the majority staff of the House Judiciary Committee in a final report to the chairman, John Conyers, Jr (2009).

Chapter 16   American Immigration Policy and Politics: An Enduring Controversy

Portes and Rumbaudt (1990) provide a portrait of American immigrants. Alba and Nee (2003) look at the impact of contemporary immigration on American politics and society, as do Zolberg (2006) and King (2000, 2005). Fuchs (1990) examines the effects of immigration, race, and ethnicity on the civic culture. Pickus (2005) looks at the relationship between immigration and civic nationalism. Borjas (1999) focusses on the impact of immigration on the American economy. Tichenor (2002) looks at immigration control. Brettell and Hollifield (2008) examine the theory of migration. Cornelius, Martin, and Hollifield (1994) place American immigration in a global perspective.

Bibliography

Aaron, H. and Schwartz, W. B. (with Cox, M.) (2005) *Can We Say No? The Challenge of Rationing Health Care,* Washington DC: Brookings Institution.

Aberbach, J. D. and Peterson, M. A. (2005) *The Executive Branch,* New York: Oxford University Press.

Abramowitz, A. and Saunders, K. (2005) "Why can't we all just get along? The reality of a polarized America." *The Forum,* 3, Berkeley Electronic Press <http://www.bepress.com/forum>.

Advisory Commission on Intergovernmental Relations (ACIR) (1981) *The Condition of Contemporary Federalism: Conflicting Theories and Collapsing Constraints,* Washington DC: ACIR.

Alba, Richard D. and Nee, V. (2003) *Remaking the American Mainstream: Assimilation and Contemporary Immigration,* Cambridge, Mass.: Harvard University Press.

Aldrich, J. H. and Rohde, D. W. (2009) "Congressional committees in a continuing partisan era," in L. C. Dodd and B. I. Oppenheimer (eds), *Congress Reconsidered,* 9th edn, Washington DC: CQ Press.

Allard, S. (2007) "The changing face of welfare during the Bush administration," *Publius,* 37, 304–32.

American Society of News Editors (2009) "U.S. newsroom employment declines." American Society of News Editors, 24 April <http://asne.org/article_view/smid/370/articleid/12.aspx>.

Anderson, K. (2008) "The first election the internet won," *Guardian,* November 5.

Appelbaum, B. and Goldfarb, Z. A. (2009) "US weighs single agency to regulate banking industry," *Washington Post,* May 29.

Apollonio, D. E. and Bero, L. A. (2007) "The creation of industry front groups: the tobacco industry and "get government off our back,"" *American Journal of Public Health,* 97, 14–22.

Apollonio, D. E., Cain, B. E., and Drutman, L. (2008) "Access and lobbying: looking beyond the corruption paradigm," *Hastings Constitutional Law Quarterly,* 36, 13–50.

Arizona Daily Star (2005) "Paying for campaigns," Tucson.

Armstrong, D. (2009) "Health insurance program for kids will get long-sought expansion," *CQ Weekly,* February 9.

Associated Press (2008) "FBI begins preliminary inquiry into Miguel Tejada's Steroids testimony," January 17 <http:foxnews.com/story/0,2933,323552,00.html>.

Austen, I. (2006) "Canadians fault U.S. for its role in torture case," *New York Times,* September 19.

Baer, K. S. (2000) *Reinventing Democrats: The Politics of Liberalism from Reagan to Clinton,* Kansas: University of Kansas Press.

Baker, J. E. (2007) *In the Common Defense: National Security Law for Perilous Times,* New York: Cambridge University Press.

Baker, P. (2006) "GOP infighting on detainees intensifies: Bush threatens to halt CIA program if Congress passes rival proposal," *Washington Post*, September 16.

Baldassare, M. A., Cain, B. E., Apollonio, D. E., and Cohen, J. M. (2004) *The Season of Our Discontent: Voters' Views on California Elections*, San Francisco, Calif.: Public Policy Institute of California.

Balkin, J. M. (2001) *What* Brown v. Board of Education *Should Have Said: The Nation's Top Legal Experts Rewrite America's Landmark Civil Rights Decision*, New York: NYU Press.

Baltzell, E. D. (1964) *The Protestant Establishment: Aristocracy and Caste in America*, New York: Random House.

Balz, D. and Brownstein, R. (1996) *Storming the Gates: Protest Politics and the Republican Revival*. New York: Little, Brown.

Balz, D. and Johnson, H. (2009) *The Battle for America 2008: The Story of an Extraordinary Election*, New York: Viking.

Banks, C. and Blakeman, J. (2008) "Chief Justice Robert, Justice Alito, and the new federalism jurisprudence," *Publius*, 38, 576–602.

Barber, J. D. (1992) *Presidential Character: Predicting Performance in the White House*, New York: Prentice Hall.

Barcott, B. (2004) "Changing all the rules," *New York Times*, April 4.

Bartels, L. (2008) Transcript of presentation in "What the 2008 election meant," Brookings Conference, Nov 14 <www.brookings.edu/events2008, 1114_2008election.apsx>.

Bartlett, B. (2006) *Imposter: How George W. Bush Bankrupted America and Betrayed the Reagan Legacy*, New York: Doubleday.

Baumgartner, F. and Jones, B. (1993) *Agendas and Instability in American Politics*, Chicago: University of Chicago Press.

Baumgartner, F and Leech, B. (1998) *Basic Interests: The Importance of Groups in Politics and Political Science*, Princeton, N.J.: Princeton University Press.

Begg, M. (2006) *Enemy Combatant: My Imprisonment at Guantánamo, Bagram, and Kandahar*, New York: New Press.

Belcher, S. (2007) Declaration of Sean Belcher in the case of *Mohamed v. Jeppesen Dataplan*, Case No. C 07-02798 JW, October 15.

Bennett, W. L. (2009) *News: The Politics of Illusion*, 8th edn, New York: Longman.

Berry, J. M. and Wilcox, C. (2008) *The Interest Group Society*, New York: Longman.

Binder, S. A., Mann, T. E., Ornstein, N. J., and Reynolds, M. (2009) *Assessing the 110th Congress, anticipating the 111th, Mending the Broken Branch, vol. 3*, Washington, DC: Brookings Institution <http://www.brookings.edu/~/media/Files/rc/papers/2009/0108_broken_branch_binder_mann/0108_broken_branch_binder_mann.pdf>.

Bobbitt, P. (2008) *Terror and Consent: The Wars for the Twenty-First Century*, New York: Knopf.

Bogus, C. T. (2000) "The history and politics of second amendment scholarship: a primer," *Chicago-Kent Law Review*, 76, 1.

Bomberg, E and Super, B. (2009) "The 2008 US presidential election: Obama and the environment," *Environmental Politics*, 11, 424–30.

Bomberg, E. and Schlosberg, D. (eds) (2009) *Environmentalism in the United States*, Abingdon: Routledge.

Bond, J. and Fleisher, R. (1990) *The President in the Legislative Arena*, Chicago: University of Chicago Press.

Borjas, G. J. (1999) *Heaven's Door: Immigration Policy and the American Economy*, Princeton, N.J.: Princeton University Press.

Bosso, C. J. (2005) *Environment, Inc.: From Grassroots to Beltway*, Lawrence, Kan.: University Press of Kansas.

Bowler, S. and Glazer, A. (2008) *Direct Democracy's Impact on American Political Institutions*, Basingstoke: Palgrave.

Bowman, A. O. M. and Krause, G. A. (2003) "Power shift: measuring policy centralization in U.S. intergovernmental relations, 1947–1998," *American Political Research*, 31, 301–25.

Brettell, C. B. and Hollifield, J. F. (eds) (2008) *Migration Theory: Talking Across Disciplines*, New York: Routledge.

Brinkley, J. (2004) "Out of the spotlight, Bush overhauls US regulations," *New York Times*, August 14.

Broder, J. M. (2007) "Governors join in creating regional pacts on climate change," *New York Times*, November 15.

Broder, J. M. (2009) "With something for everyone, climate bill passed," *New York Times*, July 1.

Bruff, H. (2009) *Bad Advice: Bush's Lawyers in the War on Terror*. Lawrence, Kans.: University of Kansas Press.

Brulle, R. J. (2000) *Agency, Democracy and Nature: The US Environmental Movement from a Critical Theory Perspective*, Cambridge, Mass.: MIT Press.

Burden, B. C. and Kimball, D. C. (2002) *Why Americans Split their Tickets: Campaigns, Competition and Divided Government*, Ann Arbor, Mich.: University of Michigan Press.

Busch, A. E. (2009) "Assumptions and realities of presidential primary front-loading," in J. Citrin and D. Karol (eds), *Nominating the President: Evolution and Revolution in 2008 and Beyond*, Lanham, Md.: Rowman & Littlefield.

Bush, G. W. (2001) "Remarks by the president on global climate change," June 11.

Bush, George W. (2001a) Speech to joint session of Congress, September 20 <http://archives.cnn.com/2001/US/09/20/gen.bush.transcript/>.

Bush, G. W. (2002) State of the Union address, 29 January.

Bush, G. W. (2002a) Rose Garden speech on Israel–Palestine two-state solution, June 24.

Bush, G. W. (2004) Comments at signing ceremony, August 5 <http://www.time.com/time/specials/packages/article/0,28804,1870938_1870943_1870951,00.html>.

Bush, G. W. (2005) The President's News Conference December 19, *Weekly Compilation of Presidential Documents* 41: 1885–96.

Calabresi, S. G. and Yoo, C. S. (2008) *The Unitary Executive: Presidential Power from Washington to Bush*, New Haven, Conn.: Yale University Press.

Calavita, K. (1992) *Inside the State: The Bracero Program, Immigration, and the I.N.S.*, New York: Routledge.

Campbell C. and Rockman, B. A. (2004) *The George W Bush Presidency: Appraisals and Prospects*, Washington DC: CQ Press.

Campbell C., Rockman, B. A., and Rudalevige, A. (eds) (2008) *The George W Bush Legacy*, Washington DC: CQ Press.

Campbell, J. E. (2008) "Editor's introduction: forecasting the 2008 national elections," *PS: Political Science and Politics*, 41, 679–82.

Canada (2005) Commission of Inquiry into the Actions of Canadian Officials in Related to Maher Arar, Report of Professor Stephen J. Toope, *Fact Finder*, October 14.

Cannon, L. (2008) *Reagan's Disciple: George W. Bush's Troubled Quest for a Presidential Legacy*, New York: Public Affairs.

Carr, D. (2008) "In mourning for a man, and his era," *New York Times*, June 16.

Carter, B. (2008) "An election to laugh about," *New York Times*, October 9.

CBS (2009) "Transcript of Steve Kroft's March 20 interview with President Barack Obama" <http://www.cbsnews.com>.

Census Bureau News (2008) "An older and more diverse nation by mid-century," August 14 <http:wwwcensus.gov/Press-release/www/reelases/archives/population/012496.html>.

Census Bureau (2008a) *2008 National Population Projections*, Washington DC: US Census Bureau, August.

Census Bureau (2009) "Table 414. Federal Grants-in-Aid to State and Local Governments: 1990 to 2008," The 2009 Statistical Abstract, US Census Bureau <http://www.census.gov/compendia/statab/tables/09s0414.pdf>.

Center for Responsive Politics (2008) "Open secrets: money in politics data," Washington DC.

Chertow, M. R. and Esty, D. C. (eds) (1997) *Thinking Ecologically: The Next Generation of Environmental Policy*, New Haven, Conn.: Yale University Press.

Chiswick, B. (2008) "Are immigrants self-selected? An economic analysis," in C. B. Brettell and J. F. Hollifield (eds), *Migration Theory: Talking Across Disciplines*, New York: Routledge.

Christian Science Monitor (2009) "Obama's faith in faith-based works," February 6.

Cialdini, R. B. (2009) *Influence: Science and Practice*, Boston, Mass.: Pearson Education.

Cigler, A. J. and Loomis, B. A. (eds) (2007) *Interest Group Politics*, Washington DC: CQ Press.

Citrin, J. and Karol, D. (2009) *Nominating the President: Evolution and Revolution in 2008 and Beyond*, Latham, Md.: Rowman & Littlefield.

Climate Action (2002) *Climate Action Report: 2002*, Washington DC: Department of State.

Clinton, H. (2009) Senate confirmation testimony, January 13.

Cohen, J. and Balz, D. (2009) "Reform opposition is high but easing," *Washington Post*, September 14.

Collins, S. R., Nicolson, J. L., Rustgi, S. D., and Davis, K. (2008) *The 2008 Presidential Candidates' Health Reform Proposals: Choices for America*, New York: Commonwealth Fund.

Congressional Budget Office (2009) "Additional information regarding the effects of specifications in America's Affordable Health Choices Act," Washington DC: CBO, July 26.

Congressional Research Service (2004) *Election Reform: The Help America Vote Act and Issues for Congress,* Washington DC: Congressional Research Service.

Conlan, T. (1998) *From New Federalism to Devolution: Twenty-five Years of Intergovernmental Reform,* Washington DC: Brookings Institution.

Conlan, T. and Dinan, J. (2007) "Federalism, the Bush administration, and the transformation of American conservatism," *Publius,* 37, 279–303.

Conlan, T. J. and Posner, P. L. (eds) (2008) *Intergovernmental Management for the 21st Century,* Washington DC: Brookings Institution.

Connelly, C. and Jeffrey Smith, R. (2008) "Obama positioned to quickly reverse Bush actions," *Washington Post,* November 9.

Conyers, J. Jr. (2009) *Reining in the Imperial Presidency: Lessons and Recommendations Relating to the Presidency of George W. Bush,* House Judiciary Committee, March.

Cornelius, W. A. (2001) "Death at the border: the efficacy and unintended consequences of U.S. immigration control policy, 1993–2000," *Population and Development Review,* 27, 661–85.

Cornelius, W. A., Martin, P. L., and Hollifield, J. F. (eds) (1994) *Controlling Immigration: A Global Perspective,* Stanford, Calif.: Stanford University Press.

Cowger, T. and Markman, S. (2003), *Lyndon Johnson Remembered,* Lanham, Md.: Rowman & Littlefield.

Cox, G. W. (1997) *Making Votes Count: Strategic Coordination in the World's Electoral Systems,* Cambridge: Cambridge University Press.

CQ Today (2009) "Votes mostly go Obama's way," July 6 <http://www.cqpolitics.com>.

Dahl, R. A. (1961) *Who Governs?* New Haven, Conn.: Yale University Press.

De Grazia, A. (1969) "The myth of the president." in A. Wildavsky (ed.), *The Presidency,* Boston, Mass.: Little, Brown.

De la Garza, R. O. and Desipio, L. (2005) *Muted Voices: Latinos and the 2000 Elections,* Lanham, Md.: Rowman & Littlefield.

Denzau, A. T. and Munger, M. C. (1986) "Legislators and interest groups: how unorganized interests get represented," *American Political Science Review,* 80, 89–106.

DeParle, J. (2009) "As ranks of unemployed swell, wait for benefits worsen pains," *New York Times,* July 24.

Department of Justice (2004) Office of Legal Counsel, U.S. Department of Justice, Memorandum for James B. Comey, Deputy Attorney General, "Re: Legal Standards Applicable Under 18 U.S.C. §§ 2340-2340A," December 30.

Department of Justice (2005) Memorandum in Support of the United States' Assertion of State Secrets Privilege. Arar v. Ashcroft (E.D.N.Y.), January 18.

Department of Justice (2006a.) Brief for Respondents. Hamdan v. Rumsfeld, on writ of certiorari to the United States Court of Appeals for the District of Columbia Circuit, U.S. Supreme Court, No. 05-184, February.

Department of Justice (2006b) *Legal Authorities Supporting the Activities of the National Security Agency Described by the President,* Office of Legal Counsel, January 19.

Derthick, M. (2007) "Going federal: the launch of medicare part D compared to SSI," *Publius*, 37, 351–70.

Desipio, L. (1996) *Counting on the Latino Vote: Latinos as a New Electorate*, Charlottesville, Va.: University of Virginia Press.

Dionne, E. J. (2008) *Souled Out: Reclaiming Faith and Religion After the New Right*, Princeton, N.J.: Princeton University Press.

Dodd, L. C. and Oppenheimer, B. I. (eds) (2009) *Congress Reconsidered*, 9th edn, Washington DC: CQ Press.

Domínguez, J. I. and de Castro, R. F. (2009) *United States and Mexico: Between Partnership and Conflict*, 3rd edn, New York: Routledge.

Downie, L. Jr. and Kaiser, R. G. (2002) *The News about the News*, New York: Random House.

Dudziak, M. L. (2004) *Cold War Civil Rights: Race and the Image of American Democracy*, Princeton, N.J.: Princeton University Press.

Durant, R. F., Fiorino, D. J., and O'Leary, R. (eds) (2004) *Environmental Governance Reconsidered*, Cambridge, Mass.: MIT Press.

Eck, D. (1997) *A New Religious America: How a Christian Country has become the World's Most Diverse Society*, New York: Harper.

Economist (2008) "Off to work they go," November 27.

Edwards, G. C. and King, D. (2007) *The Polarized Presidency of George Bush*, Oxford: Oxford University Press.

Edwards, G. and Wayne, S. (eds) (2006) *Presidential Leadership*, 7th rev. edn, Belmont, Calif.: Thomson Wadsworth.

Edwards, M. (2008) *Reclaiming Conservatism: How a Great American Movement got Lost and Can Find its Way Back*, New York: Oxford University Press.

Environmental Protection Agency (EPA) (2002) *Latest Findings on National Air Quality: 2002 Status and Trends*, Washington DC: EPA.

EPA (2008) *EPA's Report on the Environment 2008*, Washington DC: EPA.

EPA (2009) "Air trends" <www.epa.gov/airtrends/sixpoll.html>.

Epstein, L. D. (1986) *Political Parties in the American Mold*, Madison, Wisc.: University of Wisconsin Press.

Epstein, L. and Knight, J. (1998) *The Choices Justices Make*, Washington DC: Congressional Quarterly Press.

Fallows, J. (2008) "The $1.4 trillion question," *Atlantic Monthly*, January/February <http://www.theatlantic.com/doc/print/200801/fallows-chinese-dollars>.

Federal Communications Commission (2006) *Annual Assessment of the Status of Competition in the Market for the Delivery of Video Programming*, 12th annual report, MB Docket no. 05-255, Washington DC.

Fetzer, J. S. (2000) *Public Attitudes Toward Immigration in the United States, France, and Germany*, Cambridge: Cambridge University Press.

Feuer, A. (2008) "Court dismisses rendition suit," *New York Times*, July 1.

Finn, P. (2009) "Justice Dept. uses 'state secrets' defense," *Washington Post*, February 10.

Fiorina, M. (1981) *Retrospective Voting in American National Elections*, New Haven, Conn.: Yale University Press.

Fiorina, M. (2005) *Culture War? The Myth of a Polarized America*, New York: Pearson Longman.

Fish and Wildlife Service (FWS) (2009) "Threatened and endangered species system," <http://ecos.fws.gov/tess_public/DelistingReport.do>.

Fisher, L. (2004) *Presidential War Power*, Lawrence, Kans.: University Press of Kansas.

Fisher, L. (2008) *The Constitution and 9/11: Recurring Threats to America's Freedoms*, Lawrence, Kans.: University Press of Kansas.

Foley, M. (2007) *American Credo: The Place of Ideas in US Politics*, Oxford: Oxford University Press.

Franciosi, R. J. (2001) *Is Cleanliness Political Godliness?* Phoenix, Ariz.: Goldwater Institute.

Fraser, M. and Dutta, S. (2008) "Barack Obama and the Facebook election," *US News and World Report*, November 19.

Freedman, L. (2009) "A subversive on a hill," *National Interest,* May/June.

Friedman, B. (2006) "Taking law seriously," *Perspectives on Politics*, 4, 2.

Frymer, P. (2003) "Acting when elected officials won't: federal courts and civil rights enforcement in U.S. labor unions, 1935–1985," *American Political Science Review*, 97, 3.

Fuchs, L. (1990) *The American Kaleidoscope: Race, Ethnicity, and the Civic Culture*, Hanover, N.H.: Wesleyan University and University Press of New England.

Gamm, G. and Smith, S. S. (2009) "The dynamics of party government in Congress," in L. C. Dodd and B. I. Oppenheimer (eds), *Congress Reconsidered*, 9th edn, Washington DC: CQ Press.

Garber, K. (2008) "McCain and Obama take on environmental concerns," *US News and World Report*, July 10.

Gellman, B. (2008) *Angler: The Cheney Vice Presidency*, New York: Penguin.

General Accounting Office (GAO) (2003) "Campaign finance reform: early experiences of two states that offer full public funding for political candidates," Washington DC: GAO.

Genovese, M. and Han, L. C. (eds) (2006) *The Presidency and the Challenge of Democracy*, Basingstoke: Palgrave Macmillan.

Gerstenzang, J. (2003) "Book offers rare look into Bush presidency," *Los Angeles Times*, January 7.

Gerstle, G. (2001) *American Crucible: Race and Nation in the Twentieth Century*, Princeton, N.J.: Princeton University Press.

Gertner, J. (2007) "The future is drying up," *New York Times*, October 21.

Glaberson, W. (2009) "Changes planned for Guantánamo trials may lead to familiar challenges," *New York Times*, May 19.

Goldberg, B, (2009) *A Slobbering Love Affair: The True (and Pathetic) Story of The Torrid Romance Between Barack Obama and the Mainstream Media*, Washington DC: Regnery.

Goldberg, J. (2006) "Breaking ranks: what turned Brent Scowcroft against the Bush administration?" *New Yorker*, October 31.

Goldenberg, S. (2008) "Obama breaks with Bush oil bosses and puts environment at top of agenda," *Guardian*, December 16.

Goldenberg, S. (2009) "The worst of times: Bush's environmental legacy examined," *Guardian*, January 16 <www.guardian.co.uk>.

Gonzales, A. (2005) Press briefing by Attorney General Alberto Gonzales and General Michael Hayden, Principal Deputy Director for National Intelligence, December 19.

Goodwin, D. K. (2005) *Team of Rivals*, New York: Simon & Schuster.

Government Accountability Office (GAO) (2007) *Fiscal Stewardship: A Critical Challenge Facing Our Nation*, Washington DC: GAO.

Graber D. (2005) *Mass Media and American Politics*, 7th edn, Washington DC: CQ Press.

Graber, D., McQuail, D., and Norris, P. (2008) *The Politics of News: The News of Politics*, 2nd edn, Washington DC: CQ Press.

Graham, M. (1999) *The Morning After Earth Day: Practical Environmental Politics*, Washington DC: Brookings Institution.

Grandin, G. (2009) "Obama in Latin America," *Mother Jones*, April 14 <http://www.motherjones.com/politics/2009/04/obama-latin-america?page= 2>.

Green, J. (2008) "The amazing money machine: how Silicon Valley made Barack Obama this year's hottest start-up," *Atlantic Monthly*, 301, June.

Greenhouse, L. and Kirkpatrick, D. (2007) "Justices loosen ad restrictions in campaign finance law," *New York Times*, June 26.

Greenstein, F. (2000) *The Presidential Difference*, Princeton, N.J.: Princeton University Press.

Greenstein, F. (2004) *The Presidential Difference: Leadership Style from FDR to George W Bush*, 2nd edn, Princeton, N.J.: Princeton University Press.

Greve, M. (2007) *Federal Preemption: State Powers, National Interests*, Washington DC: AEI Press.

Grodzins, M. (1965) *The American System: A New View of Government in the United States*, Chicago: Rand McNally.

Guber, D. (2003) *The Grassroots of a Green Revolution*, Cambridge, Mass: MIT Press.

Gurwitt, R. (2009) "Death and life in the pressroom," *Governing*, January 1.

Haber, S., Klein, H. S., Maurer, N., and Middlebrook, K. J. (2008) *Mexico Since 1980*, New York: Cambridge University Press.

Hamilton, L. F. (2009*) Strengthening Congress*, Bloomington, Ind.: Indiana University Press.

Head, S., Sterling, C. H., and Schofield, L. B. (1984) *Broadcasting in America: A Survey of Electronic Media*, Boston, Mass.: Houghton Mifflin.

Heclo, H. (1977) *A Government of Strangers: Executive Politics in Washington*, Washington DC: Brookings Institution.

Herring, G. C. (2008) *From Colony to Superpower: US Foreign Relations since 1776*, Oxford: Oxford University Press.

Herszenhorn, D. M. (2009) "In shift, leaders of senate reject Guantánamo aid," *New York Times*, May 20.

Hetherington, M. J. (2009) "Putting polarization into perspective," *British Journal of Political Science*, 39, 413–48.

Higham, J. (1955) *Strangers in the Land: Patterns of American Nativism, 1860–1925*, New Brunswick, N.J.: Rutgers University Press.

Hogan, R. E. (2000) "The costs of representation in state legislatures: explaining variations in campaign spending," *Social Science Quarterly*, 81, 941–56.

Hogan, R. E. (2005) "State campaign finance laws and interest group election-eering," *Journal of Politics*, 67, 887–906.

Hollifield, J. F. (1992) *Immigrants, Markets, and States: The Political Economy of Postwar Europe*, Cambridge, Mass.: Harvard University Press.

Hollifield, J. F. (2004) "The emerging migration state," *International Migration Review*, 38, 885–912.

Hollifield, J. F., Hunt, V. F., and Tichenor, D. J. (2008) "Immigrants, markets, and rights: the United States as an 'emerging migration state,'" *Washington University Journal of Law & Policy*, 27, 7–44.

Hopkins, D. J. (2009) "No more Wilder effect, never a Whitman effect: when and why polls mislead about black and female candidates," *Journal of Politics*.

House of Representatives (2007) "Political interference with climate change science under the Bush administration," Washington DC: Committee on Oversight and Government Reform.

Howard, C. (1997) *America's Hidden Welfare State*, Princeton, N.J.: Princeton University Press.

Huffington, A. (2008) "The internet and the death of Rovian politics," *Huffington Post*, October 20.

Huntington, S. P. (2004) *Who Are We? The Challenges to America's National Identity*, New York: Simon & Schuster.

Iaryczower, M., Spiller, P. T., and Tommasi, M. (2006) "Judicial lobbying: the politics of labor law constitutional interpretation," *American Political Science Review*, 100, 1.

Ignatius, D. (2009) "What a 'reset' can't fix," *Washington Post*, July 5.

Ikenberry, G. J. (2001) *After Victory: Institutions, Strategic Restraint, and the Rebuilding of Order after Major Wars*, Princeton, N.J.: Princeton University Press.

Jacobson, G. (2008) Transcript of presentation in "What the 2008 Election Meant," Brookings Conference, November 14 <www.brookings.edu/events 2008,1114_2008election.apsx>.

Jewell, C. J. and Bero, L. A. (2008) "Developing good taste in evidence: facilitators of and hindrances to evidence-informed policymaking in state government," *Milbank Quarterly*, 86, 177–208.

Joffe, J. (2009) "The age of nice, or politics as psychiatry," *Commentary* [web only] (October) <http://www.commentarymagazine.com/viewarticle.cfm/the-age-of-nice—or-politics-as-psychiatry-15235>.

Johnson, C. (2009) "Appeals court rejects 'state secrets' claim, revives detainee suit," *Washington Post*, April 29.

Johnson, S. (2009) "The quiet coup," *The Atlantic*, May.

Jones, J. M. (2009) "In first hundred days, Obama seen as making a bipartisan effort," Gallup <http://www.gallup.com/poll/117874/first-100-days-obama-seen-making-bipartisan-effort.aspx>.

Jones-Correa, M. (1998) *Between Two Nations: The Political Predicament of Latinos in New York City*, Ithaca, N.Y.: Cornell University Press.

Judis, J. and Tuxeira, R. (2002) *The Emerging Democratic Majority*, New York: Sara Drew.

Kagan, R. (2003) *Paradise and Power: America and Europe in the New World Order*, London: Atlantic.

Kagan, R. (2008) *The Return of History and the End of Dreams*, London: Atlantic.

Kearns, D. (2005) *Team of Rivals: The Political Genius of Abraham Lincoln*. New York: Simon & Schuster.

Keith, B. E., Magleby, D. B., Nelson, C. J., Orr, E., Westlye, M. C., and Wolfinger, R. E. (1992) *The Myth of the Independent Voter*, Berkeley, Calif.: University of California Press.

Kempton, W., Boster, J. S., and Hartley, J. A. (1995) *Environmental Values in American Culture*, Cambridge, Mass.: MIT Press.

Kennedy Jr, R. F. (2003) "Crimes against nature," November 18 <www.rollingstone.com/politics/story/5939345/crimes_against_nature/print>.

Kettl, Donald F. (ed.) (2002) *Environmental Governance: A Report on the Next Generation of Environmental Policy*, Washington DC: Brookings Institution.

Kettner, D. (1978) *The Development of American Citizenship, 1608–1870*, Chapel Hill, N.C.: University of North Carolina Press.

King, D. (2000) *Making Americans: Immigration, Race, and the Origins of the Diverse Democracy*, Cambridge, Mass.: Harvard University Press.

King, D. (2005) *The Liberty of Strangers: Making the American Nation*, Oxford: Oxford University Press.

Kingdon, J. W. (1984) *Agendas, Alternatives and Public Policies*, Boston, Mass.: Little Brown.

Kintisch, E. (2008) "Nobelist gets energy portfolio, raising hopes and expectations," *Science*, December 19.

Klarman, M. J. (2004) *From Jim Crow to Civil Rights: The Supreme Court and the Struggle for Racial Equality*, Oxford: Oxford University Press.

Klyza, C. and Sousa, D. (2008) *American Environmental Policy, 1990–2006*, Cambridge, Mass.: MIT Press.

Koblin, J. (2009) "New York Times considers two plans to charge for content on the Web," *New York Observer*, May 15.

Kornblut, A. (2009) *Notes From the Cracked Ceiling: Hillary Clinton, Sarah Palin and What it Takes for a Woman to Win*, New York: Random House.

Kornblut, A., Citrin, J., and Karol, D. (eds) (forthcoming) *Nominating the President: Evolution and Revolution in 2008 and Beyond*, Lanham, Md.: Rowman & Littlefield.

Krauthammer, C. (2004) *Democratic Realism*, Washington DC: AEI Press.

Kritzer, Herbert M. (2001) "Into the electoral waters: the impact of Bush v. Gore on public perceptions and knowledge of the Supreme Court," *85 Judicature*, 32–8.

Kuo, D. (2006) *Tempting Faith: An Inside Story of Political Seduction*, New York: Free Press.

Kurtz, H. (1997) *Hot Air: All Talk, All The Time*, New York: Basic Books.

Kurtz, H. (2004) "Dan Rather to step down at CBS," *Washington Post*, November 24.

Kurtz, H. (2009) "That shrinking feeling: *Time, Newsweek* narrow their focus," *Washington Post,* January 19.

La Raja, R. J. (2003) "Clean elections: an evaluation of public funding in Maine legislative contests," Amherst, Mass.: Center for Public Policy and Administration, University of Massachusetts.

La Raja, R. J. (2008) *Small Change: Money, Political Parties and Campaign Finance Reform*, Ann Arbor, Mich.: University of Michigan Press.

Ladd, C. E. and Bowman, K. (1996) "Public opinion on the environment," *Resources*, 124, 5–7.

Langbein, L. I. and Lotwis, M. A. (1990) "The political efficacy of lobbying and money: gun control in the U.S. House, 1986," *Legislative Studies Quarterly*, 15, 413–40.

Leffler, M. P. and Legro, J. (eds) (2008) *To Lead the World: American Strategy after the Bush Doctrine*, Oxford: Oxford University Press.

Leichter, H, (1997) *Health Policy Reform in the United States: Innovations from the States*, Armonk, N.Y.: M. E. Sharpe.

Leuchtenburg, W. (2001) *In the Shadow of FDR*, Ithaca, N.Y.: Cornell University Press.

Levinson, S. V. (2003) "Why I do not teach Marbury (except to Eastern Europeans) and why you shouldn't either," *38 Wake Forest Law Review*, 553.

Lewin, J. (2008) "How Barack Obama beat John McCain with new media," *New Media Update*, November 5.

Lichtman, A. J. (2008) *White Protestant Nation: The Rise of the American Conservative Movement*, New York: Atlantic Publishing Monthly.

Lieber, R. E. (2007) *The American Era: Power and Strategy for the 21st Century*, Cambridge: Cambridge University Press.

Liebschutz, S. F., and Palazzolo, D. J. (2005) "HAVA and the States," *Publius*, 35, 497–514.

Lipset, S. M. (1996) *American Exceptionalism: A Double-Edged Sword*, New York: W. W. Norton.

Long, S. K. (2008) *On the Road to Universal Coverage: Impacts of Reform in Massachusetts at One Year*, New York: Commonwealth Fund.

Loomis, B. A. (2007) "Does K Street run through Capitol Hill? Lobbying Congress in the Republican era," in A. J. Cigler and B. A. Loomis (eds), *Interest Group Politics*, Washington DC: CQ Press.

Lopez, M. H. and Taylor, P. (2009) "Dissecting the 2008 electorate: most diverse in US history," Philadelphia, Pa.: Pew Hispanic Center <http://pewhispanic.org>.

Lopipero, P., Apollonio, D. E., and Bero, L. A. (2007) "Interest groups, lobbying, and deception: the passage of the airline smoking acts," *Political Science Quarterly*, 122, 635–56.

Lowenthal, A. F., Piccone, T., and Whitehead, L. (2009) *The Obama Administration and the Americas*, Washington DC: Brookings Institution.

Lucas, E. (2008) *The New Cold War: Putin's Russia and the Threat to the West*, London: Palgrave Macmillan.

Lynch, T. J. (2004) *Turf War: The Clinton Administration and Northern Ireland*, Aldershot: Ashgate.

Lynch, T. J. and Singh, R. S. (2008) *After Bush: The Case for Continuity in American Foreign Policy*, New York: Cambridge University Press.

Lyon, T. P. and Maxwell, J. W. (2004) "Astroturf: interest group lobbying and corporate strategy," *Journal of Economics and Management Strategy*, 13, 561–97.

Mailer, N. (1976) *Some Honorable Men*, Boston, Mass.: Little, Brown.

Maisel, L. S. (2007) *American Political Parties and Elections: A Very Short Introduction*, Oxford and New York: Oxford University Press.

Maltzman, F., Spriggs, J. F., and Wahlbeck, P. J. (2000) *Crafting Law on the Supreme Court: The Collegial Game*, Cambridge: Cambridge University Press.

Mann, T. E. and Ornstein, N. J. (2006) *The Broken Branch: How Congress is Failing America and How to Get it Back on Track,* New York: Oxford University Press.

Mann, T. E. and Ornstein, N. J. (2008) *The Broken Branch: How Congress is Failing America and How to Get it Back on Track,* 2nd edn, New York: Oxford University Press.

Marshall, T. R. (1999) "Why PAC? Why bundle? Patterns of interest group donations," *American Review of Politics,* 20, 245–60.

Martin, P. L. (2009) *Importing Poverty? Immigration and the Changing Face of Rural America,* New Haven, Conn.: Yale University Press.

Matheson, S. (2009) *Presidential Constitutionalism in Perilous Times,* Cambridge, Mass: Harvard University Press.

Mayer, J. (2008) *Dark Side: The Inside Story of How the War on Terror Turned into a War on American Ideals,* New York: Doubleday.

Mayer, K., Werner, T., and Williams, A. (2004) "Do public funding programs enhance electoral competition?" Fourth Annual Conference on State Politics and Policy (Laboratories of Democracy: Public Policy in the American States), Kent State University.

Mayer, W. G. (1993) "Poll trends: Trends in media usage," *Public Opinion Quarterly,* 57, 593–611.

Maynard, M. (2009) "A green-thinking president makes his first move," *New York Times,* January 25.

Mazzetti, M. and Shane, S. (2009) "Memos spell out brutal C.I.A. mode of interrogation," *New York Times,* April 17.

McChesney, R. W. (2004) *The Problem of the Media: US Communications Politics in the Twenty-First Century,* New York: Monthly Review Press.

McCormick, R. L. (1986) *The Party Period and Public Policy: American Politics from the Age of Jackson to the Progressive Era,* New York: Oxford University Press.

McCright, A. M. and Dunlap, R. E. (2003) "Defeating Kyoto: the conservative movement's impact on U.S. climate change policy," *Social Problems,* 50, 348–73.

McGuinn, P. J. (2006) *No Child Left Behind and the Transformation of Federal Education Policy, 1965–2005,* Lawrence, Kans.: University Press of Kansas.

McKinley, J. (2009) "California fails to break budget impasse as states struggle to meet budget deadlines," *New York Times.* July 2.

Mearsheimer, J. J. (1990) "Why we will soon miss the cold war," *Atlantic Monthly,* August 2.

Mearsheimer, J. J. (2002) *The Tragedy of Great Power Politics,* New York: W. W. Norton.

Mearsheimer, J. J. (2005) "Hans Morgenthau and the Iraq war: realism versus neo-conservatism," *Open Democracy,* May 19 <http://www.open democracy.net/content/articles/PDF/2522.pdf>.

Mearsheimer, J. and Walt, S. (2007) *The Israel Lobby and US Foreign Policy,* New York: Allen Lane.

Montgomery, L. (2009) "Once considered unthinkable, U.S. sales tax gets fresh look," *Washington Post,* May 27.

Mooney, C. (2006) *The Republican War on Science,* New York: Basic Books.

Mooney, C. (2008) "After Bush, restoring science to environmental policy," *Yale Environment360*, June 25 <www.e360.yale.edu/content/print.msp?id= 2033>.

Morris, C. R. (2008) *Coming Apart at the Seams: The Collapse of Private Pension and Health Care Protections*, Washington DC: Brookings Institution.

Morris, C. R. (2008a) *The Two Trillion Dollar Meltdown: Easy Money, High Rollers, and the Great Credit Crash,* revised and updated, New York: Public Affairs.

Mundy, A. and Meckler, L. (2009) "Drug makers score early wins as plans take shape," *Wall Street Journal*, July 17.

Mutter, A. D. (2009). "Newspaper share value fell $64B in '08. *Reflections of a Newsosaur,"* <http://newsosaur.blogspot.com/2009_01_01_archive.html>.

Nathan, R. P. (1975) *The Plot that Failed: Nixon and the Administrative Presidency*, New York: Wiley.

Nathan, R. P. (1983) *The Administrative Presidency*, New York: Wiley.

Nathan, R. (2008) "Updating theories of federalism," in T. J. Conlan and P. L. Posner (eds), *Intergovernmental Management for the 21st Century*, Washington DC: Brookings Institution.

National Conference of State Legislatures (2009) "Children's health reform," March.

National Governors' Association (NGA), National Conference of State Legislatures (NCSL), and American Association of Motor Vehicle Administrators (AAMVA) (2006) *The Real ID Act: National Impact Analysis*, Washington DC: NGA.

NGA and National Association of State Budget Officers (NASBO) (2009) *The Fiscal Survey of States*, Washington DC: NASBO.

Nelson, M. (ed.) (2005) *The Presidency and the Political System*, 8th edn, Washington DC: Congressional Quarterly Press.

Nelson, M. (2007) "Politics of tribal recognition: casinos, culture and controversy," in A. J. Cigler and B. A. Loomis (eds), *Interest Group Politics*, Washington DC: CQ Press.

Neustadt, R. (1960) *Presidential Power: The Politics of Leadership*, New York: Wiley.

Neustadt, R. (2000) "'Organizing the transition' and Neustadt advises the advisers," in C. Jones (ed.), *Preparing to be President: The Memos of Richard E. Neustadt*, Washington DC: AEI Press.

New York Times (2005) "Bush on the Patriot Act and eavesdropping," December 18, p. 30.

New York Times (2009) "Taking the Hill," June 2.

Newspaper Association of America (NAA) (2009) *Trends and Numbers*, Arlington, Va.: NAA.

Newsweek (2006) "The race is on," December 25.

Nicholson, S. P. (2008) "Direct democracy and the public agenda: ballot initiatives and public beliefs about important problems," in S. Bowler and A. Glazer (eds), *Direct Democracy's Impact on American Political Institutions*, Basingstoke: Palgrave.

Nivola, P. and Brady, D. (eds) (2006, 2008) *Red and Blue Nation? Characteristics and Causes of America's Polarized Politics*, 2 vols, Stanford, Calif.: Hoover Institution, and Washington DC: Brookings Institution.

Nordhaus, T. and Schellenburger, M. (2007) *Break Through: From the Death of Environmentalism to the Politics of Possibility*, New York: Houghton Mifflin Harcourt.

Norris, P. (2005) *Radical Right: Voters and Parties in the Electoral Market*, New York: Cambridge University Press.

Nossel, S. (2004) "Smart power," *Foreign Affairs*, March/April.

Natural Resources Defense Council (NRDC) (2005) "Rewriting the rules: the Bush administration's first-term environmental record," New York: NRDC.

Nye, Jr., J. S. (2002) *The Paradox of American Power*, Oxford: Oxford University Press, and Lanham, Md.: Rowman & Littlefield.

Obama, B. (1995) *Dreams from my Father.*, New York: Random House.

Obama, B. (2002) Speech in Chicago, October 2.

Obama, B. (2006) *The Audacity of Hope*, New York: Random House.

Obama, B. (2007) "Renewing America's leadership," *Foreign Affairs*, 8, 2–16.

Obama, B. (2008a) AIPAC speech, June 4 <www.whitehouse.gov>.

Obama, B. (2008b) Berlin speech, July 24 <www.whitehouse.gov>.

Obama, B. (2009a) "Inaugural address," January 20 <www.whitehouse.gov>.

Obama, B. (2009b) "Address to Joint Session of Congress," February 24 <www.whitehouse.gov>.

Obama, B. (2009c) "Responsibly ending the war in Iraq," February 27 <www.whitehouse.gov>.

Obama, B. (2009d) "Remarks by the President on a new strategy for Afghanistan and Pakistan," March 27 <www.whitehouse.gov>.

Obama, B. (2009e) "Press briefing, April 29 2009," <www.whitehouse.gov>.

Obama, B. (2009f) NATO press conference, April 4 <www.whitehouse.gov>.

Obama, B. (2009g) "Speech in Cairo," June 4 <www.whitehouse.gov>.

Office of Management and Budget (OMB) (2009) *A New Era of Responsibility: Renewing America's Promise*, Washington DC: Government Printing Office.

OMB (2009) "Historical tables," *Budget of the United States, FY 2010, Historical Table*s, Washington DC, February.

Opensecrets (2009) <www.opensecrets.org>.

Orren, G. and Polsby, N. W. (1987) *Media and Momentum*, Chatham, N.J.: Chatham House.

Orrenius, P. M. and Solomon, G. R. (2006) "How labor market policies shape immigrants' opportunities," *Economic Letter—Insights from the Federal Reserve Bank of Dallas*, 1/7.

Parmar, I., Millar, L. B., and Ledwidge, M. (eds) (2009) *New Directions for American Foreign Policy*, London: Routledge.

Passel, J. S. (2009) "A portrait of unauthorized immigrants in the United States," Philadelphia, Pa.: Pew Hispanic Center <http://pewhispanic.org>.

Passel, J. and Cohn, D'Vera (2008) *US Population Projections: 2005–2050*. Philadelphia, Pa.: Pew Hispanic Center, February 11.

Patrick, S. (2009) *The Best Laid Plans: The Origins of American Multilateralism*, Lanham, Md.: Rowman & Littlefield.

Pedersen, C. (2009) *Obama's America*, Edinburgh: Edinburgh University Press.

Perez-Peña, R. (2008) "Papers facing worst year for ad revenue," *New York Times*, June 23.

Peters, B. G. (2009) *American Public Policy: Process and Performance*, 8th edn, Washington DC: CQ Press.

Pew (2002) *Pew Research Center for the People and the Press*, June 9 <http://people-press.org/report/?pageid=617>.

Pew Center for the People and the Press (2009) "Independents take center stage in the Obama era: trends in political values and core Attitudes 1987–2009," May 21 <http:people-press.org./report/517/political –values-and-core-attitudes>.

Pew Forum on Religion and Public Life (2009) "A contentious debate: same sex marriage in the United States," Pew Forum on Religion and Public Life, July 9 <http:pewforum.org/docs/?DocD=422>.

Pew Foundation (2008) "The demographics of faith," August 20 <http://pew-forum.org/?DocID=333>.

Pew Foundation (2008a) "US religious landscape survey: religious affiliation: diverse and dynamic," February.

Pfiffner, J. P. (1996) *The Strategic Presidency*, Lawrence, Kans.: University of Kansas Press.

Pfiffner, J. P. (2007) *The Modern Presidency*, 5th edn, Belmont, Calif.: Thomson Wadsworth.

Pfiffner, J. (2008) *Power Play: The Bush Presidency and the Constitution*, Washington DC: Brookings Institution.

Phillips, K. (1994) *Arrogant Capitol: Washington, Wall Street and the Frustration of American Politics*, Boston, Mass.: Little, Brown.

Pickus, N. J. (2005) *True Faith and Allegiance: Immigration and American Civic Nationalism*, Princeton, N.J.: Princeton University Press.

Pierce, E. (2007) "A bill, a 'hold' and a (possibly) lying senator," *Roll Call*.

Pious, R. M. (2006) *The War on Terrorism and the Rule of Law*, Los Angeles, Calif.: Roxbury.

Piven, F. F. and Cloward, R. A. (1997) *Regulating the Poor: The Functioning of Public Welfare*, 2nd edn, New York: Vintage.

Polsby, N. W. (1980) *Community Power and Political Theory*, New Haven, Conn.: Yale University Press.

Polsby, N. W. (1983) *The Consequences of Party Reform*, Oxford: Oxford University Press.

Polsby, N. W. and Wildavsky, A. with Hopkins, D. A. (2007) *Presidential Elections: Strategies and Structures of American Politics*, 12th edn, Lanham, Md.: Rowman & Littlefield.

Portes, A. and Rumbaut, R. G. (1990) *Immigrant America: A Portrait*, Berkeley, Calif.: University of California Press.

Posner, P. L. (2007) "The politics of coercive federalism in the Bush era," *Publius*, 37, 390–412.

Posner, P. L. (2009) "The stimulus hot seat," *Governing.Com*, February 25 <http://www.governing.com/mgmt_insight.aspx?id=6470>.

Posner, P. L. and Conlan, T. J. (2008) "Conclusion: managing complex problems in a compound republic," in T. J. Conlan and P. L. Posner (eds), *Intergovernmental Management in the 21st Century*, Washington DC: Brookings Institution.

Priest, D. (2004) "Ex-CIA official defends detention policies," *Washington Post*, October 27.

Prior, M. (2007) *Post-Broadcast Democracy: How Media Choice Increases Inequality in Political Involvement and Polarizes Elections*, Cambridge/New York: Cambridge University Press.

Project for Excellence in Journalism (PEJ) (2009) *State of the News Media: 2009*, Washington DC: PEJ.

PEJ (2009a) *Winning the Media Campaign: How the Press Reported the 2008 Presidential General Election*, Washington DC: PEJ.

Public Campaign (2002a) "Clean money campaign reform," Washington DC: Public Campaign.

Public Campaign (2002b) "Clean money, clean elections comparisons: an inventory of clean money, clean elections legislation," Washington DC: Public Campaign.

Pyle, C. H. (2009) *Secret Government, War Crimes and the Rule of Law*, Washington DC: Potomac Books.

Rabe, B. G. (2004) *Statehouse and Greenhouse*, Washington DC: Brookings Institution.

Rabe, B. G. (2008) "Regionalism and global climate change policy: revisiting multistate collaboration as an intergovernmental management tool," in T. J. Conlan and P. L. Posnan (eds), *Intergovernmental Management in the 21st Century*, Washington DC: Brookings Institution.

Rasmussen Reports (2009) "Republicans like GOP's conservative direction, Democrats don't," January 29.

Reid, T. R. (1980) *Congressional Odyssey: The Saga of a Senate Bill*, New York: W. H. Freeman.

Renshon, S. A. (2009) *National Security in the Obama Administration*, London: Routledge.

Revkin, A. (2008) "New climate report foresees big changes," *New York Times*, May 28.

Rice, C. (2005) "U.S. Secretary of State, remarks upon her departure for Europe," December 5.

Rosenbaum, W. A. (2007) *Environmental Politics and Policy*, Washington DC: CQ Press.

Rosenberg, G. N. (2008) *The Hollow Hope: Can Courts Bring About Social Change?* 2nd edn, Chicago: University of Chicago Press.

Rosenstiel, T. and Kovach, B. (2009) "Lessons of the election" in *The State of the News Media: 2009*, Washington D.C.: PEJ.

Rudalevige, A. (2005) *The New Imperial Presidency*, Ann Arbor, Mich.: University of Michigan Press.

Rudalevige, A. (2009) "'Therefore get wisdom.' What should the President know and how can he know it?" *Governance*, 22, 2.

Rudolph, C. (2006) *National Security and Immigration: Policy Development in the United States and Western Europe since 1945*, Stanford, Calif.: Stanford University Press.

Russell, J. W. (2008) *Double Standard: Social Policy in Europe and the United States*, Lanham, Md.: Rowman & Littlefield.

Samuel, H. (2009) "France will not send any more troops to Afghanistan, says Nicolas Sarkozy," *Daily Telegraph*, October 16.

Sanger, D. E. (2009) *The Inheritance: The World Obama Confronts and the Challenges to American Power*, London: Bantam.

Santora, M. (2007) "Global warming starts to divide GOP contenders," *New York Times*, October 17.

Savage, C. (2007) *Takeover: The Return of the Imperial Presidency and the Subversion of American Democracy*, New York: Little, Brown.

Schappach, P. C. and Shafroth, F. (2008) "Intergovernmental finance in the new global economy: an integrated approach," in T. J. Conlan and P. L. Posner (eds), *Intergovernmental Management for the 21st Century*, Washington DC: Brookings Institution.

Schelling, T. C. (1960) *The Strategy of Conflict*, Cambridge, Mass.: Harvard University Press.

Schick, A. (2000) *The Federal Budget: Politics, Policy, Process*, Washington DC: Brookings Institution.

Schlesinger Jr., A. (1973) *The Imperial Presidency*, Boston, Mass.: Houghton Mifflin.

Schlozman, K. L. and Tierney, J. T. (1986) *Organized Interests and American Democracy*, New York: Harper & Row.

Schreiber, R. (2008) *Righting Feminism: Conservative Women and American Politics*, New York: Oxford University Press.

Schuck, P. H. (1998) *Citizens, Strangers, and in-Betweens*, Boulder, Colo.: Westview.

Schuck, P. H. and Smith, R. (1985) *Citizenship Without Consent: Illegal Aliens in the American Polity*, New Haven, Conn.: Yale University Press.

Schwartz, J. (2009) "Obama backs off a reversal on secrets," *New York Times*, February 10.

Segal, J. and Spaeth, H. (2002) *The Supreme Court and the Attitudinal Model Revisited*, Cambridge: Cambridge University Press.

Shafer, B. E. and Claggett, W. J. M. (1995) *The Two Majorities: The Issue Context of Modern American Politics*, Baltimore, Md. and London: Johns Hopkins University Press.

Shipan, C. R. and Lowry, W. R. (2001) "Environmental policy and party divergence in Congress," *Political Research Quarterly*, 54, 245–63.

Sinclair, B. (2006) *Party Wars: Polarization and the Politics of National Policymaking*, Norman, Okla.: University of Oklahoma Press.

Sinclair, B. (2007) *Unorthodox Lawmaking: New Legislative Processes in the U.S. Congress*, 3rd edn, Washington DC: CQ Press.

Sinclair, B. (2009) "The new world of U.S. senators," in L. C. Dodd and B. I. Oppenheimer (eds), *Congress Reconsidered*, 9th edn, Washington DC: CQ Press.

Singer, A., Hardwick, S. W., and Brettell, C. B. (eds) (2008) *Twenty-First Century Gateways: Immigrant Incorporation in Suburban America*, Washington DC: Brookings Institution.

Skerry, P. (1995) *Mexican Americans: The Ambivalent Minority*, Cambridge, Mass.: Harvard University Press.

Skocpol, T. (1998) *Social Policy in the United States*, Princeton, N.J.: Princeton University Press.

Skowronek, S. (1982) *Building a New American State: The Expansion of National Administrative Capacities, 1877–1920*, Cambridge: Cambridge University Press.

Skowronek, S. (1997) *The Politics Presidents Make*, Cambridge, Mass.: Harvard University Press.

Smith, A. (2009) *The Internet's Role in Campaign 2008*, Washington DC: Pew Internet & American Life Project.

Smith, R. (1997) *Civic Ideals: Conflicting Visions of Citizenship in U.S. History*, New Haven, Conn.: Yale University Press.

Smith, S. S. (2007) *Party Influence in Congress*, Cambridge: Cambridge University Press.

Smith S. S., Roberts, J., and Vander Wielen, R. (2009) *The American Congress*, 6th edn, New York: Cambridge University Press.

Smith, S. S. and Springer, M. J. (eds) (2009) *Reforming the Presidential Primary Process*, Washington DC: Brookings Institution.

Social Security Administration (SSA) (2008a) *The 2008 Annual Report of the Board of Trustees of the Federal Old-Age and Survivors' Insurance and Federal Disability Insurance Trust Funds* <www.ssa.gov/OACT/TR/TR08/tr08.pdf>.

SSA (2008b) *A Message to the Public* <http://www.ssa.gov/OACT/TRSUM/tr08summary.pdf>.

SSA (2009) *The Future of Social Security*, Baltimore, Md.: SSA, April 29.

Stateline.org (2009) *State of the States: A Report on State Policy, 2009*, Washington DC: Pew Center on the States.

Steinfels, P. (2009) "Despite a decade of controversy, the 'faith based initiative endures," *New York Times,* July 31.

Stephens, G. R. and Wikstrom, N. (2007) *American Intergovernmental Relations: A Fragmented Federal Polity*, New York: Oxford University Press.

Stirland, S. L. (2008) "Propelled by internet, Barack Obama wins presidency," *Wired*, November 4.

Street, P. (2009) *Barack Obama and the Future of American Politics*, Boulder, Colo.: Paradigm.

Struck, D. (2006) "Canadian was falsely accused, panel says," *Washington Post*, September 19.

Sullivan, K. (2009) "Freed detainee in U.K. tells of abuse by U.S.," *Washington Post*, February 23.

Switzer, J. V. (1997) *Green Backlash: The History and Politics of Environmental Opposition in the US*, Boulder, Colo.: Lynne Rienner.

Tanner, M. D. (2007) *Leviathan on the Right: How Big-Government Conservatism Brought Down the Republican Revolution*, Washington DC: Cato Institute.

Teles, S. M. (2008) *The Rise of the Conservative Legal Movement: The Battle for Control of the Law*, Princeton, N.J.: Princeton University Press.

Thaler, R. and Sunstein, C. (2008) *Nudge*, New York: Penguin.

Thiesen, M. A. (ed.) (2009) *The Record of the Bush Presidency 2001–2009*, Washington DC: White House.

Tichenor, D. J. (2002) *Dividing Lines: The Politics of Immigration Control in America*, Princeton, N.J.: Princeton University Press.

Tremoglie, M. P. (2009) "Poll finds Congress approval ratings are equal to Cheney's," *The Bulletin,* May 14.

Union of Concerned Scientists (UCS) (2009) "Voices of federal scientists," <www.ucsusa.org/scientific_intergrity/abuses_of_science/voices-of-federal-scientists.html>.

Uslaner, E. M. (1996) *The Decline of Comity in Congress: Representatives and Ideologues in the Senate.* Ann Arbor, Mich.: University of Michigan Press.

Vargas, J. (2008) "Obama raised half a billion online," *Washington Post,* November 20.

Vig, N. J. and Kraft, M. E. (eds) (2010) *Environmental Policy,* Washington DC: Congressional Quarterly.

Walt, S. (2005) *Taming American Power: the Global Response to US Primacy,* New York: W.W. Norton.

Wall Street Journal (2008) "In crisis, opportunity for Obama," November 21.

Ware, A. (2002) *The American Direct Primary,* Cambridge: Cambridge University Press.

Ware, A. (2009) *The Dynamics of Two-Party Politics,* Oxford: Oxford University Press.

Warren, J. (2009) "When no news is bad news," *The Atlantic,* January 21.

Wattenberg, M. (1991) *The Rise of Candidate-Centered Politics,* Cambridge, Mass.: Harvard University Press

Wayne, S. (1978) *The Legislative Presidency,* New York: Harper & Row.

Weissert, C. S. and Weissert, W. G. (2008) "Medicaid waivers: license to shape the future of fiscal federalism," in T. J. Conlan and P. L. Posner (eds), *Intergovernmental Management for the 21st Century,* Washington DC: Brookings Institution.

White House (2009) *Highlights of Accomplishments and Results: The Administrations of President George W. Bush 2001–2009,* Washington DC: White House.

White, J. (2005) "Making connections to the appropriations process," in P. S. Herrnson, R. G. Shaiko, and C. Wilcox (eds), *The Interest Group Connection: Electioneering, Lobbying, and Policymaking in Washington,* Washington DC: CQ Press.

Whitlock, C. (2006) "European probe finds signs of CIA-run secret prisons," *Washington Post,* June 8.

Wickert, T. (1997) "Broadcast news," *New York Times,* January 26.

Wilkinson, J. H. (2009) "Of guns, abortions, and the unraveling rule of law," *Virginia Law Review,* 95, 253.

World Bank (2009) *Russian Report,* March <http://siteresources.worldbank. org/INTRUSSIANFEDERATION/Resources/rer18eng.pdf>.

Wright, J. R. (1995) *Interest Groups and Congress: Lobbying, Contributions, and Influence,* New York: Longman.

Xiao, C. and Dunlap, R. E. (2007) "Validating a comprehensive model of environmental concern cross-nationally: a US–Canadian comparison," *Social Science Quarterly,* 88, 471–93.

Zakaria, F. (2008) *The Post-American World,* New York: Norton.

Zeidel, R. F. (2004) *Immigrants, Progressives, and Exclusion Politics: The Dillingham Commission, 1900–1927,* Dekalb, Ill.: Northern Illinois University Press.

Zimmerman, J. F. (2007) "Congressional preemption during the George W. Bush administration," *Publius,* 37, 432–52.

Zolberg, A. R. (2006) *A Nation by Design: Immigration Policy in the Fashioning of America,* Cambridge, Mass.: Harvard University Press.

Index